# LAOISM

To: phyllis:
The journey of Transforming
stones, and yellow flower, is
within the bones, and invisible
space of heart

1-20-04

# LAOISM

## The Complete Teachings of Lao Zi

by

### MASTER TAO HUANG

Humanics Trade Group
Atlanta, GA

Laoism
A Humanics Trade Group Publication

Humanics Trade Group Publications are an imprint of and published by Humanics Publishing Group, a division of Humanics Limited. It's trademark, consisting of the words "Humanics Trade Group" and a portrayal of a Pegasus, is registered in the U.S. Patent Office and in other countries.

Humanics Limited
PO Box 7400
Atlanta, GA 30357-0400

Printed in the United States of America

Library of Congress Catalog Card Number: 00-103454
ISBN: 0-89334-325-0

*For my spiritual father*

# CONTENTS

# Contents

# ACKNOWLEDGMENTS

As I finished writing, the Tao is still alive in my heart, directing my journey by providing me with awakening information. I feel so fortunate to be Chinese by birth and to be establishing my Taoist roots in America. My will is filled with the ancient untraceable Taoist tradition, and my life is vitalized by the American Qi of the freedom of spiritual expression. Together is the birth of Laoism, my personal connection with the spirit of Lao Zi and his works. Laoism is how I have awakened into the spiritual root of Taoist tradition, and it also is how I can express myself to the Western mind. When the East seeks eagerly into the Western technological advancement, the West is tranquilized peacefully by the Eastern wisdom tradition. Together, machine and elixir are unified, and a new century begins.

I would like to thank especially Marion Knabe for her in depth editing work. My transmitted message is alive with her gentleness, my conscious thoughts turn into the readable information under her numbed writing fingers, and my spiritual love vibrates with the fruitful insights through her motherly nourishment.

My "old poetic buddy" Kenneth Warren has filled me with invaluable and thoughtful input. Our elixir-making conversation will never end. Also special thanks go to Colette Ide for her medical advice and Robert Ridgell and Rubystine Marshall for their biblical insights. My deepest appreciation goes Kelly Farrell and Jennifer Hargreaves for their essential contributions on illustrating the Laoist's characters with simple but expressive images. Time has beautifully reconnected my anthropology teacher Ron Reminick to be the proof-reader. A man's work is birth-conceiving work. Last but not least, thanks my wife Mei, son Ingold and daughter Amy for forgiving me for not spending many nights and days with them at home.

My warm greeting goes to Christopher Walker, the Production Manager at Humanics Publishing Group for his timely evaluation of the work. Without his spiritual eye, Laoism could not have presented itself publically.

# INTRODUCTION

Taoism is defined in the Webster's New Twentieth Century Unabridged Dictionary as, "a Chinese religion and philosophy based on the teachings of Lao-tse (6th century B.C.) and advocating simplicity, selflessness, etc." This, however, is not true. What the above definition truly refers to is Laoism, which is the transliteration of the Chinese characters "Lao Zi" into English. Just as Buddhism is recognized as the teachings of Buddha, and Confucianism is based on the words of Confucius, we must now realize the difference between the ancient philosophy of Taoism and the application thereof written by Lao Zi, namely, Laoism.

The two have become synonymous in English, but it is important to realize that what the West has known as "Taoism" is in fact the philosophies of Lao Zi, or Laoism, which, while based on Taoism, is more of a spiritual path and stresses different aspects than those of traditional Taoism. We will separate the philosophical understanding of Laoism form the shamanistic practices of Taoism in this book, as the differences between the ritualistic practices of Taoism and the personal view and philosophical teachings of the Tao that arise in the Tao Te Ching are significant. Lao Zi paved the way of the Tao through his personal cultivation and ultimately refined his path into a work that has transcended the ages. But he was not the first practitioner of the spiritual path of Taoism. Lao Zi, in fact, belonged to the third generation of this spiritual development, following Fu Xi, inventor of the "eighth hexagram" and creator of the philosophical understanding, and Guang Cheng-zi, who was the second generation, and from whom the Yellow Emperor begged the teachings to enlightenment.

Based upon the history of its cultural practices, it is fundamentally necessary to use two separate words in English to denote the differences between the personal/philosophical and the spiritual/ethereal understandings of the Tao. In Chinese, the personal and philosophical understanding of the Tao is called "daojia." The spiritual/ethereal Taoism is called "daojiao." "Jia" [家] means "family," and it is personal, philosophical and private in nature. "Jiao" [教] means "teaching" and it is collective, ethereal, and public in nature. Lao Zi's personal, philosophical, and private interpretations are what we call Laoism. That which is Taoism is from what Lao Zi worked-the collective, ethereal, and public teachings of the Tao. It should be clarified that Laoists follow the path of the Tao and practice the teachings of Laoism. However, not all Laoists practice Taoism. Laoists meditate on the void of emptiness, position themselves with softness and practice simplicity. Laoists neither worship deities nor pay tribute to the personified images and statues. To them, the human body is the statue and mind is the image. In contrast, Taoists follow rules, perform sacred duties and worship holy statues. Taoists have a simpler mentality but practice sophisticated ritual and shamanistic techniques.

Lao Zi's philosophical understanding of the Tao is collected in the Tao Te Ching. In contrast, his spiritual practices of the Tao are represented by the fourteen Chinese Characters which are called couplets. The Couplets were meant to accompany the Tao Te Ching, as they provide clarity and help the student towards understanding and enlightenment. The Couplet is antithetical to the Tao Te Ching, and after being engraved on a stele, it sat, and still stands today, inside the Lao Zi Hall next to the stone carving of the Tao Te Ching. The couplet is the key to true understanding of the Tao Te Ching in its complete pictorial and spiritual aspects.

Lao Zi's couplet was constructed through the use of fourteen combined Chinese Characters. Each of these characters has elementary sub-characters. Some of the combined characters in the couplet have two elementary sub-characters, while others have three or more. The fourteen standard Chinese characters represent their pronunciation, which are antithetical in meaning, rhythmic in pronunciation, and mystical in interpretation.

According to the teachings of the couplet, as it was passed on orally from generation to generation by those within the community of the Watch Tower Temple, all these characters were not only meaningful in each of their own distinctive ways, but they were also viewed as a valuable collective summary of Taoism meditation practices. When comparing this couplet to all of the world's spiritual teachings, these fourteen characters offer one of the most concise and complete descriptions of meditation practices and spiritual cultivation ever conceived.

The first half of the couplet teaches us how to preserve the inner life forces according to the mechanism of the Tao, just as do the first thirty-seven chapters of the Tao Te Ching. This mechanism represents a very complicated systematic change of metabolism in the physical body. By using this mechanism, the crystallized life pill can be produced according to the principle of interaction between the micro and macro physical environment and the principle of yin and yang. The micro-physical environment refers to an individual's organic systems and their harmonious integration with emotional and spiritual health. The macro physical environment refers to the interaction among everything existing in the universe.

The second half of the couplet emphasizes the practice of Te, as do the rest of the chapters in the Tao Te Ching. It deals with the pure action of human behavior through the cultivation of mind which enables the perennial life pill to be preserved. This preservation relies mainly upon the virtue of actions, such as kindness, frugality, giving and sacrifice. This virtue of action is under the control of the pure spiritual mind since it is this mind that generates all the fruits of human behavior. All in all, the couplet represents the extract of the Tao Te Ching by presenting the Laoist philosophy and its spiritual practices. The approach of this book is to blend the descriptive materials of the Tao Te Ching with the graphic illustrations of the couplet, enabling readers to not only feel the familiarity of words but also the strength and character of Laoism.

The first part of this book portrays the first seven Laoist characters in the couplet according to the descending order of the Tao. The second part presents the second seven characters as the ascending order of the Te. In Taoist inner alchemy, the descending order deals with gathering the infinite cosmic power of the Tao into a finite spiritual seed within through conscious awareness. Upon completion of planting the spiritual seed, cultivation toward the following seven ascending principles begins. This is characterized by the couplet as the returning process where the seed of the Tao manifests through virtue, love, compassion and kindness. These two orders sum the complete teaching of the Tao Te Ching.

Since the Tao Te Ching was first translated from French into English in the 1860's, there are now over two hundred translations circulating in the English market. One could enter a bookstore or your local library and find at least several translations. Yet the tragedy is that in the minds of many people, including many Chinese scholars, the Tao Te Ching is no more than just another text on philosophy. It is not treated as a meditation guide or a spiritual work. Among all the translations, few provide spiritual explanations. Most of the translations are merely literal interpretations of the Chinese characters. The efforts of my sealed-love laboring are meant to combine the Tao Te Ching and the couplet together as a collective work of Laoism in order that the readers may unify the philosophical understanding of Laoism with the spiritual aspects of the Tao. The Tao Te Ching is a philosophical and spiritual understanding of the Tao, while the couplet is the sacred and mystical experience of entering into the Tao.

It is the intention of this book to bring you a step closer to the ultimate understanding of the Tao Te Ching to achieve an awakening to the Tao. Each of the fourteen Chinese characters of the couplet forms a chapter in itself. Together, these fourteen characters will, step by step, reveal the true workings of the Taoist inner alchemy by explaining the meaning of the Tao Te Ching.

# PART ONE

# The Descending Order:

# *TAO*

身寶

# STEP ONE: *JADE*

Structure: body 身  + treasure 寶
Sound: yu
Meaning: jade

## The Introduction of Value

**T**o value and cherish are the most highly qualified and ideal characters of man. It is impossible to live a life without treasuring, regardless of the importance of the treasure or the monetary value placed upon it. To have a mind-set that values nothing eternally or objectively is highly unlikely. In the mind, nothing other than the mind is valued; within the body, everything is of consequence. No other objects could be found, in Lao Zi's time, to better explain the similarities of the human body and jade.

The human body is the most valued object in life. Jade is the most treasured compound on earth. This is the Laoist belief regarding that which was treasured and valued during his time. In the construction of a value system, an individual's life is thought to be a valuable contribution in itself toward the culture in which he lives. The culture, collectively, is represented by the images which shape individual lives. A natural life must be personally experienced, culturally determined, and spiritually defined. Therefore, when the Laoist statement is interpreted by one born and raised in the West, one may say that a mechanical structure, such as a satellite, is more valuable than a human body because it is worth more than an average person could possibly earn during a life time. It may also be argued that marble is more valuable than jade. Equally, a Laoist mind's reaction would be that the emperor's jade-seal is the most important tool in the world, certainly more valuable than all other tools put together, since it symbolizes all the decision making and power ruling in the country. At any time, all definitions are the result of one's personal understanding. All arguments arise from different opinions and lead to specific interpersonal understanding. All cultural practices are the result of objective values of subjective understanding.

When Lao Zi constructed this character, he mentally attributed a natural price to the body with a natural attraction to jade. The human body is the highest representation of organic life on this planet. Jade is the most condensed and concentrated form of inorganic matter on earth. This is why the body is valued and the mind treasures itself. In the animal kingdom, fish swim, animals hibernate, frogs leap, and birds fly. In contrast, we human beings are capable of doing all of these things even though our body cannot compete with the innate ability those animals possess. We invent things that enable us to perform these activities: a boat allows us to move on the water, a house protects our body from becoming weathered, an elevator enables us to go up and down, an airplane flies us through the sky, and a satellite orbits us through outer space. These things are made possible because we have an adaptive body, mechanical hands, inspired emotions, constructive mind, and soaring spirit. We want our bodies to be more "duty free" so we can enjoy the ensuing convenience, the peace, the happiness, and the ecstasy.

Aside from the body, jade is as beautiful as the evergreen color of spring. It is more solid than plants, more radiant than any color spectrum, and more lasting than any organic matter. Yet, it is more fragile than our body, more solid than rock, and more brittle than our bones. We humans can make many imitations of an original object, and invent and produce an infinite variety of things meant to enhance our lives, but we cannot replicate the color of jade, nor can we copy the natural construct of jade. When the two coalesce, the elixir pursuing wisdom purifies the body and envisions the attraction of heavenly spirit. The reddish solar light ossifies the blue-green algae, the substance of the earth, into jade and displays its transparency as an eternal presence. Thus, Lao Zi uses the body and jade to validate the beauty and transparency of our eternal physical presence.

In the beginning of his Tao Te Ching, Lao Zi chooses the single word Tao to encompass his explanation of the original meaning of the practice. He calls upon the power of the body and the force of jade to demonstrate the elements which are valuable in understanding his couplet. Since the colors, sounds and structures are the three manifests of the Tao, Lao Zi relies on the body and jade to structure his teachings. They are useful in representing our biological experiences and our spiritual practices as we enter the Tao. Through effortless ("effortless" because anything we seek is an illusion of mind) search, he can find no other objects to alarm the reality of the ego, to cool the agitation of the organs, to inspire the vision of the mind, and to awaken the tranquility of the spirit. The body is beautiful yet fragile, jade is valuable yet brittle. The body is attractive but the mind sometimes opposes it: at times to be honored and admired, then ignored, forgotten, and taken for granted. Jade is invaluable but the mind recognizes it as sometimes sharper than a knife, easily damaged, and often more perishable than food.

Finally, in his search through all physical objects, Lao Zi selected the body and jade, which are more graphic and representative than the linguistic construction of the word Tao, to commence his teaching. Tao is silent, yet body and jade have their natural structures and appearances which are capable of echoing sounds, displaying colors, and demonstrating characters. The invisible Tao then manifests itself as the visible objects, the inaudible Tao becomes the uttering sounds, and the intangible Tao becomes tangible. Through mindful quest into cosmic nature, Lao Zi embraces the cosmic blue water with the earthly green land. Upon realizing the nature of the mind, he then unifies the beauty of the body and the ever-presence of jade into the oneness of self. Beyond any doubt, his body was as shabby as a beggar and as pure as a newborn baby. He asserts "The sage wears shabby cloth, but holds a treasure within." (72:4) This treasure is the vitality of the stomach, the prime of youth, and the substance of the Tao. Without bias, his mind is "as resonant as jade and as gravelly as stone." (39:7) It is resonant as in the sound of chanting and preaching, and gravelly in resonance when relieved from the obsession of biting and chewing.

## Body, the Troublesome Beauty

Our body provides the structure for our physical and experiential existence. It attracts and reflects the colors of our spirit by echoing and vibrating the sounds of being and becoming. Our physical existence represents the biological process of an organic being. Our experiential existence represents the manner in which the subjective individual and objective society interact, emerging in the manifestation of the mental processes. Both the physical and mental processes are well grounded in their existence in a biophysical body and psycho-spiritual mind. The body experiences (feels) and the mind is aware (senses). The biophysical body senses, processes, and experiences itself. The psycho-spiritual mind alters, projects, and guides both the experiential body and the intellectual mind. Interacting, the existential body processes the experiential body. The experiential body directs the existential body. The ensuing process is somewhat more mechanically oriented, while the experience, in its condensed form, is a process. Yet, the intellectual mind unravels the existential body, and the wise mind makes good use of the experiential body. Essentially, all experiences are processed at the physical level. The body holds and transforms them. Without the foundation of the body, both our physical and mental experiences are formless and meaningless. As independent as it is, without the existence of the body, the spirit is groundless and has no basic foundation to process itself.

The brain is an integral part of the physical and structural representation of mind. The brain is organic and the mind is mechanical. Brain function is essential to the organic function processing within the body, and mental activity is carried on through the systematic operation between the body and the mind, and between the self and the universe. The brain functions, the mind operates. Function is mechanically preprogrammed, and operation is systematically situated. Any organic being is a functional being, yet each living being's operation differs dramatically. This makes humans develop more human-oriented traits and other animals exhibit more animalistic traits. Among humans, those who are sexier, quicker, faster, and smarter perform more effectively and dramatically than those who are slower, the more withdrawn and introspective. Some may operate creatively, others kindly, and the rest more expansively. No one person possesses all these attributes, nor could they possibly handle them all in a single lifetime. We are able to manifest our unique individuality, yet retain our collective common ground.

The personal and social operations of the human system are based on the chain interaction of affective attraction, operative proficiency, and rewarding power. In this interaction, the attraction must be affective. Otherwise no stimulation occurs. Once the attraction is in effect, it must be both operable and proficient to sustain itself for its transformation into the next level. The operable proficiency leads necessarily to the last stage of this chain interaction. At its completion it proceeds to the next cycle. This is the rewarding stage based upon the success, satisfaction, and quality of the products. Again, if this were not so, there would be no reward granted. Effective power, in itself, is not sufficiently rewarding.

It is impossible to exercise these three stages at the same time. If the attractive affection, the operable proficiency and the rewarding power exist simultaneously, there would be no waiting and working and recovery periods in this chain interaction. There would be no differing dimensional realities. Duration is its required procedure.

Human interaction cannot exist in this condition. Even though the spirit is eternally beyond the creation of time, each individual soul is timely fashioned. Although the light is forever present, the psychobiological process of life manifests in the present with the condition having been created from the past and the expectation being designed for the future. Life is defined by time, experience requires the presence, success builds upon wishful projection, and enlightenment completes all the transformation.

In many situations, love and spiritual connection are affected. Alertness, swiftness and effectiveness operate. Success, satisfaction and gratification are the reward, the ultimate outcome. Meanwhile, mental stillness and tranquility stimulate the affective attraction, the patient and steadfast balance necessary to promote the operable proficiency. Letting go with no restraint by either the projected or rewarded outcome can change the entire process of the human systematic chain interaction into no more than a playful experience, leaving the memory as a meaningless blow on the cosmic wind. Certainly, between the inner stillness and attractive affection, between the almost unbearable patience required and the operative proficiency, between the forgetfulness and rewarding power, the mind must be ever attentive to what the body can do, and the body must be operative upon what the mind directs.

In a practical sense, we are aware that religion uses the power of affection and the discipline of love. Politicians are capable of making things operable. The mass population follows along with the operation and is therefore controlled by the economic and social power structures. Selfishness and patriotism are rewarded even if the price paid is the death of the body and affection of self-sacrifice. Forgiveness and letting go liberate the spirit, escalating the life journey to a higher level. During the complicated process of the mechanical operation of the mind, those who have power and position issue the awards, and those who do not have are rewarded. To have is the power and benefactor, not-to-have is the efficiency and usefulness.

Along this experiential process, there exists a difference between the organic body and the graphic mind. Each has its own special features and is an irreplaceable entity. The organic body is earthly and the graphic mind is holy. The organic body functions between purity and murkiness, drifting between successful flow and contaminated illness. The graphic mind falters between clarity and restlessness, is aware of objective reality and subjective consciousness. Naturally, they are the twins of our life, each thriving on the healthy existence of the other. When the body becomes functionless, the mind may recall some action being performed by the body, but it cannot force it. For example, when a person becomes handicapped, s/he may think, imagine, or wish the body to be productive, but without the aid of a wheelchair, the body is unable to get from place to place.

Conversely, when the brain is damaged at birth or severely injured later in life, the mechanical operation of the body may continue to function in its low quality or vegetative state. The body may continue to breathe, digest and eliminate, but the mechanical operation of the mind has lost the use of its directive power line. The entire sensibility becomes inoperative and may be completely lost. The brain is functional, but inoperative. What connects this power line? They are the mysteries of life, the wisdom of intelligence, the power of love, and capacity of talent.

Equally, when the body is sick, the mind is weak. When the mind is strong, the body is healthy. In retrospect, when the body is healthy, the mind can drift into a safe and transitional state; being aware of everything, but not actually engaged. The mechanical operation of the body is all that is happening. When the mind is sharp and strong, the body carries on its involuntary actions. The power and intelligence of the mind are enacted. Whether the mind is controlling itself or the body, the body is the center stage of the action. Whether the mind operates the brain or the entire body, it is the ego that eventually receives the rewards and the penalties of death, as the body finally succumbs to dust. The body is valued and the mind is gifted. In its yin form, value is functional, and gift is operative. In its yang form, the value is beautiful and the gift is lusty. The beauty of life forms the body and the lust for life operates the mind.

To explore this further, we need to understand that our body is the foundation for the mind and the temple of the spirit. The connection of body and mind and their power line operate within the body, among the organs, and beyond the self. When God wishes his spirit to be present on earth, Goddess renders the spirit as the physical presence. Then the soul treasures the presence, with the flesh serving as the foundation. When the spirit inspires the body, the hands build the temple. More treasured than anything in the world, the body represents the matter that is to be measured, whether as a reward (for self) or an award (for others), whether from the provider or for the benefactor. Human performance, in its entire energetic process, requires the presence of the body to be pursued, conducted, and perfected.

Most importantly, the body represents the beauty of form to be appreciated by the understanding mind, to be touched by the sensual mind, to be glorified by the egoistic mind, to be destroyed by the destructive mind, and to be reassured by the spiritual mind. Without the body, how do we expand the mind and cultivate the spirit? Without the body, how would the nutritious food be processed, the nurturing education take place, the healing medicine perform its task, and shining light vibrate? Without the body, where should the human materialistic and spiritual possessions be embraced? Without the body, how could the beauty of human life be valued any more than the state of dust? Without the body, how would human life continue and go forward in its eternal struggle to become one with God?

## Trapping in Justifying Body

In human life, the entity of the body and mind cannot exist by and for itself. They are interactive individual, inter-personal and cross-cultural components. The interactive elements deal with social, cultural and political aspects of human life. In this interactive macro human environment, the body of an individual could be represented as a statue holding the scales of justice in its hand. It is a container that recycles what the mind wishes to justify or has already done. When the mind's intention is to justify something, for example, a physical material or a mental space, it utilizes the body as a storage unit to manage and justify it. However, the mind sets such a mental configuration that the body can never prove itself, regardless of how strong or beautiful it may be and what it has been given, whether fresh or contaminated. The body can never escape the trap planned or designed by the mind. It simply serves as a vehicle to demonstrate that the mind is either intelligent and reasonable, mindful or egoistic. Ordinarily, the ego will be pacified but the body will be poisoned. The mindfulness is lost to the reasonable assessment of the price being paid; the price being illness resulting in death. In the history of the world, many political figures, revolutionary heroes and patriotic fighters have proven this many times. What they have done is demonstrate will power over body with the mind-set that others may appreciate what they have advocated. Objectively, a high price must be paid to establish justice. A much higher price must be set to regain the lost justice. Nevertheless, this action is taken for the purpose of obtaining the position of the mind's further promise.

In a culture where an individual or a group imposes all the actions of a new justice to preserve the already established system, what will be sacrificed once again is the body. This time, however, the scope is larger and the influence greater. The self is preserved upon what others have lost. For those who are anti-government, their only recourse is either to obey the imposed rules or re-establish the system with their own regulations. To kill the rival, to destroy the enemy, and to brainwash the masses is the manner in which they preserve justice. After their re-establishment, new rules represent the content, the means and the legislation of a new (same as the old) justice. This then becomes more validated than the virtue, the conscience, and the kindness.

In the face of justice, God remains silent. He has no need to justify Himself before the justice of mankind. God needs no justice to empower Himself or His transcendental consciousness among all the creatures. In the manner of justice being carried out, there are benefactors and victims on both sides. One side justifies, and the other is enslaved. With justice, the body is a tool, a smile, and an agreement. The mind makes the plea, the bargain, and executes the outcome.

According to Laoism, "Eminent justice engages, but does not respond adequately to situations. For that reason it is frustrated." (38:2)

When the spirit enters into the soul, the wisdom into the mind, the soul into the selfhood and ego into the selfishness, there is a total abandonment and rejection of Tao and Its Action. Only justice and priority are being exercised. The teaching of Laoism concludes that "When Tao is lost, it becomes Action (Te); When Action is lost, it becomes benevolence. When benevolence is lost, it becomes justice. When justice is lost, it becomes propriety. Propriety is the veneer of faith and loyalty, and the forefront of troubles." (38:3) Where does the trouble lodge? In the biological body, emotional soul, and spiritual mind. They are all there, languishing in the breathing flesh of the body.

Laoism advises us on this matter by explaining that "There is no right lawfulness. Justice tends towards the extreme. Kindness tends towards evil. People have been familiar with this for a long time." (58:3) As a matter of fact, people are so inured in the politics that they numb themselves into the comfort of their "little" justice, their individual freedom. What is the way out of this morass? Laoist's passage continues: "Be rounded without cutting. Be compatible without puncturing. Be straightforward without trapping. Be bright without dazzling." (58:4) This passage on kind action does not advocate the teaching, but admonishes it. It does not advise, but merely suggests. It is not a warning as to what should or should not be done, but a simple explanation. Cutting is painful, puncturing is distrustful, trapping is unreliable, and dazzling is cheap. When a person behaves in such a manner, everything is a loss and nothing gains. S/he sells all and benefits nothing. When one is confronted with such situations, only hostility and betrayal are the means of action. In contrast, "be rounded" recognizes all, compatibility displays all, straightforward discloses all, and bright penetrates all. These right techniques deal with the central point and the neutral ground. Lao Zi himself practiced this philosophy. Buddha awakened himself with this philosophy. Confucius established his disciplines through following this philosophy.

## Oh, What a Body!

The body is such a field that it awakens the spirit, electrifies the love, legalizes the responsibility, and individualizes the self. The body rotates the awareness, arouses the intention, processes the stage of becoming, stores what has been experienced, and hides what remains. Inwardly, the body conceals the creative genes, evokes the curious impulse, liberates the unknown reality, and fully expects the perfection. Outwardly, the body circulates the energy, transmits the memory, echoes the mirroring, and provokes the lost self. Beyond, the body designs the invitation, expresses the hope, shares the experience, and transforms the secrecy. Life is being lived in all its intricacies.

In the present time, although you love your body, imperfection gnaws away at it. When you betray your body, honesty protects it. When you ignore your body, thirst cannot create urine and hunger cannot create the process of elimination. When you glorify yourself with your body, illness results. Then the body rises from the hellish darkness it creates, stands upon the gravitational force, walks through the exploitive journey toward its unavoidable death, and changes once again into a state of dust. When, at last, you take leave of your physical body, spirit smiles down upon it. It is then reformed by the conditions of water droplets, the swirling of endless blowing, the forces of penetrating lightening, and sparks of self-wavering.

How can we possibly imagine life's experiential realms without the existence of the body? We sense and breathe with it, walk and sleep with it. It is exceedingly precious. It is disgusting. It is breath taking. Safe and free, no, it is not. What can we do with it, and what could we do without it? We must stay with it, explore it, learn from it and finally, let it go.

## The Evergreen Jade-body

Jade is often judged by Chinese to be the most valuable substance in the world because of its natural highly prized quality, artistic beauty, symbolic [green for life] representation, mystic formation, ritual practice and cultural evaluation. The clearness of its transparency, the purity of its color and the force of its attraction are the standard qualities so meaningful and symbolic to both the being and the becoming of life. Gold cannot compete in natural quality with jade; spring cannot surpass jade's eternal color of new growth; the sky cannot attain the clarity and deep degree of transparency. Physical body cannot appreciate itself enough without the mystic protection of jade. Personal value cannot be upgraded without the highest symbolic representation of jade being presented by the emperor. Healing does not enhance its miraculous performance without the sensation of touch with the jade. Physical longevity cannot be preserved beyond death without the artistically extended presence of the carved jade. That is why the first character of the Couplet translates as the sound of jade and represents its obvious meaningful value. We thrive on green vegetables and plants and treasure the color green. We are the treasures of the evergreen jade-body. Consider the most beautiful and artistic display of our body. It is carved in jade. Jade in turn, protects it. Beyond any semblance of a doubt, it embodies the exquisite perfection of humanly jade-body.

In contrast, the human body is always vulnerable to the invasion of a virus, helpless before the ego confrontation, and numbing in its confrontation of emotional disturbances. The human body is both solid and tangible. The solid aspect applies to the perfection of human form. As a baby develops, its physical structure becomes more solid, as does the development of its master, mind. At the end of life, the body becomes so solid that it atrophies, and the mind so rigid that eventually it ceases to function.

Each individual has a specific psychic structure unique to her/his individuality. This psychic structure is as old as its ageless spiritual soul, and as sharp as its penetrating light. This psychic structure may co-exist with the body, but it does not really care about the body. It is a sympathetic reaction to the body, quite uncaring. The body is dying, the mind is crying, the psychic is smiling. The body is unendurable, the mind is untamable, and spirit is imperishable.

The tangible side to this is that the human body-mind often becomes weak, frail, lame and disabled. It requires merciful acts of kindness, attention, care, and patience in order to cultivate and maintain it. Any misuse of words, action, judgment, and evaluation may completely destroy the beauty and value of it. Consider the time it takes and the effort needed to make the body-mind readily playful, workable, and tractable. The body's fears, however, remain hidden: sickness is concealed; while death stands by, waiting peacefully.

To make matters worse, the mind wishing to be pleased at all times, serves only to accentuate the fear. It changes sharply, jumps madly and flies aimlessly. It is the spirit that protects the body, encourages the mind, nourishes the love and uplifts the soul. Therefore, the body has been proven to be unreliable. The mind is untrustworthy. The spirit remains unbroken. The body exists, the mind possesses, the spirit releases.

In describing jade's immutable beauty and power, we observe the smooth appearance of its surface, soft, tangible and caressing to the touch. Yet, when carved, it is hard, fragile and brittle. A slight misuse of the knife could easily cut the hand that holds and shapes it, completely destroying the usefulness of the carving. It is an extremely difficult skill to carve the natural pieces of jade into works of art. Enormous energy is needed to then display and preserve these art works, since they are no longer regarded as natural pieces of jade. They are beautiful to our eyes and are an attraction to our mind. To understand and utilize this skill enables us to bring forth and express the art of right cultivation which differs from the process of education, civilization, and institutionalization. This art of right cultivation does not deal with right or wrong, but develops through processing something to the right point, the right degree, and the right perfection.

## Characteristic Representation

The first character in the couplet combines the body and jade in order to emphasize the value, the virtue, the quality, and the longevity of life. The two sub-characters, "body" for shen and "treasure" for bao, are constructed by Lao Zi to represent the descriptive character of body as jade. All statues and sculptures using jade or marble represent the treasured values of our physical presence and evergreen land. Our physical body represents all that is to be valued, and jade symbolizes the enduring growing power of earth's land masses. Lao Zi was very insightful in the aspect of constructing his own language. Very few people in Chinese history have been capable of accomplishing this. Not only does the first character have its own pictorial representation of Tao and its power, but the following thirteen characters in the couplet do as well. All the words employed in his teaching come from the standard Chinese characters. These fourteen characters in the couplet do not belong to Chinese language. They belong to Laoism; they belong to the teachings of Lao Zi.

Intelligent and influential as he had been, Confucius himself was unable to achieve this.

As Laoism is presented, the correct form of meditation should begin in the body. Spirit lives within the temple of biological body, actualizes itself through the bodily experience, and finally realizes its true essence beyond the existence of physical body. Due to this, meditation cannot be defined as the creation of worship by the mind, nor can it be seen as a conscious effort to raise the invaluable spirit skyward by separating the mind from its mutually existential body. Its meaning exists in the process of grounding the cloudy and restless mind into the abdominal area. The meditative experience builds upon the transformative spiritual wisdom in the midst of the biological process. The religious practice liberates the spirit from the mixed experience of good and bad, of earthly and holy.

The abdominal area centers the body and the spirit. In this area, God's realization actualizes upon the tiny drop of groundless space called caldron. Both biological experience and spiritual awakening need to establish themselves within this groundless space. The physical transformative experience awakens in this groundless space. The energy derived from wisdom rises from this groundless space. The essence of biological regeneration is discharged from this space. A more detailed discussion will be contained in the following chapter.

The pivotal meditative question regarding the body is: how do we treat our body when we can neither worship nor abuse it? How can we take possession of our body while we are abusing it? How can we talk about the value of our body when it is known to be the heart of all disasters? How can we think about living a long life when the body begins dying at a young age? The teaching of Laoism states that the body is the heart of all troubles. The heart here indicates the groundless space in the abdominal area, the troubles are the turmoil of the mind which sink deeply into the body. The heart is the invisible space of all the illnesses, disasters and trials of life. This reminds us that body is not only the most valuable thing in the world, but also the seed and source of all disasters. Values are the yang forms of representation, and disasters are the yin forms of manifestation.

To remove ourselves from disaster and dissolve the troubles, we should follow in the footsteps of sagehood by using our body as a caldron to cultivate the spiritual self. The experiences of sagehood in both choices are: "Relaxing the body, the body comes to the fore. Beyond the body, the body comes to the fore. Beyond the body, the body exists of itself." (7:3) This does not mean that we should shy away from the reality of life by abandoning our mental responsibility, which is the care-taker of our body, both emotional and spiritual. This does not mean that our mind should operate in a Utopian-like state. Nor does it mean that we need not think about dealing with the real world, or that which is real in the mind and in all natural operations. The main thrust is that we should not let the ego dominate our lives by separating our spiritual world from our physical existence; we should not permit our emotional world to hinder or hamper our physical and spiritual world; and we should not let our biological world degrade and diminish our spiritual world by rendering it to ashes and dust.

Rather, we should apply the useful methods to preserve ourselves and to be present with the reality of the world. To be present with reality is to abandon egoism completely. "Blunting the sharp edge, unraveling the tangles, husbanding into the light, being as ordinary as the dust." (4:3) When the need for striving is restrained, superiority and fame lose their importance; when the complexities and conflicts in the mind are unraveled, one can emerge into the light by viewing egoistic life and physical body as the state of a world of dust. When one lives without selfishness, one's physical body will become freed from restraint, the mistreatment and the oppression being carried out by one's ego.

Actually, our physical body knows innately how to feel and relax, and how to exist in a danger-free world. However, our minds either worry too much, are too deeply involved in our situations or we tend to become overly possessive. The ego drives our body and spirit into this state of emotional turmoil, exhausting our energy. It is not our body that ends our lives, it is the action of our unrelenting ego that destroys our lives, and it is our emotions that exhaust our life force.

Awakening possibility establishes the use of body as a smelter of the immortal self-elixir. It relies upon the abdominal area to serve as a caldron in which to cultivate the spiritual self. This is the message we will now explore.

## Meditation Practice

1. Seek a comfortable environment, with as few distractions as possible. Perhaps this may be right where you are now. Position your body in either a standing posture or be seated. Join your hands together horizontally, with the left hand on the outside for males and right hand outside for female. The first joint of the thumbs should be touching each other. The hands, properly postured, are placed in front of the thymus gland right between the two breasts and the joints of the rib cage. Feel the relaxed but structured sensation of your bodily rhythms.

2. Become aware of your breathing now. Don't try to control it. Just feel the presence of the breath.

3. Visualize the three most important facts about yourself, your birth date (year, month, date and time), your name (first name, given name, professional name, last name, and any other names related to you), and your address (the present address or the most memorable one). Recall consciously, remember truthfully, and recite silently.

4. Take a deep breath and put all the information you have recalled and recited into the hands. Feel the energetic vibration around the hands and chest as though are just coming into existence, calling yourself by name, and stepping into the door of that comfortable environment.

5. Take another breath, and push the hands from the chest down to the abdominal area. Exhale, feel the warmth in that area. Practice this continuously until you sense the circulation of the energy from the abdominal area and place it wherever you consciously direct it. Make the above steps a daily practice.

6. You will acquire an energetic power by following these steps but always place yourself mentally with the physical presence, especially the sexual desire, the mental ability, and intellect. Keep them all under the control of the "cooking vessel," or inside the caldron of our cosmic reality.

# NOTES

# STEP TWO: *BODY*

Structure: body 身 + elixir 丹
Sound: lu
Meaning: body

## Understanding the Form

In this character there are two sub-characters, one for "body" or shen, and the other for "cinnabar [elixir]" or dan. The word dan is rooted in the Taoist's alchemical practices. According to its description in the Chinese dictionary, dan firstly represents the raw substances of cinnabar that are used by outer alchemists to smelt elixir. Secondly, dan is the outcome of the alchemical process, the elixir itself. In inner alchemy, the character dan represents the groundless space within the body where the pure and immortal self is produced and cultivated. The space is called Cinnabar Field, or dantian. It is "groundless" in the sense that there is no organic correspondence and has nothing to do with specific energy patterns produced by the body and mind. It represents the outcome of energy transformation. In Qigong and martial arts practices, the abdominal area is called xia dan tian, xia meaning "lower," dan meaning "cinnabar," and tian meaning "field." Dantian is a term very often used in both meditation and martial arts practice. It has the same connotation as the chakra in Yoga tradition. There are seven chakras in yoga but only three dantian in Qigong. The centers for chakras are located around the spine, while dantians align themselves along the central channel in the body. We will discuss this more fully throughout the book.

In Taoism, the human body is not just a vehicle upon which the mind and spirit exist, but also a "cooking vessel" into which an eternal life form could possibly be transformed before the body deforms. The word "form" [xing] in Chinese is structural, conditional, observable, and tangible; its character involves a changing state, and its function evolves into a condition of stability.

The character of "life form" is a changing form. The function of life is formless. The meaning of life is a functionless changing form. The formless form is the womb, the vision, and the cosmic image. The forming form retains the virtue, conceals the essential feature, and evokes the readily involving. The changing form is the mutation, the perception, and the transition. Altogether it represents the invisible, the inaudible, and the intangible of the Tao. The teaching of Laoism explains this notion by saying "Look for it and not see it, it is called invisible; Listen to it and not hear it, it is called inaudible; Reach for it and not touch it, it is called intangible. These three are beyond reckoning. When these three merge, they are One." (14:1,2) Here "one" is the beginning of forming form, the readily changing form, and ultimate formless form. This "one" is not one drop of water, it is the forming model of water. This "one" is not any visible appearance, it is the ever changing image of nature. This "one" is not the reliable connection, the wishful hope, and returning point. It is the changeless void. This one is not one, but three; not three, but a multitude; not a multitude, but a formless seed of the universe.

For example, each of us represents the one, the duality and the multitudes of human form because we are the combination of heaven and earth with their dualistic harmony. Each of us represents the oneness of God's divine image. Each of us contains the natural makeup of duality: masculine and feminine, affirmative and negative, birth and death. And each of us is but a picture of the multitude, and a member of the entire population. We are the three, because we came from the union of our biological parents. They are the harmony of yin and yang. Because of such, we have the potential of both, masculine and feminine. That is why the Taoist's notion of "virgin boy" and "virgin girl" is reliable, practical, and meaningful. We are also the two. Since we are the two, just as our parents are two, we have the potential to become either the three or the one. The three is the manifestation of the two, and the one is the unification of the two. We are also essentially one, since we are the undivided and inseparable one.

We are the complete structural and functional representation of a human being. One, two and three are the descending power which creates. Three, two, and one are ascending power which returns. Left, center and right represent the horizontal dimension. It also stands for the hearing power, the gravitational force, and the cosmic wind. They are the function of shoulders, arms and hands.

Bottom, middle and top represent the vertical dimension. It functions as the sound, the penetration, and the rotational explosion. They are the power of thighs, legs, and feet. Front, in between and back represent the cosmic Qi circulation of water and fire and their harmonized element, sweet dew. It also refers to the structural manifestation. Yes, the mystery of trinity.

Aside from the trinity, there is still another aspect more mystic, more powerful and more magnificent than anything else in the world. It is the mystic wonder, the God, the Allah, the Brahman, the Void, the Tao. According to Laoism, "Tao gives rise to one. One gives rise to two. Two gives rise to three. Three gives rise to all things. All things carry yin and embrace yang by drawing qi together into harmony." (42:1,2) In mathematics, these four things represent zero, one, two, and three. Zero is the beginning and where everything finally returns. God is positive zero, Goddess is negative zero, Void is emptiness and Tao is nothingness. One is where all the creatures partake, every form stands, and each individual obtains. But two and three do not necessarily follow the mathematic formulae of multiplication or division. Two is the duality of co-dependence, the polarity of independence, and the unification of harmony. Three represents both the beginning of manifest and the end of a revolution, both the starting point and enclosing circle, both the unbelievable initiation and absolute resolution.

It is a fact that all things under heaven are one, all creatures in the world represent the three. This is why each of us has our own version of God, and this God is no more than the empty blank, the nothing-as-such void, the all powerful structureless form, and the ever-present nonspecific image. God comes before the form forms, prior to the energy circulates, above the completion matches and beyond the change catches. While Goddess is behind the why of darkness, after the how of death's destruction, beneath where the light shines, and within which the everlasting is sustained.

In our body, the yin and yang are the widow and the orphan. The widow has no food, no child, and no love. The orphan has no family, no home, and no comfort. This is why we are hungry and homeless. The Qi is the light, the spiritual energy, the nutrition, and the physical power needed to sustain life. Everything that is formed depends on Qi. Anything that moves begins with the function of Qi. In order to express the mystery of trinity and the maker of mystery, which represents God, Laoist employs the word "great" to describe them. It says that "Tao is great. Heaven is great. Earth is great. Kingship is great. These are the four great things in the world, kingship is one of them." (25:3) Kingship is the image of widowhood and orphanage. King has everything, yet he is nothing. He has all the rooms but nowhere to sleep. He speaks for all the voices but no one listens to his inner silent loneliness. He projects all the power but no other person could bear his burdensome suffering. Everybody obeys his order but no one processes his disorder. Everyone worships his glory but nobody cares about his misfortune. He is the image of the world yet nothing bears his absolute image.

Are we all like that? Yes, we all are and it is inherent to our nature. We all are the kingdom of our own cosmic humanity, individual selfhood and absolute oneness. No other person has all that we have, and no other person can understand what is in our inner peace by viewing our smiling or crying countenance. We are great, unbearably great, incompetently great, senselessly great.

Laoist's idea then conveys that "Humankind takes its origin from earth. Earth takes her origin from heaven. Heaven takes its origin from Tao. Tao takes its origin from Nature." (25:4) Where does it come from and/or go? Are we that earthly? Besides the land we walk, sleep and rest upon, in spite of the multitudes we have become, we can still see the sky in our openness and view the stars through our hopes and in our dreams. We are not earthly to the exclusion of all else. We are the mixture of heaven and earth. The sentence "Humankind takes its origin from earth" indicates the nature of the biophysical body that we possess, not the conscientious mind we perceive, nor the spiritual beings that we are. We are not that earthly; we are holy as well! And yet, we are murky, mixed, confused, and distorted. That is why we need to build a temple within, where our spirit can be secured, protected, encouraged, and surrendered. That is why we need food for nourishment, to eat humanly, express soulfully, and elevate spiritually.

The word "form" can also be viewed from various perspectives. Mystically, the form is the void, the big valley; in evolution the form is the embryo, the cradle; philosophically the form is the wordless insight, mindless wandering; and scientifically the form is the undetectable big bang, the unavoidable black hole.

The formless form holds, dissolves, embraces, and qualifies; it represents the evolutionary dissolving, it performs the endless changing patterns, and it contains the unitary trend. It is what the inside out is, what the creativity generates, and what the descendant drops. That is the eternal, the self-continuity, and the collective. The forming form breaks, evolves, spreads, and quantifies: it activates the silence, voices the vibration, and suffuses into the multitude. That is the external, the self-evolving, and the specific. The external life form constitutes the mass and the multiplicity of all the individualized creatures. The changing form shapes, displays, protects, and governs: it runs in between the river beds, vibrates between the breath and sweat, and rotates between the light and sound. That is the central, the medium, and the neutral. They are the co-existence, the negotiation, the bargain, and the fighting for identity.

The eternal human life form is the pure self, resulting from the cultivation of combined selves. Since it is eternal, it differs from the multitudes of external life forms, which represent the unique and diversified individuals constituting the collective eternal life form. Viewing these two interdependent aspects of sameness from the experiential results, Laoism describes vividly: "Being at peace, one can see into the subtle. Engaging with passion, one can see into the manifest. They both arise from the same source with different names. Both are called the mystery within the mystery. They are the door to all wonders." (1:3,4) Peaceful subtlety is the forming form, and passionately manifesting is the formless form. The same source carried different names. The mystery within opens the door to all wonders and closes the gateway that is beyond penetration.

In this life, we possess the enormous potential of building, making and contributing everything to the world by tapping into the inner peace and stillness. Yet, we are nothing, we have done nothing, and we will become nothing. This is due to the nature of our collective individuals being a formless form. Every one of us is a perfect concrete form of a living being, yet each one of us is a useless form due to the varieties of personality, and the uniqueness of each individuality. To us, the word "form" is individual by nature, and multiple by manifest. The selves that utilize the pure self represent dual beings of human nature, yin and yang, feminine and masculine. Yin is the forming form, and yang is the formless form. The forming process is never ending, and the formless manner is never extinguished. This is the Chinese mentality in the description of duality. They place the yin forward since yin is the form of all forms, and the mother of all mothers. Yet yang sleeps inside her, exists aside from her, leaps around her, and transcends beyond her.

## Caldron—the Self-germinating Cooking Vessel

By understanding the vehicle to be constantly transporting the process of life, we can comprehend the usefulness of the vessel. The vehicle represents the action of four corners, that is, hands and legs: hands drive and legs roll; hands are the tools and legs are the marks; hands hold the signs of inspired vulnerability, and legs stand upon the frictions of relaxed groundlessness. In contrast, the vessel represents both the container that cooks and digests the needed nutrition for the body, and the model that reforms, reproduces, and recycles what the abdominal field requires. The abdomen has the utilities for the final food processes. It also has the organs, or vessels, to reproduce the new life forms. The utilities include parts of the digestive system and excretory system, while the vessels exemplify the kidneys and the bladder. The Chinese noted that the kidneys have both yin and yang.

By using the modern anatomical and physiological terminology, the kidney yin includes both the kidneys and the bladder, while the kidney yang is constructed by the adrenal glands for both sexes, ovarian glands for the female and prostate glands for the male. The kidneys contain, distill, and recycle the leftover dust, the earthly matter. The bladder functions as a lake for a regional land, or as a sea for a continent. It deals with the watery materials. In terms of kidney yang Qi, the sexual desire of adrenal glands works simultaneously with the mental conscious desire of the pituitary glands and the emotional fluids of the thymus glands. This so-called fight-or-flight syndrome originating in the adrenal glands has the ability to empower the opposite sex, or the rivalrous enemy. This is the will power of the kidney, the power to dominate and the ability to overcome. This is the power of fight. The inability to demonstrate this power causes the person to withdraw, become fearful and numb. This energetic manifestation of flight is a result of the inability to stand up for oneself, to be fearful toward the outside world. The flight's eyes are closed, the body withdraws, and one becomes numb and/or vulnerable.

Essentially, the kidney yang organs deal with sexual reproduction, while the kidney yin organs filter, excrete and reabsorb the food products and the kidney Qi. In the household environment, the kitchen represents the kidney yang organs, and bathroom represents the kidneys yin organs.

## Recording the Cooking Vessel

Historically, the "cooking vessel" in the couplet was not an ordinary ancient Chinese cooking vessel with two loop handles and three extended legs being used for cooking and occasionally sacrificing. It was a tool for enlightenment. The outer alchemists viewed this tool as a huge vessel made with forged iron or as calcined metals which were used at that time to smelt the life-pill, life-elixir or "philosopher stone." In the Inner alchemy, this "cooking vessel" was named Caldron or Cinnabar Field. To Taoist outer alchemists, there was nothing more important than smelting the life-pills. There was no mechanical product superior to the elixir they could forge. The techniques in metallurgy were the only means known to crystallize those life-pills.

From the scientific point of view, the outer alchemists gained much detailed information regarding the varieties of inorganic substances. They were then prepared to absorb the knowledge of the smelting operation. They also discovered certain inorganic substances that had pharmaceutical applications for several diseases. For example, HgS can be used to tranquilize one's mind, Fe3D4 is effective in treatment of epilepsy and carbuncle, As2S2 can be used to cure parasitic and skin diseases, and As can be used to heal parasitic disease and soften the skin. A marked historical contribution (or disaster as it may be termed) was the accidental discovery of gunpowder. This discovery altered the human fighting capacity greatly. Fists and arrows and knives escalated into bullets and cannons and rockets.

The process of producing golden elixir is the earliest practice of chemistry of sorts on this earth. When the Arabic nations became aware of this practice, they renamed this "golden elixir" "alchemy." The idea then traveled to the West where the alchemical practice of producing philosopher's stone took a remarkable leap forward during the eleventh and twelfth centuries. Even today, the word elixir remains as the general name for a myriad of household remedies.

The financial support for those findings came from the tax money granted by the emperors. Ironically, these so-called-life-elixirs poisoned more emperors in the history of China than the total number of the assassinated U. S. Presidents. Seven emperors were poisoned to death during the early Tang Dynasty (618-907 A.D.). Yet, no one blamed the alchemists for their "wrongdoing," perhaps because of their honest intention or the emperors' insurmountable desire to become immortal upon power. That was the cultural norm at that time. People reacted to the death of an emperor poisoned by the elixir in the same manner in their time, as our modern men and women may react to the death of an astronaut in an exploding spaceship or a lab researcher poisoned by a chemical leak.

## A Cultural Norm

Contrary to modern scientific pragmatists, these alchemists never dreamed of mass producing their ideas. Nor did they imagine making a living organism or living in an environment made controllable through the use of machines. They thought only of the process of smelting minerals into elixir, or cultivating the biological hormones into nectar. Nothing other than the elixir (material and spiritual) was desired. The only reward they sought was to continue their devotion to the practice toward enlightenment. Due to their single-minded proclivity, there could be no mass production of any sort, since an elixir is not a scientifically labeled nor economically produced product useful in any trade. Enlightenment is not for the purpose of making life convenient: it is beyond the ideal and practical usage of convenience; nor is it a merchandise that can be commercially traded: the true self can never be commercialized.

Judging from the modern scientific point of view, these alchemists never visualized the possibility of systemizing their mental ideas into certain fixed and tested objectives to be mechanically operated, scientifically demonstrated, and commercially traded. To them, the elixir is the medium between biological life and spiritual existence, and nothing more. It is a product that represents both the subjective longing for and objective holding on. It is God's vision within man's defective mind, and it is man's hands-on power working within God's invisible transformation. Most importantly, the elixir represents the spiritual transformation of physical matters, as well as the process of elevating a man's life on earth into becoming a holy one in heaven.

This phenomenon of immortality is not unknown to the masses in Chinese culture. Aside from their political and social economic system, as well as their family structure, the Chinese mind has never desired anything beyond the Tao, the Ultimate Nature. In their collective mind, the final process of the finest practice of life has never veered from the immortal. This mentality traces its origin back to the myth, the legend, the cultural practices of primitive worship, and personal accounts of attaining immortality. The documented materials range from the first man on earth to the detailed descriptions of the eight immortals, and from the first emperor of China to more recent self-determined individuals. Always considered to be the one closest to this stage of sagehood is the emperor (or so it was believed). The Chinese mythological descriptions and their legendary practices inform that reaching this position is the necessary first step to entering the Tao of heaven. The practices of obtaining this state are those of alchemical refinements, both inner and outer.

In Chinese culture, an emperor or a king is considered the intermediary between man and god. He acts upon God, speaks for the Great, acts through his super power, and obeys his own divine law. He personalizes the power by embracing the impersonal nature of spirit. His personal power demonstrates the ruling authority, and the impersonal nature mystifies the "crowning" position. Power governs the country; discipline promotes the temple. In the country, he administers the reality. Within the temple, he worships the Divine Order. He is egoistic to the unruly and merciless in his authority over life and death. He is spiritual to the selfless and humble. He is the cultural hero within the national race, and he is the ritualized image of human self. He is: a self imbued with power, knowledge, and wisdom; a self that utilizes the beauty and lust of human physical appearance; a self that is capable of destroying all enemies; and a self that would protect the physical environment where the population can then live in peace and happiness.

The image of a Chinese emperor differs from the rest of the world, now as in the past. For example, the first emperor of China, Qinshihuang (259-210 B. C.), would not support any ideas of mass mechanical operation in the society nor would he establish a political system that would separate itself from religious practice. Although he did not worship God he did abide by the Tao. He wanted to go to heaven, not by following God's invitation, but by achieving immortality himself. In its entirety, the king represents the will power of the human mind. This will power is sum and substance of the life force it is, what the rest of us, collectively, strive to achieve.

In this respect, in Chinese culture, individuality merges inside the communality. Democracy is the spiritual practice of the individual and family belief system. Temple is the sacred altar. No one rules the spirit. Everyone desires to be the master-controller of one's reality. There is the sense of freedom of birthright which is governed by the dogmatic fine art of Confucian intellectual practice. Family name is the spiritual name, national pride is the collective ego: ethical but generous, homogeneous but incestuous.

Spiritual belongings and religious worship are but individual endeavors and diverse beliefs. In the history of China, no institutional religion that could possibly override the power of an emperor has ever existed. There has never been an official religion that completely controls the imagined or practical directions of worship aside from family temples. The Chinese have never been given freedom of action but have always been endowed with freedom of belief. Therefore, their diversified practices range widely from worshiping a kitchen god to honoring a patriotic hero, from primitive worship of gods (such as thunder god, ocean god, etc) to an idealized respect for Buddha, and from polytheistic believers (anything that helps the believer's wishes come true) to unified believers (the unification of Confucianism, Buddhism and Taoism). There has always been someone ruling the reality of their way of life, but no one can ever rule their inner minds. It is in this form of society that any religious group may attempt to get a foothold, whether it is indigenous Taoism or foreign religions such as Buddhism, Islam, Christianity, or even Communism.

## Historical Lesson

In this particular land, the idea of being immortal and becoming a sage is deeply rooted in the conscious activation and subconscious instinct. The final episode is reaching the "Heavenly Country." The literal description of the holy person's life style becomes the highest peak and most essential purpose for the writers' imagination to dwell upon. Ironically, it is the only therapeutic method for writers and readers to step beyond the reality of life controlled by the emperor. The desire-free action of sagehood represents the archetype in the minds of people. Sage has greater power to symbolize the hope of relief from pain and suffering, which is orchestrated by the ruling authority. The sage's spiritual nature awakens the people's conscious suffering, personally and culturally.

In the history of the Chinese mind, the machine (or qi, which has the same pronunciation as the "qi" for life force, but is done with a different character) is never placed above the Tao and the Self. The machine can never replace the responsibility and duty of one's natural life for any reason whatsoever. Science is a subject not connected to living out one's life. Life itself is an objectified subjective system with no separation between the flashes of mental ideas and the physical performances. Whether subjective or objective, it is nothing other than the mutual transformation from one to the other and from end to end. The Chinese do not think about being and becoming, they are rooted with yin and yang. The final transformation from earthly yin life to heavenly yang life is the act of taking the final step into the realms of immortal life. This has been demonstrated scientifically by the outer alchemists and practiced diligently by the inner alchemists. The outer alchemists have faith in obtaining a scientifically based outcome, while the inner alchemists rely individually on the spiritualized self.

The lesson learned from the outer alchemists is that the golden elixir smelted in the "cooking vessel" has no power to enable them to become immortal but is an effective way to commit suicide. Consider the possibility that the future of our science may follow in exactly the same footsteps once walked by the Chinese outer alchemists. We will never be truly happy nor step through the portals of heaven by relying purely on science, but we can certainly kill ourselves en masse. A nuclear war in the near future could radiate the world, destroying our planet's forgiving, regenerating, and life supporting qualities. If we are somehow prepared to escape this earth's atmosphere, it remains for us to return to earth physically. Earth is our mother. Our bodies have no place to stay and live other than on our earthly mother's flesh (land) and blood (water).

## The Inner Alchemists' Forming Trinity

To the inner alchemists, the ultimate proof of their life long practices being effective over time is derived from the transformation of the individually isolated self into a complete self. This is accomplished by combining the true self with the other self. Taoists call this the unitary play between the "virgin boy" and the "virgin girl." One is the true self, the longing and lonely self. The other is the lost self, the wishful and invited self. Regardless of the gender difference, every individual has the potential of these two selves. The conscientious awareness and conscious intention share the same source, but manifest in different directions. The true self and the lost self represent the two extremes, the two dots, and the two ends of oneness. The practical difference is that, as anatomically independent individuals, each of us is endowed with only one true self. This true self is accompanied with the other which is our driving force, our playful mate, our dependable resource, and our rewarding partner. The true self endows us with confidence, ensures our security, and cares for our biological existence. The lost self provides the hope, attracts the longing, and sacrifices the true self in order to be unified within and without. This represents both the objective matter and subjective transformation. This is the unity of Tao, the harmony of yin and yang, the embracing of the two opposites. We will see the detailed discussion and practices in the following twelve chapters.

Since there must be a central point in which the vessel is located, a neutral ground and common agreement is necessary for the two to meet and unify. There must be a connection where the minds interact, the bodies unify and the souls integrate. This connection is the vessel. In Taoist inner alchemy, there are three distinguishing places in our body: these places are called Cinnabar Fields or Elixir Fields. The lower Cinnabar Field is the actual place for the vessel to be set, where the caldron is located. It is the center for biological manifestation. It is in this empty place, or the groundless space as we discussed earlier, where all the abdominal organs are unified. The Middle Cinnabar Field is located in the thymus gland. It is the center for displaying both the emotions and personalities. The Upper Cinnabar Field is located at the central joint where the two sides of the brain split and then rejoin, between the pituitary glands and pineal gland. It is the center for intellect and spirituality.

This is as close as we can come to sharing, without heart-to-heart connection with the true meaning of the Tao. Its true meaning is shrouded in secrecy and cannot be disclosed. When the mind is not distilled and the body is not purified, the time has not yet come to ensure the information of true understanding and complete transformation.

## The Contribution of Three Cinnabar Fields

Just as water has three states: frozen, fluid and steaming, so, too, does the body. The three Cinnabar Fields represent the three states of the same source but with differing manifestations. Each has its distinguished role, but none can exist by itself. They are inter-dependent. Ultimately, they are the same with no essential difference in terms of their source of energy. In the inner alchemical tradition, the practitioner's faith is derived from, entrusted by and rewarded by her/himself. According to Laoism, "If you value the world as you do the body, you can be entrusted with the world. If you love the body as you love the beauty of the world, you will be responsible for the world." (13:4) Taoists treasure the belief that, in human life, the body is the country, and the mind is the king. When the body can no longer exist, the entire country vanishes. When the body has blockage within, the mind needs to remove the blockage to enable it to run smoothly again. When the body can no longer tolerate the stress coming from the mind, the entire kingdom becomes psychotic; when the body cannot recycle what the mind creates, the country will be poisoned to death.

In comparison, when the winter snow covers the remains of a glorious harvest of the fall, this "white funeral dressing" recycles all and nourishes the new growth that is due in the spring. The earth mother has its innate capacity to recycle its own products, including our human bodies. By the same token, we are responsible for recycling whatever our mind creates and our hands have fashioned. Nature does not have this obligation. This is the uncertainty that faces us. Who knows where modern science will lead us. We reap what we sow. What we have reaped is poisonous. Who can survive a nuclear disaster?! Should that day arrive, life as we know it now will cease abruptly. It will be the demise of all living things on earth, the death of mankind. The blissful spirits will rise above our mother earth and hungry ghosts will dance in the silent darkness.

In the final analysis, history has proven that all the combined efforts exerted by the outer Taoist alchemists can be transformed into the inner alchemy. The inner alchemy performs the very complicated procedure which deals with the transformation of the life-force into golden elixir, through meditation practice. The golden elixir is called "life-pill." It is the second Laoist's character representing the body as the foundational laboratory in which to produce the life-long-pill [elixir]. The body itself is the laboratory. The mind charges the energy surrounding it and then proceeds to regenerate it. An example of the simplest procedure that this energetic cycle performs begins when the body feels hungry and mind enters the process of satisfying the hunger. The body is an energy device conducted by the mind. The signals between the two are ever present and ever true. In an extreme situation, when the body requires an energy supply, the mind may find it necessary to drive the body many miles distant, crossing the intra-cultural land into a fearful zone in its effort to obtain this needed supply. It may be just a bowl of soup, a matter of currency, or a comfortable support, a tender and selfless love. The body is busy processing, and mind is constantly supervising. If all goes well, the "dissolving" process will function after the food is consumed. Fluids, such as sweat, urine, feces and sexual fluid, and leftover matters are then discharged from the body as waste products. If the body does not respond as it should, the mind calls upon the healing power to encourage the natural flow. Should the body become permanently inoperable with time, the mind will leave the body as it returns to its original state, the holy or ghostly spirit. If holy, there will be a greater, more intense light. If ghostly there will be impenetrable darkness.

Body is such a remarkable lab that it enables all the human activities to flow within. All these activities are energetic in essence, and healing is its potential. Hua Tuo, who lived in the 2nd century A.C. and was one of the most illustrious doctors in Chinese medical history, tested the clinical results and healing potential of hundreds of herbs by using his natural lab, once he gained the ability to allow his meridians to channel the energy circulations of various herbs. Through this process, he learned the different functions of various herbs and how they could effect specific diseases. He thought of himself not as a doctor, but a patient with different types of organic malfunctioning and various ailments. It was this unique energetic channeling that allowed the insights to reveal themselves, as well as clinical evidences which enabled him to prescribe herbs and treat patients. Despite having this immense knowledge, Hua Tuo would never have considered the use of other methods which we know today as animal testing and placebo practices. To use such methods in his medical practice would be unethical and unthinkable. As a doctor, if you cannot tell the different results the herbs may cause within yourself, mentally and energetically, how could you prescribe them to a patient? How could you possibly make a determination without any first hand experience? In the same manner, the inner alchemists have been utilizing their own natural labs, under the influence of the mind, to produce their own "life-long-pill." To them this is the one, singular approach to meet the light, go to heaven, become immortal and be one with God. We are all endowed with a similar lab. It is within our own perfectly operating bodies that connect directly to their source. It awaits only our surrender to it.

## An Expression of Body

Oh, this body, this precious Lord of life, you are the earth of being, the organ of sensation, the memory of knowledge and the seat of worship. You are an illusion of awakening and a darkness of night, intertwined with pain and ecstasy. The body is an atheists' God and a theists' sacrifice, the artist's ink, the teachings of a master and lessons learned by a student, an object for draping and sculpture of nakedness, strength for the heavy and flexibility for the light, vibration of passion and witness to gratification, beauty for youth and container for death, parents of new life and techniques for doctors, enjoyment for the healthy and healing for the sick, demonstration of the power and exploitation of the weak, information of a culture and identification of a race.

For all the human beings who have a relatively complete organic functioning system, the body provides a means of income to support the ongoing activation of its organic system, a device that permits all the organic manifestations to be fully experienced, a place where the action of care-taking can touch its heart or where abusiveness can grasp its negativity, an attraction where the co-existence of opposites come together and a possession the self can never identify.

Life is for the existence of the body and the fantasy of the mind. The body is where the war is fought for the treasure and peace forgives with acceptance. It is where the color of difference resides and the space of sameness unifies. It is a Lord for possessing and a devil for releasing. It is a friend for identification and an enemy for separation. It is where intelligence rises to an amazing height and stupidity sinks into the abyss. It is as simple and as complicated as we make it. Living with it is a fixation, while departing from it is to enter nothingness. To be with whatever it may be is unsettling at best, to be desensitized from it leaves a blank in its history. Loving it too dearly makes life exciting and not loving it enough makes it seem worthless. Altogether, the body is where our life resides and death is the ultimate victor. Body is a flesh for breathing, a reality for existence, a future for imagination, and an illusion in the mystic field.

## Meditation Practice

This character deals with the process of building a caldron for storing the one Qi of yin and yang. This caldron we refer to is an empty space in the abdomen that utilizes the flow of essential energy or biological Qi. It is inside the belly button, in front of the adrenal glands and kidneys, above the ovarian glands and bladder. It is an empty zone, an imaginative land, a perceptive awareness, a groundless space, and a focal point. Many practitioners mistakenly assume that the caldron has an organic connection or attachment. It connects to the conscious awareness of everything, the heart-driven intention, the bodily action. Its power is to concentrate on an idea inwardly, feeling and sensing and being in touch with the mental inspiration and intellectual creativity permeating inside the gut, forming the urge and accomplishing the unconscious act. That is the mystery that lies in the emptiness that exists within.

The function of this empty caldron is the personality of the Tao, the character of non-attachment, and the function of wu-wei. The teaching of Laoism uses the hollowness of a vessel or the empty space within a hub or a room to demonstrate the power and usefulness of emptiness. It says that "Thirty spokes join at one hub, yet it is the emptiness inside the hub that makes the vehicle useful; Clay is molded into a vessel, yet it is the hollowness that makes the vessel useful; Windows and doors are cut out, yet it is their empty space that makes the room usable." (11:1)

In a vehicle, the hub provides the propeller for a heliacal surface, allowing the wheels to move. In life, the hub ensures a central point to prevent the mind from deviating and the body from losing its balance. In cultivation, it refers to the emptiness of heart, the stillness of mind, and the animation of the abdomen. When the heart empties itself, the tranquil spirit flows downward with the breathing circulation. The abdomen is not filled with the mixed Qi of food, but with the pure yang force from heaven. When the pure yang force vitalizes the abdomen, the kidney yin Qi is activated, particularly upon the ovaries and prostate glands.

Together, the Tao of yin and yang will fill the empty space inside the abdomen, and the oneness of self will be produced. When this oneness of self becomes fully matured, it will manifest inside the stomach as rich food, within the heart as pure love, and inside the brain as a tranquil spirit. When the stomach becomes enriched with this special food, there is no desire for ordinary food, and there is no waste product to pass through the excretory system. The mind doesn't concern itself with seeking food, and there is no need to expend energy gathering, cooking and digesting food. As a result, the total expense of bodily energy is reduced to its minimal level. There is no toxic material to poison the temple of the spirit, our graceful and beloved body.

When the heart is filled with pure love, there is no separation between selfless love and intentional love. All the fragments of love scattered in life are unified, the heart radiates with an innocent pursuit, presenting a happy face and child-like smile. This is the earnest expression of self, the true love of the Christ conscience, and the absolute joy of God's smile.

When the tranquil spirit guides the body and mind, there can be no harm to self and others. It doesn't intentionally prevent the body from harm, but there is no cause, no bad karma and no negativity arising from spiritual awareness and conscious intention. Life may still meet with danger, but true energetic reaction of danger arising from the fear of self, will be completely purified, and negativity will be transformed into positivity. This doesn't mean that the soul is not lonely, but that the true spirit has met its oneness, the center of all centers, and the form of all forms. Where does this invasive energy reside? How could the fear manifest itself? And why is there such a thing as a lonesome cry?

# STEP THREE: *SMELTS*

Structure: one $\frown$ + enter $\lambda$ + door $\bigcap$ + fire 火
Sound: shao
Meaning: smelts

## The Ecological Structure of the Character

**T**his is a very valuable rich, ritual and mystical character containing two additional sub-characters, for the total of four individual Chinese characters. The first sub-character at the top is called bing, which is the third heaven's stem in the Chinese calendar. This character consists of three individual characters: yi for "one," ru for "enter" and men for "door." "One" is the single drop of light, the unconscious awakening, and the original desire. In I Ching, the "one" represents the unbroken line, the single sprout, and the lasering light.

"Door" represents the gate of life and the valley of spirit, while "enter" refers to the harmonious action involved with the one and the valley, between the solid and the empty, and water and fire. The character "enter" personifies the spirit descending in a human body, co-existing with the creation of body. It resembles the unified action between yin and yang, or the harmonious work between screw and nail. The entire character bing indicates that as the one-drop of cosmic essential yang Qi enters the door of life, it begins to decrease as it is being replaced by the transformative growing yin Qi.

This character represents the shoulder, describing the position of the brain or head standing upon the shoulders and entering the door of the cosmic opening, the valley spirit of heaven. The extension of shoulders form the wings, but not the arms and hands. Shoulders are the area where the will performs the function of action and mind takes the responsibility for it. They are where the light falls and the mechanism flows through. The symbolic meaning of this character is that we entered this world with head down, and our brain turned one hundred and eighty degrees in order to face the sky, from where it descended. During our lifetime, we stand on the shining edge between light and dark. We move along the transition between formation and transformation, and we sometimes leap into the cosmic zone of heaven and earth. In this zone, the cosmic light penetrates into the holy water. The North star points to the returning journey and its final destination that is beyond the formation of life. So the heaven's third stem, bing, represents "the God of light, the eternal involution of life, and the transition of spirit into the souls."

The second character huo, appearing at the bottom, symbolizes "the fire and the southern madness of growth." The combustible material which makes the fire is the solar light, the heat of sun, the passion of love and urge of transformation. The growing power is the exothermic combustion between the light of the one essential yang Qi, the seed of life, and the valley-gate spirit of the Milky Way or the earth's water. When the body was formed, either by spirit and love between Heavenly God and Cosmic Goddess, or by connection and love-making between father and mother, the seed of cosmic essential yang Qi died immediately by transforming itself into a new form of life, our individual life. At that time, its cosmic decreased, and this decreased force materializes itself into spiritual and intellectual form, from whence our spiritual tranquility, intellectual wisdom, and protective discrimination evolve. Contrary to this, the reddish growing yin Qi became more dominant. This reddish growing yin Qi represents the biological fire, emotional madness, personal passion, and egoistic control in our body and mind.

Together, these two characters represent the common saying "Water and fire harmonize each other" in the inner alchemical practices. It is the earliest formation on earth, manifesting before anything was created. On the one hand, water represents light, the white color and the north direction. It conveys the image of form and power of growth; it is the sensation of solidarity, the circulation of lucidity, and the power of purity; water begins the work of initiation by displaying the magic of healing.

On the other hand, fire represents the God of power, the longevity of life, and the transformation of form into a multiform. It represents the heat, the red color, and the south direction; it stands for the image of penetration and the power of transformation. It is the vibration of heat, the vaporization of flame, and the character of inner stillness. Its undertaking is to conduct our journey to resurrection.

Biologically, when the masculine and feminine energy embrace one another, the yin Qi of egg and yang Qi of sperm form the cellular growth and development of the fetus. Beginning with conception, normally, the fetus is upside down, facing the bottom of the womb. This is the true application of the third character of the couplet. It means that the heaven's yang Qi decreases, transforming itself into a new form of life, and yin Qi then takes on its role of nourishing the process of growing and developing. By the time the fetus develops fully, the head drops down toward earth, the face turns to the sky, looking to its return journey. The pure spirit then diffuses into conscious behavior and instinctive action. The body takes in the earth's growing nutrition, breathes in and out with the circulative energy between heaven and earth, and is attracted by the light.

Then, linguistically, the character bing is combined with "one," "enter" and "door" respectively, meaning the One-drop of Primordial Yang Qi enters the heavenly gateway or drops into the mystic valley. "One" is the one-and-pure-seed of holy spirit or holy son. "Enter" represents the process of dropping, descending and penetrating. The heavenly gate or mystic valley stands for the black hole of the earth, and the vagina of the female. This character symbolizes: 1) The spiritual wind entering the human soul, as represented by the shoulders, the swinging and flying wings; 2) The sprouting of a plant reaching out of the ground charged by the growing and penetrating spring power. The yin Qi then manifests due to the growth, and yang Qi begins to decrease because of its transformation from its original state as a seed into a new plant; and 3) This character continues from the second heaven stem, yi, representing the neck or the whirling-through-sprout. The character bing means literally that "the one-and-pure-seed of holy spirit enters the heavenly gate of earthly black hole, or the one-and-pure-seed of holy son penetrates through the mystic valley of a female's vagina."

In human evolutionary and biological development, this drop of seed is the undivided substance of sperm and egg. Sperm and egg are the water that emerges from this drop of essence to form a new seed inside mother's womb. Her opposite, the "fire," is the energy of conscious mind such as desire, arousal, passion, and ambition. "Fire" is the force of libido that drives the sperm and egg together to form a new seed. It is the passionate love and selfless sacrifice of the heart. It is the power of mating and hoping for continuous existence as a physical being after a person has reached one's prime. This is why many parents experience the feeling of "rebirth" after they have their first baby.

Ecologically, the character bing represents the third ordering character in the Chinese calendar. In its design, there are ten stems representing heaven and twelve branches representing earth's monthly cycle. One complete cycle encompasses sixty years' time, beginning with jia of the heaven's stem and zi of the earth's branch. The next cycle repeats exactly the same pattern as the first. The heaven's stems represent the complete numerical functioning of heaven's manifest, counting from zero to nine and signifying the illumination of heaven and sun's yang Qi. The earth's branches stand for the twelve months of the earthly cycle, or the twelve cycles of the moon. The ten stems and the twelve branches combine to define each and every creature's life cycle, from our mother earth to all her children on earth, including ourselves.

Along the way, there are beginnings and endings. There are precise indications of the birth and death of each creature, but there is no demarcation except for their conscious living and awareness. This means that the twelve cyclical functions are destined, as is our physical life journey. Our physical life is preprogrammed before the course of our life and death, and predestined in the process of formation and deformation, but our cosmic and spiritual essence is unchanging. It is eternal. In the case of the human being, heaven's third stem symbolizes the transitional state between the growing power of yin Qi and the decreasing influence of yang force. This is the reasoning in Lao Zi's creation of the third character in his couplet. The "one" that constructs the third heaven's stem is the eternal oneness of our spiritual life. The "door" is the formation and deformation of life. And "fire" is the growing, changing, and transformative power that manifests from the harmonious action between the eternal oneness and life-gate.

Finally, in Taoist's inner alchemy, the water represents the abdominal and digestive yin Qi, while the fire is symbolic of the cosmic and conscious yang force. During meditation practices, the practitioner should always center her/his consciousness inwardly and direct with devotion her/his heart internally by gently "warming and cooking and boiling" the "water" of kidney yin Qi. The "water" will transform into steam or gas and be reabsorbed by the cells in the body. Gradually, with the passing of time, there will be a decline of mature sperm or eggs produced. This is because the water and fire function fully and waste nothing, defining the true nature of energetic circulation and recycling. For females, menstruation will cease and consequently provide a complete energy preservation. In males, semen will circulate inside the body instead of being ejaculated as a waste product. This practice would be an effective method of changing the behaviors of sex offenders. It is also the most harmless and effective way to prevent conception, correct irregular menstrual cycle, cure impotence, and prevent sexually transmitted diseases.

In advanced stages of meditation, through mindful and dedicated practice, the meditators can purify the oceanic state of abdominal sexual yin Qi into its pure force, the holy water or cosmic water, then place it in either chest or brain area as the image of Lake or Dui in I Ching. This is the condition of joy and peace. Departing from the state of natural development, the meditators can regain their youth by regressing to this pure stage of seven or eight years of age. The ego self will be purified, emerging as a complete self, a selfless self, and a cosmic self. The pure self, the virgin self, will then be preserved. The longing self or the lost self becomes the force of attraction. Together, they form the true and complete self of oneness. In essence, water is the "virgin girl" and fire is the "virgin boy." During the course of cultivation, the water and fire harmonize each other energetically, the virgin girl and the virgin boy dance together joyfully, the self and the other embrace one another fruitfully. This is, perhaps, the most complete pictorial demonstration of this third character in the couplet.

## Lao Zi On Water

In Taoist practice, purity and stillness are its defining qualifications: purity signifying the watery body, and stillness as firing mind. The body must be pure to become receptive and productive, and mind must be still to be creative and transformative. This is why Lao Zi characterizes water and fire as the primary elements for cultivation. To be more precise, Lao Zi is a water-type person with a firing character. He refers to himself as "I am a fool at heart, as a water droplet is to the spring." (20:5) The "fool at heart" is the passion of fire, the emptiness of ego and the character of selflessness, while "a water droplet" is the value of life, the direction of planning and the hope for the future.

Lao Zi also uses water to represent the goodness, the kindness and virtue of the Tao. He says that "Eminent goodness is like water. Water is good at benefitting all things, yet it actively competes. It retires to undesirable places. Thus it is near to Tao." (8:1,2) Mistakenly however, the standard text of Tao Te Ching defines the water as "uncompetitive," rather than "actively competing." The sentence "it is uncompetitive" has many scholars interpreting Laoism and Taoism as being passive and quiet. This is a misleading conception. There are passions in Laoism and there is madness in Taoism. We do not understand the nature of water thoroughly if we say that its character is inactive, and that its motion is passive. Water is the most active element on earth and in the sky. It is everywhere on earth and circulates constantly in our organism. It is active in its performance and competitive in occupying its own position. Water never ceases to battle with fire and light over the space it occupies. It peacefully competes against the chaos caused by the fire, and actively transforms the resulting murkiness, poison and contamination.

Lao Zi further explains that "Nothing in the world is softer and more supple than water. When confronting strength and hardness nothing can overcome it." Then he advises that "Using nothingness simplifies. Using water overcomes hardness. Using weakness overcomes strength." In reality, as Lao Zi indicates "There is no one in the world who does not know it, but no one can apply it." Finally, Lao Zi concludes that the usefulness and meaningfulness of water can be explained by "Whoever can bear the disgrace of the country is the ruler of the country. Whoever can bear the misfortune of the world is the ruler of the world. Truthful speech seems paradoxical." (80:1,2,3,4) This final truth awakens us to the heart of spiritual practice as well as the richness of life. Normally, everyone expects the outcome of situations to be good, yet few people realize the value of working through the bad things that happen. Everyone hopes to reap the benefits of teaching without learning the power of mastering the bad. Everyone knows the difference between good and bad, yet no one embraces the deeds occurring between them. Whoever understands the paradox knows the game of life. Those who remain in the paradox have yet to awaken to the mystery of life.

## The Prime and Combustion Of Water And Fire

There are several explanations relating to the power of water and fire. Firstly, water serves as the biological base and the essential life drop that produces both eggs and semen. It is the womb for all the seeds and the form of all forms. Fire represents the conscious desire in the head (intellectual), the heat in the heart (conscious), and the instinctive urge in the gut (spiritual). It is about their dynamic functioning and active programming. In theory, water and fire represent two of the five elements in Chinese philosophy. Water represents the winter season, the black color, and the kidneys. Fire represents the summer season, the red color, and the heart. The other three, wood, earth and gold, relate to the fourth character in the couplet. We will discuss these in detail in the following chapter. In mythology, when the one-and-pure-white drop of the holy spirit descends on earth, the winter snow in the ice state of water buries it and freezes it. This drop is the first heavenly stem, jia, meaning the head raises upward. The time for its first interaction with yin Qi on planet earth is zi, which occurs during the Winter Solstice on the 21st of December, and the first hour-period of the day, 11:00 p.m.

Before our knowledge of the body and mind became known, we were aware that water and fire were the first powerful materials existing on earth, or created by God. In all the cultures throughout the world, water and fire are the inescapable substances which exist in mythology, philosophy, and legend. Greek, Arabic, Indian and Chinese mythologies all referred to the primary substances of earth, water and fire. Northern and Indian mythologies declared that water and fire were the first visible materials existing on earth after the explosion and resulting chaos. Plato speculated that "God, when he began to put together the body of the universe, made it of fire and earth"... and "placed water and air between fire and earth, and made them so far as possible proportional to one another, so that air is to water as water is to earth; and in this way he bound the world into a visible and tangible whole." (Timaeus and Critias P.44 by Penguin Classics)

Of all the substances on earth, water is the most valuable. Without water, there could be no essential substance to construct life, especially organic life. Without water, all creatures on earth could neither come into existence nor survive. Consider the percentage of water in our body, the important role it plays in our daily life, and the space it covers on earth. What would happen if there was no water to sustain life, both individually and ecologically? Contrary to water, fire is the energy that activates, energizes, cooks, and digests. Without fire, the cosmic and solar light, there would be no energy supply on earth, and no way for proteins and sugars to be produced. Without the invisible fire of God's light, we could not think and would have no consciousness. Without fire, the heart couldn't vibrate. Water makes the darkness of earth and our body useful, light makes the God's power visible within.

In the course of our human development, this period of time represents the pubic stage, the yin form of the second developmental stage. Each stage consists of two sub-stages, the psycho-spiritual and biophysical. The psycho-spiritual stage must always come first. The first stage is the formation of life between sperm and egg, and the birth process between the mother and her child. This first stage is more individually determined than gender based. During the thirty-seven-weeks of gestation, there is no precise indication of which gender develops more quickly, even though there is speculation that boys will enter the world earlier than girls.

In reality, our birth is not the beginning of the first stage of life, but its maturation. The first stage of our life is the action of our parents' lovemaking which ensures the formation of our cellular life. Our parents' unconscious awakening and unspoken intuition were the unknown catalysts for their desire to make love for the purpose of creating a family. Similarly, before a child acts, verbally or physically, something has already formed in her/his mind. Primarily, before our body acts, our mind already knows what to do.

In the second developmental stage, the ego-construction begins as the yang form. For girls this occurs when they are about seven years of age and eight years for boys. The yang form of the second stage deals with the mental identification of self. This is the psychological moment when there is a clear separation between the self and an object, and I and God are closely unified. This is the stage of wondering and questioning.

Consider the endless questions children ask, including the one "Who is God?" We all understand the question but no one knows the answer. During this period, if the child's mind is more active, s/he becomes more rational and analytical as time goes on. S/he may become a philosopher or a mathematician in that magic play of spiritual imagination. In contrast, if s/he is more sensational and more hand oriented, s/he becomes more intuitive and creative. S/he may become an inventor or a magician (the father of science) in that magical play of spiritual construction. There the God manifests either as the mental construction of the mind playing a head game with words and pictures, or as the mechanical construction of the hands manipulating their toys and machines.

The yin form of the second stage is the biological maturation of the self, which occurs for girls at fourteen years of age and at sixteen years for boys. For girls, it is the secretion of blood, and the beginning of menstruation. For boys, it is the ejaculation of semen, the starting point of killing and returning. They have no way to experience "bleeding" (menstruation) other than by engaging in war and opening the gate of blood flow, sometimes, into death. Killing performs the death that results in the liberation of spirit from its living temple. The girls have a predestined base in their biological makeup. The fixed ratio of eggs in the beginning of their lives directs them to go either with the moon or a man. Going with the moon is the menstruation, and going with a man is the pregnancy.

From the moment this second stage is effected, both girls and boys are biologically mature. The sight of blood can reveal to a young woman the beginning of her menstrual cycle. During war time, it is the females who are saying goodbye to their loved ones, either a husband or son. It is also the girls and women who welcome home both the victorious and the conquered. The heroes are stained with the blood of their enemies. The vanquished carry their vengeance, wounded bodies, and dead spirits into their bleak futures. The women bear the burden of the death of their loved ones and the building of a new ruling power.

Laoist describes this paradoxical mystery "From within the murky comes the stillness. The feminine enlivens with her milk." (15:4) War is the murky fight, and peace is the still ground. The murky fight is driven by the reddish and black fire, and the still ground is shielded by the blue and white water. The feminine is the womb of life, and milk is the nourishment of life. The womb heads towards the valley of darkness, and milk supplies the spirit of hope.

The coming or appearance of the second stage is emergence into the prime of life. It is a transitional stage of life as well. The prime is reached at the peak of our youth, and the transitional phase represents the onset of aging. When we begin to think seriously about ourselves and attempt to accomplish things by ourselves, our primal force decreases.

At this defining moment, the God within becomes alive. Whether this God is a visionary image or ideal model, it is the eternity of our life at this time. Whether we have the symbolic connection with the words and pictures of God or the objective connection with God with structures and machinery, our life is being constructed with a fixed pattern of life force from this time forward. Whether we enjoy the rest of our lives or struggle through with it makes no difference once the decision is made and the image is connected. The story of our life repeats itself until the life is over or the enlightenment is achieved. Whether it be the first time of that inseparable and peaceful connection between the two spirits and their living temples or the final unbearable separation after decades of marriage through divorce or death, the inseparable feeling and unforgettable memory unify the God and Goddess, the masculinity and femininity into one. The record of our human history remains unchanging. Each of us is biologically predestined as the creation is made. It matters not whether we know God when we are seven years old or seventy. Neither does it matter which of us knows God and who speaks through God. The journey of spiritual awakening is the beginning of the journey and ultimately the liberating path. The part we do know is the attraction and separation, and the part we don't know is the mystery and wonder.

This second state, the prime of our life, is also a transitional stage. In the yang form of his stage, our belief system, our religious values and our spiritual nature are already manifested within, although it may take years or decades to accept and understand it completely. What contributes to this delay is the continuation of parental practices passed on, the systematic teaching of the government, our cultural conditioning, and the turmoil of living. These are the conditions responsible for precipitating our loss of freedom, our inner connection and our natural belief system. Through this conditioning, we are all delayed, misinformed and can be ultimately destroyed. In the yin form of this stage, women will have thirty-five years of reproductive life, followed by menopause and aging. Men will live through passing the power and dominance and control to finally accepting and understanding and letting go.

Laoism acknowledged that "When things reach their climax, they are suddenly old. This is 'Non-Tao'. 'Non-Tao' dies young." (55:3,4) This exemplifies the swift and sudden climax of primal youth, just as a blossoming flower, a dreaming moment and a wishful illusion drift into the past. In human life, aging doesn't begin at menopause or after retirement. It begins immediately after the pubic stage. As the body grows, the freshness is lost; youth is gone when the person matures. S/he then carries the burden of her/his life, experiences the sickness of the body, and is fearful of the reality of death. That is all. In this vein, Laoism states that "Matter becomes strong, then old. This is called 'Not-Tao'. Dying young is 'Not-Tao'." (30:5) This is, perhaps, the most valuable advice this character suggests, and the most honest description that the teaching of Laoism provides on returning, going back from youth and aging.

## The Practical Value of Water and Fire

The practical reason behind this alchemical cultivation is that in life, the water is constantly fired by the conscious urge to satisfy desires, i. e., sexual, emotional, or egoistic. It must be made clear that water does not represent regular drinking water, but the essential yin Qi that forms the life along the heat or fire of yang force. The first breakthrough of this union of yin and yang within the body is the birth process, since the fetus is no longer viable in the mother's womb. A life living on mother's energy emerges into a life dependent on air, light, food and water.

The second breakthrough is at the age of seven (girl) or eight (boy). At these ages, the ego establishes its identity, and the body demonstrates its gender characteristics. The third breakthrough is the pubic stage, when the individual biological development reaches its maturity. The fourth breakthrough is at age eighteen for girls and twenty-one for boys. These ages display the full maturity of biological growth and mental development. This is the true beginning of an individual independent life. From this age on, the water and fire are separated by the mental anticipation, the emotional devotion, and physical interplay.

The theory behind this practice is that, in life, each individual has a fixed amount of water and fire stored in her/his body. Water is the kidney energy, and fire is the spiritual and intellectual energy. This water and fire are the pre-heaven life energy, not the nutritious energy being supplied throughout the lifetime. In regard to the water it is understood that a female carries a fixed amount of eggs from the time of her birth. During the first seven years of life, the eggs are inside the ovaries. At the second stage of her growth, the eggs become fertile. They are either prepared to unite with the sperm to form new life, or are discharged. Over the course her lifetime, the total number of eggs being carried decreases. By the time a female reaches forty-nine, or perhaps earlier, there are few eggs remaining in her body and the menstrual cycle slowly winds down.

In the male, semen is produced at age sixteen and the force that produces the semen is also proportional inside the body. In one lifetime, there can be no more than whatever can be generated within, regardless of how the person attempts to acquire more of this energy. During adolescence and adulthood, each sexual discharge, or ejaculation, contains millions and millions of sperm cells.

The irony is that, for both men and women, the more active they are, sexually and egoistically, the more water they will lose. Finally, the fire is distinguished, and the water dries up. Bones become brittle and teeth fall out. The abdomen becomes stiff, and the hair turns white or falls out. This is the natural process from birth to death, and from the whole to nothing. Laoist summarizes that "We live, we die. The companions of life are three and ten. The companions of death are three and ten. That people live their active lives necessarily leading to the ground of death is three and ten. Why is this so? It is the nature of life itself." (50:1,2,3)

The numerical description of "three" is the symbol for mass production, multiplication and dissolution. Anything mechanical, systematic and numerical has the structural and functional domains of three. Laoist explains this by saying "Three gives rise to all things." (42:1) "Ten" represents the complete manifestation of heaven's ten stems. It signifies the complete presence, the absolute interaction, and the constant changing. Through this interaction, three gives, develops, and matures, while ten touches, fires, and transforms. There is no end to this cyclical course, but there is an end to its distinguishing stages and performances.

The interpretation of Laoism in summary is that following after is the nature of life itself. The welcoming of the new life process reaches its demise when death approaches with the last stroke of our aging time clock.

## A Hope For Life

The above summarizes the Taoists' method of dealing with human growth and development. While complete, it lacks the details and depth that modern biological and psychological research can produce. In terms of child and adolescent development, there have been detailed and documented descriptions of both clinical findings and social applications. From Darwin's evolutionary point of view to Freud's depth psychology, from clinically observed stages of growth to socially programmed education, and from gene research to biotech practices, the myth of human birth has been reduced to an observable and tested experiment. The mysterious water and the cosmic fire of life is scientifically replaced by cloning and gene-re-mutation. Besides having the right chemistry during mating and love making, everything in life has been mechanically demonstrated. Each step can be predictably controlled. All the natural processes of growth and development are being reduced into the quantifiable and explainable, from IQ tests to licensing programs, and from legal justification to moral constraint.

However, through adolescence and aging, the developmental/experiential theory becomes distorted during mid-life crisis. The mentally projected wishes to live a stable life are destroyed by the presence of illness, the uncertainty of the future and forgotten meaning of the past. The present becomes a ruthless struggle, and the goal of life becomes a fearful escape. The idea of human growth and its happiness meets its own challenge on the road toward the final outcome. In medical science, experimenting with human organs and various body parts cannot serve as a final solution, regardless of how many times the body has been surgically operated on and transformed.

In contrast, the religious and spiritual practices of the Taoist inner alchemy stresses that in order to preserve the Tao of yin and yang, the life of water and fire, one should always direct the conscious fire inwardly, placing it beneath the water of holy seed. The water of holy seed will then move up internally through the spine to the brain, unifying the pure self of spirit with the cosmic light and spiritual guidance. This reverse process is described as "Humankind takes its origin from earth. Earth takes her origin from heaven. Heaven takes its origin from Tao. Tao takes its origin from Nature." (25:4) Laoism also amplifies this notion by stating "As a matter of fact, I hear of those who are good at preserving their lives: Walking through, not avoiding rhinos and tigers. Entering battle without wearing armaments. The rhino has no place to dig its horns. The tiger has no place to drag its claws. The soldier has no place to thrust his blade. Why is this so? Because they have no place to die." (50:4,5)

In meditation, a meditator, female or male, can regenerate this drop of essence within her/his own body without the required physical effort to join the sperm with egg. Everyone has both of these types of energy within and everyone can get "pregnant" by her/himself without biological sexual unification. Today, biologists and doctors question the possibility and probability of a male getting pregnant. In Taoist meditation, this is a customary practice. The Taoist slogan "like-a-man-being-pregnant" is neither a psychological wish for a male to become like a female, nor that a male desires to be a female. It is the reality of oneness by combining the virgin boy and virgin girl that can result with daily and life long meditative practice.

The structure of this third character symbolizes the passionate desire for this sexual union which resembles a kettle of water being boiled over a fire. Also, in terms of energy circulation, water as yin or murky energy flows downward while fire, as yang or tranquilized energy, rises. This constitutes the yin form of energetic circulation. The yang form suggests that the water molecules rise into the sky, forming clouds to disperse the rain or snow which nourishes and preserves the dried earth and plants. The cosmic light and solar energy shine down unceasingly. As a cosmic entity and spiritual being, we humans can lose our desire to return to our original source.

Similarly, the earth's gravitational force and nourishing power can never abandon her attachment. The essence of Taoist inner alchemy lies in the manner of returning from the yin form of life (biological life) into yang form of life (spiritual life) through a cleansing process and ascending principle. The final outcome occurs when the earthly water in the body is replaced by the holy water and the conscious fire becomes illuminating light. In I Ching, it is the harmonizing of Kan (the abysmal, water) and Li (the clinging, fire). Within our body, water is the qi (chi), the basic substance of life, while fire is the instinctive impulse, representing the beginning of consciousness, the arousal of emotion, the longing for knowledge, and the desire for food intake and sexual gratification. When the qi and instinctive impulse is harmonized, we experience the completion of the melting process, or life-pill.

## Utilizing Water and Fire Within

Being the most valuable elements, water will never be totally vaporized as long as the earth lives, and fire will never be distinguished as long as the sun shines. In our life, the substance of our body, which is mainly water, is always proportional in maintaining a healthy foundation. The nature of consciousness, which is the illumination of fire, never lives away from the will power of its spiritual root.

How to utilize water and fire has been the essential quality to identify the meaning of our human life and to distinguish our human lives from animal ones. In the human history, making use of water and fire has been the earliest and the most powerful actions ever achieved by humankind. All animals need to drink, but only we can use river and lake water to irrigate the land and rely on spring and well water to prepare food and fine spirits. All animals need to eat, but only we can make fire to boil water and cook a meal. No other animals can build the dams to control flooding, only humans are capable of this conception and its construction. Forests regenerate themselves by burning the old trees naturally, only humans can make weapons to fire and create destruction instead of engaging in nature's cycling process. We build houses with wood and make fire with wood, and we make use of natural gas (the holy air) and purify the natural oil (animal water) to make machines, such as automobiles, operating. Most animals rely on plants which grow and die seasonally for their food supply. Only humans can make full use of plants (leaves and bark) and their products (fruits and seeds), and other animals, as well. All these human activities are based upon the utilization of the primary elements— water and fire.

From spring water to milk, from river flows to blood stream, from oceans to bladder, it is all the circulation of water. Between spring and ocean and between bladder and milk, water produces and purifies our lives. From light to inspiration, from sun to fire, and from explosion to instinct, it is all the work of fire. Between light and fire and between love and passion, fire generates and distinguishes our lives. Without water, there would be no life source for human to civilize ourselves; without the aid of fire, there would be no productivity exercised upon life, nor destruction to the living life. Without the proper use of water, we would be either poisoned or dehydrated. Without the proper management of fire, we would be either burned or frozen.

Unquestionably, out of thirst and stagnation, we drink water and swim with the streams of river-life-force. Out of blue and urge, we make fire to boil the water and cook the meal, to keep us warm and to see ourselves present in darkness. Sun is bright and right above the face, providing us the life force. Mountain's cry is peaceful but frightening, flowing us through all the streams of life. Valley's silent, breath-taking, and impenetrable force of echo returns us to the bricking edge of life existence. Sky is high above the land, and ocean is far distant from the cave. They are the image of blue. The mist awakens our soft consciousness; the sunrise directs us into our passionate action. Darkness surrenders our activities, and moonlight smiles at our dreaming consciousness. These are the urges of life force.

Consciousness pacifies the silent, awakening surprises the self, yet water softens them and heart maddens them. Fire exists between cold and hot. Water swims between dry and wet. From breath taking to life saving, work is done. Between contraction and expansion, life is experienced. The mystery of life is but the wondering of moon upon the sun. The meaning of life is but the wandering of mind through will. The beauty of life is but the steams of water under the sparks of white light.

## Meditation Practice

1. Sit in a chair allowing the knees to form a ninety degree angles between thighs and shins. Keep back and neck straight but relaxed. Extend the lower jaw a bit forward.

2. Relax the arms and hands for a second, then bend the index and ring fingers by pressing the thumbs on them, allowing both thumbs, middle fingers and little fingers to touch each other in a closed posture. The four realms of the world are thus separated. Water of little fingers and fire of middle fingers form open structures, and wood of index finger and gold of ring finger are integrated by the thumbs. The earth of thumbs promotes the transformation of water and fire between wood and gold.

3. Draw a connection among the middle fingers, the thymus gland and the yin third eye (the cross between eyes and nose). Feel the energy rising from the third eye and thymus gland and join together at middle finger point.

4. Visualize a purple light flaming through thumbs, index and little fingers.

5. Make a connection between middle fingers and artery, and little finger and vein.

6. Feel the middle finger point becoming the apex of the heart by moving the hands downward. This helps body structure to return from post-heaven state to pre-heaven state.

7. Feel the right arm becoming the vein and the left arm becoming the artery.

8. Slowly picture the three-paired structures, artery/vein, middle fingers/little fingers, and left arm/right arm. They all become the circulation of breath, of heartbeat, of life.

9. Feel the fire flame around the body, within the fire is the steaming water. In the center is the empty stillness.

10. All the muscles are firing muscles, all the organs are watering organs, and all the glands are white glands.

11. In the middle is the center of white light. Around is the green/blue colors, and surrounding are the red/orange colors.

12. Allow the body to become completely integrated with all that is happening, keep the mind still and alert.

13. Feel the tip of the fire becoming the crown of the brain. There is a hole opening connecting the root of the body with the root of the heaven.

14. Observe the paired oppositions swirling and revolving and changing and circulating until there appears a natural stoppage.

15. Awake to the regular consciousness, and give a message to any desirable areas and parts.

# STEP FOUR: *CHEMICALLY*

Structure: wood 木 + stone 石 + earth 土
Sound: lian
Meaning: chemically

## The Picture of Five Elements

The three substances in this character represent the productive and transitional elements between water and fire, winter and summer, cold and hot, body and mind, solid and empty, matter and force. Water holds and chills the temperature in the atmosphere. It also transmits, scatters and dissolves the heat that comes directly from the solar light, thereby placing in the sky a sheet of filtering clouds protecting the earth's surface from extreme temperatures. It is hard to imagine that our mother earth rotates herself with all the living creatures on her surface with the protection and comfort being provided by the clouds in the sky. The clouds enrich us with their ever-changing presence that can be viewed as mystic or severe, floating or gathering, transparent or gloomy. Without clouds, especially their free-form movement, their flash of lightning, their gentle cover, their releasing of rainfall, and most blissful of all, their blanket of snowfall, we cannot survive. When they become identified with the flakes of whiteness, the heavens are white, the earth is white, the mind is white, and the abdomen is white. The ice, semen, the milk, the flour, and the salt are white as well. The entire world proceeds at an indestructible pace in its motionless peace.

We are thankful for the changing nature of water, and the mirroring tranquility it reflects. Regardless of its state, it benefits all who are in need of it. In our living atmosphere, water in its "spiritual" form –cloudiness becomes the source of consciousness. Light, in its female form wind directs the conscious alternation. This second stage of cosmic circulation is more powerful and yet more subtle than the direct harmony of water and fire. The moving clouds in the sky regulate the open space between the expansive blue sky and the shimmering ocean reflecting its color, while the circulation of the solar wind is generating the frictional or gravitational forces.

Water molecules move up and down, producing mist. The solar wind shifts the water molecules to a quieter and more peaceful arena. Together, they smooth and balance the energetic circulation on earth and in the sky. The earth's surface, particularly the North Pole, is then tempered between the coldness and darkness surrounding its two poles. It is circulated by the moist and dry air along the horizontal line, its belt meridian. Between these two atmospheres we see the four seasonal changes that ensure the growth of all living things, their maturation, death, and reproduction, season after season and year after year. The cold becomes warm, and the darkness becomes light. The dampness vaporizes, and the dryness becomes moist.

We are also thankful for the light that shines upon us. It is the light that gives us the visibility, cooks our meals, digests our food, and finally opens for us the door into heaven. It is also the light that transmits the energy, heals the wounds, illuminates the darkness. Whether we perceive and work with its energetic form during the daytime, or dream and wonder with it at night, light informs us, ensures us, and finally transforms us. We are charged by the sunlight, pulled by the stars, yet light reveals our reality, draws us into our imagination, encourages us with its illumination, and illuminates our puzzled confusion. Without light, the form of life would not change into a living organism. Without light, there would be no wind blowing, no circulation of temperature, no vision of spiritual illumination, no seed of love, and no mood of emotional expression. We cannot exist on earth without light.

One yin and one yang makes the Tao. Yin is water and yang is light. Because of water and light, the mother earth is smoothed and moistened with her own milky water while the heat generated by the light is altered and vaporized. It is between these two rotating poles on earth, that light and darkness alternate between day and night on the earth's surface, and also between the awakening and dreaming consciousness in our mind. On the earth, moisture rises from the east, dryness engulfs the west. Rain and snow make their appearance in their scheduled or unexpected time and place. The cold and white and dark open and close the two poles. The hot and humid dance and languish in the middle.

Physiologically, the four directions are the skeletal system of arms and legs. The four seasons are the four stage of life, fetus, youth, adolescence and aging. The breathing patterns, inhalation and exhalation, provide the tropical wet and dry, hot and cool conditions. The pre-heaven sexual energy represents the power of the North Pole, and the creativity is the power of the South Pole. These are the three dimensions and the six angles of life. Two arms and ten fingers drive the cosmic yang force, representing the gravitational force and the cosmic wind circulating between east and west, right and left. Two legs and ten toes generate the descending power of light and ascending force of water, moving up and down, back and forth. The abdomen is the Northern Hemisphere, the brain the Southern Hemisphere, the chest the tropic region. The primordial yang Qi is the cosmic egg. Unconsciousness is its Milky Way. The intellect is the creative force; the wisdom is the guiding light. The tailbone is the North Pole, and crown is the South Pole.

According to Taoism, the location of the North Pole on earth is amazingly parallel to the caldron in our body. Since it is only one degree away from the North Star, it is the place closest to the spiritual light. The Taoists' literature advocates that the North Star is the pointing star of human spirit. It is from the North Star that the cosmic consciousness shines into the earth's valley and within every creature's unconscious realm as well. When this cosmic light is enlivened in the human body, located in the caldron within the abdomen, it becomes the primordial yang Qi, or bindu as it is in Hinduism. The primordial yang Qi is the essential yang force, the cosmic womb, and God's light. When this primordial yang Qi is awakened, it moves up from the biological instinctive center, crosses the emotional agitation, and manifests as spiritual illumination. The poetic wisdom, the intellectual aspiration, the instantaneous intuition, and accompanying healing dancing are all coming together, working, drumming, inspiring, and transforming.

This primordial yang Qi is God's light descending into the human soul and is conditioned by the light of the North Star. The North Star is the stabilizing force for rotation of the earth. Without it, the earth would be a swirling planet with no stationary orbit. Without the caldron, this primordial yang Qi would not be restored to rise up through the spine. This human energy would manifest itself in most people as a condensed urge or distracting purge. The true value of our essential force would then be extinguished through various energetic devices such as instinctive attachment, emotional disturbance, personal preference, fragments of love, and intellectual confusion.

It is the body of earth that forms, houses and recycles creatures like ourselves. It is also the body of earth that channels the flowing water and receives the abundance of rain in order that all the creatures can exist and survive. Through its meridians, such as the riverbeds and pressure points, or ponds and lakes, the spring water milks all the new creatures, while rainwaters and snow purify. Along the way, all living things are watered and nurtured, poisoned and purified, washed and recycled by the flowing streams. Finally, the water is mixed with dust and poison as it recedes and begins to merge again into the oceanic environment.

For every meditation practitioner, it is very essential to realize the power and transition between water and fire, and cloud and wind. Without this realization, the entire meditation practice is fruitless. Nature and its manifest are such that we must tap into the harmony of energetic circulation of vibration and the comfort of stability, between the mystery of darkness and the awakening of illumination.

After the practitioner harmonizes the water and fire within the body and mind, it is time to come to terms with the minerals, the earthly stuff. The living earth is made up of flowing water and earthly minerals, and is spotted by the light. The minerals form the structure and dynamics of the earth. They also make up the physical structure and energetic transmission of all the creatures living on earth, including ourselves. In our body, the genetic construction is the visual map of our body. A framework of minerals constructs this visual map, their energetic circulation manifested with water and light, air and nutrients. Our mental activity is analogous to the weather temperature, while the minerals make up the staggering mechanism in our organism. Inside this genetically constructed, emotionally and intellectually sparked environment, water expands and contracts our organic frame. Light touches and transforms our energetic space. Together they function between the energetic circulation and living consciousness, between the digestion and re-absorption, and between the maturation and replacement.

Minerals constitute the third most abundant element on earth. They can be divided into three categories: wood elements, earth elements, and golden elements. When a solid seed, representing a golden fruit, buries itself under the snow covered earth, it is nourished by the earthly minerals, and ultimately becomes a wood-like plant. The earth element serves as the medium between the wood and golden elements, between that which is soft and that which is hard, and between that which grows and that which matures. In our human body, the wood element represents the skin, tissues, muscles and organs, anything that is soft, murky and tangible, capable of being expansive and contractive. The golden element represents the skeleton of our body, bones, teeth and nails. It represents everything hard and firm. The earth element stands between cellular growth and replacement, energetic circulation and balance, and the deformation of our body as it returns after death takes place. The earth element represents those minerals that energize and stimulate both the formation and deformation of our body.

## The Minerals Of Modern Society

The above describes the Chinese way of defining nature. Specifically, the wood element contains the expansive minerals, the earth element holds the scattering minerals, and the gold element condenses into solid minerals. Water, fire and minerals each have three states. The three states apprizing water are the frozen, the fluid and the gas state. The three states (or degrees) existing in fire are the heating, the igniting and the lightning energy. In regard to the minerals, the three conditions consist of the wood element carrying the growing and forming states; the earth element containing the cooling and condensing states, and the gold element which enables the rocking and dissolving states.

In one respect, the minerals circulate in our body in a way that the currency flows in our society. Without minerals, our life has no mobility; without currency, there would be no monetary exchange between the supply and demand factor of life. Minerals consist of both inorganic elements and energy-transferring substances. The power contained within them is the capacity and ability to utilize the space, communicating the interaction between water and fire. It is a matter of fact that fire and light have their atoms, and water and air contain their substances. These atoms and substances can never act independently but they remain individual by nature. It is the minerals that bond and transfer the atoms of light and the substances of water through fire and air. Conversely, the minerals engage in the biological life as do the individuals in social life. Biologically, minerals form bacteria and nucleus, grow cells and organs, create and transfer energy, strengthen and protect the systems, and finally reproduce and recycle their lives. In our social or cultural life, each of us is an individualized element. With these elements unified, we become the minerals of our unique social and cultural environment. In our individualistic society, we remain as the independent individuals, although we are also inter- and co- dependent living beings.

In our human evolutionary history, the only period when we lived as truly independent individuals was during the time of an agrarian society. It was a time Laoist referred to as "The neighbor countries are in sight. The sounds of dogs and chickens are heard. People grow old and die without interfering with each other." (67:3) The difference now in industrialized societies is that the neighbor's apartment or house is in sight, but people do not interfere with one another.

Even though we are still independent individuals, we could never exist independently by ourselves. The more industrialized a country becomes, the less its citizens depend upon each other. The more highly a person is educated, the more independent s/he becomes. The more commercialized a society becomes, the more skills it requires to sustain itself and the more kindness is transferred into cash flow.

It seems that one person's pain can become another person's advantage, momentarily, and one individual's demand is met by another individual's supply. As working individuals, we perform in a confined area, yet we can not separate ourselves from one another. The material supplies we collect and use have already been developed or prepared for us, from consumable goods to machines and utilities. We strive to become successful in our professions in order to enable us to earn a "decent" income allowing us to buy food, educate ourselves, pay the bills, and maintain a "comfortable" environment. Without the necessities of life, we cannot survive or become proficient. Therefore, we live not only with biological minerals but the social requirements as well.

Biologically, minerals are the essential constituents of all cells, organs, and systems. From the construction of a cell to the pigments and enzymes of a cellular or organic system, minerals are such that if the minerals within a cell willingly absorb and work with other resourceful energies, such as sugars and proteins, the cells remain alive and the organs will be capable of maintaining their normal functioning. Over time, as these minerals are depleted from our bodies, our organs and tissues gradually atrophy. Minerals are the parts, the batteries, the protectors, and the destroyers of the body. Without minerals, water cannot conceive and light cannot reflect. Without minerals, cells cannot mutate and organs cannot function; without minerals, the body can neither stand firmly as a rock nor sit relaxed as a sponge. Without minerals, the mind can neither think as quickly as it normally does nor can it be preserved slowly throughout its eternity. Life is the green land of ever-changing minerals.

Love is the red fire of burning minerals. Glory is the reassuring display of golden minerals and death is the black ash of dusty minerals. The speed of life depends upon the bio-electric charges transmitted by the various minerals. The harmony of life is the result of the interaction of the minerals inside the body. Essentially, the object of life is to use these inorganic matters and minerals; stones and rocks are the construction of minerals; worms and bugs can exist because minerals, eggs and shells are made from minerals, and the body and mind communicate with the aid of minerals. Minerals are to our living body what light, especially the colors, is to our mind. In the smallest place and largest space, minerals and lights exist in an inseparable oneness. Minerals and nucleus are the biological yin and yang, lights and atoms are cosmic yin and yang. Nucleus and atoms are yin, and minerals and lights are yang.

## Minding the Minerals

In our modern society, the ancient Western philosophical speculation upon the four elements, water, air, fire and earth have been decon-
structed by various specialists in their own fields. The spiritual trinity has
been statistically calculated along the information highway through our
technological advancement. Paleontologists use the fossils they recover
to piece together our own evolutionary history. Biologists reproduce the
cellular life structures by technically coding and cloning the DNA in
selected secret action with experimental subjects. Chemists combine and
experiment with various elements enabling other specialists to reproduce
and reconstruct anything bio-chemically possible, such as growing food
and vegetables, making tools and machinery, and building containers and
weapons. Physicists quantumize the madness of inflamed lights and the
vapor-like dancing forms of water molecules into a black hole, thinking
ahead to where the whiteness will be by turning their faces towards new-
age UFO quarks. Religious zealots preach, holding the satellite-connect-
ed microphone in one hand and reaching out with the other to collect their
tax-free contributions. Finally, spiritual seekers have been known to
inject drugs into their hungry bodies for the purpose of materializing and
hallucinating with their inner spirits.

The beauty of our human body has become a receptacle for disease. The meaning of our life is reduced to nothing more than scientifically determined labels and numbers. While pursuing perfect health in
our living environment, our body has become conditioned, our mind programmed, the water contaminated, the earth poisoned and the air pollut-
ed. We face an enormous crisis: our water is unclean, the ozone layer is
torn and impure, and our earth is not refreshing, but slowly eroding.

## Minding in Organic-Mind

In contrast, there exists a tradition that relies upon simplicity and
flexibility to carry us through to stillness and peacefulness. According to
the tradition of this fourth character in the couplet, life itself is a flow of
energy, an ideal of awareness, and an anticipation felt in the present. This
flow of energy is the neutralized, utilized and crystallized flow of the five
elemental Qi, the water Qi of the kidneys, the wood Qi of the liver, the
fire Qi of the heart, the earth Qi of the spleen and the golden Qi of lungs.

This awareness is how the mind perceives the body and why the
body interacts with the mind and world. Verily, the world is what the
mind is minding. This anticipation of the present is how the body and
mind work in peace, live with cleanliness, and return to tranquility. To be
able to "go with the flow" allows the spirit to be present, the mind to
remain intent, and the body to participate. It is the flow of Qi inside the
spirit of Shen, the vitality of Qi, and the essence of Jing.        I    n
Chinese philosophical and medicinal language, wood is the son of water
and the mother of fire. It represents the spring season, the green color,
and the liver organ. The earth is the son of fire and the mother of gold.

It represents the later (Indian) summer, the yellow color, and the spleen organ. Gold is the son of earth and the mother of water. It represents the fall season, the golden color, and the lung organs. This is the major difference between Greek or Indian mythologies and the Chinese. The first two, Greek and India, regard the four substances on earth as earth, air, fire and water. Chinese mythology declares that all the material forms are based upon the transformation of the five elements of wood, fire, earth, gold, and water.

There has been no evidence to explain why the ancient Chinese added stone or gold to the other four elements. We can speculate that gold represents the fall season and the color of earth and the yellow race. According to one of the Taoist classics, The Emperor's Mystic Incantation Text, the five elements represent the five fingers of a hand. The body represents heaven and earth. Human beings stand with their feet on earth and face to the heavens. All the decisions and actions in life are executed by the intricate movements of hands and fingers. The five indicates the completion of all the creatures in the world, and is an ongoing manifest of the universal evolution.

The other difference between the Taoist inner alchemical cultivation and the western religious explanation is that the Taoists gather all the five elemental Qi from the liver, heart, spleen, lungs and kidneys into a place called the Yellow Court. The seat for devotion, sacrifice, and unification (resurrection) is the heart chakra, which is near the thymus gland. There are two places for the Yellow Court, the yin court and the yang court. The yin court is located slightly below the thymus gland, the organ which distinguishes, differentiates, and discriminates. In the alchemical practice, instead of separating what is good from what is bad, the yin part of the Yellow Court accepts both and embraces them rather than letting the thymus complete the job. The thymus then becomes either an intimate receiver by spontaneously recognizing and storing them in the gut, or a friendly facilitator in the function of the gut. By using the lowest level of spiritual light, yellow, this gathered energy is then condensed in the yang side of the Yellow Court located around the number five thoracic vertebrae. This is the major contrast between the Taoist teaching and the Western religious practices of Christianity or Islam.

## The Practical Value of the Character

The practical application of this forth character in the couplet deals with the function of the Qi flow in the chest. Essentially it teaches us how to crystallize the elixir of love, which is the combination of the passion of love and the fairness of consciousness. Passion of love makes the truthful love; a love that cannot be distracted, distorted, misled, or specified. It is the impetus of the awareness, before the action, above the engagement, and beyond the attachment. In detailed practices, it is the true manifest of love formed in the chest area through purification but not through the discrimination executed mechanically by the thymus gland. It deals with the true nature of the heart, the complete emptiness of the fire, and the absolute contentedness of being truthful and selfless. This fairness and consciousness leads toward truthful consciousness; a consciousness that can neither be discriminated against nor grasped. It is a consciousness in its pure form. It is seen in the blossoming of the golden flower in the back around number five of the thoracic spine; a flower of illumination in understanding, of recognition of purification, and of preservation leading to crystallization.

This character imparts the method to unify the animated soul and the human conscious soul into a pure spirit, a spirit which is pure in its original nature, universal by its structure, and eternal by its content. When the truthful love and truthful consciousness combine, guard each other, and are indifferent to one another, the truthfulness of the self and of the spirit is unified. When these two are indifferent and inseparable, there exists no selfishness, no egoism. Emotion works the selfless love, intelligence is the pure understanding, and consciousness manifests the truthful expression of self and spirit. Therefore, earthly Qi diminishes and cosmic light permeates.

## The Extinction of Five Thieves

The Taoists term the five organic Qi as five thieves because they invade the spirit, diminish the vital Qi, and dry up the essence. They are the secret of illness, the cause of sickness, the intruders of the health, and the ghosts hidden behind the holiness. Laoist's meditation formula for these five thieves is: "Five colors blind the eyes. Racing and hunting madden the heart. Pursuing what is rare makes action deceitful. Five flavors dull the palate. Five tones deafen the ears. Therefore, the sage's method is for the belly, not for the eyes. He abandons the latter and chooses the former." (12:1,2)

This is our understanding of the formulas of Laoism. Other than the breath, the most immediate and noticeable objects we perceive are lights and their colors. Lights and colors are the decorations of God's invisible form. They are the source of Image, which is the dynamic form of all things in the world. Lights and colors represent God's consciousness in all living things, from stars and planets to bacteria and organs. Before our spirit is formed, there are lights and colors of joy, pleasure and hope visibly demonstrated by our parents. That is their spiritual Shen Qi which represents the exact duplicate of the Heavenly Father and Mother's union of oneness. Our parents' spirits also serve as a representation of them. When these two spiritual forms are unified during our parents' love-making, emotional touching and spiritual longing, we have not only the oneness of our parents' union but our God and Goddess's union, as well. Their spiritual light stands between the ultraviolet light and infrared ray, which are the representation of the North Star and the sun. Radiating in between are the seven rainbow colors, representing the time and order of the creation of the universe.

Since we are the representation of God and Goddess, of yin and yang, we are the loving union, the meeting point, and defining line. We are coded within truthful love and truthful consciousness. We stand between the heaven and earth. We embrace the lights of the sun with the colors of the moon, and we integrate the visions of our intellectual wisdom with the vibrations of our individual demand. Our visibility is limited to the seven colors, and our vibration is restrained within the five organic sensory receptors. As we become independent individuals, we breathe in the void of the universe, the substances of the air, and the sensational vibrations of our consciousness. We then draw in the consciousness of the sun and the motion of the moon. Afterward, we exchange the energy between earth and food. The sun provides us with inner stillness, the moon balances our outer stability. The inner stillness manifests as the passionate action through the liver and the truthful consciousness in the lungs. The outer stability vibrates along the truthful fairness of the spleen and pure vibration of love in the heart. When the sensational vibrations of consciousness descend into each organ, they are altered into emotional vibrations and personal characters. The Chan hexagram (# 1) changes into Kan (# 29), and kung hexagram (# 2) turns into Li (# 30). The holy oneness manifests as the human oneness.

At this time, the truthful consciousness becomes discriminative and identifiable. Emotional love and organic consciousness surround us. We wish to be free, but our organs drive us into a self-protective state. We wish to move forward, but emotional love blocks us and we return to the same patterns again and again. We want to be our own beings, but the visual attractions and lust for love keep us in the center of these two extremes.

We are limited, cut off, and restrained from the unified oneness, because we must rely on external energy resources to live and survive. We use the five sensory receptors to receive and transport the energy and the five organs to digest, translate and transform the energetic circulations between the inner organs and the external world. Gradually, the truthful love drifts into organic love, and truthful consciousness becomes egoistic consciousness. Step by step, we become fixated. Layer upon layer, we become contaminated. We go from sickness after sickness until we become useless. By the time we are aware of where our life has led us, we are facing death.

Laoist points out that the eyes are the door of distraction and trouble, and the belly is the seat of stillness and immortality. Much of what the eyes receive is of no importance but distractive stimuli. When the eyes see something, the heart is stirred, the concentration is interrupted, and the energy is depleted. The chapter on the five thieves is the only biological description of illness that the teaching of Laoism has summarized. The eyes see the wrong colors, the ears listen to the wrong information, and the mouth tastes the wrong food. Instead of becoming clean, healthy and energetic, the body and mind become cloudy, sick, and exhausted. Essentially, it is the thief of the heart that causes all the trouble to the body. If the heart is kept clean and still, no evil can enter our thoughts or actions.

The five thieves work together, under the direction of the main thiefthe heart. When the five thieves are transformed into positive energy, the divine thief of the heart becomes a selfless love, a pure love and a Christ love. This is the biggest task of cultivational practices. If the heart is not clean and still, all other efforts are useless. The heart is the master of all organs. It is the mirror of spirit and the organ of disaster. It is also the seat of love and the seed of hatred. In life, even if the eyes are blind, the ears are deaf and the mouth cannot taste, they cannot be as detrimental as the heart. Those sensory receptors are attracted to the forms. They will cause no harm to the body and mind if the heart is clean and still. The heart is the organ of truth, the vibration of trust, and the sensitivity of understanding. The five elemental Qi circulate through the heart and are rewarded by the heart. If the heart is content, the Qi flows serenely. When the heart is clean, the sensory organs work exclusively on the positive side. When the heart is still, the five facial organs are inactive.

## Transforming the Five Thieves into Selfless Love

The third and forth characters in the couplet together complete the work of refining the five chemical elements in the body. The five chemical elements are the five organic functions, from the kidneys and liver to the heart and spleen and lungs. These five organs correspond to the five openings in the face and the five extensions of the hands. In the first stage of cultivational practices, the work begins with the water of the kidneys and the fire of the heart. When the kidney water Qi is boiled by the fire in the heart, under the caldron, the heat rises up along the spine through the life-gate pressure point to the brain. This is called returning the essential Jing to nourish the brain. This practice can take from a few months to possibly many years, depending upon the spiritual talent and biological foundation of the practitioner. The caldron is the cooking vessel in the Lower Cinnabar Field. It is the battery of life essence.

By gathering consciously the cosmic force from above the head, the brain combines the energy coming from the spine and the sky. This combined energy then travels downward to the mouth to stimulate the salivary glands. This combines with the digestive and healing enzyme to produce sweet dew. When this healing enzyme is produced, the fluid of sweet dew flows down into the chest and the thymus glands. The second stage of refinement is now activated.

In this second stage of cultivational refinement, the energy of the wood liver Qi, the energy of the earth spleen Qi, and the energy of the golden lung Qi are processed and refined. After going through the systematic organic process, or the mechanism of smelting, the five thieves transform into the vibration of pure love and the illumination of conscious inaction. The vibration of pure love is the yin form of manifestation in the Middle Cinnabar Field, and the illumination of the conscious inaction is the yang form of that manifestation. The love is to seek resurrection, the power of returning. The illumination is the selfless expression, the flow of Tao. The process of refining the essential Jing of life force into the vibrant flowing Qi is then completed. This total process of "chemical smelting" has accomplished its holy purpose.

At this moment, the meditator receives the seed of true love, the selfless love. S/he will no longer cling vigorously and hopelessly to the obsession of loving the ideal image. The love vibrates between the genders and across the generation with no bias. The subjective attachment becomes the objective respectfulness. The selfish obsession becomes selfless transformation. The romantic love becomes cosmic love. The private satisfaction becomes mutual liberation. Sperm manifests itself into cosmic awareness, and the milk transforms into an everlasting substance.

Do not think that a person then loves the loved one less, for the love is deeper, more abundant. This doesn't mean the person no longer plays the game of love; one is self-responsible in a way that s/he respects the other as an equal to her/himself. No more jealousy, only kind wishes. No more fighting, only mutual transformation. No more hatred, only selfless love. No more fear, only eternal happiness. When a meditator reaches this state, s/he is a happy, healthy, and lovable individual.

Be joyful as your transformation journey continues. Wish you the best in your earnest desires. Hopefully you will no longer think of love as a game, or that love is only for the sake of love, or that love is the best wish with the worst reward. When you reach this state of true love, you will become a beloved individual, and people will love you unconditionally, since you love yourself and others unconditionally. Love is not for receiving only, it is for giving as well. Love does not sacrifice the self, it is the act of abandoning the ego self. Love is not making love with someone, but circulating the loving energy through the body and mind. Love is not expressing outwardly, it is to be experienced inwardly. Love is not holding the loved one captive as a personal possession, but letting go of the obsessive desirable attachment. Love is not clinging to just one person or one thing, its purpose is to mutually respect all people and all creatures. Love is for one and love is for all and love is forever!

## Meditation Practice

1. Sit comfortably on a chair; relax the entire body from head to toes.

2. Press thumbs upon ring fingers, and close thumbs, little fingers, and middle fingers. Let the index arrow fingers point outward, and little finger withdraw and connect the ring fingers.

3. Picture the color(white) and locate the position (center of the brain) of the pineal gland.

4. Establish a connection of eyes (body aura), nose (breath) and ears (inner voice). All three are centered by the pineal glands.

5. Connect the eyes to index fingers, and mentally visualize the aura of your body, your personal color, and your psychic power. Recite silently your name and number of your home or apartment address. Provoke the presence of your physical energy.

6. Connect the nostrils with middle fingers, and mentally examine the breath of your life, your emotion, and your character. Recall inwardly

your full name, first name, middle name, and last name (all name you name). Reconnecting to your soulful energy.

7. Connect the ears with little fingers, and mentally feel the inner vibration of your body, your mind, and your prayer. Remember your birthtime, time, day, month, and year. Return to the state of your psychic expression.

8. Picture the yoke within the connection between thumbs and ring fingers. Gradually, you will see the golden color shining within and around the thumbs and ring fingers.

9.Drawing an energetic connection between the golden color in the hand and the sensational third eye. Let the energy lasering in and out, back and forth between the two points.

10. Connect the eyes, nostrils and ears to the pineal glands by drawing consciously the energy within the fingers and hands upon the brain. Allow the chest to open itself up to the cosmic emptiness.

11. Be ready to perceive what it may present, lights, colors, images, animals, and deities, etc.
Take your time allowing the energy to speak for itself.

12. Visualize the wheel-power of the circulation within the chest, and upon the brain.

13. Feel the volcanic vibration coming through the ears, allowing the sonic vibration to channel the power of pineal gland.

14. Picture the walnut shape of the brain (the integration of pineal gland, thymus gland, and prostate gland). The structure of the brain becomes the hive-shell, the nut-shell, and the light-bulb, centering through the white light of pineal gland.

15. Mentally gaze down upon the gut center above the umbilical cord, reading through all the biological construction of life, from worms, insects, bugs, organs, muscles, emotional memories, and personal histories.

16. Picture the presence of a dove, a chick or a swan sitting peacefully upon the hands, presenting itself as the worldly being.

17. Finalize the three centers, the gut, the hands, and the pineal gland. Let them speak their own thrust, present their own worldly matters.

18. Picture a white streaming light straight from the cosmos to the pineal gland, the chest and caldron (the empty center of the abdominal area).

19. Stay with the color change between the left body and right body. Enjoy the rainbow-colored transformation.

20. Picture the golden light encircling the upper back and shoulder area. Feel the oceanic flow within the abdominal area. Understand the transformation of conscious mind.

21. Awaken yourself to your ordinary conscious state when it is ready.

22. Massage any desirable areas.

23. Recollect what you have experienced, enter your permanent memory by letting it go. Ground yourself in your minute by minute presence.

# STEP FIVE: *LIFE*

Structure: life 命 + heart 心
Sound: yan
Meaning: life

### The Designative Ming

Two sub-characters are used to construct the fifth Laoist character. The one on the top means "life" [ming] while the bottom one is "heart" [xing]. The oral tradition of this character is, as its translation signifies: "to continue, to last, to extend, and to elongate." The character reveals the importance of the unitary harmony existing between the mind and body, the sound and message, and the tongue and order. This importance deals with the purpose of distilling the flaming sensation of the heart in order that a man's action, physically, mentally and spiritually, illuminates itself in harmony with not only one's inner consciousness but the worldly/cosmic orders as well.

When the inner world and external world are harmonized, the knowledgeable understanding becomes pure, authentic, and truthful. When the life and heart are one, there is no difference between the spiritual inspiration and conscious awareness within and the conscious projection and the physical process evolving with the connection. When the man's action truly represents the pure flow of these two ends of the body-mind bridge, nothing is lost and nothing can further be destroyed. The entire process of action is the way of water flowing, the wind blowing, and the sun shining. The penetrative power of light and the purification power of water harmonize into the wonder of the Tao, the magic of power, and the wondrous mystery of life.

Ming in Chinese depicts as "a person obeys, exercises, and practices the order expressed through the mouth." This order is verbalized either through one's own mouth or that of others'. When the order arises from one's own inner world, crossing the conscious bridge of the tongue through the mouth, it is the order of will, the message of the power of God within. When the order comes from others, it is the lawful discipline, the unavoidable destiny, and the surrendering journey. When a person is pure enough to obey her/himself, God is within the presence of life. When one's mind is murky, consciousness is cloudy, the heart is maddening, and body is contaminated. In this condition, there is no way that the pure spiritual consciousness can speak for itself, that the inner light can illuminate itself, and that life can walk its original path. When the lower and condensed forces are controlling the body and mind, the spiritual consciousness is lost into the conditional habits, personal and social, resulting inevitably with no choice but to listen to others and obey their orders.

One then becomes submissive to man's power instead of God's; is fooled by the tricks and enslaved by the destructive forces.

In such a life as this, one has surrendered one's power, become submissive, and is living a life of enslavement. Either God's power or man's power must enslave all lives. God is the ultimate self-enlightened master; man is the self-destructive monster. The power of God lies within; the power of man is derived by the outside sources. The power of will is eternal; the power of ordering manifests externally. To be the slave of God is to be the slave of Self. To be the slave of Self is to willingly serve all beings with unconditional love and compassionate action. To be the slave of man is to be the slave of others whereby one has completely lost the true self within.

God is not out there in the unknown above the sky, He is forever inside the heart. There is no God in the sky but only the penetrating light and ever flowing water. The creator does not exist beyond the life, but always within every living creature.

Goddess is not the opening Window in the Cosmos. She is not the ultimate sacrificial being, but the containment of ultimate Love within. There is no Goddess beyond peace in the universe, and there is no sacrifice beyond the unconditional love existing in our hearts. To surrender to the power within is to surrender to the divine law; to love oneself is to liberate oneself from the worldly orders.

The power of will exists not through acting forcefully but embracing unconditionally. The order of the world does not maintain itself through the power of man's will, but processes itself rightly within his conscious surrendering choice. We are endowed with the freedom within, to follow unconditionally but not to choose consciously. Consciousness is a God-given awareness. All existing conditions arise from Goddess' creative power with no prior condition existing. The wheel-of-life force is not discharged from any other force, but emerges only from the inner conscious journey of spontaneous flow. This spontaneous flow is the mist of loving presence.

In life, the choices are already being made, either by the power of the Creator, within the lawful order of life, or by the force of man following the journey of others. A person must listen to the order from the Heavenly Emperor even though s/he is not obliged to obey the ruling emperor's ordering power. Obeying oneself is submitting to one's destiny, which is assigned by the heavenly order being spoken through the God-designed message. Obeying others is being compliant to the power, discipline, demand, and control of others, including the heavenly ones. To obey oneself is to be governed by the character of self, the power within, and the beauty of life as it is being expressed. To obey others is to surrender oneself with either complete faith or submission to the destiny of life, from the practice of breathing to the activity of footsteps, and from conscious awareness to physical actions.

Therefore, when one listens to the silence within, peace is one's world. When one obeys the power within at that moment, the will is extremely powerful. Peace knows no time and there is no will involved with the second thought. When peace ceases, lust follows after. When hesitation falters, fear ensues. When lust replaces love, conditions occur. When conditions arise, duality emerges. Within the duality, God is conditional, Goddess is emotional, life is situational, and love is personal.

In spiritual practice, it is the combination of both obeying and listening that allows one to be with all and one to be with the true self at the same time. Each one of us is a messenger of God. No one else can live her/his life or fulfill another's life destiny. Ming, then, means to listen and obey the journey, the destiny and the pilgrimage within the power of will. The more one chooses to be guided by her/his inner self, the more one will be freed from the outside forces. The more one is influenced by the outside forces, the less capable s/he will be to listen to oneself. When one's life journey, whether in inner consciousness or physical activity, is directed and influenced by others, the will of self reflects only through the will of others, and one's own destiny is shaped by the expression of others. One then becomes not the slave of Self but the slave of a conditioned system, habitually or socially, personally or politically. The freedom of will is converted into the freedom with no choice. The freedom of spontaneous flow of love becomes the conditional expression between love and hatred. Love is an extinguishable fireball. Hatred represents the negative force emerging from the extinguished force of love.

## The Power of Order

In animal life, the tongue selects the food, the teeth chew to digest it while the saliva is produced by the reflex from biting and chewing and swallowing. The mouth, therefore, becomes the gateway to the storage house, the stomach. All animals use their mouths and tongues for communications. Each animal relies upon its unique signs and signals that no other animal species can fully interpret, thereby preserving their secrecy and protecting their lives. All the signs and signals are biologically built in. No special training process is required to develop such skills.

In human life, the mouth is an organ that allows the food to enter in and verbal messages to be expressed. Teeth represent the drumming hands. Tongue represents the post-heaven swinging spiritual tail. Hands are both the decisive executors and food collectors. When an inner vibration quickens, the mouth releases this informed message through its breathing activity. The air released from the mouth drums the vocal cord enabling this spiritual drummer to echo the various inner consciousness impulses. The mouth renders the empty space of this spiritual drummer contracting and expanding its mechanical muscular vehicles in order to clearly express the message. In spiritual practice, the "mouth" represents the inner cosmic silence where one can hear clearly and act accordingly, where the cosmic sweet dew is produced to nourish the work of unconditional love. Silence reveals the orders of the Heavenly Emperor or God. Sweet dew is the ultimate healing medicine.

In human development, language, as a tool, is the highlight of civilization. To transfer and expand from the oral form of communication into a combined form involving oral reading and handwriting, necessarily requires education. In this ensuing process, one's name is inter-connected with the educational system and its effects on one's identity. Discrimination occurs. Possession takes its place in life. Inner will power and executive power become distinctive. Inner voice and external expression are usually incongruent, due to the shift of mental projection and control. Spiritual life and material life become separated entities. Gradually, one's distinctive oral voice becomes the identification of one's written name. Inner consciousness is expressed in egoistic behavior. Spiritual consciousness yields to intellectual property. Unconditional love turns into conditional lust. Energetic flow is restrained within the property of materialistic and manageable controlling power, which in turn, is cyclically controlled by the inevitable reaction of fear.

Essentially, the order expressed through the mouth originates from either transcendental spiritual awakening inspiration or one's conscious and egoistic desire. The former is the Order from the Heavenly Emperor or God, and the latter represents one's eternal will or ego power. In life, there exists two types of will, that of God and that of man/woman. When the will arises from God, it is the free choice of spirit, the destiny of spirit with faith and submission, an awakening path within. When the will is formed from self or others, its origin is the destiny of karma. This karmic destiny deals with the obsession of controlling the force of karmic interaction in all phases of personal, family, social, and political function. Obsession can be classified as both personal and individual, while karmic interaction is mutually and co/interdependently motivated. However, if one lives beyond the karmic interaction or has accomplished the karmic work, the orders of others would not effect one's inner journey, either spiritually or consciously. The light power coming from within is more powerful than any external influence. The dark forces cannot exert any influence upon the undivided force integrated between the spirit and light.

The karmic interaction is the condensed and mutually bonded energetic interaction. Whether the interaction be willful on the stimulating side or willingly accepted on the responding side, the energetic forces remain the same. These karmic energetic forces represent the two persons' interactive streams of consciousness. They are the echoing power of conscious breathing. The more one is conscious of self and world, the more subtle the experience of this conscious breathing. The conscious inhaling is consciously willful. The conscious exhaling is willingly energetic.

With this karmic energetic interaction evolving during spiritual practice, only the state of purification can occur. No replacement is needed in the aftermath. If a conscious condition is liberated and its vibration is transformed into a higher level, no replacement can occur afterward. Nor can any repetition exist. Qualitatively, it is a leap. Quantitatively, it is a new beginning. In terms of personal communication, for example, if one side is free from this energetic bondage, the opposing side would either be liberated by this higher force or withdraw itself in an effort to retain the old energy pattern. For the side that is completely liberated from this old chain of energetic interaction, there can be no turning back. The gate into the darkness, the addiction, and the fixation, is finally obliterated from its very root cause for all time. Only the lighter, the higher, and deeper realms of conscious power are re-born. In effect, the spiritual self is re-born.

If one is free from any addiction, smoking or drinking or enslavement by others, the energetic patterns arising from those acts would not affect the person's true destiny, the Will of God. When one is free from any social, political, and religious organization, one is then exercising the work of God's will, intertwined with one's own freedom of action. When one is free from one's own built-in energetic karma of conscious duality, no fear can exist in life, only a momentary response and reaction to the world of self and others. One is truly a free spiritual being.

In the spiritual journey, the order is the function of the double-edged sword, the tongue. The double-edged tongue can either save or destroy life through its ordering power. Each order involves both reward and sacrifice. In a higher conscious realm, the one edge destroys the old energetic pattern through the power of light and penetration of self-discipline. In this area the action of sacrificing is essential. The opposing edge enacts the healing and purification and liberation, enabling a new world order to occur. This new world order follows the spiritual law which exists beyond the causality order governed by the conscious realm.

However, in ordinary consciousness, this double-edged sword rarely functions harmoniously. It may destroy one's precious vital force by projecting externally. When the projected mentality becomes reality, one's own vital force is extinguished and the responding party is also destroyed. It is then a double loss. One's verbal expression brings catastrophe to both sides, self and company. That is why in karmic interaction, each form of negativity, such as hatred or violence, entails only more negative consequence. Hatred breeds more hatred, violence promotes more violence.

## The Rising of Conscious Second Thought

This ordinary consciousness can be soulful, egoistic, and selfish. It originates from one's being either too excited or too fearful. The spiritual thought as an instant vibration is reexamined and reinterpreted by the creation of time, the second thought. When this second thought surfaces, there exists discrimination between new and old, this and that, above and below, self and others. As this second thought occurs, the spiritual force descends into soulful or personal awareness. The creative peace arises as a physical sensation or emotional understanding.

Each side then generates another three dimensions. Together dimensions occur. The top, the back, and the right represent the spiritual trinity. The brain stores the spiritual intelligence. The spine restores the rocking groundedness. The right side of the body follows the earth's rotation.

The bottom, the front, and the left represent the physical trinity. The abdominal area is the unconditional oceanic peace. The front body expresses the personal character and emotional vibration. The left side follows the earth's orbiting order. Thus, heaven and earth are separated,

God and Goddess are divided, masculinity and femininity are extinguished, male and female are created. The past and future are divided by the hesitation, the doubt created by the second thought. The moment is conditioned by the old habit which in turn is projected as a new hope. The vital force is divided into either mental and physical forces, or spiritual power and lustful desire.

The six realms of the life wheel co-exist within their inherited duality. The spirituality at the top is charged by the sexuality at the bottom. The emotional and the personal expression is governed by the conscious and conditional understanding. The receptive and repelling force of femininity on the left side balances the penetrative striking power of masculinity on the right. The body/mind, the heart/soul, and the consciousness/spirit all work together as an inseparable entity. The six realms of the life wheel work the wonder between God and Goddess, male and female, spirit and soul. Respectively, they emerge as spiritual sensitivity and wisdom understanding, mental awareness and physical sensation, awakening consciousness and dreaming consciousness.

Therefore, in spiritual practice, one necessarily becomes liberated from either side of the world. One must harmonize, neutralize, integrate, and unify the co-existing forces into the pure, the truth, the love, and the oneness. The spiritual liberation deals precisely with the murky forces which have been sustained in their own small encapsulated environment. Conditional love remains with the conditionally loved environment. Wishful thinking exists with the hopeful dreaming environment, inviting addictive behavior to manifest through a repetitive cycling environment.

To liberate from the old karmic interaction of fixated patterns and addictive behaviors one must enter and practice faithfully a process of self-discipline, complete submission, and personal sacrifice of that which one likes most. This is called martial/military fire (wuhuo). All the likes must be abandoned; all the dislikes must be viewed as teachers. This must not be considered a mean feat since reward is the eternal spiritual freedom within the realm of cosmic content. In personal and social life, one sacrifices the vital force which is spiritual in its purest form. The life force permeates as the conscious effort, timeless devotion, and interpersonal bondage. Its rewards are the illusion of mind, the temporary sensational and emotional satisfaction, becoming a promise toward future fixation. In spiritual practice the essential vital force, which is the spiritual and loving and sexual force, never dies, just as unconditional love never dies. It is a gentle fire silently extinguishing the old fixated patterns, encouraging the selves to love mutually, and the creative freedom to liberate passionately. It is called intellectual/compassionate fire (wenhuo) in Taoism.

## The Empty Xing

Xing, in contrast to ming, depicts the organic flaming fire of the maddening heart. The original Chinese character xing resembles the heart organ. The inflamed energy arises from the earth's spleen and descends from the passion of soulful liver. Within the madness, there is emptiness that does not connect with the cosmic void but with the personal loss. It is not summer heat that steams and vaporizes the kidney water. It is the force of the red fire, the drying heat, and the self-sacrifice. Wind has not yet cooled it down. Peace has not yet found its residence. The wind is the conscious awareness based upon the spiritual inspiration. Peace is the tranquil mind, the cosmic water, and valley womb. Therefore, the red firing madness represents the directionless urge and uncontrollable compulsion for earthly pursuits, without foundation or support, serving only to inflame and madden.

Cosmically, this reddish flaming fire represents the solar light, especially its arousal moment in the sunrise. Rather than reflecting the moonlight as it lifts up the soul, the solar light pours down onto earth to awaken and liberate the spirit within the body-mind. That is why the blood charges us, just as are all the members within the animal kingdom. Blood is the transitional vehicle between birth and death. When we were born, there was a blood exchange between our pre-heaven and post-heaven life. The pre-heaven blood originated from the sacrifice made by our parents and by our old soulful energy. When our parents initiated our life, our former soul, being pure spirituality or a mixture between spirit and soul, was watching and waiting, anticipating the moment of involvement. During their secret love making process, our spirit flies, invisible to their flesh eyes but visible in their spiritual communication, into their confirmation. As the fetus then grows, our spirit resides placidly within.

The post-heaven blood represents the rebirth of our old soul, resulting from the dissolved relationship between our mother and our new life. It is the stream of the life force itself. Passion and love and sacrifice are its vehicle. Liver, spleen, lungs and kidneys work together to ensure the normal healthy circulation of the heart. Most importantly, the biological organ of the heart facilitates the spiritual organ of the thymus gland. Together, the physical nutrition and mental understanding make the heart the master of spirit.

Tao is the form of heart and body is its function. The form is empty and function is its understanding. If the heart is not empty by itself, nutritious blood cannot flow, and mental understanding cannot occur. When the space of heart is not empty, the flow of the Tao, which is the meaning of spirit, cannot reside in its rightful place. There can be no true understanding. The spiritual power cannot be transcended into mental function; the sacred meaning of life cannot manifest physically.

Precisely when the heart is empty, the ego becomes non-existent and the mind becomes pure. The message of life is clear and the unconscious reality within the abdominal area can be awakened into spiritual consciousness and wisdom understanding. This is the message of the fifth character, that when the heart is empty, the spiritual light and conscious fire can descend upon the valley of body and the root of fire, just as cosmic light and sunshine descend upon the earthly mother and the heads of all living creatures. The valley of body is the unfathomable power of the kundalini awakening force, the spiritual awakening within the sexual power. The root of fire is the function of the tailbone which is the spiritual head of life. It manifests as the yang spirit. The brain, in contrast, represents the yin spirit.

In life, it is the functioning of the empty heart that allows the play of magic five, the Pentateuch. From the five Qi in the Cosmos to the five colors in the world, to the five organs (kidneys, liver, heart, spleen, and lungs) and their five sensational and emotional expressions in the body, to the five fingers on each hand, and toes on each foot, enabling the sustenance and maintenance of the body-mind. Unlike trinity that manifests in ming, xing contains and works the wonders of five. Xing must be empty, by itself, in order to regulate the four corners of the world. That is why, in its Chinese description, xing of the heart's fire is stored in the spleen's earth, representing the center of body-mind.

When xing is unencumbered, no conscious thread can be produced, no calculating time can be created, no secondary thought can be generated, and no loss can result. Do not misinterpret this to mean that in spiritual practice, we must kill the heart. It signifies the necessity to retain the original state and pure functioning of xing. In spiritual discipline, from five elemental Qi to five pillars, from pentahedron to Pentateuch, the heart must be empty and pure, ensuring the unification of the five universal principles within the trinity of life's destiny. When the heart is maddened, the life becomes completely distorted, and spiritual understanding is lost. What is lost is the meaning of life and the opportunity for spiritual awakening. It is the greatest tragedy of life.

## Characteristic Representation

In pre-heaven life, ming is at the top and xing is at bottom. This is because the body is upside down in the womb, with the abdomen on top and the head at bottom. The ming represents the cosmic entity and the xing constitutes that of the growing fire. The tailbone is the guiding light and directing power. Ears are the air lifting echoing drums within the valley of the creative ozone. The brain becomes the charged swinging ball. The fire coming through the brain burns the water in the abdomen allowing the fetus to grow to its fullest normal maturity. The root is not the baby's feet but the mother's ovaries standing above the pelvic bones. This pre-heaven life stage represents the earth's image that is rotating and orbiting the sun. The water is in the north and the fire in the south.

In post-heaven life, the heat of conscious loving fire seeks its way of returning. Instead of flaming through the water first, the heat, as the brain vibration, immediately dissolves through the mental activities. Without the fire that boils the water into steam, the holy water of primordial yang Qi turns largely into biological yin Qi of sexual fluid charged by the murky oceanic water. Whether being frozen internally or discharged downward, the part of the primordial yang Qi that has not been transformed into the sprout of passion in the liver is gradually contaminated by the heavy materials sinking from the top part of the body (migraine headache). It becomes the frozen unconscious energy about to be transformed into gross sexual energy (compulsive action). The conscious yin fire gradually becomes dry and invasive (vacillating between sadness and jealousy). The unconscious yang Qi of that spiritual fire is frozen in a remote distance, somewhere that cannot connect with the reality of the spiritual world (between loss of mind and fixation of mental activity).

To many people, the body and mind rarely engage in conscious communication. The mind wanders externally in its personal and social way, while the body maintains its biological process internally. The wandering mentality arises within, but its goal is not geared toward internal transformation; rather, it facilitates the wandering process. The mind wonders along its wandering way, taking steps with no focal point. The gate of heaven remains blocked, but the gates of wondering are never closed. Finally, the life force is extinguished before connecting with the spiritual root, the inner and unconditional love. This spiritual root represents the cosmic light and wisdom fire as well.

This defines precisely the meaning of Laoist fifth character. Whether the mind leaps ahead or the body marches forward, they should never become separated. The mind should exalt the sacred position of body. Although the body is temporary and illusive to the spiritual body of universe, the mind should retain its humbleness within. The body should grind the fire down to its root with its heavy earthly entity. Even though the mind continues to ignite the firing ball containing the conscious sparks from the sun, the body should preserve her precious holy water, the primordial yang Qi, in order to unify the light within. The body contains the blue and creamy Qi within the black valley. The mind invites the red and golden Qi within the white Cosmos.

In spiritual practice, the body-minded action is essentially about obeying oneself first, foremost and continuously through surrendering to one's pure intention and conscious effort. This action then represents the purest form of the integration of the body as vehicle, the mind as conscious soul, and the spirit as the divine inspiration. The five organic and emotional Qi become spiritual and unconditional love Qi. The trinity of body, soul, and spirit will become one Qi of life force.

The meaning of this fifth character is clearly illustrated in the Tao Te Ching. It says: "Donning the spirit and soul, and drawing them into Oneness, can this come apart? Gathering in Qi and making the body supple, is this not an infant? Being clear-headed and eliminating any mystic vision, can a speck exist? Loving the people and governing the country, is this not inactive? Opening and closing the Gate of Heaven, is this not the female? Comprehending the four corners of the world, is this not knowledge?" (10:1) These six sentences unify the six realms of the world, the hexagonal prisms of I Ching's crystal structural formation.
The first three sentences deal with Godly or masculine nature, while the last three sentences express the goddess or feminine nature. The duality of triangular functioning becomes the oneness. Body and mind are one single complete entity.

Practically speaking, this character demonstrates how to experience life consciously without separating the mental awareness from the physical operation; how to live fully without discriminating between what the mind intends and the body executes; how to interact the life selflessly by treating it with understanding and acceptance. As a result, the literal meanings of this character are: "1) to be with the situation of presence, not the present situation; 2) to reach the state of longevity, not to come to grips with the boundaries of life; and 3) to enter the condition of immortality, not to be judged by the historical calculation of longevity." To be with is to be grounded. To reach is to walk through the pilgrimage. To enter is to sit in the embryonic cosmic state of consciousness.

Why is this so? First of all, the presence is the actual reality: not only the reality of mind but also of culture; not only the reality of diversified physical or mental or spiritual existence but also of a single and total existence. It is about the mind's truthful presence with whatever it is here, there, and everywhere.

Secondly, longevity is a mental state upon physical conditioning. The truth of longevity exists in the reality of a long history for each eternal life along its course from the beginning to the end. This eternal life course is, in itself, the spiritual life. The longevity lies in the presence of living and working harmoniously with this spiritual course. The more closely the physical life listens to the order of spiritual life, the simpler the course will be. Within the simplicity, longevity ensues. Along the eternal course of spiritual life, the physical form changes, life after life, just as the earth rotates around the sun, year after year. Each lifetime presents a specific function and carries a unique role into the timeless, unending river flow of that eternal life. The totality of this eternal life has its own natural longevity. Each individual life has numerous cycles of birth and death. But its eternal life, individually and collectively, has already had a long history of beginning. It lives through the present time and into eternity as though nothing has begun and nothing has yet been done. It is, actually, endless.

Lastly, each of us has a temporarily stationed physical body and death may at any time be on its way. We are surely dying each and every moment, from cell to cell, and thought to thought. But each of us has an old soul. This soul is seated within the root of longevity. Just as all the plants that have lived through cycle after cycle without varying any of their special features and uniqueness, each of our lifetimes has its own natural history. Regardless of the gender role, the soul remains essentially and indefinitely the same. Regardless of the specific character we are destined to engage within a specific role, our eternal self or soul remains forever unchanged. That is the message of immortality along the course of longevity. God's form of oneness is eternal because it is formless. The life form of oneness is eternal because of God's presence within. Goddess's creative power is ever present. The power of unconditional love is also an ever presence. That is the message of Tao and Te. That is the meaning of ming and xing.

We will view the above situations from another aspect in regard to the literal meaning of this fifth character, we must understand the difference between the situation of presence and the present situation, between the individual physical longevity and its collective one, and between the spiritual immortality and a wishful one. First of all, when the person is with the situation of presence, her/his mind remains alert, cool and distant, regardless of how the body engages. As for the present situation, it is a breath, a catch, an attention, an emergency, and a task performance. Secondly, longevity deals with the natural history of a life. This natural history lives up to the wishful projection of the mind and also to the actual capacity of the body. It deals with how long a single lifetime will last and how well it has lived at every given momentary stage.

This natural history consists of both the individual and collective styles, since we human beings are individual in character and collective in representation. Each individual's physical life must live and die, and lasts but a short time. But collectively, we human beings have lived a long life and the future will take us a still longer and endless way. Each individual life is a mere drop, a part, a single pigment, and a specific sensation along the river flow of life and death. It is like one small scene in a film and one display on the evolutionary stage of its endless course.

Our immortality enables the spiritual mind to return to its own place in the universe, its own reality. It is not about the repetition of a mental idea or a physical display. It is about the ever-present cosmic light, the forever shifting of the spiritual wind, and the eternal trust of the heartless soul. We will discuss this further by illustrating with the words of Laoism "To die, but not be forgotten, is to be immortal." (33:2) in Chapters twelve and thirteen.

These three words, presence, longevity, and immortality, are not only interrelated but also inter-changeable. Any presence has lived according to its recorded history, and is continuously recording its course as well. The role of longevity is to inspire the spiritual desire of being with its true reality, which is the eternal and spiritual reality. Immortality is defined as the true spirit, no longer abiding within the temporary living body, but beyond and outside the earthly physical pressure and karmic restraint. Again, immortality is the real presence of spirit. Presence deals with the enlivening spirit. Longevity tracks the durability, the changeability, and the persistency of spirit. Immortality returns to its absolute nature of pure spiritual condition. This is the reality of life, the truthfulness of life, and the originality of life. This is meaning of the fifth character.

## Presence of Flowing

To present this in greater detail, being with the situation of the presence is to be in touch with the reality of life, continuing from the past and living fully with the presence of any situation. To be with the situation in the presence does not require the mind or heart to be present. The mind is always present, whether with its own illusionary makeup and received information, or its instinctive demands and habitual repetitions. It is continuously going with the flow. The present is the spiritual present, and this flow is a spiritual flow.

Flow marks the precision of the energetic interaction among all things that are involved, conditioned, and habituated. Flow is an indication of a living situation continuing in its present conditioning, or more explicitly, that it has not stopped, ended, and terminated. It is eternal and ever present. Flow means too that everything involved is working at its full potential and that all things in that environment are in harmony. In the flow, the rules are present, the laws are present, the details are present, and mysteries also are present. In this harmonious flow, God is present, self is present, and love is present. At that moment, under that conditioning and within that environment, there exists no separation, projection, interpretation, repetition, nor control. Simply put: the mind and body are one, the action and interaction are the same, and the awareness and engagement remain indifferent. The so-called ego mind, the analytical mind, and intuitive mind are merged in the actual engagement. The receptive body, the sensational body, and the experiential body all participate fully. All are then put into the context of reality, being with presence of the reality, and thoroughly aware of the union of reality.

While going with the flow is to engage fully, to act passionately, and to experience thoroughly, it also has both earthly dimension and cosmic realization. The earthly dimension deals with that which is tangible, perceivable, and controllable on earth. It is the containment of the participation and interaction between body and mind, and between earth and heaven. It relates to what we are, what we have, and how we are doing.

The eternal spiritual self is the reason for our being and what we are. What we have is the psychic conditioning and biophysical body. How we are doing is how we are dreaming, carrying on, and becoming. We have the physical size, the bodily weight, and mental density. This is the earthly dimension, the tool we employ. Without this dimension, we know not what we are, what we have or how we are doing. The cosmic realization concerns itself with things that are invisible, inaudible, and intangible. It is about the Tao: the Tao of creativity, the Tao of changeability, and the Tao of eternity.

Furthermore, the earthly dimension deals with how the mind receives information, learns and uses the skills, and makes friends with rules and justice. Information is the flow of energetic interaction, considers who was born, how the weather tempers everything, and where God directs us. Skills are the representation of how the mind and body separate and unify themselves in their unique conditioning process; it is about demonstrating, displaying, protecting, and preserving what the mind grasps and what the body demonstrates. Making friends with rules and justice is about buying off the laws, frightening oneself into devotion, saving oneself in the face of fear, disguising oneself before the existing and prevalent injustice. Rules renounce oneself, and justice protects oneself. Rules are realistic, and justice is egoistic.

Going with the flow is a liberating sensation when, in an unexpected moment, you are involved in a vulnerable situation. The liberating sensation brings forth an overwhelming experience and a complete transition. It is a reward leading to the final preparation, that breath-taking evaluation and peaceful cry emanating from the inner joy. The unexpected moment announces to the void that everything comes from nothing and returns to nothing, and nothing is in everything.

In just such a moment, everything is crammed in and jumbled together at one end, yet all things are in perfect order and regulated at the opposite end: chaos and order are one, irregularity and norm are the same, good and bad make no impact. It is at this moment when everything that catches its breath survives, but anything that misses the opportunity dies. That is what is defined as an unexpected moment. The peaceful cry rising from the inner joy indicates that liberation and surrendering meet on the same track, that happiness and sadness celebrate at the same moment, crying and joyfulness are secreted in the exact drop, becoming at one with the absolute peace and vibrating ease, moving in the inseparable frequency and timeless stoppage. Oh, such a cry, such a joy!

At the same time, going with the flow doesn't abandon the sight of detective eyes or reject the waves of possibility which block the space for acceptance. In this understandable environment, anything can and will happen. It is not only the precious moment and inner peace that allow the mind to be engaged and mindful, the body to experience anticipation and become workable and pliable, and the self to be special and playful. It is also in such a moment that glory has already dissolved and the hope remains concealed behind the scene. Laoist's experience is: "Full of care, as one crossing the wintry stream; Attentive, as one cautious of the total environment; Reserved, as one who is a guest; Spread open, as when confronting a marsh; Simple, like uncarved wood; Opaque, like mud; Magnificent, like a valley." (15:3)

Lao Zi further realizes that "From within the murky comes the stillness. The feminine enlivens with her milk." (15:4) He is centered at a turning point, beneath the situation of transition, and beyond the surrounding atmosphere of neutralization. "The feminine" in this instance represents the form of forming and condition of changing. On the edge of forming and changing, it is not the seed, but the active being with its livelihood; it is not a finished product, but the nurturing power of milk. Oh, then which is with the flow of the Tao, the feminine or the milk? Here Lao Zi doesn't use the word "mother." He chooses the state of virginity within the feminine. He doesn't refer to this feminine as mother, but sustains the milky way of the Tao, that life channel and nutritious supply. In this feminine body of the Tao, flow becomes very pure, quite virgin, truly earthly, and absolutely realistic. In any other given situation, the milk will either spoil, or the child will die from hunger and thirst. In the true spiritual setting, hunger is cast off by the light, and thirst is quenched by the air. It is these two, light and air, that combine to make both the flow and all that-could-possibly-be-with-the-flow.

Lao Zi's practical evaluation of this present moment is: "Keeping such a Tao, excess is undesirable. Desiring no excess, work is completed without exhaustion." (15:50) Who cannot embrace this? Yet, how few people can achieve such a state of being, going with the flow of presence?

## The Beauty of this Character

This character implies, rather than assuming or presuming that the mind is superior to the body, that the opposite is just the case: one should never permit the heart to become maddened or to step outside of the interactive environment with the body. One should always remain peaceful and tranquil in the face of the maddening fire.

The word "one" indicates the oneness of unified spirit between the body and mind. As in the nature of a family or the invisible power of a government, this super-visionary "one" is alive and real, yet, one cannot discover the true nature of its existence. This super-visionary "one" stands on the precipice of alertness, leaps about on the edge of forgetfulness, and hides behind the curtain of ignorance. It is nowhere yet everywhere. It is you, me, her/him, and it.

There is a vast difference between getting mad and being mad. Getting mad is a readily responsive expression, while being mad is an energetic conditioning. Getting mad is self-involving, while being mad reveals an energy pattern objectively. Getting mad is a voluntary processing, while being mad is a state of non-figurative art. Getting mad emerges one in a dangerous position and a self-destructive environment, being mad is a specific type of fixated expression. Getting mad is a temporary distortion, while being mad is a sickness. Between this subjective involving and objective expression, there exists the true quality of heart. Heart, by its very nature, is empty. But the sensational fire of getting mad ignites it and brings the flaming fire to the boiling point. A person has no real reason to be mad about anything, including her/himself. But the position of frustration, the situation of misunderstanding, and the inability to control make the person think he is being necessarily mad.

What is the madness of fire and from where does it come? Typically, it is a form of selfless sacrifice coming from the heavenly destructive manner. In the sky, the shining light represents it. On earth, it is the volcanic fire. In regard to the changing seasons, it is the energy of growing (thundering power awakened by the lightening) and the power of healing (the transformation of light into heat by dissolving everything into its purest fruit and complete seed). Emotionally, it is the selfless devotion and useless sacrifice. Nature acts in this manner, and we behave as such. It is also a manner of the inability of maintaining itself in the context of a deforming and transforming situation, including the role and character that the heart projects. Madness is the truthfulness of explosion, the quickness of dissolving, and readiness of giving up. Because of this, madness has both a positive and negative side. When there is a liberating transformation, everything then becomes peaceful; one experiences the awakening peace. When there is only firing destruction, the world withers and dies within that deadly peace.

The difference lies in whether one chooses to flow with it or be pushed by it. When one flows with the fire, no sickness results, only positive growth and refreshment. Milk represents that flow and the understanding shares that flow. If one is either pushed or pulled by it, the result is, necessarily, an involuntary death. Ashes sink downward, and dust blows in all directions. This is why fire is a transitional element, just as water is a flowing element. Birth is the new era of that transition and death is its renunciation. Without fire, seed could not mature. Yet, too much fire will burn it and too little fire will allow it to freeze. Healing and transformative power emerge from the fire, and burning and destructive forces are the eventful results from the fire. Consequently, we see that there cannot be fire without inner emptiness, nor firing without acting madness. Stillness reigns within the empty fire, and madness expresses through the passionate firing. Stillness captures the spiritual sensation, and death results in the physical transformation.

The pathological nature of madness is this: getting mad is primary and being mad is conditioning. When one gets mad, one loses her/his balance and the ego is overpowered by the penetrative energy coming from outside sources. Then the process of protecting and defending oneself takes place simultaneously. When one takes on a protective position, one is driven by either fear or uncertainty, or possibly both. This is the nature of distortion within, which renders the destruction of the ego's stability.

When one defends oneself, if possible, without fear or uncertainty, it is the expression of the honest heart being driven by the kidney will. Fear invites more destruction, while willpower stabilizes both the eternal and external environments. If the energy gets stabilized easily and quickly, there is no madness circulating organically. If not, the organs, such as liver, will be colored by the maddening Qi, and the person becomes enraged and is constantly frustrated. Collectively, at its worst, the family becomes fired, the community is maddened, and the nation erupts into a destructive fire. This is, primarily, the physical interaction of madness, since the mind protects the endangered bodily environment and ego guides the instinctive behavior. Fight or flight is both a pathological reaction and a biological response.

Mentally, when the psychological environment is distorted, the body becomes the true victim. When the ego is conditioned by any specific belief system, it turns into an endless firing ball. This belief system is a conditioned pattern of specific energetic circulation. Energetically, language is a fixated expression, belief is a fixated pattern, and culture is a fixated environment. They are all the substances of a human belief system. This is, perhaps, the true nature of human confrontation, which constitutes the comings and goings of maddening heart. That is why we humans constantly fire at one another in our unceasing disputes.

Naturally, when the heart is empty, only stillness is visible. If the body is cosmically tempted by the pure spirit, peace is the presence. Even in that area there may be certain types of the firing element at play, on and off, altogether it is the expression of blissfulness. In the nature of the Tao, the spirit has no need to be fired by the forming and transforming sensation. The mind has no time to establish a belief pattern, nor to mention the belief system, because the cosmic spiritual light penetrates and recycles simultaneously in no time. And the body constantly refreshes itself leaving no trace contained within. There is no purpose in responding to the madness of fire, either seasonally or personally, mentally or physically. But sadly enough, as it has always been, the history of civilization is a conditioned interaction of madness. The culture, the religious culture in particular, is a heartfelt expression of madness. It is the highest form of ego-controlled madness brought by the mind's need to be stationed, and ego's desire for gratification.

This is the nature of fire and the emptiness of heart. But what is the nature of water, the weaving cradle for all things on earth? It is the character of instinct and the overwhelming power of obsession. The body is obsessed with food, water, light, love and all such things we consider necessary to our lives. In cultivation practices, the madness should always be positioned lower than the existence of the body, by either allowing the still body to cool the madness down or by absorbing and transforming the maddening Qi into a more useful vibration between the self and others. Meanwhile, the nature of instinct must be converted into the conscious awareness. The meaning of obsession must be reinterpreted by the power of spirit. Without this process, heart is always mad, and body is always obsessive. Madness destroys the self, and obsession extinguishes the self. By the time the self is aware of this, it is prepared to be maddened by the ghost spirit, and possessed by the lower forms of life, the life of germs or parasites.

This is why it is such an important task to put the fire under the caldron, a position for true self-rejuvenation. And it is urgent to be fully aware of what is happening, to realize the obsessive demands of the old energetic environment that is possessively controlled within the fixated habits. In its completion, this character represents what Laoism has emphasized: "The sage is for the belly and not for the mind." (12:2) and "The sage wears shabby cloth but holds the treasure within." (72:4)

What is often the situation in life for most people is that the heart-devoted mind never coexists step by step, side by side, and image upon image within the busy working body. When an idea appears in the mind, the heart drives the body into doing what the mind pursues. When the body feels hunger, the mind feeds it and tries to please its palate. When the body is sick, the mind is mad and abuses the body further. Instead of listening to the needs arising from the body, the mind tries desperately, by any means, to fix it. Instead of searching for the true cause of the problem, the mind concentrates on pacifying the suffering, thereby promoting more suffering. Instead of clarifying the true cause of problems, the mind is busy analyzing them, labeling them, and pathologizing them through its own power structure. As a result, the body becomes the carrier of sickness, the troubles caused by illness, and endless names given to identify the disorders.

In our educational training and learning process, we are systematically brainwashed to separate our thoughts from our feelings, to discriminate our perception from our awareness, and to diagnose the ill health we suffer from the very environment we inhabit. The intellect defines this as civilization, but what is felt is the suffocation of the soul. This is what the mind crams into the over burdened body which slowly asphyxiates to the state of ever present dust.

This character in the couplet illustrates vividly the meaning of "continuing, lasting and prolonging." The heart is just below the weightless breathing life. Life means the circulation of breath, the destination of passage, and character of obedience. Without such, the ego mind does not know where the weight is, or how to play the game and be responsible. The order should arise naturally from the oneness of heart. In doing so, it represents the most authoritative message and ruling power signified by the "imperial jade seal." That is the meaning of life, or more succinctly, the destination of life, which is listening to the heart, obeying the rule, and carrying out the order. Ruling the heart is the best order of ruling the people. Without rulings of the heart, there can be no respect, discipline, honor, obedience, and sacrifice in life. The power of ruling is the power of continuing, the beauty of lasting, and the meaning of prolonging.

## The True Instinctive Behavior

The only instinctive human behavior that has not been conditioned culturally is the breathing activity. Even though there are culturally specified practices such as Indian Yoga and Chinese Inner Alchemy, no culture can categorize the breathing activity into its own egocentric territory, and no one needs to tell others how to breath. We all know instantly that no one can live without breathing. However, there is a vast difference between shallow breathing and stomach breathing, and similarly between nostril breathing and bodily breathing. In a sense, the entire cosmos is a breathing void in an empty universe circulating its own Qi. Air is the medium between heaven and earth, light and water. Lungs connect the conscious spirituality with the biological cellular function. Breath circulates the temperatures between body and its surrounding environment, regulates the degree of freshness and stagnant, beats as the drummer of life and death. It is such that breath is characterized as the most addictive activity of life, particularly among organic lives. Without breathing activity, organic lives could not be organic, since they depend on air for generating and transforming the energy. If you can hold the breath in an open environment for three minutes or more, you are already a sage.

In human history, there have been some who could breathe with cosmic Qi after leaving their breathing biological bodies. They acquire their spiritual bodies by breathing with light and cosmic wind which is holy water. They no longer rely on air and water to sustain their physical body. They are now capable of breathing breathlessly. They are still alive with light as their visual attraction, air as their audible vibration, and life as their organic obsession. Daytime is a dreamed compulsive activity, and nighttime is distorted dream work. Awakening is a dreamless sleep, and confusion is a sleepless dreaming. Working and dreaming are the climax of life, and sleep and death are the renunciation of life. The activities of this life are but the breathing of air, the drumming of madness, the sleeping of stillness, and the dreaming of activities. Being mentally aware but not engaged in is dreaming the dreamwork, being mentally aware and being engaged in is the conscious activity; being mentally aware of and engaged in plus being physically activated is the meaning of life, being mentally aware but not engaged, and physically purified but not yet exhausted one, comes to the resolution of enlightenment. Being mentally engaged but not aware, and physically fixated but not resolved, is the breath of life. Before breath, there is no need to think, remember or dream. Just breathing is enough for that life.

Our birth is announced by the independent circulation of breath, and our life is terminated with the inability to breathe. During our life time, it is breathing that opens the lungs, pumps the blood, drives the cellular system, digests the food, and circulates the organism. During the last minute of life, the moment before a person breathes his last, the reality of physical existence vanishes. The spirit departs from the body, and the body departs from its living image, which is the character of soul. The dying person understands that s/he is dying but merely experiences a brief fearful feeling of approaching death. Following this, the deceased is then moved to a safe resting place, readied for the funeral service. The energetic soul body gradually detaches from its dissolved physical body, entering into the world of spirit.

When we were born, we were granted the birth by departing from our mother's abdominal area. Until we actually die, we are unable to experience our so-called death. We must simply stop the breathing activity. We can die our psychological death, but we cannot die in our physical body. The physical body deforms into its original components, water, fire, dust, and minerals. Dying is nothing more than an awareness of transforming from living spiritually with the physical existence to the singular pure spiritual existence. In dying, the spirit detaches from the body to return once again to the lonely life of one-self, the spiritual self. Dying means ascending from the body and returning to the self truthfully. Dying is awaiting another breath, whether on earth as an organism or in heaven as a cosmic being. Dying is a step toward the final goal of becoming a true self, either holy spirit or holy ghost. Dying is sinking breathlessly into the void. Dying is floating weightlessly in the cosmos. Dying is a selfless departure.

## The True Spiritual Instinct

In the longevity of the flowing river of life, the wish for continuity is unyielding because of the insistence of the ever present will. This can never die. The undying will is the true spiritual instinct. It enacts either through the members of a family or the administrative powers in a country. The will continues forever transforming as love or hate, care for self and kindness to others. The will continues moving in the direction of either attaining material possessions or some other mental obsession. In material possession, will is the bloody fight, the deadly gamble, meaningless proof of self worth. In mental obsession, wisdom is the will's demand, creativity is the will's supply, ego is the will's disguise, self-discipline is the will's appraisal, and control is the will's foolishness. Should one experience an accidental death, there continues to be a will manifesting itself into the survivor's life, whether in a dream state or a visionary quest. The departed soul or spirit will remember this everlasting breathtaking suddenness, and its will to return back to life will never stop until it reaches fulfillment.

From the dying moment forward, realistically or visionarily, religious and metaphysical groups come to the fore, promoting themselves not on the subject of dying but on the activity of remembering. They disclaim the power of will and preach on the wish of the will. The nature of this will is both close to the eternal steadfastness and the business of monetary exchange. The steadfast ensures the never-dying personhood, since the will continues forward. The monetary exchange promises the continuation of life, since the will is still active. The religious group states authoritatively that there is no final death. The person will go to heaven to receive an eternal immortal reward for goodness, or will incarnate another life form according to their concept of reincarnation. The metaphysical group declares that there is no death, only transformation. By following the ideal will in their own minds, the true will left by the deceased is truly deserted.

Concerning the willful practice towards the aspect of human life existence, the modern health profession knows well enough that good health depends ultimately upon physical, psychological, as well as spiritual well-being. But medical doctors and mental health professionals treat their patients willfully by following in a completely different direction. Medical doctors attempt to correct many physical problems, paying little or no heed to the mental causation. They divide the physical body into the measurement of depth and length so that the scalpel can be applied. Their objective is to replace the body's natural organs with similarly matched alien organs or artificial ones. Even though they are aware of the significance of the mental strength on physical well-being, doctors ignore the mind willfully as though it were an invisible entity. Mind is far less "organic" than the physical organism.

Most mental health professionals cannot take over the position held by medical doctors. At most, they analyze with certainty that the mind is as real as the body. Because they have no control over the clients' bodily existence, they expound into their mental existence. In that they fear rejection from the scientific community, mental health professionals can only acknowledge quietly that psychic energy has much to do with the spirit. In their selected practices, they are inclined to put the nature of spirit into the back of their mind's subconscious will.

This tragedy is rooted in the egoistic will of our current institutional practice. If the institution would no longer treat the body as merely the body, the mind as nothing more than the mind, if medical doctors and mental health professionals would attend lectures in the same classroom, think and work and observe with open minds (not open books) in a common work place, then the practical result will be markedly improved. The will would then become collective and cooperative.

In contrast, in a meditative life, there is never a separation between the body and the mind. The willpower sees the body and mind as equal and coexistent as they were originally. The practice of meditation involves far more than meditating a few times a day. It is not a structured lesson to be acquired from a master. It is a way of life filled with the treasure of inspiration which conceives in every second of life's existence. It manifests in waking hours and in sleeping, in happy moments and in sad situations, in physical passion and in spiritual fantasy. It is the devotion of heart, the faith of mind, and will of being eternal and becoming immortal. This is the will of life, the willpower of spiritual life, and will-fortune of eternal life.

## How Long Should the Will Be, Really!

Let me present some honest questions. How many times or how frequently do we assess the existence of mind into the existence of body? In how many situations do we allow the mind and heart to work together with the bodily participated events? How often does our mind think the same that we feel in our gut? In modern life, especially in our scientifically projected and industrially operated society, the heart or mind rarely exists simultaneously with the body. The only times they are together are: (1) when we first embrace our Self with objects, whether these objects are our body, our feelings, our parents, or our toys. (2) when our life is in an extremely dangerous situations. Even then, the mind is either threatening the weeping body or ignoring its cry. (3) when the body and mind have a deep and sound sleep. (4) when our experience is in a truly relaxed state or we are enjoying a peak performance.

During those times, the heart, or the conscious mind, does not think, presuming that the body is there taking care of things. At other times, we are not only absent from our living body, but also from our conscious mind and the heart as well. At this point we have no notion of mind separating from the heart. Actually, the conscious mind is the loving heart. The mind is conscious of what the heart loves and the heart loves what the conscious mind is devoted to. Normally, we consider the mind and the heart as two different entities because: (1) the mind is manifested in the brain and the heart is something we feel at the chest level; (2) the mind is rational and has intellectual capacity, while the heart is emotional and feels sensations; (3) the entity of mind can be perceived, studied, and objectified, while the nature of heart can be unstable, distrustful, and subjective.

Especially in modern society it is felt that the mind must be valued and respected. At the very least, it is something that can be educated. However, the heart is thought of as tangible, semi-transparent, and unreliable. Yet it is essential that it be there when the mind needs it. Yet, when the mind thinks straight, works hard, and scrutinizes madly, the heart is never the thing to be laid bare on the table, inside the lab, or involved in the fighting. Ask the scientists. They will deny it! Ask the lawyers. They abuse it! Ask the preachers. They sell it! Ask the enlightened ones. They forget about it!

## Meditation Practices

The essential meaning of this fifth character is how to retain spiritual awareness and live with unconditional love. We must be aware of things. Whether something of importance or of no account, it remains a thing. The challenge is in how to elevate ordinary personal and cultural awareness into cosmic and spiritual awareness. In order to do so, one must be in a consciously loving state. In this conscious loving state, all things are present within the unconditional loving relationship. All love relations expressed externally will be transferred internally. This is how love originated, from the inside out. Ridding oneself of the projecting and discriminating mind is the key to entering this state.

When we grew up, it was necessary to discriminate in order to separate things and people, mom from aunts, and dad from uncles. We learned to be discriminating in order to make the spiritual play mental and physical. We learned to be discriminating in order to plan things (mentally) before action (mental and physical). God then became personal to us. Love became conditional. Self became egoistic. Spiritual awareness was hidden behind the conscious awareness which is governed by the institutional training and political control. Unconditional love was forever conditionally situated. We now live with planned maps, scheduled works, projected loves, and conditioned lives. The meaning of life does not exist in the present moment, but is retrained with wishful hope, mental planning, conditioned habit, and uncontrollable addiction. Culture is itself the sum of all addictive habits, of all uncontrollable urges, and of all fragmented loves.

How to turn this projection inward is the essence of this character. To project love externally, love eternally. When the love feels right within, everybody will love you, recognizing that love. When the love feels painful, stay with it and you will heal it. When the love becomes universal and unconditional, it is the love of life, the wonder and mystery. Do not love conditionally and selfishly, but unconditionally and regardless of any other thought. Do not remain with what the memory is aware of, but be aware of what the world is aware of. Do not be sensitive mentally, but be aware of emotionally, physically, and psychically as well.

In our spiritual journey, we must unify body and mind, self and other. Love and sacrifice must be a prerequisite. The unification commits to transforming all emotional distractions into pure love and distilling the mad fire with eternal peace. When the love becomes fire eternally, the self is healed and transformed. It is inevitable that others will soon be inspired to follow your example.

When the heart becomes empty, as in its first home, the body becomes sacred, love is powerful, life is wonderful. The eternal spirit will be honored within the temple of body, worshiped within the kindness of love, and preserved within the atmosphere of peace.

No one person can teach you how to achieve this. Everyone is your teacher. Learning from each other, loving one another, having respect for each other, and worshiping each other is the way. That is the light of God, the power of truth, the magic of love, and the content of life.

## Warning!

In spiritual discipline, no one should project the sacred energy of love externally before it has been internalized. When you project your love out into the world, including emotional and sexual energy, a portion of the loving energy is lost. Even though the person or the object of your love responds to you positively, it will become a loss, because you can never regain that energy. If the response is negative, it becomes a double loss. If the energy you had projected brought a response of hatred, you will expend an equal amount of energy in an effort to balance yourself again. This is the spiritual discipline of love within and without.

Your longing partner is out there waiting for you as well, whether it be God or Goddess, or your beloved images and ideals. All it takes is the unification, integration, and harmonization into oneness. We, as individuals, have separated ourselves more than enough already. When our spiritual self descended into a physical form, we became separated from oneness. When we experienced our birth, we were further separated. We lost both Father and Mother, the Lord and Creator. We cannot afford to separate ourselves any further. We are already sadly lost.

This is the spiritual discipline of living a celibate life. In Taoist mentality, sex is wrong if there is no liberation within, yet sexual energy is precious. Lust is bad if there is no bliss within, but love is invaluable. Therefore, the male practitioner should never ejaculate unless for the purpose of creating children, nor once he no longer wants more children. Ejaculation is for the sole purpose of producing new life. To have babies is spiritual and not lustful. If not done with this frame of spiritual mind, God cannot transcend His message to the children. You are the carrier of His message. When you ejaculate for any other reason, you discharge not only the sexual energy, but the sacred God loving energy as well. Such an action results in loss, which leads consequently into violence.

The female practitioner should never sacrifice her body sexually for any reason, emotionally or physically. It is too sacred and is also harmful to do so. The body is a sacred vessel, the temple of Goddess where God can perform worship. What she is longing for is not a man, it is God's image within. To replace His divine image with a mortal man is to lose herself completely. She will receive, in return, an act of abandonment, betrayal, and worse. She will be forsaken.

# NOTES

禍

# STEP SIX: *PERENNIAL*

Structure: thousand 千 + ten thousand 萬
Sound: nian
Meaning: perennial

## The Meaning of Perennial

In the previous character, we discussed in depth the meaning of continuity, that is, how to be continuously present with the awareness of mind before/with the action of body. Longevity was revealed along with its related aspects, presence and immortality. This is the rational, philosophical, and intellectual approach to the journey of life. In this sixth character, we come to understand the nature and durability of life in its sequential order and natural cycle, which is the concept of "perennial."

Perennial accounts for one year in the earth's cycle. It is the earth's birthday. Lives on this planet all have their own anniversaries in accordance with earth's seasonal temperature and annual mood. They continue on the same course eternally but follow along a different pathway in life after life. They repeat the same image each time but each life has a different destiny. They are freshly renewed and vitally exuberant after each anniversary. Yet, their lives are beyond the cyclical formation which lasts for an indefinite time period. They have the power of recurrence and reconfiguration, because they live on the power of earth and the light from heaven.

According to the botanical definition, perennial describes a plant or a flower that will bloom or thrive at least two years, and, possibly more. By using the same definition, a person's perennial life constitutes at least two or more life cycles in its spiritual history. In Taoist tradition, there are three realms of life, the realm of eternal spirit, the realm of personality/character, and the realm of physical body. A spiritual person lives openly and heartily with her/his eternal spiritual life characterized by the will-power and embodied with the physical appearance. A person who portrays a unique personality displays the past life experience symbolizing through this unique personality. A person who has a physical body exists physically during this life time but expresses personally and reveals spiritually.

Spirit is eternal but spiritual energy remains invisible to a physical body. Only when we are in our spiritual consciousness can we begin to understand the law of spiritual energy. Spirit represents God/Goddess's specific playfulness and can be equated to the personality of a star in the universe. Each God/Goddess's playfulness represents spiritual character of celestial being, whether it be star or planet. Together, God/Goddess's full characters are the power representations of all stars and planets in the cosmic constellations. All the stars and planets represent, energetically and consciously, God/Goddess's creative playfulness. As the Ultimate Yin and Yang, God and Goddess harmonize their playfulness into the existence of all celestial beings.

Just as God and Goddess's playfulness forms both physical and characteristic construction of stars and planets, the power of stars and planets is a spiritual representation of celestial and planetary beings in the universe. A star's character represents a masculine spiritual makeup. A planet's character constitutes a feminine spiritual makeup. In Taoist tradition, a star's character is viewed by its light, and a planet's character is symbolized by its holy water. The interactive harmony between star and planet creates the physical bodies of all celestial creatures, such as our human body. The interaction of God and Goddess's shadow transmits as the personality characters of all living creatures, which are the living consciousness or living souls.

An embodied human personality is created through two life experiences. At the first life time, the person lives with the shadow of God/Goddess creation as one's personality power, together with the physical power and the spiritual power, which is God/Goddess creative power/image of star and planet. As the person is born once again, this God/Goddess shadow manifests as one's own reincarnated shadow. This shadow is the origin of soul, pertaining to the characteristics of either masculine or feminine. Thus, the personality character is completed. The spirit becomes the one and eternal seed. The personality becomes transitional, changing between angel and holiness, switching between human and animal, mediating between conscious soul and instinctive soul.

As an energy character, the personality energy body is more subtle and refined than the physical energy body, but more condensed and less crystallized than the spiritual energy body. In living creatures, the personality energy is the spiritual energy of a specific organ. All organs in the body have their own personality characteristics, and the strongest organ within the body has the most dominant personality role. In Taoist tradition, there are three centers for these energy bodies, called three dantian. These three energy bodies are the empty vessel for all the organic functions in the body-mind. Spiritual energy is the invisible battery of that personality. This spiritual energy relaxes in the abdominal area, mediates the chest area, and illuminates in the brain area. The power, the talent, and the knowledge contained within the personality is a combination of that person's past life experience and its present spiritual quality. Personalities are God's flowers planted within and blossomed through humans. Taoist funeral service is marked by chanting celestial-like mantra and offering flowers to the going-to-be-returned spirit, as a means of honoring its flower-like character, personality, and uniqueness traveled through earth.

Physical body is the most gross energy body, gross to the degree that all the physical energy bodies harbor clusters of germs and parasites within. Personality energy is represented partially by the clustered group parasites within a refined energy body. That is how the organs are grouped. In the physical body, spiritual energy integrates the conscious parasites. Personality energy manifests as emotional parasites. Physical energy guides the voracious parasites. This is the Taoist notion of three bodies of parasites. These three yin energy bodies co-exist with the yang spiritual energy bodies, generating endless power, cycle, and interaction between body and mind, consciousness and instinct, light and water.

In spiritual practice, when a person becomes born-again, her/his world changes dramatically. It is not that the s/he sees the world differently, but exists in a different world of being. Only when s/he is changed, can the world be viewed in accordance with the new image. World is an image that reflects the reality of a person's outlook. When one lives a perennial life style, there is more knowledge to be experienced than to be learned. There are more stories to be read than there are to tell. There is more love to be revealed than to project. All the news is old news. All the stories are one's personal experiences. All the knowledge is a conscious living bridge.

When a person lives a perennial life style, there is a sense that life is not only precious but enjoyable, not only short but indefinite, not only destined but unpredictable, not only meaningful but dream-like. The perception and attitude are totally different from the time when one's life was no more than a miserable suffering existence. In spiritual practice, a person unifies the two worlds, two extremes, and two selves. Everything becomes relative and is a relative thing in itself. Life carries a physical body, a spiritual body, and a cosmic body; a time when one can realize, awaken, and become enlightened through the transformation of these three. The meaning of life is no longer concerned with physical or social entities, which have already been internalized. It is now a time for developing oneself toward spiritual unfoldment and actualization.

Scholars in the West tend to categorize the final process of spiritual enlightenment into two realms: the intellectual entity of realization, and the physical process of actualization. These approaches are very tentative, even though there is fluidity. Realization will come through an actual physical process, while actualization emerges as the final stage of spiritual realization. It is in this manner that the perennial life process deals directly with the spiritual awakening of physical experience, the highest and most blissful experience.

It must be understood that this process can never become fully "programmed" until the person is completely freed of personal attachment to the earthly physical realms. After each awakening experience, one's inner world changes. Those unprocessed energy patterns remain untouched, they continue their sluggish descent. One should never belittle the usefulness of spiritual work, nor become attached to any particular awakening experience. The lower and more gross realms of life we see are but God's designed task, the personally experienced illusion, and the physically processed garbage. This is the continuous, endless perennial life experience. When a physical life ends, it moves on to the next life cycle. Until the body is burned by the light, the personal illusion awakened by the cosmic knowledge, the spirit remains at home, the pilgrimage goes on through life after life, generation after generation, love after love. Yet, the spiritual entity or soul form of that life exists continuously after the physical form dies. In the nature of spirit, it travels between heaven and earth, exists as soul and ghost, manifests as intelligence and emotion, and appears to escape from itself and again reappear time after time.

## The Perennial Spirit

In spiritual work, perennial life experience is contingent, periodic, and spiraling. It is contingent with its never-ending and eternal spiritual evolution. Periodic intervals reveal the specific moment and qualitative structure localized in the living environment. The spiral approach leaves the spiritual mind refreshed and active, and rational mind unexpected and distrustful. Out of silence and storm, human life fulfills its progressive experience. Breath after breath and stage after stage, this experience is a continuing odyssey.

Specifically, each experience takes its own natural course, renounces what it wishes to with its own particular force, and is rewarded by its own destiny. Each experience announces its own conclusive mark, particularly in the matter of spiritual experience. When a person arrives there, the experience ends unexpectedly and it is beyond any rational speculation. Regardless of how rich the experience is, how magnificently the person performs through the experiential scene, and how transformed the person thinks he has become, he finds there is nothing more to be grasped from the experience. Worse still, the life becomes uninteresting and even distasteful. This is because the lighter one becomes, the clearer one sees the dark force within; the higher one has achieved, the closer one comes face to face with the negativity and bad karma. Until there is no opposition to be met by the spiritual entity, the negativity and bad karma will become at least as strong as the positive. In other words, the cleaner one becomes, the stronger the resistance of opposition. They are proportional and each depends upon the other for its existence. The higher one develops, the worse the energy s/he encounters.

This is how Laoism has detailed: "Favor and disgrace surprise the most. Value the trouble as you do the body." (13:1) Love and hatred arise from the same source. Favor and disgrace receive an equal amount of reputable treatment. The value of body runs along the same track as the value of trouble. One will never find trouble greater than that which the body can possibly contain. Without body, God has no structured form in our human existence, and our spirits can never be encumbered by the physical existence on earth. Also, as one reaches a higher and lighter level, one faces no one but self, as the worldly others sustain their own images and energetic patterns on their journey.

Laoist uses the word "widow" or "orphan" to describe the person who is close to both her/himself and Tao. "What the world hates is the widow and orphan without support. But lords and rulers name themselves these." (14:2) Widow is the matured "virgin girl," and orphan is the abandoned "virgin boy." Why? On the one hand, eggs are fully prepared and fertile by the time the female becomes an independent being. And semen is always anxiously awaiting the opportunity to make the connection. On the other hand, the great mother is forever a widow, and we, as God's seed, always stand alone in the face of the wilderness of the world. We are homeless on earth, directionless before the gravitational force, dusty within the cosmic wind, and meaningless before the light. Lords and rulers are the most revealing representations of ourselves, as we too are the lords of ourselves and are ruled by no one but ourselves.

The final resolution is to encounter no more opposition, to practice unification and integration, and to become the true oneness of completely unified Self. "As for this one," Laoism simplifies, "there is nothing above it yet to be accounted for, there is nothing below it that has been excluded. Ever searching for it, it remains beyond naming. It returns to no-thing. Its state is described as no state, its form is described as formless. It is called the vision beyond focus. Follow after it, and it proves endless. Go before it, and no beginning is found." (14:2,3,4) This is the condition of perennial life experience.

Aside from this clarification, Laoist also signifies the importance of oneness in the matters of universe. The message is: "By attaining Oneness, heaven is clear. By attaining Oneness, earth is at peace. By attaining Oneness, the spirit is quickened. By attaining Oneness, the valley is filled. By attaining Oneness, the king puts order in the whole world. All these result from oneness." (39: 2) Among these five, the first three are the cosmic trinity of creation. Heaven is the invisible Father, earth is the visible Mother (Mother must be visible). Spirit is the harmony of these two, while valley is the "widow" and king is the "orphan." Valley is full in the sense that holy water is ever present inside the empty vessel of the Tao. King is the governor of order whose nature is self-discipline. Taken together, these five comprise the definition of the Taoist saying "five Qi return to their Primordial Origin."

The ideal way of the human symbol, the king, puts order in the world because, on the one hand, he can do nothing other than what nature has provided and what the universe cycles. All he can do is promote order in the world according to self-discipline. Without self-discipline , nothing can arise from the God consciousness. Without self-discipline, the order of nature cannot manifest in its own way, from individual consciousness to group activity. Therefore, the king feels that "Being presented with jade in front of the team of four horses is not better than sitting and entering thus." since he "allows having without asking, and allows forgiveness of wrong." (62:4,5) The word "thus" is an indication that the King, or any enlightened being, is no longer pushed or pulled by the opposition. He is in the wilderness of nowhere, yet in the center of everywhere.

Historically in Chinese, the King or the Emperor is a celestial being. His biological development is totally different from those who go through the normal process of conception. His spirit descends personally without introduction to his assigned father. His spiritual power allows the virgin conception directly with his mother, who is also a virgin maiden. The maiden's husband is an absent figure. He contributed nothing toward conception. When these two virgin spirits are unified, there is no interference of soul or personality. The Emperor's soul, as the shadow of spirit, manifests as the power of light of the image of celestial beings, such as the dragon. As for the rest of humanity, their lives are controlled by their souls, which are the accumulation of their past experiences. Therefore, the power structure between the Emperor and his people is crystal clear.

When the spiritual body quickens along its spiraling way, the union of yin and yang, or the double helix as it is labeled in scientific terms, occurs. The liberation from the opposition and the unification of the inner embracement are the playful-working and love-making of the dual universal beings. They dissolve themselves in the manner in which they integrate each other, their inner machinations with their opposing co-dependent parts. Each part lives in its opposite side, and both sides return to the central place—the empty agreement—of their mutually circulating and independently living spaces. The liberation from the opposition and the unification of the inner embracement are the two parallel and necessary steps we must clear for ourselves along the singular path of our individual life, and simultaneously, seeing and embracing our Self in a deeper and more unified way. Until every opposition has been conquered and no separation occurs between the dual existence, there exists no difference between liberation and unification, freedom and vulnerability, self and the other, and female and male. In spiritual reality, these differences lie in the natural display of trinity.

## The Three Bodies We Have

During the progression of our human experiences which are followed by the secret path of contingent revelation, the spiritual body grows in a spiraling direction, toward the liberation from the opposition and the resulting unification of inner embracement. The spiritual body is the light version of the emotional body, and it is the unearthly form of the physical body. Using earth as an example, the earth's spiritual body guides the existence of earthly body, and contains the true spiritual entity of the earth. This spiritual body is both the web and womb of all forms in the universe. The word form is being used to represent anything that has a physical infrastructure, from shining stars and spiritual bodies in the universe, to the inorganic matters and cellular structures on earth. This spiritual body is the form of Tao.

The "emotional" body of earth is the inner drive and the attraction that circulate around the earth. It is the vital Qi for circulating and transforming all things. This vital Qi is the thrust of the Tao. The make-ups are what decorate the earth's existence, which accounts for the temperatures and seasonal changes. The inner drive is the gravitational force. And the attraction is the light coming from stars, sun, and moon.

The physical body of the earth is composed of mechanical components found on this planet, and the dynamic functions which it operates. The mechanical components are those that make water, dust, and rock. The dynamic functions are the programmed operations that earth utilizes. The mechanical components and dynamic functions make up the foundation—the valley—of Tao and the selfless interaction—the empty functioning—of Tao. Laoism describes this spiritual body as "Look for it and not see it, it is called invisible; listen to it and not hear it, it is called inaudible; reach for it and not touch it, it is called intangible. These three are beyond reckoning, so when these three merge, they are One." (14:1,2) This is another way of presenting the three "bodies" or trinity of the Tao of Nature.

According to Taoists' tradition, we humans also have three bodies, or three Cinnabar Fields or dantian as they have been labeled. The three Cinnabar Fields are the Lower Cinnabar Field, the Middle Cinnabar Field and the Upper Cinnabar Field. The Lower Cinnabar Field is our biological body. It is where we came from and how we became mature enough to produce offspring. It is the center of the biophysical structure we have in our human existence. This doesn't mean the rest of the body is not physical. Our entire body is physical, even our mental body — brain—being a part of our physical body. The Lower Cinnabar Field in the abdominal area is more biologically oriented than emotional, and more organic than mental. It deals with the biological intelligence, the gut feeling. This psychological power is, basically, our will.

The Middle Cinnabar Field is the center for love and personal construct. All the emotions manifest in this center. The Middle Cinnabar Field is the seat of love, representing the love of expression and the action of nourishment. Particularly for the male, this loving energy shifts around the Yellow Court and into the action of mechanical and personal, or political and militant activities. It is very difficult for the male to open this field. Naturally, a man's energy is focused at the forefront of the brain and the tip of the penis. If he restores the loving energy within or allows the sweet dew to activate the seat of loving power, then this field is as vital and warm as that of a mother's unconditional love toward her children. But it takes years of practice. The biological power is the nourishment, either from sacrificing oneself or abandoning the ego-self. The psychological power is Love, selfless and fearless.

The Upper Cinnabar Field is the center for intelligence. Brain is where the light shines, the wisdom sparks, and the intelligence dominates. Most importantly, it is the womb for spiritual enlightenment. When a meditator reaches this third level of cultivation, thinking is no longer bothersome, and sleeping becomes trouble free. The constant pacing of the thinking mind becomes tranquil, and sleep is replaced with the meditative mentality. Objectively, there is no difference between thinking and dreaming, and there is no separation between visionary expression and illusions. The reality of man's mind merges with the reality of God's wisdom.

## Working Through with No Opposition

Let us take a detailed look at the nature of opposition in a more relaxed way. If we are not relaxed, we cannot be at ease with everything, and the body will not collaborate with the mind's intentions. When we are relaxed, we can view the nature of any particular thing, even our own self, with an open-minded fashion and self-dispatched attitude. The nature of that particular thing will then begin to appear to us by itself, without invitation. The observations made are not about the impenetrable whole, but the mechanically fragmented details and their undivided pieces. These details are the countless germs and parasites living upon the three bodies we have. Their existence is as old as our oldest ancestor, the Mother creator. The details are where God's consciousness dwells. God's light abides and His creative power is conceived within. Each detail represents one parasite, from a spark of light, to an emotional sensation and a biological instinct. Each undivided piece is a working station, a circulating energy, and a walking bridge. Seemingly physically isolated, you know instinctively the piece does not exist alone. It is a transition, an involvement, and a project.

Laoism experiences this relaxed manner and examining attitude by saying that "Knowing that the eternal action abides is to return to childhood." (28:1) "Action in its profundity is like a newborn baby." (55:1) As for this child, he further explains, "Poisonous insects and venomous snakes do not sting it. Predatory birds and ferocious animals do not seize it. Its bones are soft and its sinews supple, yet its grasp is firm. Without knowing the union of male and female, its organs become aroused. Its vital essence comes to the point; Crying all day, its voice never becomes hoarse. Its harmony comes to the point." (55:1,2)

Laoist then concludes that "Harmony is eternal. Knowing harmony is discernment. Enhancing life is equanimity. Generating vitality through mind is strength." (55:3) This means that the eternal harmony of life comes from the equanimity of discernment: all is guarded by the strength of will power upon vitality. Harmony is opposite to discernment, and eternity is opposite to equanimity. The harmony is based on the integration of various unobservable obscurities, diversified characters, and multi-dependent polarities. Discernment involves in comprehending the subtle, working toward utilizing the efficiency, and processing into reliable accuracy. The eternal has no artificial display or detectable visibility. Equanimity possesses all the eternal stillness and external balance. The two pairs of opposites are the arising forces, the playful characters, the potential extremes, and the ultimate return. Without this, there is nothing to harmonize and integrate and there is no possibility of becoming One again. This One is what the harmony integrates, where the discernment enters, how the equanimity surrounds it, why the strength flows, to what degree the eternal returns.

Since it is so critically important that in the work of healing and the journey of spiritual growth, without balancing all the opposition, it is impossible for the body to become clean and mind to be still. In daily life, the opposing forces are the rivals, the enemies, the counteractions, and the shadows. They are what the spirit embraces, the mind catches, the body feels, and self attracts. While on the spiritual journey, the opposition offers the surprising invitations, the heartbreaking opportunities, the welcome ceremonies, and farewell parties. In essence, opposition is what we thrive on, how we follow things through, and why we eventually die. Opposition is beneficial when we treat it with respect. Opposition is valuable when we deal with our innate confrontations. Opposition is beautiful when we realize that it consists of the details and pieces of our life construction. Opposition renders itself defenseless once we become spotlessly clean and motionlessly still. Opposition connects with our healing spiritual work just as it does in the co-existence of the immortality of bacteria on earth and the immortality of spiritual beings in the cosmos. In mythology, oppositions are the makeup of our Self, existing between biological self and spiritual self.

Opposition is such that it makes the universe visible, matters touchable, things manageable, and energy dissolvable. Without opposition, there would be no celebration between space and time, there would be no unifying work between matter and force, there would be no journey throughout life and death, and there would be no meaning and purpose for cultivation of spirit upon body. In Chinese culture, the mental understanding of the origin of the universe, the changeability of Nature and the Tao of flow are all related to the functions of opposition, namely, yin and yang. This is the highest summary of man and nature, the most astute, comprehensive understanding of matter and force, and the art of alchemical refinement and cultivational practice. Without this, male and female stand alone, and day and night are indifferent, and spirit and ghost are inseparable.

The introductory message of I Ching literally opens the discussion of the nature of the Tao by saying that "One yin and one yang is Tao." One yin is the pure matter, the cosmic web, and the biological womb, while one yang is the real force, the cosmic light, and the biological fire.

The final breakthrough in the alchemical practice and cultivational practice is readily that of shifting consciousness between good and bad. This is experiencing the dance of opposition in between the union. Laoist's evaluation of being at such a state is that "Without preference, Being is as resonant as Jade and as gravelly as stone." (39:7) This is because through cultivation, boundaries are eliminated, all oppositions are integrated.

## Lao Zi on Opposition

Since Tao is the function of opposition, the flow of harmony, and the dance of one and sameness, it is useful and desirable to utilize the opposition along the path of spiritual cultivation. From beginning to end, Lao Zi reveals nothing on the path of understanding the Tao other than the opposition. Examples are the spoken Tao and unspoken Tao, the nameable Tao and unnameable Tao, the Tao of the subtle and the manifest, being and no-being, difficulty and ease, long and short, high and low, voice and sound, before and after. ... All these are the pairing of yin and yang, the value of opposites.

In Chapter twenty eight, he discusses fully the work of opposition in spiritual practice. He uses male and female as the flow of the world, the pure and impure as the cleansing of the world, and white and black as the formation of the world. To go with the flow of the world is to know the harmony of male and female which is to be in touch with the eternal action of the child. This is the first phase of understanding. Truly, how many of us in life can live up to the eternal action of this flow? "I am married to God." is the summary of the true statement of this understanding. Who, among us, can make this statement?

In the process of dating, we explore ourselves; when we love someone, we betray ourselves; when we make love, we discharge ourselves; when we marry someone, we promise ourselves; when we devote ourselves to someone, we exhaust ourselves. We know the opposition, we see the opposition, and we live with the opposition. But how often do we create the flow through the opposition? Who recognizes and applies the power of this eternal action that attracts our likes, balances our dislikes and continues with our opposites? Only the person who really abides with the eternal child-like action.

Child is the flow of both male and female within. Its body is immature, and its ego has not yet developed into a subjective "I" or an objective self. Everything flows within. That is why Lao Zi applies this understanding: To be with an eternal flow. This flow of eternal child is the business of the biology of life. Self flows from here, family flows from here, society flows from here, nation flows from here, and God flows in here. The political issue is a sex issue, the love issue is a sex issue, and the life issue is a sex issue. The entire mystery of life is in this flow. This, then, is the real meaning of going with the flow, not going with the flow of opposite sex but going with the flow of the other self with and within our self. This is the biological side of spirituality.

The second understanding Lao Zi imparts is the cleansing of the world between the pure and impure. This cleansing process deals with the ongoing action of the Tao, which is the simplicity of the Tao. This is where heaven and earth function jointly, with heaven representing purity and earth impurity. This is why water and earth stand together, with water being pure and earth impure. This is how male and female live together, with male pure and female impure. In understanding this cleansing, simplicity becomes the way. Simplicity is where the ongoing action suffices and returns. This is the vital Qi of life, the action of life itself. This is the living reality of life, the interaction of life itself. The pure is the clean, the good, and the healthy part of the life. The impure is the murky, the bad, and the sick part of the life. Between these two opposites, stillness is at work. In stillness, water purifies itself, the body cleanses itself, and the mind tranquilizes itself. Stillness is a flowing state, a transitional state, and an eternally changing state. Stillness is not a condition. It moves between the structure and character, and it rotates between quality and quantity. It drifts and changes between discernment and eternal, and it travels between harmony and equanimity. Stillness is the womb of action, the mother of Qi, and the father of peace. The womb of action is the forming state, the mother of Qi is the eternal changing state, and the father of peace is the present unchanging state. This cleansing action is the notion of the Tao and the emotion of life.

The third understanding is the notion of formation of the world between the black and white. We know that the black is close to us and the white rises above us. We feel that the black is behind us and the white is in front of us. We understand that the black is inside our bodies and the white surrounds our breath. We have neither descended into the valley of the black nor ascended into the wave of light. Before we are formed, the white sperm penetrates the black form of life. After our birth, the white milk nourishes the black body of life. Before we are able to see anything, the white light penetrates the already blackened darkness. After our body is cremated, the remains are the black ashes and white bones. This replicates what our body is, and this is the way all the forms of the world are. The black and the white are the formation of the world, the vision of the infinite, and the image of the Tao. Integrating these three understandings one can discern the message, the character, and the nature of opposites. In the process of learning to apply these understandings one can learn how to go with the flow, the cleansing, and the formation of opposition.

## What Life Teaches Us

We begin life with no clue to anything, progress through learning, and believe we know it all. The hopelessness of being unable to grasp the meaning of something falls into the shocking reality of life. When we are born, we have the potential of experiencing everything we want to know, to be fulfilled and liberated. Throughout the course of life, we try our best to gratify ourselves, to magnify everything, and to objectify all we see. By the time we bid adieu to this materialistic and illusionary world, nothing makes sense (the spirit has left), and nothing is operable or sensible anymore (the body is dying), no-thing is possessive (everything returns to its origin). For those who live in the third world countries and non-industrialized societies, from their first action to the final releasing of life, everyone is bound to the earth, breathing between earth and sky, and being liberated, ultimately, to the transformation of life and spirit. How earthly the life is! In industrial societies, the elderly are often taken to a nursing home, unable to care for their own bodily functions, helpless as infants. What is the significance of this social conditioning process? How unworthy this conditioning process is! How sad to watch this!

Concerning these two differing learning environments, Laoist's approach is: "In order to know the world, do not step outside the door. In order to know the Tao of heaven, do not peer through the window. The further out you go, the less you know." (47:1,2) The door being referred to is not the door in your house, but the conscious intention you project. It is what the mind accesses, how the energy is released, and what the body stands for. The secret lock is the conscious awareness and conscientious anticipation. The treasure inside the house is the treasure of Jing, Qi and Shen, the trinity of Tao in man. The window is not the opening that transmits the light and darkness into the emptiness within the walls framing the house. It is the spiritual vision, the inner mind, and the third eye. Body is the temple of spirit and the gift of experiencing. Body knows how to breathe, since it has the windows — lungs and all the cells —into the world. Body knows how to circulate the energy: its systems are designed for this purpose, and the body has the innate ability to heal. This is how powerful its transforming ability is.

Do not misinterpret this. Life may be relaxing, rejuvenating, and preserved inside the house, but should not be restrained within the limits of the house. Even when the door is unlocked, the desire of heart and curiosity of mind still peer through the window of eyes without blinking. The window is the mirror that reflects the secrets inside the house, and within the body. When the secret door of heart is open, the possession of body then walks in and out of it, embracing the world beyond. When the window is wide open, the air can be breathed in and out, and body is then refreshed. We need to see the world, we need to identify the inner world through the universe, we need to experience the meaning of the world outside the house, and to enjoy the beauty of the body and mind within the boundaries of the world.

Laoist's realization regarding the door is not meant to project the intention outward, nor to release the vital force in the body and remove it from where it is located. The window is visualized as the opening to the spiritual world. He cautions: do not peer through the world with a curious mind, do not look at the world with the desirable eye, and do not betray the treasure of the inner self to the external world. First, look within. When the inside is clean, bright with light, the windows will be dust free. When there is no desire leaching through the window, when there is no attraction felt from the outside world, the body will freely walk in and out the door, that conscious gateway, with peace and tranquility. The spiritual light, the emotional vibration, and biological experience will fill the house with its presence. Where else does one need to look, what more does one need to know, and what else does one need to experience! Because of this, "The sage knows without moving, identifies without seeing, accomplishes without acting." (47:3)

## The True Meaning of Knowing

"Knowing the Tao seems costly. Entering Tao seems like retreating. Becoming equal with Tao gives birth to paradoxes." (40:2) Knowing the Tao comes with abandoning the desiring self, the egoistic self, the emotional self, and animal self. When life is constructed with these fragmented pieces of self, the Tao is lost, the action is lost, the righteousness is lost. Only frustration is visible, existing through denial of the gnawing inability to know and the inescapable fear of separation from the unknown of nature. In order to know the Tao, one must be free from desire, agitation, and the restraint of internal turmoil. One should make peace with the world by releasing worldly events. When the body is surrounded with those "materials," it can never pay the price of knowing the Tao. That is why knowing the Tao seems costly.

Actually, Tao is desire-free, attraction-free, and restraint-free. It is priceless in every respect. There is no monetary price to be paid but you take on the responsibility for purifying yourself completely. Quite the contrary, it can be viewed as the most expensive procedure in the world, because you relinquish everything that the mind desires, and clean out everything stored in the body. In comparison to possessing and controlling everything in the world to the price of knowing the Tao, the latter is more costly. First, you must die completely. Yet, the Tao has no price. The Tao embraces all that lives but can be detected nowhere.

What is the true meaning of knowing? Laoism explains: "Knowing what is sufficient averts disgrace. Knowing when to stop averts danger. This can lead to a longer life." (44:3) This is precisely what the perennial life experience is. Sufficiency is what is present, what is happening, and what is working. It is the inner mind being fully aware of how the world operates. It is what the mind observes, how the body partakes, and how well the body and mind interact. Sufficiency is concerned not with material things or objects, but with how the mind is pleased with the world functioning at the given moment. Knowing when to stop in following the madness of mind is the art of total participation, the mechanism of body-and-mind interaction, and the harmony of the Tao. "Knowing that you don't know (everything) is superior. Not knowing that you don't know (everything) is a sickness. So the sage's being without sickness is that he knows sickness as sickness; Thus, he is without sickness." (73:1,2) Because "There is no disaster greater than not knowing when there is enough. Knowing that sufficiency is enough always suffices." (46:2,3)

"Entering the Tao seems like retreating" implies that one needs to be refreshed, relaxed, and rejuvenated. It is retreating into oneself with nothing. In retreating, one needs nothing, desires nothing, and is surrounded by nothing. There can be no sickness nor expectation. Also, under the condition of retreating, one embraces danger, difficulty, and disagreement. There will be no threatening, no hostility, and no rivalry. Only under this condition does the true self appear with the appearing Tao. This retreating activity abides in the beauty of steadfast, and "Knowing the steadfast implies acceptance." (16:3) This is the state of becoming like a child once again. One is born-again, returning the life constantly to its beginning state. And for a child, "Without knowing the union of male and female, its organs become aroused. Its vital essence comes to the point. Crying all day, its voice never becomes hoarse. Its harmony comes to the point. Harmony is eternal. Knowing harmony is discernment. Enhancing life is equanimity. Generating vitality through mind is strength." (55:2,3)

"Becoming equal with Tao gives birth to paradoxes" means that "Everything that is good is the teacher of the good person. Everything that is bad becomes a resource for the good person. No need to honor the teachers. No need to love the resources. Though knowing this is a great paradox, it is a subtle principle." (27:3,4) This is, again, the teaching on knowing and understanding the opposition in life. Life is paradoxical, because it is pulled by the pure, the male and the white, and pushed by the impure, the female and the black. So the subtle discipline is "better to be centered." (5:3) This central position is the formation, this central point is the cleansing, and this central joint is the flow. What else can be so worthy of knowing!

## The Mystery of Perennial

This sixth character in the couplets is composed with two elementary characters, one (qian) meaning "thousand" and the other (wan) "ten thousand." What would be the sum total of these figures when added or multiplied? They are figurative to the material world but precise in spiritual practices. In material world, the numbers represent the living spirits within the bodies. In spiritual wisdom, they are used to describe "Heaven is eternal, and earth is long-lasting. What makes heaven and earth eternal and long-lasting is that they do not give birth to themselves." (7:1,2) Therefore, it is said: "Natural speech consists of few words,"(24:1) and it is unnecessary to act excessively.

Lao Zi points this out by saying that "Gusty winds do not last all morning, cloudbursts do not last all day. What makes this so? Heaven and earth will not last forever, how could a human being last!" (24:2,3) There is no contradiction in the sentences "Heaven is eternal, and earth is long lasting." and "Heaven and earth will not last forever, how could a human being last!" In the first sentence, Laoism describes the nature of heaven and earth. Their longevities are much longer than our human lives. As for the second one, heaven and earth don't give birth to themselves. How could nature's momentary motion, such as gusty winds and cloudbursts, last forever? How could our thoughts and emotions and actions last forever? But, in the universe, all the eternal creatures last, ranging in time between seconds and forever, and between permanent to eternal. All material things last for a very short period of time, to years and even centuries.

An example would be that in human adulthood, most eggs and semen become waste. Very few will form to create new life. A possible exception can be the preservation of these valuable materials in their crystallization through cultivation practices. One of the cultivation practices is to freeze the matter that forms the sperms and eggs before they become materialized. This is the method of internalization, whereby mental concentration, the material that produces the sperms or eggs will be kept inert, and there will be no chance for them to become materialized. This method is especially valuable for the female since the eggs are proportioned in life and each menstruation is a wasting period. Some women may experience joy during menstruation, while a large number experience temporary distortion, mentally and physically. It is interesting to note that the first stage of Taoists' female cultivation practice is to cut off the blood sea (to freeze the eggs and become absent from menstruation). Another practice to be applied to male is to reabsorb the matured material internally. This method is very practical and can be carried without ejaculation or wet dreams.

Among the very few sperm that will form lives, not all have the capacity to develop; some of these life forms exist for a short period of time in the mother's womb but die before they develop. The circumstances may be a miscarriage or the practice of abortion. These unfulfilled life forms have been imbued with the spirit but they lack the ability and capacity to experience their independent biological life. Those who were born into life successfully, may live through just a few months' history, while others enjoy a lifetime of more than a hundred years. Even though the potential of the life span can be one-hundred twenty years of age, the average is a mere sixty years or so. Regardless of the number, nobody can live forever physiologically.

Still another example is that our mind constantly creates ideas and generates thoughts, almost all of which are useless and wasted products. They come and go like flashing lights (each idea is a flash of light in the brain). When the ideas or thoughts become intensified and condensed, they will appear either as philosophical materials or practical substances. When these ideas and thoughts are tested and tested objectively, they characterize the creators and are socially accepted as cultural substances. Each character is a personal demonstration, and education popularizes it as a cultural substance. Plato explained his ideas and thoughts, and the culture propagated them through educational practices. All the useful ideas and thoughts have lived beyond their creators' personal life, whether partially or fully. Some live several generations or even longer beyond the creators' expectation. Only a few become permanent cultural substances. Computer science is the greatest example of this. The numbers of ideas are overwhelming, the products are exciting, the cycles are rapid, and their duration is, almost exclusively, short lived. What is the answer to this phenomena? Lao Zi says: "The person who works according to Tao unites with Tao. In the same way he unites with action. In the same way he unites with loss. Uniting with action, the Tao becomes action. Uniting with loss, the Tao becomes loss." (24:4,5)

**Biblical Answers To Laoist's Character**

"How should one chase a thousand, and two put ten thousand to flight, except their Rock had sold them, and the Lord had shut them up?" (Deu. 32:30) This is, perhaps, the best illustration of the Laoist sixth character, numerically and esoterically. In spiritual practice, the inner stillness of Rock chases thousands of spiritual, emotional and biological parasites away by Its light, Its inner discipline, and Its eternal strength. Since the light is much quicker than the creative formation, it chases after everything in the universe, from stars to planets, to bacteria and viruses, to organic cells and organic beings. The chase itself is an act of secretive formation. Without the power of chasing, there is no secret swiftness within the formative process. There is no surprise and magic, no shock and violence. In the cosmic realm, yang chases yin, light chases wind, fire chases water, male chases female.

Through the chasing power coming from the Rock, light, fire and consciousness, the spiritual parasites of conscious thoughts manifest as pure spiritual inspiration. The emotional parasites of organic sensations turn into pure love. The biological parasites of instinctive behavior change into pure water. Without the power of Rock, nothing can be chased away. Meanwhile, it is only with Rock that wisdom, love and holy water can be chased. Without the shining light of Rock, the mind is windy and cloudy, the personality is emotional and agitative, and body is greasy and murky. The three states of water within the micro-universe of body—gas, liquid and ice—will not be liberated. Without the distillation of Rock, wood of liver cannot grow to make fire. Earth of spleen will not deform to become crystallized. Metal of lungs will not be stilled, awaiting the melting process. Fire of heart will not become light. Water of kidney will not become elixir.

Rock represents the light, the penetration, the inner-discipline, the tail bone, the spine, and the will. It is the Rock which chases away all the heaviness, thickness, murkiness, and sickness resulting from the parasites in the body-mind. Rock of discipline lives through all the trials and tests enabling the spirit to become purified from galloping madness and stubbornness. The Rock of stillness will ground itself in the testing process so that the pure consciousness can chase away thousands of monkey-like thoughts and desires.

The Oneness of Lord, the combination of Holy Spirit and Holy Father, the harmony of Tao, the unification of God and Goddess, closes the Door of Duality, of yin and yang, and of masculine and feminine, allowing tens of thousands of pure spirits to take flight into their heavenly home. The oneness represents Cosmic power, God's light, spirit-consciousness. It is the undivided oneness of Tao, the form of universe, the structure of law, and content of truth. It is though the oneness of Rock that the inner power and unconditional love were sold to the Lord, the son of God, the Christ.

Lord was not only sold by the Rock, but also by the Love. Rock as "one" represents inner light and power. Rock and Love together as "two" represent the power of transformation in Christ teaching and practice. Teaching is the voice of God, the sound of truth, the vibration of wisdom, and the magic of healing. Practice is the act of being, the joy of living, the love of giving, the willingness of sacrifice. "One" is the Tao which is the Oneness of life. "Two" is the harmony of Tao and virtuous way of Action [Te], the harmony between heaven and earth, the integration between man and female, the dance between the self and the other.

Yet Rock cannot work alone. It must be transcended into the hands of Lord. It is with the power of light that spirit-consciousness is sold into unconditional love. It is through the unconditional love that innate virtue is sold to the power of spirit. A thousand forms of wisdom power of God will then become the manifestation of pure conscious spirits. A thousand prisms of energy shimmer with the vibration from the joy of love. A thousand characters of spirit display the liberation through virtuous sacrifice. The thousand stars, the thousand eyes, the thousand spirits, and thousand hearts will be completely sold to the power of Lord, the maker of love, the truth of nature.

Light is never double-headed. Tao is never alone. Power is never single. Love is never selfish. This formation is re-created in the hands of Lord, into the hands of His followers, that they may fly as ten thousand folds of creatures, from germs to vegetables, from plants to forests, and from animals to souls. The parasites of ten thousand conscious spirits become the shining lights. The parasites of ten thousand organic sensations and personalities will live together as dancing souls, the mating couples, and undivided individuals. The parasites of ten thousands of viruses and cells will represent the pure webs, life wombs, and protective shells. They all complete their journey because of light of Rock and the power of Lord.

Lord is the Christ, the son of God, the symbol of the unification between the Heavenly Emperor and the Earthly Lake. Christ's inner Rock-like discipline ordains his life, and the lives of his followers, while His unconditional Love closes the door on lust and fear, which represent the duality of sin. Lust generates distrustful ego, and fear promotes self-ish control. Within the Christ Love, Himself and His Unconditional Love are brought together as "two." Two are One, Rock and Lord are two. Christ and Love are One. Spirit and life are two. Inner marriage is one, male and female are two.

Rock is the descending power, Love is the ascending longing. Rock is the single-spirited mentality, Love is selfless devoted action. It is the Spirit that chases after the Love. It is the Love that shuts the further entrance of earthly gate. Only when the Spirit chases after the Love, is light sold to darkness, direction given to wildness, order put into chaos. Those surrendering are welcomed by the freedom. Sacrifice is embraced by the hope. Self is united with the other. Evil is imprisoned into darkness. Spirit is shot into heaven.

When Lord has Rock and Lake together, life is meaningful, love is beautiful, dance is joyful, and spirit is blissful for one and all. Light is solid, Water is soft. Heaven is clear, Ocean is murky. Rock is shining, Lake is virtuous. Power is destructive, Love is healing. Man is penetrative, Woman is receptive. Love is sacrifice, Union is embracement. This is the message of Two, the power of shutting, the love of liberating, and joy of unification.

## Realization upon Perennial

There will be a final enlightenment adding to the road of spiral growth along the last periodic experience. This enlightenment is the last sudden insight into the nature of the Tao, the body of harmony, and the function of emptiness. Because of this, perennial life force is the spiritual awakening power, and perennial life experiences are healing processes of purifying, dissolving and transforming the negative forces into positive ones. Otherwise, each experience would only serve to add to the distortion of mind and each force would transfer into the negative karmic consequence. As it is, each periodic state is an awakening process toward the healing practice, and each healing practice promotes another new, more advanced and more difficult period of the awakening process. Following an awakening experience, the person is in the state of being unified with self and the world. Nothing matters at that time, and nothing else makes sense. Elated, wonderful, absolutely exhilarated, ecstatic! Suddenly, the opposition plunders head-on, appearing from nowhere, blocking all directions, closing the gate, and sinking the flaming and vibrating heart into the suffocating valley of death.

Then comes the encounter with depression, numbness, hopelessness, sickness, and disorder flooding into the cells of awakening. There is another period of waiting for the moment, working at the task, seeking a negotiating opportunity, and continuing the perennial life style. During this period, one becomes calm, humble, clear-minded, and pure-hearted. The world is a wonderful quest, the spirit is a charming gift, and self is a smooth machine. Consequently, one lives more carefully and cautiously, and behaves more patiently and politely. Each chance is both an awakening call and a dangerous invitation. Each moment opens the door to the two directions and situations, old karma and new liberation. Then all that can be done is to perform the dutiful work. All that one can be is the self. All that one can interact with is the spiritual awareness. All that one can control is the unknown.

## The Alchemical History of the Perennial Life Force

The conscious chemical vibration is essential to be connected and we need desperately to be alone as well, to be one with self, and to be independent. How do we define this, and what is the chemistry? It is the beauty of union and the natural harmony of the Tao. Life has no break, love has no standing point, and harmony has no fixed angle. Even if we know the chemistry of life, can we ever know fully the chemistry of love? And if we did know fully the chemistry of love, could we flow perennially into the chemistry of harmony?

"The person who works according to Tao unites with Tao. In the same way he unites with action. In the same way he unites with loss. Uniting with action, the Tao becomes action. Uniting with loss, the Tao becomes loss." (24:4,5) Life is the loss, love is the action, and harmony is the Tao. That is the ultimate summation of the chemical history of the perennial life force. Should you ask a chemist to define the chemistry of life, no answer can be given. An explanation of a love relationship may be true to the relationship but not true to the love. If you question the flow to the Tao, the answer may be true to the flow of love but not-at-all true to the flow of the Tao.

Does this make sense to you? Censorship is the type of flow we know, and nonsense is the true flow.

## Meditation Practice

Virtuous deeds are the credits accumulating toward spiritual enlightenment. This is the God-defined rule of life devotion, sacrifice, and energy consumption. The other rule is simply the reality of loss, death, and reincarnation of negative karma. Without spiritual grounding, all the actions performed are waste products, inviting only the loss of life force.

The matter and force that underline this golden rule is the power of love, the virtue of unconditional love. These are the golden treasures. When a person and her/his love are unified, ten thousand spiritual deeds will be produced and ten thousand suffering spirits will be liberated and return to their heavenly home. This is perhaps the greatest gift to God's "birthday" and Goddess's "anniversary." This is the clearest illustration of cosmic perennial life force manifesting within the Kingdom of Heaven.

In order to become a Pure Person in Taoist tradition, thirty-six thousand virtuous deeds are required. If one good deed can be produced per day, regardless of how small or insignificant it seems to be, then thirty-six thousand virtuous deeds take only ten years of work. Should one awaken into the Tao later than the fortieth or fiftieth birthday, s/he still has plenty of time to become a Pure Person. The question then remains, how much energy has already been squandered uselessly? How far into debt is s/he before a virtuous deed can ever be accounted toward spiritual accumulation?

Without love, no one will sacrifice; without unconditional love, no one can stay on track; without light, no one comprehends the road toward enlightenment. These are the directions, the visions, and the power.

Enlightenment is quite simple; nothing bothers it. Enlightenment is very plain, nothing troubles it. Enlightenment is absolutely easy, no life force should ever be wasted. Practice this, and soon, ten thousand spirits will envelop you, love you, and fly aloft with you.

鯨水

# STEP SEVEN: *PILL*

Structure: self 自 + family 家 + water 水
Sound: shui
Meaning: pill

## The Nature and Triple-function of Spirit

The previous six characters are constructed for and germane to this character, which deals with the essential substance for producing the healing and transformative life pill. The derivation of this life pill is not from an herbal formula, as are other historical remedies that have been processed. Nor does it resemble in any manner the mainstream antibiotic capsules now being manufactured in the lab-converted factories of our modern society. Its makeup is a combination of God's light, the spiritual consciousness and the Goddess's holy water which is defined as unconditional love and biological fluid. This fluid is the creative form of the life formation already existing for the sole purpose of the creation of a unique individual. It is God's secret formula. It is also permeated by the Goddess's power of love and sacrifice. This fluid is the vital Qi that attracts our parents to come together for the purpose of building their love bridge, which is the essential link to each individual life. This fluid can also be defined as the growing force that makes everyone a sexual pro-moter, an emotional conductor, a soul lover, an intellectual speculator, and a spiritual loner. It is this fluid-like vital Qi that drives us mad, takes us to breathtaking heights, makes us forgetful, and renders us fearless. Finally it is this never dying vital Qi which we are endowed with that allows us to be happy, healthy, and to live a long life.

The vital Qi is the combination of our parental spiritual power, the seed of our spirit, and its biological fluid. Our parental spiritual power is the power of God and Goddess manifesting within their spirits and souls. Their bodies are the temples of this spiritual power, and their souls are the medium between their biological lives and their spirits. The seed of our spirit is a free floating energy formation existing between the sub-tle energy realm and deep conscious reality. The subtle energy is the cosmic conscious fluid existing between spiritual consciousness and soul-ful consciousness. The deep conscious reality represents God's creative law and Goddess's creative reality. Our parental fluid is the undivided conscious dancing energy form where God and Goddess's creative power manifests as the existing potential reality of a biological male or female.

The union of our parents is the flow of their harmonious Qi, which is the glory of our spirit within the reoccurrence of our new life. The longing between them creates a neutral space for our spiritual exis-tence. The masculine soul is longing for the feminine soul while the fem-inine soul is longing for the masculine soul. Each longing represents an energetic circulation from the opposite side. What the masculine longs for from the feminine is what the femininity characterizes and what the feminine longs for from the masculine is what the masculine characterizes. Together, our parental longing for the union coalesces with our spiritual longing for a new birth of life. If there exists no spiritual longing for a new life awaiting rebirth, our parental love-making process is unable to produce a new life with a true spirit within. Therefore, the union is the dance between their longings being guided by our spirit. Their union is the announcement of the beginning of our new physical life. Together with our personal and emotional characters which are interacting between our spirit and our biological instinct, our complete life is created.

Essentially, there exists an equal relationship between our parents' spirits and our own spirit. These are the trinity of the spiritual makeup. Our parents' spirits represent the harmony of heaven and earth, the Tao of male and female, the shadows of God and Goddess, as do the harmony between soul and spirit. The only difference is that before our spirit takes on a new physical body, it is still within the oneness of spirit. This specific time is determined by the quality and position of our last exhalation, discharged in the previous life. The exhalation is the flight, the separation, and the liberation of spirit from its dwelling temple, along with its unique lived and experienced and conditioned energy patterns.

Therefore, the purity of spirit and the quality of soulful energy are the defining characters for the speed and quality of reincarnation. The more pure the spirit, the faster the reincarnation will take place; the higher the soulful energy containment, the smoother the reincarnated life will be. When a celestial spirit wants to be incarnated within the human form, there is no human soulful energy yet visible in his new human body. Whether this spirit is powerful in a constructive manner or carries a destructive nature is beyond the human conscious comprehension. Many great leaders are human embodied celestial beings. Their power to save or end peoples' lives does not receive the reciprocal results as it does with ordinary people (For ordinary people, each killing brings a natural punishment to the killer's life). They exercise a higher power order. Spiritual leaders establish their spiritual/religious orders, and political leaders create their dynasties. All the religious founders belong to the first category. Mao and Hitler and Stalin were within the second category. They embodied not with an average human soul-contained spirit, but one charged with celestial power. Their celestial spiritual power is what attracted millions of followers, or killed thousands upon thousands of people within their own power structure.

The reincarnation of the Lama's spirit represents a combined figure of spiritual and political leadership, from one physical and personality body into another. The new life is determined and predestined, following immediately the exhalation of the previous life. The new personality and character requires a new learning experience, but the pure spirit remains intact. Each personality enhances and enriches its spiritual experience. Dalai Lama is both a personal and a national icon in Tibetan culture.

With ordinary people, it takes a much longer time for the spirit to reincarnate. It may necessitate a detour in an animal life before being elevated once again into the human realm. This is always the case when the death is unnatural, such as being killed in a war or being given a death sentence. Any form of accidental death is subject to this potential detour. It also occurs in the situation where one dies a normal death but the soul is not yet clean or purified enough to attain residence in the human realm. Reasons for this may be the negative consciousness having been imprinted in the previous life, or the lack of appreciation and compassion for the equality of animal life, regardless of the strength each characterizes.

Our parents' spirits are the representation of God and Goddess's spirits and their personal souls. The visible spiritual power between God and Goddess is our parental soul form, a combination of intelligence, emotionality and personality, the specific creative substances between God and Goddess. The longing power for the union and connection and being in oneness is the shadow of spiritual power between God and Goddess. In other words, our parental spirits are the model (spirit) of God and Goddess; their longing for reconnecting to their double loss (each side depending on the other for its existence) represents the shadows (transformations) of God and Goddess, and the creative potential copy of our soul within the oneness of our spirit.

In the parental union, our father's feminine loss within represents the Goddess's love, the creative power for making each and every spirit materialize. Our mother's masculine loss within represents God's light, the creative power, and the inner discipline. In reality, the father's loss is conceived with the soul of the mother, and the mother's loss is strengthened with the soul of the father. Each person mates and marries her/his soul-mate and each soul-mate is guided by the character of a spiritual being which represents the shadow of God or Goddess.

Our souls can be either masculine or feminine since they are determined by the previous biological formation of being either male or female. Our souls are the God and Goddess's shadows, the loss of our parental spiritual makeup, and the makeup of our biophysical energetic characters. Regardless of the biological makeup we inherit in this life time, if the previous biological body had taken on a female role, our soul would be destined to be feminine in this life time. Otherwise, it would be masculine. The definition of male and female is biologically determined by the creative power of God and Goddess. The difference between masculine and feminine is energetically constructed, both emotional and personal, within each and every one of us from life to life.

This also clarifies why each person takes on a specific animal spirit. Since each animal lives by its strength, the sum of this strength will compete with our emotional and personal construction, energetically and characteristically. When this energy quality becomes a surplus in the face of a particular human soul, this-going-to-be-reincarnated soul will benefit from this extra strength added to her/his own unique characteristic. Animal sacrifice has the same spiritual significance. By sacrificing the animal for the spiritual worship and cosmic understanding, the spirit of that sacrificial animal and its natural energy will be completely transmitted to the person who wishes to learn and benefit from such a spirit, providing that s/he is qualified in the spiritual journey.

We are all materialized spiritual beings, embodying our intellectual, personal and biological characteristics. Intelligence is God's creative wisdom. The personality is either God's or Goddess's shadow. The biological power of the physical body is Goddess's creative power of love. Within the God and Goddess's power, two biological bodies dwell within, representing the male and female of our physical existence. Within these two biological bodies, there exist five emotional (Soul) bodies, six desirable bodies, seven spiritual bodies, eight formative bodies, and nine constellation bodies. The God's power lies within the odd numbers, and Goddess's power is carried within the even numbers.

The five emotional bodies represent the subtle energy body that governs the five worlds, the five directions, and the five characters of organism. They are the magic five of God and Goddess's shadow. Among the five, three represent the trinity, and two the harmonious flow. In the pentagram, the upper three represent cosmic trinity, while the lower two symbolize the biological formation of one (on the right side) for construction and the other (on the left side) for destruction. In Chinese culture, these five emotional bodies represent, cosmically, the five elements of the creative power of the universe. They are wood, fire, earth, gold and water: the magic five in the Chinese cultural construction of things in the universe, from bodies to stars. In Christianity they denote the five qualities of a spiritual teacher, namely, apostle, prophet, evangelist, pastor, and teacher. These five qualities are the descending power of Christ Body, which are Wonderful, Counselor, The mighty God, The everlasting Father, and The Prince of Peace. (Isa. 9:6)

The seven spiritual bodies represent the cosmic body of four star groups, containing seven stars in each group. The nine constellation bodies are the nine largest constellations in the universe. In Taoism, the cosmic body of star groups charge the four directions in the universe, each governing one direction. For example, the north direction is embodied by the Big Dipper which rotates around the North Star. There are a total of nine stars amassed in the North Star, forming the constellation bodies of the celestial world. The nine stars represent, ultimately, the nine holes within the body. In spiritual practice, these nine holes are all charged by the cosmic fluid or holy water as well as the guiding light and discipline power.

With the Goddess's power, the six desirable bodies are the six major energy craving bodies within the six realms of the world, up/down, right/left, and front/back or forward/backward. In the hexagram we see the union of trinity, the harmony between red/orange, yellow/green, and blue/purple color structures. Each exists with and is governed by the other two. In our body, the six desirable bodies are the six hungry states for the six color realms of the rainbow order, with the exception of the violet color of the North Star. These bodies lack direction and stability. Essentially, the hexagram represents the transformation of the energy, time, and space. Its energy is flowing up and down vertically, the time shifting back and forth eternally and externally, and the space balancing right and left horizontally. The eight formative bodies constitute all the existential bodies in the universe, from germs to cells, to spirits and stars. The octagonal formation represents the eight edges of the cross, governed by the four corners of the world and directed by the central creative wheel-power in the axis.

In spiritual awakening practices, the trinity designates the self, the conscious awareness/focus, and the conscious projection or the inter-active body. The self is the subject, the source, the cause, the reason of truth, and the nature of self discipline. It typifies both spiritual and soul-ful self, egoistic and personal self. The consciousness awareness/focus is God/Goddess's awareness within the flow of vital Qi. In daily life, it represents the destiny, the journey, the way, the task, the plan, and the schedule. It is the mutual agreement, mutual engagement, and mutual sac-rifice. Cosmically, it is the energy body between matter and force mani-festing through the time existing between the ongoing formation and the stoppage. The conscious projection or the interactive body is the shadow, the mirror, the karmic body, and the partner who may be either friend or foe.

Numerically, the spiritual discipline outlined above guides the detailed energy work and conscious transformation. The five represent the five senses, the five inner organs, and the five fingers of each hand. The five Qi are guided by the five seasons. The red color is the body's trunk color, the blue color is the circulating Qi between the legs, and the yellow color is the healing power extended between two arms. Green stands at right, purple at left. They are either pulled down by orange or raised up by white. These form the trinity of color. The basic two forces are water and fire which are governed by the light and air, and the wind and rain.

The water flows up and the light shines down. In the north, it awakens gentle mist and cooling cosmic light. In the south it warms with solar light and firing heart. The right arm indicates the direction of sun moving from east to west. It represents the tempestuous (Job 27:21) and withering (Gen 41:23) wind. The left arm depicts the direction of moon rotating from west to east. It represents moisture wind of either clouds (Luke 4:16) or rain (1 King 18:44-45). The flesh eye watches the front side, which is the conscious protection. The third eye views the back side, the cosmic rocking motion circulating along the spine between brain and legs.

The seven holes in the face are protected by the seven stars in the Big Dipper. The first star, called the Heavenly Dog in Taoist tradition, is the initial water making star above the earth. The holy water from this star floods down to earth and is steamed by the sun and the southern star group. During the Ice Age, when the North Star Group was more power-ful than the South Star Group, everything on earth was covered with the ice flooding down from the Heavenly Dog. Gradually, earth's rotation was governed by the sun and moon in one area and by the East Star group and West Star Group in another, enabling wind and air to harmonize water and fire into living creatures, grounded or structured by the minerals. Each mineral represents a specific cosmic conscious formation and creation on earth, which is similar to an idea or a thought within the human conscious formation and creation.

As organic beings, we lack an unending energy supply, and are being poisoned constantly by the toxic leftovers from the energetic circulation. Therefore, six desirable thought bodies and seven deadly sinful emotions exist with conscious awareness on one side and instinctive behavior on the other. All this behavioral consciousness originated from the eight phases of cosmic wind circulation on earth within each given year. Each wind phase or period consists of forty-five day time period. These eight wind circulations move in and out of nine holes in the body, seven of which are on the face, and two in the lower body.

The makeup of our biophysical energetic character (the living soul within) is a very interesting topic that must be stressed according to the spiritual discipline involved. As we live this life time, for example, our spirit is ever God's creative wisdom within the intellectual inspiration. Our body is the Goddess's creative power of love within a materialized body. Our soul represents either/both God and Goddess's shadows. After our physical body deforms, our spirit returns to its universal creative origin. Our entire energetic body evolves into another form of loving energy circulating between heaven and earth. This energy body or the pure soul body becomes the spiritual makeup for either a male or a female in ·a future life time, predicted by the biological body we possess in this life time. In other words, the spiritual body will transcend into the soul body of masculine or feminine in order that the biological body can be attained in conjunction with our future parental union. This energy body may also elevate into the shadow form of God and Goddess, the angelic beings, or holy ghosts or animal spirits on earth. Becoming an angelic being, called holy person, the enlightened sage or Pure Person, is the ultimate purpose of spiritual practice in life.

When we die, the power of our soul, being masculine or feminine, becomes the gender maker for another life within the shadow of spirit. It becomes the energetic character of soul body, the emotionality and personality within specific organs. These organs take on the power role, are determined by the exact time of our biological formation, the union of love-making of our parents, and by the time of our birth which is the demarcation between our pre-heaven life and post-heaven life. In each given life, these organs express as characters, emotional and personal, animated and holy, until the soul is again transformed.

The transformation of soul between life and death is the representation of holy spirit and holy ghost in their energetic construction. If the life journey is geared in a more spiritual direction, this soul will turn into an angel, the spiritual body of a holy person. It can then work further with the celestial spirit in order to become the complete single Oneness of spirit. If during the life more healing work is done and energy patterns become clean and pure, there is a greater possibility of becoming a holy spirit. If the work of life has not been completed, the soul must return into life once again to continue its journey. If there is an over abundance of negative energy accumulated, the soul becomes ghostly and will take a much longer time to return to human form. When the negative energy patterns fit into any specific animal being, the soul will remain to live with that animal for another lifetime or so before being liberated into human realm. When this similar type of energy becomes scattered, it takes on its spiritual form within plant life, the inorganic form of life. If the negative energy is so intensely strong and condensed, the soul lives in a hell with no organic connection to animals nor inorganic connection to plants. They become the demonic forces. They are so condensed that they must exist for a prolonged time in this state before being transformed into lighter versions. A hellish world is the most condensed energetic force and destructive power in the universe.

Taken in descending order, our original soul within human context is the shadow of God and Goddess, masculine for God's shadow and feminine for Goddess. As the soul became a living energy within the organs, emotional and personal quality came into effect. When the first ancestor died, the soul energy was imprinted within the spiritual makeup. Thus began its search for the next life formation called reincarnation, since the soulful energy had incarnated as the shadow of spirit within. The most striking feature of the soul is that it is organically oriented, individually defined, and personally qualified. That is why there exists individual or singular souls within all living creatures. In all the organic beings on earth, souls are the conscious formation derived from the spiritual inspiration. They are the original sins towards building ego formation and self-destruction. They are the seat of self consciousness transcending from the spiritual consciousness.

In spiritual cultivation practice, these soul energy patterns are the origin of blockages leading to illness, both mental and physical. In a mental blockage, destruction ranges from personality disorders to psychotic and mental retardation. It includes deafness and blindness as well. Should it manifest as physical blockage, it becomes the source of biologically inherited problems, ranging from specific physical makeup to abnormal functions, such as cancers, high blood pressure, diabetes, and other severe physical disabilities. All these problems spring from the separation of soul from spirit.

Therefore, we see the yin and yang of energetic forms in the universe. God and Goddess's creative powers are pure light forces, while their opposing forces are destructive and hellish. All creatures exist between the two. Both creative power and destructive forces exist in the two extremes within the space of universe. They are called duality or polarity, or yin and yang. However, between are both the energetic circulation of that vital Qi and the formation and de/transformation being experienced between birth and death, physical life and energetic life.

## What is this Life Pill?

There are three forces that generate the circulation of creative formation of all things in the world. They are the vertical force, the horizontal force, and the conscious force. They represent the three dimensions of the world. The vertical force is the transformation between light and dark, the creative and destructive, the virtuous and mortal. The light force is the power of invisible creative force within the visible penetration of shining light. The dark force is the power of invisible destructive force within the destructive actions being practiced among living beings. In between is the circulation of water and fire. When the fire cannot penetrate through the action and water cannot purify it, it then becomes the demonic Qi. When the power is stronger than the blazing fire and cleaner than the state of water, it is then the pure creative power.

The horizontal line represent the lineal fashion of each and every creative being, living and reliving by itself, cycling and recycling from one form to another. Living and reliving represents the pure energy patterns of God's creative wisdom. To reiterate, this force circulates from east to west. The cycling and recycling represent formation and transformation of the material world of Goddess's creative power. It rotates from west to east.

The conscious force either marches forward or retreats backward. Marching forward is the creative force, the visionary dream, the wishful journey. Retreating backward is the repetition of conscious memory, the habitual pattern of experience, and the locked-in conscious dream. Each conscious memory constitutes a specific energy pattern. Each energetic pattern, pure or murky, is the driving force of an energetic expression. Each creative body is the physical representation and containment of that energetic expression. The idea of man is within the creative wisdom of God's power, from conscious nature to the ideal cellular formation. The manifestation of love in this energetic pattern imbued in an individual ascertains his unique God-given individuality, and a person with the changing characters is guided by the idea of creative wisdom. The idea is a flash of invisible light, the expression of the flashing invisible light lies within the expression of a form, from the visible to the audible and tangible.

Therefore, each individual human being is a specific and collective representation of this ideal formation. God's creation of humanity is carried out uniformly in all human beings. The Goddess's creative love power lives forever from body to body, from individual to individual, and from generation to generation. The genetic code of a spiritual and biological human being never changes, yet the expression and formation will differ from body to body, soul to soul, and spirit to spirit. This genetic code is the union between God and Goddess, and this difference constructs individual thoughts and their corresponding behaviors. Thoughts are the specific cosmic consciousness, the never ending creative change, and the spontaneous structural understanding. Behaviors are the expressive formation of love, the devotion of sustenance, and the sacrificial return to the procreative power.

Within God's power lies the creative wisdom and the external expression of that wisdom. Each creative code is an ideal of God's creation, and each code is an eternal expression of a completed creative wisdom. Therefore, each conscious understanding is a finished product, and each creature is a completed code. Within the Goddess's power exists the unconditional love flow of existence manifesting itself while destroying itself at the same time. Each love is a powerful expression of Goddess's love toward God's creation. Every love must die for the new love and for the change, for the recreation and for the return. The change is the breath of life, the recreation is the joy of life, and return is the meaning of life. This is the nature of the trinity of spirit.

We see a trinity also in the three types of waters that exist in universal beings, holy water, love, and water molecule on earth. Holy water belongs to Goddess's creative power of love, the water molecule is the biological basis of all living creatures, and love is the interactive water existing between holy water and regular water. It is the holy water that attracts God's creative wisdom. It is the water molecule that attracts light, and it is love that makes everything flow, consciously or unconsciously, conditionally or unconditionally. Combined, they form the life pill as described by the seventh character.

Spirit is the creative mechanism of holy water. It lives through love and is conceived within the oceanic water. Through light, holy water becomes the mechanism in the universe. Through cosmic wind, spiritual consciousness becomes the mechanism of love. Through air, water becomes the mechanism of organ. Light is the creative discipline of God. Cosmic wind is his creative wisdom, and air is his conscious manifestation. Without water, light is invisible. Without love, cosmic wind is still. Without water, air does not flow. Cosmic void is the spirit's womb. Clouds are the footsteps of wind. Fire is the workstation of water. This is the cosmic makeup of life pill.

## The Mechanism of Self-Water

Vital Qi is the Laoist's idea of self-water or life pill. Tao is the Self-Water. Spirit is the self-water. The vital Qi exists individually, manifests between time and space, and changes within the conscious reality of God's creative ever moving reality. Since the creative force can only be measured through each individual within a given time and space, the vital Qi exists between the individuals, time and space. Self-water denotes for the time. Spirit enlivens within the individual. Space is the conscious understanding and individual capacity sustaining the unconditional love.

There are three types of vital Qi, the primordial yang Qi, the unconditional loving Qi, and bio-mechanical Qi. The primordial yang Qi exists in the universe, inside the unconscious reality, throughout the creative power form. The unconditional loving Qi directs the conscious flow, ensures the bliss of love-play, and forgives the obsession of conditional love. The bio-mechanical Qi shapes the cellular formation, empowers the organic transmutation, and protects the instinctive habituation.

In the cosmic realm, this self-water mechanism is the Goddess's creative loving power, eternal, unconditional, and merciless. In the universal world, this self-water represents the white matter/hue that colors the entire cosmic appearance. On earth, it is the oceanic water that nourishes the bodies of all living creatures. In the sky, it is the cloudy ozone that protects all living creatures on earth, from plants to animals, from dreams to hopes.

On the road of the evolution progression, within the fish, this self-water is the germinating power. Within the serpent, this self-water is the power of tongue. Within the reptile, this self-water is the power of spinal fluid governing the limbic system. Within the animal, this self-water is the formation of egg between semen and milk. Within the human being, it is the unconditional love within the kingdom of God.

Among all the creatures existing in the evolutionary journey, fish have the most spiritual power. This means that God's light of that spiritual creative wisdom pierces through the fish's eyes within the oceanic water. There is no third eye, and no pineal gland, just oceanic spiritual eyes. Through the evolutionary process, the entire biological formation of a fish transforms into the biogenetic construction of all mammals, including humans. The odor of fish is similar to the odor of this biogenetic construct, which are eggs and semen.

The most interesting part of marine life is that it is not influenced by the earth's daily cycle, nor the nutritious food chain so necessary to sustain earthly life. Fish sustain themselves within the family group. Their sensitivity is created by the reflection of light and air pressure upon the water. The under-developed tongue becomes a universal symbol of a self-germinating process. When the serpent's tongue takes on the role of a self-protective device, it becomes then the power of order and sacrifice in evolutionary development. The communication takes a new leap. In all mammals, the tongue becomes perhaps the most vital organ of the body. Without tongue, God's inner conscious thinking power cannot be expressed, soulful character cannot be distinguished, food cannot be digested as it is through the first digestive enzyme produced from the salivary glands, good and evil can not be justified.

The second most important development is the cerebro-spinal-abdominal fluid. This is the trinity of self-water within the body, or the micro-immune-fluid. None of the dozens of glands within the body, their structures and dynamic functions, can be fully established without this linkage. In terms of human life, in the brain, it is the collaboration of six major glands, thalamus glands (brain bladders), the hypothalamus glands (brain kidneys), the pituitary gland (the brain sexual glands), the pineal glands (the brain adrenal glands), olfactory bulbs ( the brain dantian), and amygdala (the brain gut). Of these six glands, pineal glands and olfactory bulbs are the most significant in high spiritual practices, since air and light become the most important vital forces in themselves. In addition, the fluid-filled cochlea is crucial in interpreting the vibration of sound. Without this fluid, air waves cannot be translated into bio-electrical formation. It is a matter of fact that air pressure within the cerebro-spinal-abdominal fluid and the entire organic system ensures the first sensory perception. In high spiritual awareness, it is the combustion between light/water and air/body that generates innate spiritual vibration itself, both gene mutation and love expression. Therefore, sound is the natural interaction between light/water and air/body.

Without such, there could be way that one could redevelop and reawaken the power of third eye. Pineal gland would remain buried under the cerebral cortex of the human brain. Spiritual light would be more than the visible solar light seen during the day and remote stars twinkling at night. God's vision of eternal creativity and sacred understanding could not be revealed. God's image would be but an imaginative vision or distorted illusion, the yin form of creative lights, since God's light has descended into visible matters and their appearances. One's spiritual conscious awareness and understanding would still be altered between regular consciousness—thinking consciousness, and dream consciousness—recycling consciousness.

In the high spiritual state, there is no difference between spiritual awareness and spiritual understanding. In this state, regular consciousness and dreaming consciousness are unified and purified. They are affiliated with the cosmic wind circulation, the creative form of air, and the eternal sound, the cosmic echo. The eyes for sight, the ears for sound, and the nose for smell are all cosmically reconnected into their embryonic state. The mouth is closed tightly, and power of tongue becomes invisible cosmic vibration. The earthly gates are closed as well since there is no urine nor stool coming through. There is just breathing.

Without eliminating dreaming awareness, both day-dreaming and night-dreaming, the spiritual awareness will always seem half clear and half mystic. The ascending order of this transformative power is that the regular consciousness will be elevated into spiritual awareness, and the dream consciousness will be purified into spiritual understanding. The awareness comes from God's light, and the understanding is the vision of spiritual light connecting to God's light.

## From Oceanic Water to Cloudy Elixir

In Taoist tradition, floating in the clouds/mists is the magic play of spiritual practice, while refining bioglandular fluids into pure elixir is the necessary requirement of spiritual practice. How to refine the bioglandular fluids is the art of inner alchemy, and how to float with clouds is to enter the heavenly realm of the Tao. On earth, the body is sustained by the regular water, and it is maintained by the bioglandular fluids. The regular water makes the body conscious, bioglandular fluids make the mind conscious. Bodily consciousness is instinctive, and mental consciousness is possessive.

The clouds above form the love-making consciousness, water flow makes the life consciousness. The clouds are forever moving and changing, and life never stops changing and relocating. Clouds are the conscious wave, rain is the conscious love. They are regulated by the air and wind. Air fashions the peace of life, and wind directs the hope of life.

In Taoist practice, understanding the transformation from oceans into clouds is the spiritual awakening practice. And how to transform the biological fluid into spiritual fluid is the cultivation practice. How does nature make such a transformation from oceans to clouds? How can a sage make such an enormous leap from sexual lust to spiritual love? This is the magic play of nature and the spiritual mind. The basic difference between oceanic water and rainwater is that oceanic water contains salt and other minerals, while cloud-water blends with air and other cosmic winds. The cosmic air is the "cosmic salt" and the cosmic winds are the "cosmic minerals."

In understanding the transformation from oceanic water into cloud-rain, we develop spiritual awareness and spiritual understanding. The ability to make such a change lies within the magic play of cerebro-spinal-abdominal fluid. When the cerebral fluid moves down along the spine, it is bodily rainwater, the drive of sexual expression. When the abdominal fluid rises up into the brain through the spine, it is the elixir/life-pill/Self-water of spiritual understanding.

## Beyond Science

Modern scientific study stresses the formation of cerebrospinal fluid. It does not include, however, the abdominal fluid which is the most important fluid within the body. Without biological formation carried out by ovarian/testis fluid, there can be no opportunity for the unconscious to be awakened. Spiritually speaking, there are three flower-shaped structures in the human body. The cerebellum is the spiritual flower, the mammary glands are the loving flowers, and testicular glands are the biological flowers. The cerebellum governs the precise movement of muscles and other refined mobility practices such as writing and spacial balance. The cerebellum is the leaves of the spiritual cosmic tree, the earliest cosmic memory within. It is, in a sense, the power line of the entire bodily movement. The mammary glands deal with the nourishment of new life, and testicle glands sacrifice the seed into a new life. From the implantation of the seed, to the nourishment of the spout, to the coordinative action, these three "flowers" renew, regenerate, and recreate individual lives endlessly.

The tail bone controls the spiritual ascending power of the testicle glands. The thoracic spine controls the seasonal (monthly and yearly) function of the emotional balance of love, which is unconditional itself. Love is unconditional. Yin power of Goddess's creativity is unconditional but seasonal. The invisible flower is the thymus gland, which is the master of mammary glands. The brain stem (the limbic system) controls the bodily movement, intellectual, rational and instinctive. The perennial power of this moment is controlled by the pineal gland.

The pineal gland is the inner eye or the third eye as known in Hindu spiritual tradition. Descartes called this gland the organ of soul. It is the regulator of all glands. It reflects the light of God's creation which makes the spiritual mind visible through thoughtful actions. It secretes the spiritual hormone—melatonin—the invisible sexual growth and spiritual climax hormone which triggers the onset of the aging biological clock. The time of secretion is during the dawn (3-5 am) of the day, and in the first psychological development of rational discrimination from spiritual embracement (7 for girls and 8 for boys). During these times, night is separated from day, and spirit is divided into self and ego. Spiritual awakening and spontaneous action descend into intellectual and rational understanding. Therefore, this gland controls not only circadian rhythm but also perennial function. Through spiritual light, the pineal gland makes

God visible. Inner light is projected onto the pupils in the eyes. They form the triangular formation of spiritual light and understanding.

Through cosmic white fluid, the pineal gland makes life productive. Primordial yang Qi descends into ovarian/testicle glands. The primordial yang Qi is God's self-water. Through Goddess's love, this invisible yang Qi becomes visible, and determines the biological makeup of male or female. In the creation of the yang form, solid matter of primordial yang Qi forms the bones. Teeth are the external expression. The spiritual love is the formation of all bioglandular fluids, the water of life itself. The yin aspect of primordial yang Qi forms organs and muscles, skin and hair. Spiritual conscious love is the vital force within. Brain hair, in spiritual discipline, must be the first product of pineal secretion as is the skin and eye color. In its pubic stage, the brain hair, the bodily leaves, is extended into the pubic area and other body parts. In the aging process, the brain hair returns to its original color of white.

In circadian rhythm, the pineal glands alter the function between midbrain and cerebral cortex, thereby providing needed information for conscious thinking and conscious dreaming. Conscious thinking is charged by the reddish firing solar light, while conscious dreaming is guided by the indigo/violet cooling North Star's light. Together, they form the rainbow colors, with red at the bottom level and violet at the top. During conscious thinking activity, the information is received from both directions, the world as memory within the brain/body, and world as stimuli/measurement from the outer realm. This information deals largely with sensory information, revealing the worldly appearance of colors, density, height, and depth. Hippocampus, located below the pineal gland, processes such information and stores it selectively for permanent usage beginning with onset of life and continuing in future growth of life. All the automatic involuntary work done by body-mind represents the pre-heaven life activity. All the personal memory formed during life represents the learning experience.

In spiritual practice, there exists no conscious learning experience. All that is required is the purification practices and returning pilgrimages. Spiritual memory does not involve conscious activity. It is the spontaneous flow of love and light. Light provokes the innate memory, love engages the conscious flow. For this reason there is nothing to be learned in spiritual practice. All one needs to know is already inside the body and within the spirit. Social and civilizational learning practice are useless in this arena of life. Institutional practices are the curses that hinder spiritual awakening. Hippocampus has all the information stored within. Nothing further is needed.

In connection with the life learning experience, during the day the mind registers useful information in the hippocampus. At night, the selective activity in the hippocampus continues during sleep. When it is necessary for the information to be stored, hippocampus works in conjunction with parahippocampal gyrus, amygdala, and cingulate gyrus. Cingulate gyrus and olfactory bulbs which deal with air and smell constantly throughout life, work simultaneously with nostril and lung functioning. This is the function of animal soul or vegetative soul. Called Po in Taoism, this soul governs the entire limbic system, from olfactory bulbs for smell, to the eardrum for hearing and the pineal gland for sight. Together, these six holes in the face, two for eyes, two nostrils, and two holes for hearing are regulated by the Po of hippocampus.

When the information received involves emotional intelligence dealing with organic soulful energy, it will receive the needed advice from amygdala, which is the spiritual center of love, corresponding to the thymus in the chest. Whether or not that amygdala is involved with the function of tongue and the vocal cord remains unknown. Yet, one thing is certain, that being the ability of amygdala to detect the textures of food and drink. Food, like breathing and sleep and sex, provides emotional pleasure for the organic soul, and verbal expression is the organic soulful vibration between food and thinking. Tongue plays a major role in functioning with the emotional master gland, amygdala. This energy device connects with the heart organ, the vibration of fire and blood circulation.

When the information deals with human soul, or Hun in Taoism, it works in conjunction with the parahippocampal gyrus which lies beneath the amygdala. This organ connects to the liver organ in the chest, the largest internal organ in the body. In Taoist tradition, liver is the seat of the human soul, or conscious spirit. Happiness and rage are its emotional expression. Through parahippocampal gyrus, the negative emotional expression—rage—is executed. Also, since parahippocampal gyrus is the external coverage of both amygdala and hippocampus, conscious memory enlivens in this area, in both thinking and dreaming.

Midbrain, as in the function of spleen, alters all the functioning between the limbic system and cerebral cortex. It connects the brain stem with cerebral cortex via thalamus glands. Its function is regulated by the basal ganglia. The basal ganglia contributes partially to the subconscious activities of accessory movement and inhibiting tremor. Similar to the function of spleen, it deals with the stability of the administration within the entire organic system. It also sends the walking message to the heels. In this area, animal and human souls are communicating with each other by altering the limbic system and the advanced brain information system in this manner. Consciousness and unconsciousness become regulated.

Brain stem is the "tip of the spiritual tongue" connecting the tail bone and sacrum. In birds, it connects with the power of mouth, as exhibited by the woodpecker. Neck functions as human arms. In all animal lives, the spiritual organism and biological organism are altered through the brain stem. During a meditation practice, I received the information from the first star in the Big Dipper. My ears took the form of a dog's ears, and my brain stem was the stretched tongue of that Heavenly Dog turning back from my normal brain direction.

How to circulate the energy smoothly between the brain stem and throat is the key function during high spiritual practice. By eliminating all the seasonings in food, the throat will become clean, no longer forming mucus. When the brain stem works in union with pineal glands, no tears will be produced. When all the neck muscles are softened, there is a direct energy discharge between spine and throat, thereby connecting vision and sound via the breathing olfactory bulbs. When there is sexual arousal, tears are secreted, and the mouth becomes dry. If there is an early or abnormal ejaculation during the sexual practice, it is due to an energy discharge occurring in the entire section of brain stem. This can lead to various pathological psychological expressions, such as rage, guilt, sadness, depression, and fatigue.

In Taoist cultivational practice, when the tongue is placed in the proper position, the sexual Qi from the abdominal area will rise up to the brain stem via the spinal cord, thereby increasing the brain activity and further enhancing the production of sweet dew in the mouth as it merges with the enzymes secreted in the salivary glands. It will enrich the power of love, empower the verbal expression, and promote the loving spiritual float. Yet all the fluid flowing along the spine, between tail-bone/sacrum and brain stem, is nothing more than Self-water within the body. It is the precious dew and priceless jewel.

## A Comparative View of Water

In the Biblical context, this self-water is the power-surge of trinary formation. "Let there be a firmament in the mist of the waters, and let it divide the waters from the waters." (Gen. 1:6) Firmament is the divine law of God's creation, The discipline of Rock, and Power of light. It is through the power of firmament, that water will be divided into three layers, each containing another three layers. In the mist of waters, are three layers, Goddess's creative form or Holy water, Unconditional Love or cosmic flow, and biological fluid or cellular formation. These three layers can be defined as Peace, Harmony, and Creation. God's Self-discipline holds the Peace, His light draws Harmony, and His Law defines Creation. In the regular water, there are three states, ice, liquid, and gas.

In our human body, the three layers of water are the biological water, the love energy, and the spiritual elixir. The biological water is the essential bodily fluid. Love energy is soulful, an emotional and organic vibration. Spiritual elixir is the creative flow of wisdom. Among these three, biological water is the most significant. Without this fluid, there is no possibility for the human to grow and continue to live life after life. There can be no attraction for the spirit and no quality flow of love. The biological water develops into either milk/love or insight/intelligence. "Except a man be born of water and of the Spirit, he cannot enter into the kingdom of God." (John 3:5) Water in this regard represents the unconscious flow of abdominal water. Spirit is the vision and creative idea of God. The Kingdom of God is the impermeable space of Love, which is the unconditional flow of love between God and Goddess. In the creative order, there is first water, then spirit. Following after comes the kingdom of God, called Cosmos, Universe, Emptiness, or Void.

As the biological water is quickened, stirred, boiled, and aroused, there comes the existence of life. This life is a moving creature that has a spiritual guidance in a moving flow of water. The moving flow brings forth abundance, richness, and grace. "Let the waters bring forth abundantly the moving creature that hath life, and fowl that may fly above the earth in the open firmament of heaven." (Gen. 1:20) This is the ascending power of creative returning process, from biological/oceanic reality to spiritual/cosmic reality. Naturally, the spring must rise above the formation in order to generate further purification and creation. Oceanic water must rise into the sky to form clouds and rain. Biological water must move into the brain to create a spiritual fluid. When the seeds of spirit arise and grow, they produce an abundance of living and moving and changing creatures, from plants to animals, to humans and angels. They are one and all shimmering and dancing in the open light of heaven.

This abundance generates liberal and conscious souls in human life form. "The liberal soul shall be made fat: and he that watereth shall be watered also himself." (Prov. 11:25) The unconscious flow of abdominal power flows within the liberal soul. Love and creativity for the unique expression make each and every soul liberal and fat. Together they generate prosperous power that enriches the soul, not fat in the physical sense, but fat in the spiritual containment. Laoism refers to this as "vitalizing the stomach." (3:2) Only when it becomes fat can the soul be more powerful, more selfless, and more generous. Only when the soul becomes fat, can it invite the spirit to live within permanently and with peace. Only when the soul becomes fat, will the heart be content, and faith be strong. When faith chairs the seat, belief is the fragrance of flower. The smell and longing for fragrance is fat itself because spirit paints it and love nourishes it.

The rise of abdominal power will generate such belief. To propagate this belief is to create new life forms. To sustain such a belief is to enrich the life with love. "He that believeth on me, as the scripture hath said, out of his belly shall flow rivers of living water." (John 7:38) Laoist's version is that "the sage's method is for the belly, not for the eyes." (12:2) The river in Taoist tradition represents the bell meridian that resembles the flat ocean. Out of ocean, there flows the living water from spring, and out of oceanic flat, land is formed above the scene. These rivers represent the blood streams within the body. When the abdominal power rises, it becomes either loving vibration through its intense longing and echoing voices, or the sound of inner drumming and chanting prayers. They are spiritual in nature and cosmic in vibration. These voices and prayers are the rivers of living water. Rivers are the fire of blood, and living water is the vital Qi within the body-mind.

Laoist further defines that: "Nothing in the world is softer and more supple than water. When confronting strength and hardness nothing can overcome it. Using nothingness simplifies. Using water overcomes hardness. Using weakness overcomes strength." (80:1,2) In a similar expression the Bible describes it thus: "With all lowliness and meekness, with longsuffering, forbearing one another in love." (Ephe. 4:2)

With peace and love, Oneness is attained. "The sage holds oneness as the shepherd of the world" (23:2) since "By attaining Oneness, heaven is clear. By attaining Oneness, earth is at peace. By attaining Oneness, the spirit is quickened. By attaining Oneness, the valley is filled. By attaining Oneness, the king puts order in the whole world. All these result from Oneness." (39:2)

The Bible contains a very similar expression: "There is one body, and one Spirit, even as ye are called in one hope of your calling; One lord, one faith, one baptism, One God, and father of all, who is above all, and through all, and in you all. But unto every one of us is given grace according to the measure of the gift of Christ." (Ephe. 4:4-7)

The kingdom of God is in the spaces within unconditional love residing in the chest. They are all guided by the vital Qi. "He gave some, apostles; and some, prophets; and some, evangelists; and some, pastors and teachers." (Ephe. 4:11) "For unto us a child is born, unto us a son is given; and the government shall be upon his shoulder; and his name shall be called Wonderful, Counselor, The mighty God, The everlasting Father, The Prince of peace." (Isa. 9:6) As such, the five elements of creation and teachings are illuminated in the kingdom of heaven.

## Embodied Water

What is this vital force (Qi), fluid, pill within our body-mind? It is the essence of intellectual creativity, emotional loving vibration, and biological energy-making action. Without this vital force, the mind is numb, because it lacks the impetus of cerebrospinal fluid mediating with the pituitary glands and pineal glands, enervating with thalamus and hypothalamus glands, amygdala, and other fluid making glands. In Taoist's cultivation practices, the pituitary and pineal glands are the batteries connecting the cosmic power with the life power. They are the power plants that unify the light between the sun and earth , emitting our conscious power, and the moon, the dreaming power. They are also the stimulating organs that gather the violet light of the North Star to infiltrate the human conscious mind. They are the energy resource that receive and store the cosmic light ever-present in the yang third eye which will generate the power to transmit this light into the yin third eye.

When the energy in these organs is insufficient, there will exist either a conscious deficiency, a slower or complete lack of mentality, or many surfacing psychological problems. To have lower or no mental activation will result in poor IQ, or mental retardation. The psychological problems are those manifested deviations that leach from the inner stillness, spiritual tranquility, pure intention, and rightful projection. In spiritual practice, pituitary glands govern the yin form of third eye, and pineal glands control the yang form of third eye. The yang form is God's wisdom. The yin form is the expression and understanding of the creative wisdom. When these two glands are harmonized, the ideal is pure, the thought is clear, the understanding is self-expressive. Daily consciousness and dreaming consciousness are one, earthly water and holy water are the same, the spiritual light and wisdom air are inseparable. In the highest form of spiritual practice, when these glands work harmoniously with thalamus and hypothalamus glands, enlightenment is achieved.

When this vital Qi vibrates in the heart or chest area, it is the power of love, either the pure unconditional love or the many fragmented loves. The corresponding organ is the thymus gland, which is very independent, fiercely discriminative, and quite lonely. It stands right before the heart, the power of madness of fire. Actually, it is the thymus gland that generates the power of madness in both love and hatred. Through the activity of this gland, the notion of empty heart becomes the reality. The thymus gland has no paired system as do the pituitary glands or the adrenal glands. It is a singular organ; it will be paired but is not yet separated; it must be absolutely discriminative. It is able to distinguish self from nonself, to differentiate self from others, to separate what love is from what hate is, and to alternate between love and hate, depending upon the reality of each and every situation.

This organ is a lonely one. It is unlike other glands that are either paired or at least close to others, it is solitary. Yet, it occupies the most essential place, the center of the heart, not the center of mind nor the center of gut feeling. The thymus feels from the reactions of both gut and mind immediately recognizing what is good or what is bad, which are the benefactors and which are the destroyers. Without this extraordinary ability, we would be unable to survive for a minute.

The reaction resulting from the gut feeling is a biological and animated response. For example, when the stomach recognizes what the mouth is consigning to it, it will test it before transmitting information and instructions to the thymus glands as to its disposition. If poisons enter through the mouth, the body will die instantly before there is time for any anecdotal self-protective measures to be taken. However, when the reaction is first instigated in the mind, there will be a resultant action from the intellectual and egoistic response which may then prevent death, for human ego plays a crucial part in determining how to live and die. However, if the mind sends a message or signal to kill, someone/thing will then die.

Generally, the thymus gland manifests in two emotional reactions to the self and world. One is the conscientious love, and the other is the combination of egoistic and emotional love. The conscientious love represents the moral response, and egoistic and emotional love solicits the selfish response. The former is more universal, cross-cultural, and selfless. The latter is individual, personal, and selfish. The specific location in the body for the former will manifest in the back side of the body, exactly in the number five thoracic spine. Taoists term this area as Yellow Court. It is the unified and crystallized emotional and personal love. It is the dwelling place of Christ Love, as well.

There is an imperceptive difference between the Taoists' Yellow Court and Christ Love. The Yellow Court is selfless in the sense that the self no longer exists. There is neither devotion nor sacrifice involved within. The key word in this translation is "flow" or "going with the flow." As for the Christ Love, there is a dominant factor of either absolute devotion or fearless sacrifice. It remains, therefore, that "self" continues to convey the strongest role. The key word for this manifest is "being" or "I am." Directly in the front of the thymus gland, the distorted love, both positive and negative, permeates. This distorted love is defined by Taoists as seven emotions and six drives.

In the abdomen, the vital Qi-pill is the power of fight-or-flight, and it is the resource for the reproduction of future generations. In essence, it is the will of preservation. Without stressing the importance of this Qi-pill, it must be expressed that Taoists are not Taoists simply because they love it so deeply. Nor are Taoists to be viewed as sexists. Taoists are the matchmakers of the two sexes, the virgin girl and the virgin boy. They understand the power of this Qi-pill, never squandering it. They know the vital importance of this Qi-pill, they never misuse it. They understand that "the man of substance dwells in wholeness rather than veneer, dwells in the essence rather than the vain display." (38:6) They understand clearly that "not to lose one's substance is to endure." (33:2)

The entire practice of Taoism is an aphorism in which, as Lao Zi has vowed: "I want to be wholly different from everybody else, by taking sustenance from the mother source." (21:8) Its process can be defined as "eternalizing the qi-essence and nourishing the head," a method or practice for regaining one's youth and returning to childhood. In this manner one can "preserve the mother," because "The world begins with the mother as its source." (52:1)

## Why this Water-Qi-Pill?

This Taoist method of practice cannot be equated with an absence of sexual practice, or desexualization. It is a process of regaining and controlling the manifest or the out-flowing of the essence in the body. This essence has existed since before the formation of the physical body, and it continues its existence through the physical body, the mind, and earth itself. Since the mind is powerful enough to fight against the earthly gravitational force, the soul can become a heavenly sage. Otherwise, the soul will become a ghost, or at most an earthly sage.

Reproducing for most adults is a way to ensure the continuity of one's life. Smelting a life-pill is the ultimate achievement for know-the-practice-Taoists. This life-pill is the baby of one's own. It has neither spiritual nor physical make-up. It is the Pure Self of selves, a unified being of matter and form. Its matter is beyond any physiological transformation, and its form is above the spiritual manifestation. It is the essence of life, although it lacks any visible form to represent the image of life. Most importantly, this baby has no gender identification. It is neither male nor female even though it has potential to manifest in either directions, just as a baby who survives no longer than six weeks in its mother's womb. An individual, whether a religious or lay person, who achieves this highest level will undoubtedly live beyond the cycle of life and death. It enables her/him to attain an eternal and immortal life matching the age of heaven and earth.

In the Bible, the concept of being born again and returning back to new life—the origin of life and not the repetition of life—is identical to that of Taoist. "You must be born again." (John 3:7) and "Whosoever therefore shall humble himself as this little child, the same is greatest in the kingdom of heaven." (Math. 18:4) This passage carries the identical message as described in the Tao Te Ching. Laoist's version is "Gathering in vitality and making supple, can't you be an infant." (12:1) And "Sages always smile like a child." (49:4) Whether one is a born-again Christian, or an enlightened Buddhist monk, or a Taoist sage, it matters not. The differences are but institutional formations.

When a Taoist is unable to achieve this goal, then her/his purpose in being a Taoist would be on the second level where one could help building temples, recite Taoist tenets and live a life that benefits society. These activities accumulate the virtues that generate a future successful life for the practitioner. At the third and lowest level, one could perform as a service person in the temple. This can ensure a relatively happy life at the onset of a new life. Lao Zi defines these three types of individuals as: "When the superior persons hear of Tao, they practice it faithfully. When average persons hear of Tao, it seems they practice and it seems they do not. When the inferior persons hear of Tao, they ridicule it. (40:1)

Truthful and devotional activation is achieved by a superior person, one who has accomplished such activation and is one with the Tao, living beyond the danger of death and being born again soulfully. The quintessence of such activation is "taking my substance from the mother nature" (20:8) and "acting within the good timing." (8:3) This substance, in Taoist terminology, is "the one-Qi before heaven and earth," the vital force that generates all activities and activations of all matters in the universe. Similar concepts would be the theory of eternal flux by 'Greek Taoist' Heraclitus, shalti or spirit energy, Kundalini or serpent power. This unnamed and unnameable Great or Great Void, Primary or the Unfathomable, is the inexhaustible bellow that pushes and pulls the running fluid to all that exists in the universe. From such, the spirit and body of a human being are formed; charged by such, the essence and vitality are transformed. When this heavenly such is reduced, the spirit is vaporized; when this earthly such is limited, the body sickens; when this primary such is exhausted, the life has completed its journey.

## Laoist's Position on this Water-Qi-pill

Lao Zi explained: "The world begins with the mother as its source. When you have the mother, you know the son. When you know the son, turn back to preserve the mother. Although the bodies, there is no harm." (52:2) "Turn back to preserve the mother" has no similarity to the theory of the Oedipus-complex, the action of a son murdering his father to take possession of his mother. Nothing could be further from the true interpretation, although it is true that the child receives nutrition and protection from her/his biological mother. The Mother in Laoism is the Spiritual Mother, or Goddess of Mother.

To preserve the mother is not meant to preserve the maternal mother, but rather an action of "taking the substance from the mother source" (20:8), the source of the creation of time, space, and matter. In Taoist meditation, it is the exercise of gradually taking the yang chi of the celestial body by reducing the earthly yin Qi to zero. Unless one does so, one will be at most and at last an earthly ghost. By using these two different energies, through the process of "high/martial heat" (Wuhuo), which is the actual mental concentration, and the "gentle/intellectual heat" (Wenghuo), which is the mental awareness, the elixir-baby can be formed.

On Winter Solstice, when the solar (or yang) energy begins to return, a meditator should attempt to transform this energy into the body, if the physical condition is prepared and the time to collect this energy is set up internally. Then, by combining the energy in the Summer Solstice, the meditator, practically speaking, can obtain both heavenly and earthly energy into the baby of life-pill, the process being called "forming a pill." After ten months, the pill is ready to come out of the body, to go anywhere the spirit takes it, and stay at any place the spirit desires. The ten months represent the ten years of thirty thousand virtuous deeds.

The process of "smelting" is an actual practice in which effort is exerted for the activity of meditation between "martial heat" (Wuhuo) of energy gathering and "intellectual heat" (wenhuo) of energy saving. The "martial heat" and the "intellectual heat" are involved with the energy transformation as well as energy distribution to different parts of the organs, directing the energy of sunshine during the day and moon's and stars' light at night. They also participate in physical, emotional and spiritual balance throughout the days and nights. The whole process comes together through years of earnest inspired effort to produce the "perennial" or everlasting life-pill.

## Meditation Practice

How many of us, in our lifetime, realize that our most precious life-pill is within? How many of us can fully utilize this life-pill, to preserve it and use for the spiritual awakening?

We are all driven to seek pleasure, expect to have a good time, wishing to experience climax, longing for the union. What is there afterward? We have used up this life-pill. The more we try to reach these conditioned self-consuming states, the faster we travel the road to loss. Finally, the life-pill is extinguished, the life force shrivels, and the spiritual temple withers and dies.

God and Goddess preprogrammed these pleasurable states allowing us to be close to our true self, our own home, and to be one with God/Goddess within. The life-pill is not designed for us to have a good time, become exhilarated, then stressed and depressed. We think we want these fleeting pleasures, and chase madly in their pursuit. But the spirit waits patiently longing for the supreme.

If you know this, you know the secret of life. If you have this, you obtain God's creative power. If you own this, you own the Goddess's unconditional love. If you are one with this, you are one with yourself.

Life-pill is all we have in life and for the continuation of life. Life-pill is all we need during life and in preparation for after life. Life-pill is spirit-pill, golden-shell-elixir, primordial yang Qi, the secret formula of God/Goddess within, the evolutionary genes. It is what we are.

Don't waste it, but preserve it; don't spend it, but refine it; don't discharge it, but retrieve it; don't misuse it, but spiritualize it. That is the most forthright advice Laoism can suggest.

# PART TWO

# The Ascending Order:

# *TE*

# STEP EIGHT: *RIGHT*

Structure: right 正 + green 青
Sound: zheng
Meaning: right

## The Antithetical Beauty of Chinese Language

**T**his character and each of the following will correlate with its corresponding character detailed in the first half of the couplet. The orders are 1-2/8-9, 3-4/10-11, 5-6/12-13, and 7/14. To further explain the connection, the first and second characters covered in the first half of the couplet are phrased as "jade body," while the oppositional phrase in the second half is termed as "right mind." Jade and right are antithetical, and body and mind are opposite. Words and phrases within a couplet are antithetical in the sense that those in the second half are opposite or contrasting to those in the first half. Proposing and responding antithetically through couplets has been a tradition in Chinese culture, especially among intellectuals. The two verses or the two halves of a couplet escalate to form a poetic marriage. This form of linguistic practice is the most honorable and effective way to acquire insight into another person's character. It is invaluable in realizing one's own talent, capability, and artistic beauty. It is through this poetic marriage that the social and cultural phenomenon are expressed vividly within the verses.

In Chinese language, antithetical couplets are the foremost descriptive concepts of the yin and yang of man's understanding of nature. They are woven into a harmonious balance of the defender and the surrender. There is a perfect match between rivalries or oppositions, between the push of a rejection and pull of a reflection, between the message of mouth and the clasping of hands, or between the passion of heart and the stillness of mind. Antithetical couplets are the most complete illustration of Chinese language: they contain the highest concentration of alcohol in their natural poetic wine; and they fully utilize space, time and efficiency in human creativity, endurance, and proficiency. Even when the linguistic structures seem unsavory, the content may be illuminating.

Couplets can also serve as educational tools, interactive devices, healing remedies, and liberating visions. They provide the readers with an insightful idea, a convoluted suggestion, and a hidden message. They force people to think, laugh, cry, and release. They give the instigators the opportunity to demonstrate the master of the linguistic disciplines and techniques, at the same time elevating themselves from the restrained orders that language and society have imposed on them. For the respondents, it is a test area of swiftness, sharpness, insightfulness, adaptability, and thoroughness. All in all, it is poetic in the sense that it captures all the essential thoughts of a language; it is artistic in the unfolding of the beauty of the creative and responsive mind as inseparable from its authentic origin and swiftness. Knowledge, creativity, time and understanding are all expressed in the characters of the two antithetical verses.

Couplets have the power of demonstrating the ability spontaneously, healing the psychological wound scathingly, stating the upright attitude satisfactorily, and proving the social justice satirically. For example, in ancient China, the Board of College Examination used the couplets to test the extent of the examiners' knowledge and creativity, especially spontaneous creativity. Also, in both literature and actual life experiences, dating couples are made aware of their compatibility by proposing and answering each other in an antithetical way. Through verses, the poets themselves are recognized by their linguistic ability and poetic power. With the discovery of one another's intimate secrets, they then can play together, stimulate each other, and evaluate one another passionately and objectively.

The most meaningful use of couplets is in the intellectual battleground. It is the most effective, persuasive and competitive way to either debilitate the respondent beginning with the first verse or retaliate the proposal in the responses of the second verse. In one perspective, the proposal is initiated in a verse with such a high degree of difficulty and complexity that the respondent can not unravel the meaning. But to his credit, the respondent might answer so effectively, intellectually, and destructively that the proposer could be too deflated to regain her/his position. Above all, couplets are the most objective tools with which to evaluate things, since they invite the observers who are standing by, reading objectively the results generated between the proposer and the defender.

The most commonly used characters within a verse are seven, such as how the couplet has been constructed. Some verses may have four or five characters in each half while others may expand into ten or even fourteen in each verse. In the land of China with its cyclical mentality, the most cultural practice of couplets observed is the celebration of a new year. Every Chinese new year is marked with both feasts and couplets, both celebration and preparation. Without couplets, the mind wanders, hope fades, and life diminishes. For the new year abundant feasts are prepared, household decorations of the couplets adorn the door frames creating a joyous and holy atmosphere, just as new clothes can fashion individuals with new plans and possibilities.

Contrary to Chinese culture, American culture does not celebrate the mind during the new year holiday as the Chinese do. Every material thing in America can be purchased in the super market. During the Christmas holiday, intelligence is centered in the cash flow as the biggest asset in commercial life. In China, when you visit a family during the Chinese new year, the couplets posted on doors and door frames welcome you more warmly and honestly than the host does. From the couplets, you know all that has happened during the year, and what the hopeful plan is for the coming one (That is my motive for emphasizing that couplets at Chinese new year are the true representations of both celebration and preparation). You will also find that the couplets speak for the intellect of the family. It would be ineffective to compose an English versed couplet and post it on the door. Couplets are the annual reports in Chinese culture. The Chinese calligraphers promote an annual competition in the art of writing up couplets.

Before the Chinese new year begins, all door frames must be posted with the couplet, including animal shelters, as well. Couplets are posted on either side of the door frames, with the first verse on the right side, and second on the left. There must be one phrase posted on the top frame, and one on the upper section of the door. They may be written by friends or relatives, or purchased commercially in the market. If the doors are double, two verses must be used, also antithetical, and posted on both upper sections. The phrase at the top frame is identified as the heading, and the verses on the upper part of the door are called the body. Those on either side are called couplets, with the first verse "shang lian" or upper verse, and the second verse "xia lian" or bottom verse. The couplets must be written on red paper which invites good luck and wards off evil spirits. All this must be completed before new year's eve. The couplets cover many fields and promote greater human understanding of nature and humankind.

## The Characteristic of Laoist Couplet

Pertaining to a unique and abstract notion, Laoist's couplet serves as the true genetic codes that construct human nature and its functions. It is an evolutionary understanding in an involuted void; a presentation of completeness being formed from the inhibition of nothingness; the nature's effect upon human trustfulness. In speaking the language, the couplet can be classified as one of the most, if not the utmost, condensed yet simplest observation of human inner alchemy and its extracted elixir. The inner alchemy consists of the growth hormones for health, healing, aging, and immortality. The extracted elixir is the right way, the perfect medium, the central joint, and pointless ground.

The first verse in the couplet describes the essential chemical mechanism materialized in our human body, the biology of life. The second verse deals with the psychospritual world manifested in our mind, the immortality of life. The first verse is the source and resurrection, and the second verse is the action and returning. The first verse is concerned with the actual biophysical process of energy transformation, while the second verse deals with the psycho-spiritual illumination upon the transformation.

## A Word on Right

Instead of simply describing the quality of body and jade in the first sentence, this eighth character opens with the behavioral aspect of bodily and spiritual action. What does "right" mean? "Stay with virtuous oneness of childhood by embracing the nature of spring and the color of evergreen." This eighth character combines the character "right" for "zheng" with the character "green" for "qing." It represents the "evergreen spring color, the youthful life, and the rightful action." The structural meaning of "zheng" is "to come to or reach the point of oneness." It has one line on the top followed by a "foot" stroke at the bottom. Our basic common sense tells us that foot always comes to a halt, which is the one pointed action. The linguistic description of the character "qing" or green means "the wood green Qi in the east producing the elixir."

Coming together, this eighth character in the couplet has the structural meaning of "two feet halt at one point of evergreen elixir Qi." This is a state of an infant's behavior before any desire and evil action begins to manifest. Before the foot begins its walk, the mental passages go directly to the cosmic realm. Since there is no second thought, there can be no desire, evil thoughts, and sinful actions. This is the right way of being with the meditative life: not only practicing meditation but living a meditative life. Meditation practices deal with mental and physical performances, while the meditative life results from a mental/spiritual attitude. The character represents the best state of meditation and is filled with vitality, beauty and virtue, being without behaving, spontaneously responding without acting, performing without claiming the result.

The component "zheng" in the eighth character refers to "correct, right, punctual, pure, principle, straightforward, accurate, perfect, exact, and precise." The transliteration of the word "right" is not in reference to something being normally right or wrong, or right as opposed to left. The truthful meaning of the Chinese character zheng indicates: correct but not absolute, right but not exclusive, punctual but not cutting, pure but not dazzling, principled but not lawful, accurate without binding, perfect without giving it up, straightforward but possessing the capability of yielding, exact with more required space and opportunity, and precise to the complete understanding and thorough liberation.

The character zheng is constructed with five strokes, indicating a right composition, a perfect grouping, an accurate summary, and a recognizable break. It is often used for counting, voting, and grouping. When I was in school in China, we would use this character to count publically the votes or diversified decisions. An elected or appointed scrutineer would stand in front of the blackboard, to first write the candidate's name or the subject at issue on the blackboard. S/he listened to the announcer's counts, posting them next to the candidate or subject. Each stroke stood for one count. Every five counts were grouped by one zheng character into a complete unit. After the counting, the scrutineer summed up the total and wrote the arabic letter(s) at the right end of the counts. It is simple and creates no confusion as everyone observes the process with their own eyes. It is a democratic tool, is it not!

## Where Did Lao Zi Go Afterward?

According to legend, after the completion of the Tao Te Ching and couplet and before his departure from the Han Gu Pass, Lao Zi told Yin Xi to meet him in Sichuan Province one thousand days hence. When the time approached, Lao Zi's spirit transmitted itself into that of a baby boy in a Lee family, by transforming his green dragon into a green sheep that would accompany him daily. One day, this green sheep suddenly disappeared, and the Lee family searched everywhere in horror of what they might find. Fortunately, Yin Xi happened to be passing by at that time and saw the little boy with the green sheep. He instructed him to go to the Lee family with the message that Yin Xi was arriving. As soon as this baby boy heard the news, his body turned into a giant spiritual being. Laughing at Yin Xi, Lao Zi acknowledged that Yin had successfully cultivated himself into the body of the Tao. Nowadays, there exists a temple in Chengdu called Qi-Yang-Gong, or Green-Sheep-Temple. This is one version of the story that green always signifies something mystic in Taoist legendary literature.

Following this, Lao Zi continuously reincarnated into human forms. Some Taoists believed Lao Zi to be the spiritual body of Buddha. According to Hua Hujing (Scripture on the Conversion of the Barbarians preserved in Donghuang Caves), Lao Zi continued his wanderings through Central and South Asia after passing through the Han Gu Pass. His teaching influenced Buddhism, the person of Confucius, and even Christianity in Mani.

After Yin Xi, He shang-gong, man-on-the-riverside, became the first spiritual interpreter of the Tao Te Ching. He was himself the reincarnation of Lao Zi, according to one version of the Taoist literature. He shang-gong compiled the two volumes of Tao and Te into one book embodying eighty-one chapters, representing double yang or double nine. He created a title for each chapter as well. The truth is apparent, after all, Lao Zi never dies, since he has "no place to die." (50:5)

## A Religious History on the Character Zheng

Heavenly Master Zhang was the person most closely related to the character zheng in Taoist tradition. His name was Zhang Dao-ling (34 -154 C. E.). He was the most powerful shamanistic Taoist healer of all times. He was the founder of Wu-Dou-Mi-Jiao, or Five-Pecks-of-Rice Taoism. This school was the first shamanistic religious Taoism in China. The Heavenly Master Zhang was a healer and a spiritual leader in Sichuan Province, curing the sick by reciting the magic formulae of mantra-like spells, then serving them sacred water. All his followers were required to donate five pecks of rice as the initiatory entrance into the Tao. Zhang wrote twenty four volumes on Taoism and worshiped Lao Zi as the ultimate founder of Taoism, creating the reverent name Tai-Shang-Lao-Jun, or the Supreme Master Lao Jun. This name became an honorable religious title and remains so to this day.

In the mountain where I was baptized, Mountain Qing Cheng (Qingcheng Shan), also in Sichuan Province, not far from Qing-Yang-Gong in the city of Chengdu, there is an area where a sharp valley appears unexpectedly. Legend has it that when Zhang Dao-ling stayed in the mountain, he cut it into two pieces with his magic sword. The evil spirit then occupying the mountain has since disappeared. Zhang Dao-ling's Wu-Dou-Mi-Jiao later became Zheng-Yi-Jiao, or Right-One-Taoism which is commonly translated as the Way of Right Unity. The Zheng-Yi-Jiao can also be interpreted as Five-One-School. The word zheng came into existence after Heavenly Master Zhuang's appearance and became part of the Taoist's essential understanding and conduct. It pertains not only to a moral explanation but for a spiritual discipline as well. Zheng represents not just one right conduct in a life time, but the right conduct forever throughout the life.

Among his writings are two books entitled with Zheng-Yi (Right/Five-One). One of the interpretations of Zheng-Yi is that, according to the Yellow Court Classics, the bible of the Shang-Qing School of shamanistic Taoism, or the Supreme Magic Jewel, "Zheng-Yi contains the golden flower that nourishes the all." This sentence means that when the five elemental Qi are unified in the chest and crystalized into a golden flower in the Yellow Court, the entire body is fully nourished. Therefore, there is no need to have sex, to obtain food, or to sleep at night. All day and night, this cosmic water nourishes the entire body with its golden flower shining at the back and vibrating in the front. In its literal sense, five Qi are the centralized, integrated and unified love Qi. One stands alone, pointless, and without reference. In action, when the activity of five fingers and intention of one heart are unified, there can be no difference between the internal intention and external action. It is the oneness of right intention and right action.

Another description is that "Destiny manifests with four, and root abides to one. Concentrate on oneness and you would not attain it. Abandon it and it would not disappear." This is called Zheng Yi. Four represents the four skeletons in the body and four directions in the world. One is the central point, the vital joint, and the elixir caldron. The four squares and one point make the perfect completion. This is the application of Zheng-Yi (see detailed explanation about the machine-qi in chapter 14).

The historical background of this is that during the Yang Dynasty, or more exactly, in 1304 C.E., one of Zhang's thirty-eighth generation disciples named him after Zheng Yi. He headed several shamanistic Taoist schools that unified various practices of talismans. Also, because he helped establish the Yang Dynasty by explaining the new dynasty with the characters such as Zheng and Yi, he was titled as the founder of the Zheng Yi School. He combined the Five-Pecks-of-Rice Taoism, the Lin-Bao-Pai, or the School of the Magic Jewel, and the Shang-Qing-Pai into one unit, Zheng Yi School, which is now the standard shamanistic school of Taoism.

While in practice, this religious school concentrated on autowriting (like the still practiced sand writing), magic, talisman, exorcism, ritual healing and many other techniques. Those practices range from conducting funeral services, to healing psycho-spiritual problems and performing fenshui (geomancy) service. This school exists everywhere in China. Historically, it is the first mental health profession in China. Psychologists in China today cannot separate the roles in these religious and spiritual practices. In dealing with spiritually and ghostly related psychosomatic problems, these Zheng-Yi-Jiao practitioners are much better suited to handle such conditions than any qualified professional psychologist.

## A Historical Understanding of Zheng-Yi

There are historical differences between the shamanistic schools mentioned above and the orthodox schools of the inner alchemical practices in the history of Taoism. The differences began after the Brother of Fu Xi and Sister of Nu Wa were married and their children came to be populated into different families. They were the first two children whose virgin mother was the Western Mother, and they were the ancestors of the Chinese race. During the time of this historical expansion, there were two distinguished families overpowering the rest. One is Lee, and the other is Wu. The Lee family flourished along Huang He or the Yellow River. The Wu family practiced mystically along the Chang Jiang or the Long River/the Yang Zi River. The Lee family was more intellectual and analytical in terms of human understanding and practices. The legendary family name for Lao Zi is Lee, as well. His birthplace was in Henan Province of central China. When the mouth of Yellow River ran through Sangdong Province, it highlighted these intellectual practices through Confucius's teaching.

Quite oppositely, along the banks of the Yang Zi River, the culture was more spiritual, shamanistic and ritual, due to the influence of Wu's family lineage. Symbolically, Wu represents the pictorial image of a female's chest. The meditative meaning of this Wu character is a bit divergent. It means that when the brain energy and abdominal Qi are unified in the chest, the two-breasted heart will be opened. Virgin boy (the masculine nature) and virgin girl (the feminine nature) will dance together in the chest, each occupying one breast. In the Wu character, the line on the top stands for the spiritual energy, the line at bottom represents the biological Qi, and the line in the middle signifies the central channel which connects man with heaven's light and earth's vibration. The two triangular parts represent the two breasts, from which the mother enlivens the twin-boy-and-girl.

This branched family lineage was the cradle of Chinese healing tradition, the spiritual practice, the magic dance, and the ritual performance, due to the transcendental power coming from the Sister Nu Wa. That is also the historical connection whereby Master Zhang could form the first shamanistic Taoism in China. Even today, northern China is more comfortable with intellectual or mental interpretation, whereas in the south, magic and rituals remain very popular, especially in the central south and southwest of China. This accounts for another practical application of yin and yang of Chinese family and their culture.

### What Means Right?

Let us look one more time at the definition of the eighth Laoist's character zheng or right, which means that the two feet halt at one point of evergreen elixir Qi. The one point is the one inch size of the Tao within the body, which will be discussed in more detail in the following character. This point is colored by the evergreen elixir. Actually this evergreen elixir has bluish and yellowish colors in it, which are the ranging colors of jade and the first character we have studied. According to modern biological language, there exists an organelle giving birth to all the lives on earth. "Organelles" means "little organs", and they are the organs of cells. To be more explicit, organelles are the specialized internal compartments or molecular structures that host the energy reaction. Nucleus is the biggest organelle, occupying as much as one-tenth of the cell's volume. Organelles give life to cells and all living things in the world. They all differ in shape and size; each having a specific task to perform. Organelles are the battery makers for life, so to speak. Evolutionarily, organelles make the single celled monera, bacteria and blue-green algae, into protista with one nucleus and other membrane-bounded organelles.

Fungi are the highest development of this evolutionary process. What makes fungi so special from plants and animals is that they lack the ability to photosynthesize, drawing light from sun and stars to energize water and air. Fungi are not green, since they do not have the chloroplast; they are often black, similar to Chinese or Japanese black mushrooms, or white, as are the ordinary mushrooms or the poriae used in Chinese medicine. Fungi represent the natural black and white biological illustration of Taichi; black denoting the earthly matter and white the cosmic way. Fungi are also the byproducts of the winter season, with white at the top and black at bottom. Fungi hate light. Laoist defines it as: "Understanding the white and holding on to the black enables the formation of the world." (28:3) The familiar representation of this is the mushroom growing from the root of a tree during the rainy season and being transformed into mud after being penetrated by the sunshine. But, evolutionarily or cyclically, they are endowed with the capacity to deviate into green, red or yellow coloration. That is why biologists define monera as blue-green algae which is the short, sudden, or temporary transition from winter to approaching spring. They are about to transform into a new seed of the nucleus, but they have the ability to photosynthesize.

When I came upon this biological information, I was extremely happy to be a Taoist. I am also a biologist of sorts, not one who studies the evolutionary process of life, but as a meditator who practices and personally experiences the process of returning to the oldest form of life, fungi. Fungi are the mother of plants and animals. Taoists feel reverence to fungi, as one of my friends informed me. More strangely, Taoists thrive on fungi during their fasting practices. They survive on fungi for as long as twenty years or more according to some sources of written literature. When I started my first longtime fast, to honor the Jade Emperor in San Francisco Chinatown, I was so moved by some of the Taoists' literatures that I longed to experience this myself in the future. One writing stated that: if you consume poriae for ten days, you will constipate; if for one hundred days, you will embrace the spirit. If you continue to consume poriae and similar herbs for twenty years, your intestines will fossilize into bones. In fact, many legendary stories revealed that the successful Taoist practitioners turned their bodies into "white bones" by elevating their spirits into the sky during the daytime.

How wonderful it would be! Create an image of a cave with water trickling over the stones and fossils. The air there never stops circulating, yet the fossils retain their basic structures for years and even centuries. They are much older than any living creatures on earth. Couldn't the same truth hold for the longevity of our biological life?

On this subject, Lao Zi advises us "Husbanding into light, being as ordinary as the dust." (4:3) This means that the spirit hubands into light when the body deforms into the state of dust. Lao Zi does not mention the white bones, but does advise that you should envision the state of your body as the state of dust if you are unable to fossilize them into white bones. When the body ceases to operate as a worn-out machine, the most visible things that continue to exist are the water-weight-body which is blue, the transformed hair which is white, and bones which are also white. Everybody's hair will eventually turn white from whatever the original color had been because the spiritual light will transform it. White hair, white Christmas! Lao Zi further realized that: "Ah! Limpid, it seems to exist forever. I do not know whose son it is, this whom is exceeding the Heavenly Emperor." (4:4,5)

The true application of the above mentioned is that we should live physically as fossils once lived, but never spiritually. This is exactly what Lao Zi experienced "Tao functions in itself empty harmony. When used, it remains full. For sure, this source is the very ancestor of the myriad things." (4:1,2) What is the technique to know such and to be with such? The answer is: "Blunting the sharp edges, unraveling the tangles, husbanding into the light, being as ordinary as the dust." (4:3) What does right mean? Bacteria is right, blue-green algae is right, and fungi is right. That is the longevity of life. Scientists have been unsuccessful in detaching or eliminating the bacteria existing in the organs. I think they will never succeed. To do so they would have to discover a substance much older and more powerful than the bacteria on earth. And if this were possible, then what would happen to earth? Earth cannot be shorn free of bacteria. To fight against the substance of the earthly mother is an act of futility. Our body is useless without the bacteria, and our mind is useless without the electron.

## Jade or Chlorophyll

To a biologist, the comparison of this sub-title may seem ineffective and useless. Even the biologists may decorate with a piece of valuable jade in their office or hang a carved image around their necks. Under the mechanically made biological lens, they would determine that the composition of jade is either jadeite or nephrite. The differentiation of jadeite and nephrite is in the chemical structure. Jadeite is $NaAiSi_2O_6$, with the essential elements of sodium aluminum silicate, varying from whitish to dark green. Nephrite's main element is actinolite, which is in hues of whitish to dark green. The jadeite forms a tough mass, while nephrite has a structure which is either compact or fibrous. Their existing structural difference is based upon the exact amount of elementary minerals each contains.

Yet, there is no difference in terms of color. Nevertheless, Jade is the guardian angel among dust, stones, rocks, and gold. Even though gold is a precious treasure, it doesn't exist independently in the natural environment. It must be extracted from other minerals. Jade exists independently from stones and rocks, and needn't be extracted through such an educational or civilizational process as gold does. Laoist's evaluation of this matter is that "Being presented with jade in front of the team of four horses is not better than sitting and entering thus." (62:4) Because "It allows having without asking, and it allows forgiveness of wrong. Thus, it is most valuable to the world." (62:5)     According to Laoism, the practical insight is "Without preference, being is as resonant as Jade and as gravelly as stone." (39:7) What a beautiful liberation! How superior this mentality is! Be as exuberant as a jade and as clicking as a stone at any time and in any given environment. The solution to understanding this puzzle, as Laoism indicates, is: "Esteem is rooted in the humble. The high is founded upon the low. This is why the lords and rulers call themselves widows and orphans without support. Is this is not the root of being humble? Much praise amounts to no praise." (39:4,5,6)

But why chlorophyll? Without jade, we cannot know how to value stone or rock. Jade is the combination of both. Without chlorophyll, the earth cannot vibrate with green color. Plants and trees would not be dressed in green. Chlorophyll is the green soul of mother land, it is the heart of green plants. Chlorophyll is the source of the organs of plants which receive its love, the sweet sugar. They must be touched by its photosynthesized transformation, the energy battery. We know, in life, it is the heart that effects the change, the heart that changes the entire makeup. The same is true in plant life. The chlorophyll provides the nutrition with its sweetness of love, the sugar molecule. And it is again the chlorophyll that produces the peaceful transmission, due to its stillness of heart, the green filaments.

Green makes the peace, accepts the reality, and understands the endurance. Everything green on earth comes not only from the rainbow radiating with a green color, but through the green molecules in the natural makeup of plants and trees. We don't yet know how during the evolutionary process, plants and trees took on immediately and precisely the green color from the hope of sunrise. It may have been a shift from monera, such as in blue-green algae, that forms a combined package of blue for sky and green for earth. We know with a certainty that sky and ocean are blue by their nature, and plants and trees are green by their virtue. Through imagination, when the rainbow colors make use of their specific function, the plants and trees absorb the green color and choose it as both an energy supply and personality identity. Because of such, whether with the sun rising on the east coast or the moon rising on west side of the mountains, green makes the peace. Whether we step on the land of green color, or consume the green vegetables, we are connected to the green world.

Green also represents the soft morning, early childhood, tranquil mind, and the spiritual color in liver. The sun does not burn a plant into ashes in the morning hours. A five-year old child would never fight to the death over the fire of love. The liver spirit would never participate in the animated fight of egocentrism. In the early morning, we are filled with the freshness of peaceful mind. We are channeled by the fresh air. We are greeted by the sweet dew. Our mind is unlike the blazing sun during high noon, not as blue as during the afternoon. In our early life, we were afraid to fight. We were fearful of blood and darkness. Our actions were as soft and gentle as the wind-blown grasses. Also, experienced in the eye of our liver spirit, we avoid feeling empty in the heart: green is contentment and red is emptiness. We can not calculate in such a detailed fashion as the spleen does: yellow is solid. We would not feel the shortness of breath as the lungs constantly do: white is pale. We could not be threatened by the black kidneys: black seems deadly.

This is how we relate to the green in our organic body. This is how our emotions embrace the growing land. This is how we clasp tightly the invaluable jade. Jade can be comparable to our envisioned lady. We feel her gentleness, but we cannot cling to her softness; we can penetrate her shyness, but we cannot invade her quietness; we can hold her with tenderness, but dare not embrace her with forcefulness; we would sense her melodious voice through her distinct tone, but we cannot surprise her with thunder lightening eyes or threaten her with earth-shaking muscles; we can communicate with her clear mind and slender body, but we cannot capture her psychic power and extreme sensitivity; we would be content with her pure refinement, but we don't want to deal with her poor conditioning. This is what our body is about, a piece of jade and a virtuous lady, precious water and eternal void.

## Where Does the Green Qing Stand in Our Body?

We discussed the physical structure of jade-like-our-body in the beginning of the couplet, explaining its character as it relates to our physical life. In this chapter, we will further explore the psychological nature of green, psychoemotionally and psychospiritually. With the green, we pair oceanic feelings of clarity touched by the moon light, the heart-driven emotional feelings in the chest. Through the passion of green, the sound reverberates from the mouth, which is the outer manifest of the inner drive. Chest is the center for emotional intelligence, and the mouth is the gate of linguistic expression. The reason the nature of green is at work within these two areas is that when the human soul forms, it relies on the evergreen to present its truthfulness, to display its vigorousness, and to announce its youthfulness. The mental awareness is the truthfulness. The conscious vibration is the vigor aroused. The passionate heart depicts the youthfulness.

There are three very important Chinese characters that contain qing or green in their construction and are related with the notion of spiritual green. This spiritual green is the soul form of our being human. They are all regarded as root character qing or green. The first character relates to the clarity of water, the second with the motion of heart, and the third connects the vibration of voice.

1. The first character arises from the abdominal area of the ocean and appears in the tranquil sky reflected in the moon light. Oceanic water is the life substance on earth, the holy water in the tranquil sky is the substance of cosmic void.
2. The second character has to do with the desirable yin Qi manifestation, representing all the emotional feelings, sentiments, and moods. They are the yinful turmoil of life.
3. The third character comes from the combustion of lungs. This combustion is eager to speak, open to invitation, prepared to explain, and is helpful in consultation. This is due to the immediate and accurate sensations manifested through the lungs.

As a result, these three characters represent three seasons: the winter of oceanic coolness and the night of clarity, the summer of fire and the madness of passion, the fall of echoing and the spirit of responding. The green qing character remains at evergreen spring time and represents the penetrating growing power. In Chinese language, each of these characters is constructively represented by one unique character. In turn, all live inseparably with the green qing character. Let us now take a look at these three pictorial characters and their psychsomatic functions one by one.

## The Clarity of Qing: Water Plus Green

The nature of this qing character is clear, limpid, stainless, and bright. Its behavioral character is clean, honest, and upright. Its expressive tone is melodious and distinct. Its mental state is clear-headed, sober, elegant, and refined. Its physical conditioning is thin, lean, spare, and poor. Its flexibility is its refreshing quality and thoroughness. Its adaptability lies in washing, cleaning, and vanishing. Its required state is purity and freshness. Its reservation is faint or scant. This is the oceanic state and night time. Most importantly, this is the true physical state, as pure and clean as the still water in the ocean, and as cool and tranquil as the bright night. In Taoist meditation, understanding this character is the first requirement in dealing with biological conditioning of longevity. If the body is not as pure and clean as that of a newborn baby, all the cultivation practices become fruitless. All the mental effort will be contaminated by the sick body.

When the body is pure and clean, the mind can release its responsibility of making the biological process work. The body performs naturally in its biological process, by constantly receiving and transmitting and rejuvenating the energy in and out, back and forth. Only when the body is pure and clean, can the mind be still and tranquil. Purity represents bodily refreshment. Cleanness stands for the vital circulation. Stillness is the mental conditioning. Tranquility is the spiritual eternity.

This is, perhaps, the biggest disparity between Taoists' practices and those of Buddhists. This may be due to the historical fact that Buddha consumed a poisoned meal in his final physical experimentation, and Lao Zi deformed his body into the state of dust. Buddhism tends to neglect the usefulness of body, the temple of spirit. It denigrates the body as carnal flesh, waiting to be poisoned and discharged. In a practical sense, the Middle Path does not reserve much space for the transformation of body. It focuses mostly on psychological awareness and spiritual realization. The teaching on suffering is, by its nature, a mental fixation and attachment in the beginning, and is always assumed to be a projected outcome. In order to end the suffering, Buddhists are eager to seek enlightenment with no regard to the physical existence. Even the temple is temporary, it is the color of spirit. Even the body is transitional, soul weathers it. Even the body will deform, the mind must live through the deforming process before attaining enlightenment.

In Taoism, biological purification is the first step of cultivation, cultivating essential jing by transforming it into vital Qi. To purify the body is to cultivate the entire immune system with the eternal strength to defend against the foreign viruses and protect its biological existing space. One must have the innate clarity to expel murkiness before its transformative power. The immune system entails the entire glandular structures and functions in the body, ranging from digestive system to reproductive system and ultimately to nerve system as discussed in the previous chapter. The three Cinnabar Fields are the cultivational centers and the representation of the outcome. The biological center or the Lower Cinnabar Field is the foundation for the emotional center. The Middle Cinnabar Field is the residence for the spiritual center, the Upper Cinnabar Field. The emotional center is the steaming vibration of the biological process and the soulful expression of the spiritual liberation. The spiritual nature is rooted in the biological center and illuminated through the emotional center. Three are One. The biological process is the spiritual liberation acquired on earth. Emotional experience is the soulful expression of the spirit. Spiritual awakening is God's awakening in the human form.

## The Motion of Qing: Heart Plus Green

The nature of this qing character ranges from feeling and sensing as an engaging state, to mental and emotional diversities resulting from emotional, personal and egoistic love. The feeling side energizes the ability to feel, to affect, and to favor. The loving side relates as love, appealing to the emotional, the passionate, and to the lust. Entering into mental conditioning requires being situated, kind, and possessing an even temperament. To interpret the feeling aspect is to be with the action, to be in the sight of, and within reason to the state of affairs. On a higher scale, it is the enactment of goodwill and moral conditioning. It is the summer season, the prime time of life, and the emerging state of emotional conditioning.

Basically, this character marks the yin form of heart's action, which is not the true state of heart in its empty formation, but the combination of distorted situations that the heart deals with. These contrived situations are pleasant to the emotions but bitter to the taste, easy to arouse but difficult to stop, cheap to purchase but expensive to repay. It is food for the passion but poison for the action, powerful to connect with but earthshaking to break loose, and wonderful to live with but horrible to die for. This qing character is the weathering condition of life, the temperature of the heart, and the climate of the soul.

Emotional love and expression is an integral part of life, containing a mixture of light and water, fire and steam, soul and spirit, consciousness and instinct. This emotional character represents both the stagnation and flow. Between stagnation and flow lies the purposeful business and the pursuit of life. The stagnation is the fixated state, the habitual conditioning, and the animated instinct. In the forefront of this stagnation, love is selfish, life is materialistic, and body carries a price-tag. At the opposite extreme, the flow represents the spontaneous state, easily aroused and spiritually anticipated. In this flowing state, love is selfless, life is dimensional, and body is transformative. Being with this qing character, the beauty of life is displayed from this point. The tragedy of life, thereafter, has its beginning in this environment. The mystery of the life experience is expressed here as it permeates through our ordinary life.

## The Sound of Qing: Speech Plus Green

The nature of this qing character ranges from the urge to ask and request, the state of being engaged and pleased, to the condition of petition, the openness to invitation, and the further approach through consulting. This natural invitation welcomes the new hope, the new seed, and the new mentality. The new hope is for the change, the new seed is the power of changing, and the new mentality is the strategy of dealing with change. This qing character deals with the acceptance of the heart, agreement of the mind, the vibration of the soul, as well as the initiation of the action. It is an element of readiness, a touch of quickness, a sense of relaxation, and the desire of expression. It welcomes the challenge: open to learning and change and being conclusive with its appraisal. It is the biology to please, the psychology to be with ease, the policy to release, the reality to immobilize, and immortality to be.

If we could add another character Qing (sun + qing), meaning the clear sky cloudless and non-threatening, the nature of Qing of green extends into evergreen by encompassing all the seasonal elements, plus the bodily experience, the emotional expression, the linguistic vibration, the mental reasoning, and the spiritual tranquility. It would encompass a beautiful complete picture of evergreen! No wonder Lao Zi wished to make an elixir of it.

## The Position of Right

The position of right is an energetic feeling, a perfect response, an accurate measurement, a mutual interaction, and finally a result of a good timing. Laoist explains:

Dwelling in good places,
Drawing from good sources,
Supplying from good nature,
Speaking with good trust,
Governing with good rules,
Conducting with good ability,
And acting within good time. (8:3)

This Laoist explanation is much like the right intention in the Buddhist Eight Foldpath. This rightness is the right conscious effort, the right conscience, the right ideal, the right thought process, and the right mental projection. It is the seed of drive, the consciousness of behavior, the origin of mind, the power of creativity, and the spirit of wisdom. All the human history and their evolving civilizations have arisen from this. The ideal difference in characteristics of human beings and our animal friends (being one with) is centered here. The mental creation and spiritual unification manifest here. From this, the thought of identification and differentiation separate one flash of energy impulse from the others, project one thing from another, and form prejudice in viewing one beauty to another. It is the birth of mental creation and its accompanied consequences: mental and physical disorders. It is where the voice begins to communicate, where the name comes into existence, and where the belief begins to overtake the mind.

## A Word On Emotional Qing—the Drive

The notion of drive and motivation in modern psychology connects with the gross material of human intention and conscious activation. Yet it remains rooted in the concept of ego. The outcome of drive and motivation are unlike the refined form of action resulting from the truthful intention and conscious activation. What psychology cannot explain is how does one differentiate right drive from a wrong one, and how does one determine what motivation is a right motivation. Of course, the modern psychologists would reply that it must be universal since ego is universal; it is cultural since we are all cultural beings; it is also individual because we are individual by nature. Speaking from a Taoist mentality, these interpretations are at most ego gratification emitted from energy exhaustion. Drive theory and motivation theory have nothing to do with the right intention, nor the right conscious effort flowing from the guidance of the Nature of human action.

The word "right" does not deal with the common notion of right from wrong, is not connected with possessing one thing by sacrificing another, or swinging between the extremes of dualistic aspects of human perception. To further clarify the meaning think of it as being Natural or Action of Nature. In Laoism, it is described as: "The goodness of water benefits all things, yet it actively competes. It retires to undesirable places. Thus it is near to Tao." (8:1,2)

If a person can act like water, being the source of supply and the essential substance of purifying everything on earth, then her/his action would be the"right action." However, who likes to dwell in undesirable places? Not ego! Not the name! And not the satisfaction! Should a person actually do so, it would be considered the result of bad luck or a matter of no other choice. Comparing this to other translation, the standard text describes the water as "noncompetitive (non-action)," not "actively competes." This historical error occured because: (1) when later generations attempted to interpret the Tao as noncompetitive through using the notion of water, they were carried to the extreme in both theoretical interpretation and its practical application; (2) human mind always seeks perfection and the absolute; (3) anything in human mind, resulting either from forming a mental creation or searching for an ideal archetype, would be labeled as absolutely good or absolutely bad. How can the goodness or badness of Nature ever be defined?

Water is always active, and actively compatible. Observe the historical records of humanity struggling against the floods. When water is rampant, the world is mad. Yet, water always flows to a lower level, never upwardly. Even in its steaming state, it continues its downward journey but upward liberation. Why so? Nurturing and clarifying. Water nourishes all the earthly creatures by washing away "dirt" and "dust" refreshing and refining all living creatures. Can we say the same about our human expectation and action derived and projected from our drives? Can our emotions be as pure, clean and useful as water? Can we retain the power of water for enlivening and nurturing and cleansing and refreshing?

## Laoist Further Advice

There are many chapters in Tao Te Ching espousing right action that a person should mindfully perform. The following lists are the most vital. You may find them useful to employ:

A) The work is done, the body withdraws.
  This is the Tao of Heaven. (9:2)

B) Begetting but not possessing,
  Maintaining but not dominating,
  This is the Superior Action (Te). (10:2,3)

C) Don't seek gain from losing, nor loss from gaining. (42:4)

D) Peace and tranquility can be the measure of the world. (45:2)

E) You are not distant in not acquiring.
  You are not profiting by acquiring it.
  You are not at loss in not acquiring.
  You are not ennobled by acquiring it.
  You are not disgraced in not acquiring it.
  This enables the nobility of the world. (56:4,5)

F) Be rounded without cutting.
   Be compatible without puncturing.
   Be straightforward without trapping.
   Be bright without dazzling. (58:4)
G) Therefore the sage is self aware but not introspective.
   He has self respect but does not price himself. (74:3)

    The above are the actions of sagehood. It is the action where the ego and desire and attachment are completely out of mind. There is a right action for all human kind, embracing love, health, and happiness. There is also a right action for a sage, which is, peace in the mind, action according to the Tao, and being one with Nature. Even though the human mind always wishes to maintain a peaceful state, it is never entirely possible to achieve this goal.

    We may have a peaceful mind for a short period, but not over months or years. We may reach that state often, but our human action will eventually destroy it. We may think we have a clear picture of ourselves and the world around us because of the eternal quality of peaceful mind, but the elements of our emotional attribute, the addictive behavior and possessive desire drive this peaceful mind into a war of passion, self satisfaction, and cultural protection. Constantly and forever, we engage in wars. Peace, as is often the case, becomes a time of retreat or preparation for future war. Even in our sleep stage, the mind is in combat. There is some truth to be found in war. It is what we would presume to know about things in the world that are unknowable in our present capacity or our highest intellectual understanding. We never cease to search and fight for these truths in our habitual fixation. Whether our mind is a tabula rasa when we are in childhood stage, or later when we imagine ourselves to be experts on various subjects, we learn nothing because we cannot know anything more than we do in our present state. Or perhaps, we do not want to know any more. We are smug and content within our limitation.

    This is not to say that we can no longer learn anything at all. Our basic intelligence equips us to better know ourselves and our surroundings enabling us to live a healthy, happy, and danger free life. Our innate ability recognizes and separates the good from the danger to be avoided. Viewing any toddler's behavior, we are aware that because they cannot recognize people, they can easily be taken from the home. They could ingest poisoned food or unmindfully place themselves in peril. In life, moment after moment, we constantly engage in dangerous life-threatening situations. There is an enormous amount of information (needed and/or available) for dealing with these situations. Sadly enough, beneath the surface of this widely exposed knowledge exists the psychological pressure of fear, which is the source of most needed information. This input drives us all into the imaginative conflict between two realities, the mental and physical. Fear cannot protect us and death is ever present in all consciousness.

    In our present environment we must protect ourselves from each other more  than even the destruction of nature. We have created cultural environments where each individual is locked in this mental creation, from fearing one's physical safety to psychological expectation to spiritual worship. We have created our own god as well as our own "living organism." This does not diminish the reality that heat, cold, earthquake and flood are a threat to life and well-being. They assuredly are. Relatively speaking, however, we live in a much safer natural environment than our ancestors, and we have greater technology to protect ourselves than our ancestors could possibly have imagined.

In the yesteryear, people had no fear of being burned by electricity, killed in a car accident or an airplane crash, being poisoned by nuclear waste, or having AIDS. Nuclear weapons, as we know through the destruction brought on by the bomb, can now kill more people within a second than the thousands upon thousands killed by outdated weapons, knives, swords, arrows used in the numerous battles constantly being fought during any part of our human history. How destructive we have now become! Our minds are intelligent and destructive, honed by past experience. The end of our super world will not be the end of the earth life, nor even the end of earth's surface life, never will it be the end of the world as we know it. It will, inevitably, be the end of our own life and our own world. We may not live to experience a natural death, but projecting into the future, we may then choose to live through a spiritual journey.

What is the use of mind if through it we have lost our heart, the conscience heart. Nature creates itself, enlivens itself, balances itself, and revitalizes itself. And we, of course, are part of this nature. As the most intelligent creatures on earth, we humans wish to be unique ourselves, with no realization that we are an integral part of nature. How could we survive without water, air and seasonal changes? Can we live a better, healthier and more spiritual life in anything other than following the way, the "right" way? Return momentarily to the beginning where everything under the sun is right, has its rightful place and will remain right, where the only right will be that of spirit.

## Meditation Practice

It is time to re-establish and reconnect with our spiritual rights. That is all we have besides the love we live consciously and the temple in which we breath instinctively. Understand and accept that there is no absolute right, only relative right. There is no permanent right, only present right. There is no exclusive right, only situational right.

To live with spiritual lawfulness is the only right way to be. This lawfulness will not come from the outside world of our personal, social, and cultural rights. It is the unerring rights of heart's devoted consciousness. This consciousness is the right for self-discipline, self-understanding, and self-adjustment. This consciousness is the spiritual requirement to be good and generate virtuous deeds in the society.

When you feel that you are the only person to initiate right action, to process the right conduct, and to evaluate the right conclusion, you are on the right track. At this point, society does not affect you, others are but mirrors of your journey, and inner consciousness becomes your true guidance. You will know in your heart what right is from wrong, not by how they are culturally and socially labeled. You possess only your conscious presence. When you accept your conscious presence, the world benefits from the gift of your presence. There will be more space for kindness to replace justice, there will be more energy to embrace acceptance of everything rather than rejection of anything, and there will be more forgiveness than self-condemnation.

Your rights are god's rights, and your rights are your individual rights. Your rights are situational, are your very own personal rights. When you are the recipient of the unconditional love, health, honesty, innocence, and self-discipline, you have all the rights in the world. Right is a good feeling, a comfortable breathing, a common-sensed meaning, an energetic moving, and a Christ-like loving. Right?

傳

# STEP NINE: *MIND*

Structure: person 亻 + dao 道 + inch 寸
Sound: dao
Meaning: mind

## Tao: Everything Right Rises and Returns

**T**he cultivation of mind upon the body has been our prime goal from the onset of the second verse of the couplet. In the previous step, the eighth character in the couplet is a depiction of right between zheng and qing both seasonally and environmentally. We have closely examined the nature and function of zheng in all that is right due to the evergreen Qing elixir. After viewing this picture, we were warmed by the light and able to digest the green chlorophyll within our organelles. Yet, we cannot but ponder such questions as: what makes any right? What is the purpose of right? Where does right reside? The answer is found in Nature and Its Action in God's creative consciousness. It is the Virtuous Action of the Tao that creates both the great and small, encompassing both complexity and simplicity, and embracing both the magnificent and ordinary. The Action of the virtuous deed originates in the Tao and is the highest expression of human conduct, whether charismatically spontaneous or profoundly cultivated.

By extending this human action into other natural life forms, the conclusive picture of the total action can be interpreted as "that particular combination of qualities belonging to a person, animal, thing, or class by birth, origin, or constitution." We are not only a part of nature, but exist with nature in all its wondrous forms. We live with all things in the universe, from light and air to water, fruits and animals. We are the form of the Tao, behaving in accordance with the natural action of the Tao.

The body and spirit we possess are the body (yin and yang) of the Tao, the harmony of nature. Our conscious behavior and biological process are the Action of the Tao. Because of the Tao, we exist in our complete form, physical, emotional, and spiritual. Because of the Tao, we behave in the manner that we do, which is both human and inhuman, personal and selfless. Our human behavior distinguishes us from animals and plants and stars. Our inhumane nature is a reflection of God's creative beings on this earth and within the cosmic constellations in the universe, as well.

In terms of this interaction, the Taoist classic Yin Fu Jing (The Secret Evolution Text) states that "Heaven and earth are the thief of myriad things. Myriad things are the thief of man. Man is the thief of myriad things. When these thieves mutually benefit each other, three talents completely settle." The word "thief" may seem inappropriate, obscure, and shocking. This is only because we have not yet liberated ourselves from the three realms of the energetic cycle in the universe. Thief and talent are the yin and yang of all that interact in the universe. Thief deals with the yin form, being more subtle, dependable, secretive, and adventurous. Talent as the yang character is expressed in a more creative, independent, liberal, and transformative manner. The two stand side by side within the three realms in the universe.

The three realms are presented as heaven, earth and man. Between the realms of heaven and earth, humans are the most harmonious combination and the highest representation of life form on earth (but not among constellations and galaxies). As humans we can neither survive as long as tailed fish under the dark force of water, nor fly as high and free as the winged creatures. Yet, we are able to utilize all the creative talents endowed in the animal kingdom and celestial bodies. Myriad things refer to all creatures and their creative living talents existing in the universe, including heaven and earth. Human beings can employ the greatest use of the collective creativity of all God's creatures. No other creatures on earth, as a family group, can compete with human capability, with the possible exception of the earth itself constantly in motion, exhibiting its natural phenomena: floods and volcanoes and earthquakes. As individuals, we can be chased by lions and threatened by tigers, stung by bees and bitten by snakes, and attacked by dogs and stalked by cats. We can not always outsmart them, they live by their instinctive and swift actions for survival. Yet our minds are stronger than our animal friends, though we may not be, most of time, as faithful as dogs are, and as fearless and dedicated as horses can be. Our spirit is more powerful than that of any other creature, albeit its radiance is not as brilliant as the stars and planets.

Since we are all God's creatures, we live on God's creative power within ourselves, and we rely upon stealing each other's creative energy both consciously and unconditionally. Stealing is a chosen act of submission in not relying on awakening one's own talent but passionately disclosing others' talented actions. Talent is a single-headed fire ball; it lives on itself, by rising from the stealing action of the piercing eyes. Talent is a gift from no one knows where and cannot be transferred from place to place. It is the presence of God's creative circulating energy manifesting within as a sparkling sensation, a quickening understanding, a spontaneous realization, and a complete actualization. Those who are endowed with talent must pay the price by sharing it. They do not own it. Rewarded in their accomplishment, talents are enabled to sustain themselves (sell them).

The vital Qi necessary to this talent belongs to all creatures in the universe. This Qi contains both creative talents and their gifted understanding. Each creature relies on this creative Qi to sustain its life. This secret Qi is granted by God's creative power and charged by Goddess's love power. We have paid for the death of the meaning and the understanding of our life Qi. Since payment has been made, the talent is conceived within, and stealing is the most passionate life-threatening tapping into this secret gate. This vital Qi goes far beyond what our ordinary mind can comprehend, regardless of how talented and successful we are. The mind just cannot untangle it. Able to share each other's talents promote the power of love. This power opens the door to the mystery. Stealing each other's talents brings about one's own self-destruction, since others flourish on these talents as well. Just open the heart and promote the love. It is the most powerful tool for awakening the wonder of talent. When the innate talent is discovered, the sinful action of stealing is transformed into the power of mutual growth and enhancement as they are joined in the adventure of love.

This love further invites the light of creation. When the light shines, everything is visible, evident, and meaningful. This is the presence of life within the frame of time and space where life is an energetic force (a battery) existing within time and space. That is the Talent of God. When life becomes individualized, and its meaning personalized, then life existing as formalized energy is over. All the individual forms can do is to steal everything from one another, from talent, to techniques, to love, and to the context and the very meaning of life itself.

When the individual talents become the objects of stealing, various similar minded people may institutionalize their own talents into a collective power in order to safeguard them. In a modern civilized environment, an institution represents an authorized space where all the individual life forces are being sold or stolen, bargained for willingly and leached from voluntarily. We all thrive on God's talented tricks. We all thrive on each other in the world where we pay everyone for what is, in reality, the vital force belonging to the creative power of God's wisdom.

In spiritual journey, there is no need to steal, only awakening transformation. What has been transformed is the talent that has been reopened by longing, re-charged by love, and re-experienced through union. When we demonstrate our talent, we willingly display God's creative talent and we express our love. To understand this talent is to understand God's creative secretive formula. To express our love is to demonstrate our innocent yet pure action. The positive way is to submit onself, to surrender oneself, and to die in it with grace and joy. Then God's creative secretive formula is self evidential (through our love). Nothing needs to be hidden secretively, controlled vigorously, and glorified deadly. Everything is visible to the spiritual eye, essential to the soul, and vital to the gut. Flow is the mechanism; each flow is a crossing bridge that leads to the next land which is built upon another bridge, and each flow is an expression of love which invites more loving expression. Willful stealing behavior becomes willingly expressive action. The flow never stops, love never dries (it is fat and rich), and mechanism never dies. This is the individual way, the spiritual way, and conscious way.

The negative way is found by stealing (which belongs to God anyway) God's secret formula from other creatures, whether they be minerals or living beings, spiritual understanding or intellectual formulation. This has led to intellectual rationalization, systematic formation, numerical formulation, profitable manipulation. The technique is to first decode, deform, and deconstruct, followed then by repeating, researching, and retesting until the mechanical operation within a system becomes as automatic as the instinctive behavior in any organism. In this way, there can be no spiritual or emotional selves visible since these energetic qualities have already been transformed into mechanical automation. Fearfully and conditionally, those living in this way cling to their thinking habits, they embrace their conditional operations as the way to consume themselves, and they trust their technological advancement to the degree that the invisible God within emerges as the visible machine. This is the fearful way, the institutional way, and the stealing way.

In between these two ways, one discovers God's creative hidden talent within the darkness of disparity, through the vulnerable excess, by means of compulsive discharge, or after the death of all conditional efforts. In this order, love becomes the will power, emotional expression manifests intellectually as charged instinct, spiritual awareness emits the guiding light. To be perfectly honest, this order is inspired by the sheer power of will for survival, not for the pure purpose of sustaining the existing body, but maintaining voluntarily the conscious presence and loved reality.

When we are controlled by the negative way, we cling tightly to the understandings of these talents, fearful not to release them, and suspiciously inviting more stealing power. Consequently, our fear and selfishness invite more stealing actions, instigating an endless battle of violent actions. We label each other thieves, aware that others want to steal the same talents which we have stolen, discovered and inspired from God without our permission, or without exorbitant payment. The only right remaining is the act of stealing. The most joyful and rewarding power to steal is borne of love, the passion of love, hidden behind the curtain of love.

The origin of this phenomena began with Adam and Eve. The apple "represents" God's creative secret formula. The content of the apple is Love. The juice within the apple is the loving vibration. The appearance of the apple represents God's illumination and self-destructive invitation. Adam and Eve stole God/Goddess's secretive formula of Love, the most powerful combination of talent. That is how the five thieves (five elements) have mutually benefitted one another since the beginning of the cosmic evolution.

It is in this context, therefore, that this stealing power demonstrates the power of talent, and it is the power of talent that provides the opportunity of stealing. Within each given talent, there exists numerous acts of stealing, yet the action of stealing never moves beyond the talent created within. As soon as there is a complete understanding of the gift following the procession of thefts, the gate into the creative talent is closed tightly and permanently, nothing can be further known until another creative talent establishes its new environment. Talent descends from nowhere, while the incessant act of stealing abounds everywhere.

As God's creative creatures, we have nothing in ourselves other than God's built-in creative formula. Within this formula, the mind is filled with wisdom and talent, the body is a hungry thief. Love is a gift, intellect plays the role of the thief. Talent is the visible light and the thief will find it inside the secured box within the dark room. The consent is given from God to his creative talents of active and secretive stealing power. These permissions are in the form of the vital flow of cosmic Qi.

Stealing and stealing, until we reach a point of no return, we then enter into the secretive creative talent. Undetectable love, invisible love, the knowing that God's light and Goddess's dark force are constantly stealing from one another, embracing one another, and promoting the mutual creative power in the Cosmic universe, we are forever one with everything, life, time, and space.

Taoism treats nothing as either good or bad. Rather, it views everything as neutral, allowing one to approach it and constantly benefit from it without possessing or harming it. To fully display the potential talent is a talent in itself, and to successfully steal what the talent conceives requires an equally talented pursuit. Knowing how the talent works by stealing is more adventurous and challenging than learning it is concealed within itself. The theft harbors the talent and its mastering talented formula as well. The talent is the master, and its talented formula is the process to master. When the talent displays itself openly, theft becomes the follower. When the talent displays its power secretly, theft follows. When love is expressed unconditionally, it draws more love. When love becomes selfish and lustful, it destroys the virtue of love, inviting only ongoing hatred and violence. "Everyone recognizes beauty as beauty, since the ugly is also there. Everyone recognizes goodness as goodness, since evil is also there." (2:1) Talent must meet its challenger, the counter-active-talent of stealing. The two feed upon each other mutually, relatively, co-operatively, and co-dependently. The talent will defend itself fully, and the thief then discovers it inexhaustibly.

Yet, there is something that "is exceeding the Heavenly Emperor." (4:5) It does all the jobs, plays all the tricks, and resolves all the solutions in the universe. More precisely, it is the simple and magnificent Tao. Laoist defines this as "Tao is the conductor of all things. The treasure of the good. The protection of the bad." (62:1) Thief and virtue are the interactive devices circulating between the good and the bad. Treasure and its protector become the sacrificial devotees, through their exchange of the good for the bad. Knowledge and virtue advance each other from bad to good. "Using knowledge to govern the country, knowledge itself becomes the thief of the country. Not using knowledge to govern the country, knowledge itself is the Action of the country." (65:3) Between the two is the "subtle principle" and "being in the tow of enlightenment." The teaching of Laoism makes full use of this principle by declaring that: "For everything that is good is the teacher of the good person. Everything that is bad becomes a resource for the good person. No need to honor the teachers. No need to love the resources. Though knowing this is a great paradox, it is the subtle principle." (27:3,4)

The good in a good person is personalized by kindness, virtue, and oneness with the Tao. A good person performs good deeds by positioning her/himself at a neutral place, and by then working on the bad through the good. The word thief in both the Secret Evolution Text and Tao Te Ching has a positive connotation. The force that attracts the thief is the force containing the secrecy. Without secrecy, what is there to be stolen? Myriad lives depend upon each other's secrets, since secrets inspire uncontrollable curiosity, unspeakable excitement, adventurous exploitation, and passionate pursuit into the hidden truth. This hidden truth is the secrecy. If not by stealing, how could one attain it by any other means. Adam and Eve knew this. The CIA knows this well. As did former KGB. Love knows it all, penetrating every aspect of it.

## Before the Secrecy of Stealing

Human action is mystically balanced between openly displaying the talent and carefully hiding the secret. The most powerful talent is to reveal God's discipline and the most deeply hidden secret is the Love. Love is the inexhaustible talent that you must live with it, and a priceless weapon worth dying for. Love is an unfathomable fountain. Love is the breath of life. Talent is a gift and Love is sacrifice. When the gift from God and the sacrifice made by the Goddess are unified, mystic wonder blossoms into spontaneous action, sacrifice becomes unconditional love and the cosmic vital Qi of life itself.

Two types of people operate behind the secrecy: one group feels that everything they know is the secret because they either guard it selfishly or exaggerate its simple importance. They selfishly withhold from God's talent. They clutch whatever their selfishness desires, unaware that it will gain them nothing. It is a futile endeavor. God's secret opens only to those who stand by the gate of the secretive talent. When someone presumes to know everything through their intellect only, without tapping into the creative talent, nothing will be disclosed. Should they go so far as to claim God's creative talent as their own, the vital Qi within the priceless gift of talent withers and dies. Selfishness can only serve to close the gate to the gifted talent.

The other group of people takes the position that everything they possess is God's mercifulness and everything they do not know is God's secret. They never hold onto what they have already understood and experienced. They know how to free themselves and start anew. Each time they encounter God's given miracles, they liberate themselves through their understanding of God's disciplined talent. To these people, the drive itself is the hidden truth, the undiscovered territory, and inexperienced reality connecting God's invisible discipline and Goddess's unconditional Love. Goddess's creative loving force can never be conditioned nor will it ever be. God's invisible talent is never selfish and cannot be personalized.

In our human consciousness, to display is the action of will, and to hide comes from the fear that lurks in us all. Truth lives with secrecy. Talent exists with fear. Secrecy is both mystic and imaginative. Fear is both egoistic and realistic. Talent is fearful before the thief, it dreads the loss of its power. Thief is fearful before the talented power, because it fears being further exploited and controlled by the talent. In life, fear stands between death and loss: death is unknown, and loss does not want to define its self-truth. We are fearful of dying. We do not want to lose our "conditioned predictable" life and enter the unknown. Because we cling to our fear, we are unable to grasp the true reality of the consciously dying process.

Fear is both the hidden treasure and life destroyer in our life, the self protector and powerful defender. How many of our actions have already been precipitated by fear? Why do we continue to use so much of our energies protecting ourselves from our projected mind game? What are we protecting ourselves from? How can we protect ourselves from the imagined and unknown? What is the point of defending ourselves? It is nothing but fear that drives us in our habitual thinking process. Fear must be overcome before one can be born-again. Fear can be the means and momentum, giving rise to the drive behind many ambitious business endeavors. And it can also conversely stifle our inner creativity.

Laoist's wisdom is that "Through discrimination, I have the knowledge to walk in the great Tao. The only fear is what is other than that." (53:1) This discriminative power does not refer to the conscious and conditional ego power, but to the power of light and the Rock of self-discipline. Through this discrimination, the path of the Tao and the drive of fear are naturally separated. Before one walks on the great path of the Tao, s/he is surrounded by fear. After receiving the seed of faith, one is guided by light, love is the power, and virtuous deeds are the succulent juice of the great apple. Liberating oneself from fear is liberation from the fear of death. When one walks on the great path of the Tao, death is nothing other than sustaining more deeply with the great source within the Mother. The Mother is a Widow, She never dies, but is dying into every living creature. Our body is a widow, never dying but ever changing through all the experiences and changes.

Laoism sees this as a fearful societal reaction. The message is "The great Tao is quite smooth, yet people prefer a short-cut. The court is so busy legislating that the fields go uncultivated and granaries are all empty. They wear the magnificent clothing, girdle the sharp swords. They are gorged with food and possess many brides. Their bounty suffices but they do not quit stealing. This is utterly not Tao." (53:2,3) The drive of fear and the price of lust fester in all the actions taken. People want more and more of everything, regardless of how little the body-mind can digest at any given time in any given situation. The mental fear constantly drives us into the vicious mental VCR-player of continuously reacting with fear, being conditioned and reprogrammed.

In Taoist mentality, fear can be transformed. It is the finest tool we have to liberate ourselves. When we become self-enlightened, we need nothing, and there is no need to please others. Everything we need we already have. Everybody we interact with has mutual interests. When we become fearless, what is fear then useful for? It is pointless, groundless, and meaningless. Without fear, there is no desire to conquer the world, since the world of selves has been conquered. The world continues to be a mixture of yin and yang, the absolute good and bad. This is the Laoist method of using the power of discrimination. He first separates himself from the world in order to embrace the world fully. He transforms fear into kindness and goodwill, rendering himself fearless. Since he has "no place to die" (50:5), he is fearless. The Rock of light pulls him out of the death valley, leaving his already softened white bones as the transformed conscious white mist which awakens seed after seed, spirit by spirit, faith upon faith.

This doesn't completely quell his underlying caution. It is not the fear that provides the cautious mentality, it is the mentality of being Small and Simple. To be cautious is not necessarily being fearful. Caution is a watchful mentality, fear is a will-derived protection. To be fearless is not meant to be bold, daring, and reckless. All Laoists, Lao Zi and other sages, are: "Full of care, as one crossing the wintry stream; Attentive, as one cautious of the total environment; Reserved, as one who is a guest; Spread open, as when confronting a marsh; Simple, like uncarved wood; Opaque, like mud; Magnificent, like a valley." (15:3) This reveals the true psycho-spiritual conditioning of Laoists' experiences. What else could it be! "This is the Tao of having a deep root, a strong stem, a long life, and an enduring vision." (59:3)

## Involutionary Tao

Aside from any particular features, and beyond its combined qualities, the teaching of Laoism concludes that: "Humankind takes its origin from earth. Earth takes her origin from heaven. Heaven takes its origin from Tao. Tao takes its origin from Nature." (25:4) This is the involuntary returning, which is the meaning of knowing and understanding its origin. It is the inspiration to ascend our spirit into its original place. Science remains puzzled with the first sentence "Humankind takes its origin from earth." The conclusion of the scientific evolutionary map is that we are as immortal as bacteria and fungi, and we are as old as the original substance on earth.

Science has not moved one step beyond the second sentence in the teaching of Laoism. It far surpasses the scientific imagination and technological advancement. Our space program can place our bodies, the earthly matters, onto other planets, such as the moon or Mars. Scientists ponder water conditions and other elements that would effect living organism but give no thought to the human body which belongs to no other planet than mother earth. Our spirits had lived together agelessly with the celestial stars, before descending to earth. Solar light is our conscious power. Our spirit communicates with the moon every night. There is no reason or necessity to spaceship our human bodies to other planets. From the dawn of our own biological and spiritual history, we have always been influenced and controlled by the power of moon. What would the nighttime be without the Jade moon? What would the female manifestation be without the moon-rotation?

We cannot classify the moon as primarily feminine, and the sun entirely masculine. Actually the sun is masculine-feminine or yang-yin, and moon is feminine-masculine or yin-yang. Why? The sun's masculine power and its feminine murkiness obscures our vision into the universe. We cannot see stars and planets during daytime. At night, even the moon uses the yin Qi (shadow) of the sun as its reflective light, her masculine power awakening our female nature (dream consciousness) and directing us into the cosmic twilight. We can hide our fear under the blanket hoping to be engulfed in safety, but it proves to be a false safety net. Our spirit detects everything, our body, our behavior, and our egoistic disguise.

Only at night do we truly feel our desperate aloneness, are we aware in our deepest consciousness that we are homeless, and that we understand truly that we are spiritless. That is why we gather together with our loved one(s), gazing into the North Star, and searching for our true spiritual entity somewhere in the Milky Way. Our biological mother's milky breasts cannot sustain us. We know then the Milky Way is our true spiritual mother, the light is our true spiritual father. Through them we have descended to earth, and are constantly longing to return to our original home.

During the day, we think we are conscious, we are aware of our actions, and we are dreaming about our activities. Truly, it is the dark night of the soul. We continuously fight and abuse and betray one another. We just assume that we are conscious, creative, and even spiritual, yet the sun's red fire demolishes our true spiritual functions during the course of the day. We are empty of heart. What can we do about it? Look beyond the sunlight and peer into the cosmic twilight to get a glimmer of what we long for.

Only when we are alone with our inner consciousness, are we free and one with God's creative power and Goddess's loving power. Only when we are aware that we should be with light and dark at the same time, do we become free and complete. Only when we become the gifts of God's creative talent, can we consciously steal God's secretive formula and liberate ourselves thoroughly. Without desiring to hold and hide them, can we transform our stealing behavior into the oneness of the Cosmic Play of God and Goddess.

## Evolutionary Fusion of the Tao

The evolutionary course is described thus, "Tao gives rise to one. One gives rise to two. Two gives rise to three. Three gives rise to all things. All things carry yin and embrace yang. Drawing chi together into harmony." (42:1,2) Taken step by step, Tao weakens; stage after stage, Tao returns. That is how "Tao moves by returning. Tao functions by weakness." (41:1) the returning is an inactive process, and weakness is the way of simplicity. In our human existence, we are moved by our drives, and develop understanding through our inner stillness. This drive pushes us to the edge where stillness stands guard preserving our truth.

Meanwhile, we act through our strength and inspiration, being directed by our will. Our strength is our character, our inspiration is our self-produced food, and our will is our own image. Strength is the character of light, inspiration is the spirit of wisdom, and will is the image of love. Our strength can be measured, our inspiration can be felt, and our will can be envisioned. The strength is the director of the physical demonstration, the inspiration is the power flow, and the will occupies the mental capacity. The strength makes one stand tall, the inspiration fires one to jump up and down in the spirit-train, and the will enables one to move under diversity. Standing before the strength is the self acceptance. Firing by the inspiration is the self-understanding. Surrendering within the will returns the self back to its home. When the self accepts the will, the Tao presents itself; when the self returns, we see that the Tao functions by itself.

The reason Laoism states that "all things carry yin" is that yin is the form of all forms, and it is the formless form. To "embrace" is an action of longing, an activity of returning, an understanding of acceptance, and a submission to the truth. All these are by the empowerment of yang. No thing (object or situation) can encompass yang since it is formless, without structure, and intangible. In conclusion, "All things under heaven are born of being. Being is born of non-being." (41:2) Being is yin (image) of the world. Non-being is the image of the Tao. Tao is the image of Nature.

## Spiritual Action of the Tao

"If Tao is utilized to manage the society, its ghost will not become spirit. Not that ghost is not spiritual, but that the spirit harms no people. Not that the spirit harms not the people, but that sage is harmless. As those two cause no harm, they are united in Action." (60:2,3) This is the only chapter in Tao Te Ching where Lao Zi refers to spiritual action in the ghostly world through the channeling of a sage. And it is the clearest description of the spiritual trinity: spirit, sage, and ghost. In Christianity it is often referred to as Holy Spirit, Holy Father, and Holy Ghost.

There are ghosts in the world that are spiritual in harmful ways. They look constantly to the light power and positive forces to feed them. They are voracious and as powerful as spirit, but lacking in virtue. They desperately need soulful realms, sacred vessels, and whitish matters. They need life, love and light. There are spirits in the universe that cause no harm but sell the living souls/spirits into the spiritual home. They cause no harm to other spirits, yet, are very harmful to the degree that all spirits must be sold. They do not provide an alternative path, only the spiritual one. All the living spirits on earth must be sold to the Kingdom of Heaven. All spirits are powerful, and loving. Ghost knows only how to pull the embodied spirits down, spirit wishes only to raise them up. Only the sage carries these opposite forces and embraces the two into harmonious action.

The sage's body resembles the holy ghost and his spirit symbolizes the holy spirit. Through the sage, Holy Father transcends His Power and Love. Power is the force of Holy Spirit and Holy Ghost. Love is the Action within and between, since both Holy Spirit and Holy Ghost have only love within, can do no more than love each other fully, completely and absolutely. Only when they are united with the sage-like action does, this love cause no harm either to spirits and ghosts or sage and people. Only when the constructive force and the destructive force are united, does virtuous action become the enactment in the universe. Only when one becomes sage-like, does one unify the two oppositions within. Love is seeded to promote a proliferation of loveable spirits. Body is the living temple where all sickened souls can be healed, all the suffering spirits liberated, all the cells crystalized, and all the selves enlightened. Only when God and Goddess are in their eternal and constant harmony, will the universe run its forever changing yet eternally unchanging course. This course is Action, virtuous deed, or unconditional Christ-like love.

Holy Spirit is the yang form of spirit while the earthly spirit is its yin form. Human spirits descend from these two spirits. Evil ghost is the yin form of ghost in hell and on earth, while holy ghost is the yang form of ghost on earth and in heaven. Sage is the embracement tempering the two. In the presence of the sage, ghost diminishes its power. The Christ-like body purifies the murky Qi within the ghost, forging it into a kinder form. Standing before the sage, spirit is more than just spiritual as it takes on a human form bearing its spiritual image thereby embracing its attracting force, the yin or ghost spirit.

Lao Zi doesn't deny the existential and harmful nature of a ghost, nor does he underestimate the power of a spirit. By its very nature, ghost is destructive. This is its natural disposition. Ghost is more harmful than spirit because it feeds on human connection, permeating its presence into human form. Its objective is to destroy the human spiritual connection with light. Ghost reveals exceedingly the dark force in human nature. If a human spirit could avoid becoming a ghost, it would be, at the least, very holy, possibly above human soulful manifestation. Also, spirit has no need to become human in order to deal with intellectual understanding and emotional loving activity. It prefers to remain in its pure form and clean state of spirituality in the heavenly realm.

Holy spirit, however, is bound to perform its duty here on earth, to prevent the living spirit from becoming ghost. That is why spirit is harmful to individual people. The conscious shocking alarm shakes all the conditional habits, destroy them completely. It can and will sell the individual living spirit to God. In order to illuminate what the spirit imbues in the midst of human and animal world, it exercises its powerful nature to still people's consciousness and to awaken their lives to the spiritual transformation. Only through the sage's embodied life and love, will peoples' conscious spirits be altered but not shocked, shocked but not harmed, harmed but not destroyed, destroyed but not punished by being forced into the ghosts' world. It is the holy spirit's role into which the living body is sacrificed, the living consciousness distilled, and the living personality tempered. That is why holy spirit does no harm, but harms the existing individuals. It harms not the people's true spirit, but it destroys all false and ghost-like spiritual identities. Without receiving help from the sage, spirit will burn every living spirit into dust. If this happens, holy spirit does harm so great, it cannot be measured or qualified.

The inescapable truth that there is a need for the sage to interact between the ghostly and the spiritual worlds is that both ghost and spirit must exercise their necessary power. And they are equally powerful. The two powers are the essence of dark and light, the destructive and the creative, the material and the spiritual, and finally, the earthly and the heavenly. In one respect, ghosts wish to teach human and animal souls the lesson that their soulful nature must encounter the ghostly world in order to serve as the dark ground, the evil power, and the destructive force. Hell is the ultimate destination of these souls. The dark force has the power of deforming without reason, killing without mercy, and remaining without transformation. Opposing this force, spirit does not wish to relinquish its realistic hope of returning the human and animal souls to their original spiritual creation. That is why the light force illuminates without invitation, knows without understanding, and exists without becoming.

Fortunately, sage embraces both worlds by appeasing both sides. Sage is the justice circulating between yes and no, a healer between the healthy mind and the sickened soul, a medium between the inner conscious thoughts and outer expressive actions, a bridge connecting both sides of a river, and a rainbow arching splendidly displaying its light connecting earth and sky, water and rain, color and light. Because of the sage, ghost is elevated and thus reduces its hellish power. The holy spirit drifts into our realm, and becoming less spiritual than it was in the heavens.

Sage is a shaman, a channeller, a medium, and a healer. Sage makes the ghost gentler and less harmful by raising it up into the holy forms, either human or animal spiritual forms. Sage also draws the holy spirit down to earth to demonstrate its kindness and dispel its aloofness. That is the essence of the holiness of a sage engaging in Taoist action. He enlightens the world and all its inhabitants. Nothing rejects him and he abandons nothing. He is there for all lives and within everything existing. He embraces God's consciousness and Goddess's love within. What a sublime role God has cast for him, what a magnificent body Goddess has bestowed upon him!

## The Tao in the Couplet

This ninth character in the couplet can be rightly interpreted as "the nature of self always acts in conjunction with the power of the Tao without distancing itself from the virtue of Action." The literal meaning of this character can be roughly interpreted as "A right person is a person who has the inch large Tao within himself." Or "The right mind is the way that enables a person to stand on the inch-large space within the body." Comparing this to the second character in the couplet, we see this one, too, is about the mind, which is the resource of the Tao and the sound-like-vibrating-Tao of universe itself. The mind manifests with the Action through attaining true quality toward the bodily growth and its nourishment.

The holy spirit is the cellular formation of a cosmic body which is governed by the seven cosmic star bodies (e.g. our emotional bodies) and nine constellation bodies (the nine holes within our bodies). The seven facial holes (spiritual) and the two bottom holes ( biological) are the visible holes in the heavenly constellations. Within the seven facial holes, there are three paired holes, two eyes for sight, two nostrils for smell, and two ears for hearing. They are constructed above the upper jaw, working together with the lower jaw's action of biting and chewing, babbling and belaboring. We are micro-cosmic bodies.

The entire function of our body is governed by one tongue and two hands. The tongue announces its presence and capacities to the world. The hands manipulate and destroy the world. In animal life, the mouth, teeth and tongue are the main food carriers and processors. Feet are the walking wheels. Lips and tongue collect the food and direct the teeth's biting and chewing process. Tongue, at times, also serves as the washing tool (Taoists has developed a saliva producing exercise based upon observing animal washing behavior). In contrast, the human hands collect (including planting and cultivating) and prepare the food, tongue stimulates the secretion of digestive enzymes emitted through three pairs of salivary glands located around the lower jaw. The stroke for "inch" that makes up part of the eighth Laoist character represents the proximal phalanx of the pointing index finger.

An adult's proximal phalanx is about an inch long, which is the oldest standard measurement in Chinese calculation. Two hands together form ten digital proximal phalanxes, representing the division of ten. There are twenty seven bones in each hand: eight in the wrist, five in the body of the hand, and 14 in the fingers. The total number of 54 is one number short of the sum of the addition from one to ten which is 55. The missing number is in the hand of Goddess's creation. God forms five creative disciplines, and Goddess makes one body for the existence of all bodies in the universe. Physically speaking, the thumb has two finger bones instead of three so it can unify the other four three-boned fingers.

In the oldest method of I Ching practice, the total practiced number is 49. Of 55 numbers, five are for heaven, and one is for earth. The five elemental numbers can never be used by man. They belong to God's creative power elements. The division is always based upon four, representing the four corners of the world and four skeletons in the body-mind. Therefore, the five metacarpals or metatarsals are God's creative formula, for the unitary creative discipline of holding and directing and gathering and returning. God's measurements are within the five metacarpals, especially the pointing index metacarpal. This completes the biological illustration and psychological measurement of the term "inch."

Each finger has three bones with the exception of the thumb, which has only two. The missing "bone" within the thumb is the missing power of Goddess's creation, which represents the mystic widow in the heaven's longing, since the beginning of creation of the world, for the connection of oneness. This longed-for oneness represent the completed projection of all creative formation within each and every creature in the world. It also signifies the never ending ongoing process of earth's creative recycling process. In the hand, it is the power of thumb. Two bones within the thumb work together with the other four fingers, representing the twelve seasons (twelve bones). The thumb stands in the midst of creative power, controlling the four directions, and administering the cycling and recycling process.

Each finger represents one season from index finger to the little finger, and each bone represents one month. They work together with the twelve thoracic bones governing the five organic Qi. These five organic Qi, in turn, regulate the twelve seasonal reactions, and the twelve cranial nerves which channel the twelve meridians. In Taoist tradition, the index finger designates the spring season, the liver organ, the greenish blue color/plant, the consciousness/human soul. The middle finger represents the summer season, the heart organ, the reddish brown color/warm animal, passion/spiritual seat. The ring finger stands for the fall season, the golden pink color/spiritual insight, happiness/successful accomplishment. The little finger represents the winter season, the blackened white color/ash and transformation.

All the finger bones, total fourteen, work together with seven cervical bones. They form spiritually grounded awakening, and they transform the physical and emotional bodies into intellectual and wisdom bodies. When the conscious thoughts are transmitted through the twelve cranial system and their never ending processing, the message divides at the fifth thoracic spine and is released through the two hands. The seven cervical spines shine the energy of rainbow color into five organic Qi. The body then becomes the action, the executor, and the pilgrim. Everything then ties in with the work of the thumb. The two bones of the thumb agree with everything, including itself.

In Taoist tradition, the calender is mapped with the twelve joints of the four fingers. Starting from the ring finger, the joint between metacarpal and proximal phalanx, the left hand thumb counts clockwise the next eleven joints, including four finger tips, circulating around the four fingers, and stops at the little finger. The twelve animals, twelve earth's branches and twelve months are all in the circulation of four fingers. By adding eight hexagrams and nine palaces, the complete calculation of the Chinese calender is moving and rotating magically and mystically within the left hand.

The eight wrist bones represent the eight joints within the body, three in arms and legs and two in the body trunk. They also equal the number of cranial bones in the brain skull. The five metacarpal bones represent the body of five creative elements. The fourteen finger bones represent the unity of the creation of seven, with one side being yin and the other side yang. There are also fourteen bones in the face. The total number of joints again make up fourteen: six along the shoulders, six along the hips, one for the neck and one for the abdomen. The number of bones between hands and feet is equal, making up a bit over half of the entire number of bones in the body, which totals 206. These 108 bones are the 108 martialists that guard and protect our body-mind. The two extra bones above the half are part of the mystic function of thumb. Where is the single extra bone above the half? (103 is the half, with thumbs occupying four among the five extra bones)

As for the tongue, it is the measurement of speech and the indicator of the condition of our health. The tongue can punish people more psychically than the hands could do physically. (E.g. The order of execution is exercised not through the hands but through the tongue.) Food processing is organized by the tongue in the activity of mastication (chewing) and deglutition (swallowing). The double (or double-edged) function of the tongue makes speech tasteful, detects the various conditions and tastes of food, such as warm, cold, sweet, sour, bitter, and salty (stubborn). "But the tongue can no man tame: it is an unruly evil, full of deadly poison." (James 3:8) It is not because the tongue is evil by nature, but because "out of the same mouth proceeded blessing and cursing." (James 3:10) Without tasting abilities, physical security cannot be ensured, emotional conditions cannot be measured, intellectual capacities cannot be detected, the spiritual heart cannot be perceived. The human tongue is such that it gives birth to all human actions with the exception of the biological birth process. In all other areas as well as in sexual activity, the tongue plays a major role.

In the eyes of spiritual practice, it is the function of tongue that builds the bridge between heavenly line (governing meridian) and earthly line (protective meridian) enabling the biological water and spiritual fire to circulate internally without leakage. Diseased Qi, materialistic or mental, will not enter the body-mind. The spiritual Qi, sexual or soulful, will not be exterminated. Taoists call this "building the bridge." The technique is to place the tip of the tongue on the hard palate to reconnect the two meridians. In pre-heaven conditioning, these two meridians (the energy lines) are eternally connected through one channel, the umbilical cord. In post-heaven conditioning, the unbiblical cord extends into nine holes in the body. If poisoned food enters the body through the mouth, the diseased Qi is expressed through the mouth. They are both governed by the ability of the tongue.

In life, it is the tongue that carries out the invisible order, and it is the metacarpal carrying out the visible measurement. The Chinese character Tao is the construction of "head" stroke and "foot' stroke. In this eighth Laoist character, the "inch" stroke is placed at bottom, representing the grounding point and the Rock-like standing position. The Tao of consciousness is alternated by the tongue, and the Tao of action is projected by the hands. The head part of the conscious Tao is controlled by speech, and the feet part of the active Tao is extended by the hands. The interaction between head and feet is coordinated by the tongue and hands. The trinity of the Tao (invisible, inaudible, and intangible) is expressed by the trinity ( head, foot and metacarpal) of the body-mind. Collectively, the Way of life is secretively and invisibly controlled by the "inch large Tao" of tongue and "inch size Tao" of finger bones. Tongue provides the direction, and bones calculate the measurement. The inner spiritual consciousness, the vibration of thought, the stream of emotions, the vocal power and communicative, expressive hands act in harmony of One.

This is the pictorial representation of the Tao, with head, foot and inch-size-measurement. This is the "inch" size passage for the right existing everywhere. Human beings are right within the six realms of the world. The head looks up, the feet stand down. The male (the right hand/body) rises from the east, the female (the left hand/body) shines from the west. The consciousness (willful action) moves forward, Spirit (peaceful solution) reaches backward. This is the right Tao, and this is the right "inch" size Tao.

## What Is Tao?

The word Tao is probably the single most important yet difficult character in this book and in the entire history of Taoism and Chinese culture. It is so not only in the mind's absorbing of the Tao, but also in the eye's envisioning the Tao; not in the ability of acting through the Tao, but the inability to detect the Tao, as well. In the Tao Te Ching, there are 35 chapters and 62 sentences using the Chinese character "Tao." Still, Lao Zi had never completed his teaching either in conversation or by recording his teachings of the Tao. His work is done, yet his teaching goes on forever. His writing is completed, yet, his spiritual message will never be understood fully. No living creature can fully interpret the Tao, and no human can completely express the Tao.

Yet, the structure of the Tao is always complete universally. The content of the Tao has already been characterized ideally. The function of the Tao has forever been expressed individually. God has completed his Work. Goddess has completed her Creation. Spirit has finished its journey. It is done, here, now, and forever.

Still, God's light is always shining, and Goddess's love remains alive in each and every creature, from ideas and thoughts, to wishes and longing. These never die, and will never face death. They are the presence, the timing, and the interactive space between matters and their forces, and between inner consciousness and their vibrant expression. The power of the Tao never disappears. The Love of the Tao never dies. The harmony of the union is never extinguished. There is always someone waiting in the Silent Spirit. There is always someone listening to the inspiration of creative messages. There is always someone of a new mind/spirit/generation continuously speaking the Tao which remains unfathomable, beyond total comprehension.

In the history of Taoist tradition as imposed upon the Laoist mentality, Lao Zi's literal interpretation of the Tao was naturally limited; if not, there would have been nothing more to express. Ever and still, Lao Zi could not have envisioned the interpretation of the Tao as a cultural ongoing enterprise. Regardless of any assumptions on his part, the way of life is ever the way of life, and the way of transforming the life is forever the way of transformation of life. National or international, cultural or cross-cultural, we all speak and write according to our cultural and human behavior, individually and collectively. The Tao is such that there is never enough to form its completion: its void remains empty. There can never be enough-as-such to conclude the function of the Tao: its ever returning motion remains ever-changing. There is never an absolute mentality to convey the true meaning of the Tao: its eternal weakness remains untouched. There is never an everlasting spirituality to replace the power of the Tao: its nature of the forever and always Nature remains present. Tao is beyond everything, above all things, and includes No Thing.

Having reached this point, the most difficult area to describe is pinpointing the exact location of that "inch large Tao," which indicates the size, the grounding spot, the focusing point, and the conscious intention.

The biological representation is the unification between the pineal gland and the tail bone where cosmic light fires up the fossilized crystal bone within the pineal gland through God's conscious state. The final outcome of the glandular purification is the measurement of this "inch large Tao," called golden elixir.

Yet, there is no way that it can be located in a specific place within the body as long as the spirit is alive. Before it can be identified, it is always there; when you focus on it, it disappears; when you cease to concentrate on it, it reappears. It is in no place but it is everywhere. It doesn't abide in any specific location but is boundless. It is God's conscious fire within the Goddess's creative love. Nobody can grasp it and no one ever will! This golden elixir governs both spiritual and conscious life, both masculine and feminine energy, both understanding and love, both self-discipline and self-sacrifice. It is the most singular power substance in the universe. The secret meaning and power of all lives reside in this wishfully detectable but unknown space.

## Tao and Nature

Because "Tao enlivens. Action nourishes. Matter forms. Mechanism completes." (51:1) This Tao is Nature, since "Tao takes its origin from Nature." (25:1) But how to define Nature is the puzzle. The Random House College Dictionary states the Nature is, for example: 1) "the universe, with all its phenomena," 2) "the sum total of the forces where these exist at work thorough the universe." These two definitions can be combined into one complete meaning, that is, "all the phenomena and forces occur in and exist through the universe, including the Universe Itself." But it engenders a distanced feeling with a remote sensation and a passionless view point.

In contrast, in Yong Ji Chi Jian the condensed Taoist encyclopedia, is contained one of the best descriptions I have encountered, more accurate than any of the scientific explanations proposed. It says: "I do not know why It (Nature) is so, and I do not know why It is not so; I cannot make It as such, and I cannot make It as not such." The subjective explanation is that we could never know completely what Nature is. Nature is beyond the limits of knowing and extremes of comprehension. What can be the use of "knowing" It? The objective side of the story is that Nature is beyond the manipulation of human minds (structural) and their hands (mechanical).

According to the description of Laoism, the space and time of the substance of the Tao is "boundless and unfathomable," within such a spaceless and timeless center are "form" and "object." Form is the creative image, the constructive system, and the transformative trend: it is the Great Mother's creative loving force. Form is Oneness. The object is the spirit of nature, the power of the Tao, and self of God. Thereafter, there exists the life force that ensures the embryonic growth out of darkness. The power that generates this life force is the purity of trust. Trust is the utmost important insurance for the substance of the Tao. It is the returning point of being One again with the true nature of that substance, which is itself the substance of Nature. Because of this trust in the substance of Tao, "From now to the day of old, its name never dies." (21:2)

In standard text, the sentence "From now to the day of old." reads as "From the day of old till now." which translates as the typical linear notion and sequential order of the human thinking pattern. The fact is that Tao is always present, God is always present. Our human life is nothing but a four-to-six generational group running endlessly along the course of our eternal spiritual life and external experiential life, as the changes of day to night and again night to day. Before this, the history of time was stored in the memory, either through biogenetic mutation and transformation, or through oral communication and linguistic symbols. Since then, the future became an imaginative land, a mechanical calculation, and a biological destination. The present is the condensed energy form, the extracted substances, and the highlighted demonstration. Now is the show, the play, and the perfection. Everything that has happened in history is happening now, since history as an energy cycle repeats itself. All the historical information, whether recorded or not, is reappearing. Energetically, there is no difference between information being experienced million of years ago and its refreshed experience being lived in the present. The only change is the role played and the form taken. The role is the personal play, the form is the individual and cultural makeup.

For example, we have been eating the same food for thousands and thousands of years: wheat is always wheat, and rice is never wheat. Whether to burn the wheat from the freshly harvested ground or to collect it and mill it into flour, the basic chemical elements remain unchanged. The same truth applies to our body and life. A love story which happened centuries ago may be exactly re-experienced by someone here and now. An idea flashed in someone's mind in the past may manifest now. Yet, the basic information contained in the idea remains the same. Dalai Lama is always Dalai Lama. Christ's Love is forever Christ Love. The harmony of the Tao is the endless Way.

Another example might be that traveling is traveling. Whether by air or by sea, walking barefoot or driving a car, the essential meaning involved in traveling is unchanged. Whether personal, commercial or spiritual, traveling is a pilgrimage. It is always driven by the mental desire, hope, and expectation. Most importantly, it must consume the energy generated in the body in order to cover the distance. If walking, the energy is spent from the body itself. When driving, we spend the money on the car or pay the cost of a ticket to get to our destination, which is in turn the energy exchanged, saved or owned by the body and mind. If you have no desire to make a business trip, there is no need to invest the time and money. Life is an energetic ball game. The present moment is the running, operating, playing, and experiencing moment. Your whole world is here and now. When you sleep, the world sleeps with you. If you kill something, the world shares the killing. This world is the world of your mind, our mind, and everybody's mind. If you do not sense the existence of your life, bodily or spiritually, what then is the existence of life?

Before the existence of our present living group, biological memory had already been stabilized. This means that, basically, our eyes or lungs are no different than that of our ancestors millions of years ago. The mobility of eyes toward light and darkness has taken numerous generations of timeless practices. This organic mechanical movement of contraction and expansion becomes a biologically stored automatic behavior. This is the evolutionary explanation. Creatively speaking, this behavior is genetically coded and biologically constructed at one time from the very beginning by some higher power creator.

Equally, oral tradition has similar fashion. It is a socially enabled learned process, as mechanical as the biological process of the eyes or the knees. Oral tradition takes more side tracks since oral memory creates countless misimprints. Each individual recalls events differently and in each time it reflects specifically. Also, oral tradition evolves with numerous changes along its course. These changes are both personal and cultural. Personal and generational influence play a crucial role in these ongoing changes of usage in the oral, as well as written, tradition. Normally, these changes do not necessarily destroy the biological existence. Sometime, as a result of the mis-imprint of the oral message received, turmoil or disasters occur. But if we receive a false message about war and disaster, it would not necessarily be destructive. Y2K is a prime example of impending misuse of communication possibly causing havoc or chaos.

Along the line of oral communication, when something we say is misinterpreted, we then need to explain it more clearly. And if the listener then understands our intentions, and is pleased, this oral message would take on a new and different meaning. Gradually, from one person to another and one situation to another, the oral messages proliferate and become more sophisticated and confusing. The message given by a crying voice in the beginning of life develops itself into a completed picture of a linguistic system. Ever so, this system constantly changes and never completes itself. Worse than enough, it is only half truth.

When all is said and done, it depends primarily on the adaptability, and more importantly, the mental intention and choice of communication. Laoism states eloquently that "The person who works according to Tao unites with Tao. In the same way he unites with action. In the same way he unites with loss. Uniting with action, the Tao becomes action. Uniting with loss, the Tao becomes loss." (24:4,5) In this way, belief is seen as a choice, longevity is a choice, and immortality is also a choice. They all depend on what we are united with. Tao is a choice toward immortality, action is a choice toward longevity, and belief is a choice resulting in loss.

## Naming the Nameless Tao

In order to discriminate various things, we name them. In order to identify them, we label them. In order to make use of them, we possess them. Name then becomes the mentally identified reality, label creates the controllable identity, and usage becomes the practical obsession.

Essentially, that is how we discriminate ourselves. In the end, as in the beginning, God loses His great image. God becomes an empty network of a mental system whereby everyone defines her/his own God within. Goddess becomes a victim of hateful, violent, and criminal actions. The humanity is then lost into the professionally identified labels. We are no longer human, we are labels. Love is a label, success is a label, sickness is a label, and death is a label. Following the usage becomes the make-believe personification. We make and operate machinery to perform what we have done manually in the past. We make love by enacting a loveable and attractive performance. We let our life proceed miserably. We choose to suffer in the name of religion. We are forcing God to struggle madly to entangle and reroute us. In a name-constructed society, the name becomes the self-induced and self-seeking God. That is what our ego calls upon and eventually destroys. When one ego designates a god, another ego flares up in defense of its own named god. Above all others, God, in his infinity, watches as an ego-defined and ethnocentric identity. He becomes all God and then No-God. This is not the case with the Tao.

"Tao is eternally nameless." (32:1, 37:1) Therefore, "When the Tao is spoken forth, plainly: It has no flavor at all. Look, but that is not sufficient for seeing. Listen, but that is not sufficient for hearing. Use it, but it is not exhausted." (35:3,4) Being nameless and undetectable before the human perception, Tao remains in its undivided and unsuffused simplicity. It is so simple and so plain that it enables the source of all things in the universe.

When people ask me what my religion is, I reluctantly reply "Taoism," for there is pain within the heart. It is so difficult to call it by name. But what else can I call it? I am a Taoist by name, but not a Taoist by nature: Tao is nameless. I am a Taoist by choice, but not a Taoist by voice: Tao is nameless. I am nameless. Who am I? God answers the silence with silence. What am I as I stand before the Tao? Tao is plain, simple, silent. I cannot picture myself with any other choice. I ask Goddess, why am I here? The Goddess Widow sheds tears without showing any sign of direction. Where will I return to? What can I do? I identify the God as the self in order to be identified mentally. I make the Goddess the Widow to glorify my sexuality. I make myself miserable , knowing that there is suffering beyond suffering

Before the eye of Tao, everything is "simple, like uncarved wood." (15:3) including the Tao itself. What can I then do? "Observe the plain and embrace the simple. Do not think much and do not desire much. Get rid of learning and worry will disappear." (19:3) I realize, as Lao Zi did, "Though simplicity is small, the world cannot treat it as subservient. If lords and rulers can hold on to it, everything becomes self-sufficient." (32:2) "If lords and rulers would abide by it, all things would evolve of themselves." (37:1) Oh, the Lord within me! Oh, the Lords of selves! How can abide by it? The distance voice echoes: "For the world, the sage keeps the mind simple." (49:3)

To this Lao Zi responds: "When I choose non-desire, people remain simple." (57:4) He is speaking the truth by saying that: "Those who practiced Tao in olden times did not enlighten people, rather they made people simple. What makes it hardest to govern people is what they know." (65:1) Also, people are the images of me as themselves. When I know what I know, I control the situation. I feel safe and I am protected. But if I acknowledge my unknowing to the knower, I would be banished as a fool and treated worse than a fool. I am truly "a fool at heart, as a water droplet is to the spring." (20:5)

By the time I know in my heart that I have no desire to know what I don't know, I am locked in a prison of self destruction. Finally, by the time I close my distracted eyes, the instinctive lungs and hell-bent maddening heart, I would know nothing before the knowing, the knowledge, and the known. Simplicity, I feel, is truly the way. Is it too late? No, never. I can return to life again to tell people that simplicity is the way. What I have found is that it is too late: people don't want simplicity, they want to know more; they don't want clean water, they just want drink; they don't want organic food, they want to contaminate themselves; they don't want to preserve their health, they want to label their diseases. Knowing how they are killing themselves, I realize that I am truly a fool at heart.

I am happy to be a fool at heart. I am great, as the world is great. "Tao is great. Heaven is great. Earth is great. Kingship is great. These are the four great things in the world, kingship is one of them." (25:3) "I am a fool at heart" tells me: "Great refers to the symbol. The symbol refers to what is remote. What is remote refers to returning." (25:4) I am a kingship, but don't tell the dictator, s/he will kill you, if you dare say that "I am Great." The symbol I envision is what the Great I am actually is. The symbol I envision is the remote. Standing at the seashore and gazing at the remote, everything returns. The sky returns, the sea returns, and my envisioned symbol returns. This Is Great!

I then stand at the edge of the calming echoless sea and shout into the endless blue sky: "All things return, yet there is no claim of ownership, so it is forever without desire. This can be called small. All things return, yet there is no claim of ownership. This can be called great." (34:2) I am free and having no ownership, I desire nothing. Here, right here is all. The mind is without desire, the feet are without desire, the sea is without desire, the sky is without desire, and the returning, whatever it is, is always without desire. This is the quintessence of what can be called great. It is that simple!

## The Tao of Mind

Tao is produced from the stomach, announced through the mouth, and extracted by the mind. Within this sameness, there exists the differences. The differences are no more than the desire for more of everything and the will of continuously existing. This is why people should never be bored with their lives. This is why life is always an inspiration, a challenge, a hope, and a reward itself. When we do feel bored, it is in the condition of mind; when we get excited, it is the excitement of mind. Mind is such that we can never have enough of it, it is so vast that is ever expanding and new. We can never estrange ourselves from it.

If we claim that we don't have the mind, then what is the drive, the direction, and the purpose of our life? When we seek adventure or travel or make appointments, it is the mind that programs and directs all by evaluating everything. Body is just a service person to be the carrier of the constant orders and supervision of mind. All human action originates in the mind, is projected through the mind, and rewarded by the mind.

When we speak of having the mind, we are unable to identify its independent existence except through the energetic waves being emitted among people. The religious persons say that mind is spirit. It is mind that engages the actual work of worship. It is the mind that initiates the reunion between man and God. Heart is at least as important as mind, if not more so, for heart is blinded by mind. Praying and chanting and meditating are the real workshops for the mind. Heart is its honest companion watching silently, ever at its side.

Scientists assume that mind is an invisible inventor of machine. Because they have stated that Universe Is A Great Machine, scientists propose another hypothesis stating that mind is a thinking machine. They think that all the human commodities are natural objects. They do not realize that they are nothing other than an objectified model of mind.

Without the input of thought, how can envision going to the moon in a spaceship; without thinking of healing ourselves, how could we have discovered medicine; without the desire to communicate, how can we establish a global telecommunication system? All these come about through the power of mind. Our Mind is a sexual device that generates, produces, and accumulates the elements of our human cultural products. Mind becomes a machine. It is the machine, the object of our mind, that generates our cultural life, and especially the industrial life. All these are started not from the source of life but from the mechanism of life. If there were no thought pattern to communicate mental and physical information, there would be no purpose for language. If there were no desire for stable temperature in the living environment, how could we have devised mechanical devices to condition heat and air-conditioning to regulate the room temperature.

We have restrained our mind to such a degree that everything existing in the world is like a mechanical device. When the mind reduces the form, or the momentum of universe into its projected device, the machine, the whole world lives in that mental structure, that is the creation of its existence and prediction of its duration. The mind becomes the object. Neither the universe nor its creatures are objective; nor is the mental idea and the machine it has objectified.

Human understanding and accumulation of his knowledge of the universe is purely subjective to the motions of the myriad creatures. The motions of these myriad creatures become the pictures being perceived through human sensation. The ability to diversify the sensation of the perception quantifies these motions into a creature composed of human statistical calculation. The statistical calculation then transforms subjective experience into an objective mechanical device. The more closely the mechanical device runs parallel with the motions of myriad creatures, the more powerful the human mind becomes. Therefore, it is impossible to describes without an explanation. Description involves a directive response of how one subject feels or envisions about another. Explanations form mental abstractions about how the thinker regards both the overall picture and any details of another object, whether this object is a mental flash or merely a vibration.

This is, in essence, the license for the human race to gradually emerge as the modern dinosaur on earth. The human mind has never before been this powerful, human life has never been this vulnerable. In lieu of trust in Nature and worship of God, humankind is now trusting itself more than ever before. But can they trust their natural destination, death? They place more value on their minds' creation, ignoring the mystical God's creation. Yet, this God, as we envision Him, is a humanly creative interpretation of the power beyond that of the nature and surpasses the capability of human beings.

As a result, instead of changing the diversified functioning of Nature, which is not humanly possible, mankind is changing its own functioning by manipulating the functioning of Nature and the energy transformed from the resulting functioning of electronic devices. From this conduct, human beings are becoming more sensitive, since their mental devices can receive, transform, and direct the energy of natural transformation more easily than their physical body can perceive. Those individuals who can do so become the center of intellectual waves, the headquarters of economic concentration, that result in the evil action of exploitation of others, engendering the victimization of human life.

In another respect, human life becomes more vulnerable to the mental creation and mental exploitation. The mind becomes the facilitator of our life. We cease to live a natural life with God as supreme. We live in a mental environment created by our own distorted egoistic perceptions. Our physical lives are dependent upon the creation of our mental lives, and our spiritual lives live within the limitation placed by our mental lives. In between is the emotional life that controls the balance between the extremes of human life and the natural life of all its creatures. Natural life can no longer be considered natural. It has become mental. It has been reorganized into a mental creation, the product of mind's projection and prediction.

## Meditation Practice

Tao is close to the heart, the mouth, the toes and finger tips. Arising from the heart, Tao is the vibration of love. Expressing through the mouth, Tao is the sonic tone above the silence. Standing on the ground, Tao is the Rock-nailed-light. Flying through the finger tips, Tao is the magic play.

Tao is never out there somewhere, it is inside everywhere. Tao is never the force of a matter, it is the thought of that matter. Tao is never the indication of time, flow is its timing. Tao is never the image of a space, it is the image of silence.

Tao pulsates around the finger tips, tumbles out of the lips, dances with the hips, secretes through the nipples, shines above the pupils, and all the way it tingles.

Tao speaks the silent, tastes the plain, senses the dull, dampens the numb, drinks the wine, emits the dew, blows the air, scatters the dust, bases the abyss, governs the sky.

Tao chases the love, ignites the silence, chills the flame, steams the water, drives the clouds, pours the rain, drifts the snow.

Through signs and symbols, Tao enlivens upon forms and sub-stances, Tao energizes through consciousness and intention, Tao displays by trust and faith, Tao unifies with one and all.

Running through meridians, blood streams and conscious chan-nels, Tao is the vital Qi within; becoming organs, viscera and skin, Tao is the dynamic construction of organism; strengthening into muscles, bones and joints, Tao is the power supply; crystalizing into glands, hor-mones and enzymes, Tao is the maker of the body-mind; illuminating through speech, movement and silent prayer, Tao is the wisdom of light.

Down and down, Tao becomes visible; forward and forward, Tao continues to manifest itself; smaller and smaller, Tao is the essence of all things; softer and softer, Tao is the purifying detergent; empty and empty, Tao becomes invisible once again, returning to its own creative home.

# NOTES

德

# STEP TEN: *CULTIVATES*

Structure: human 亻 + follow 法 + heart 心
Sound: xing
Meaning: cultivates

## Where Is The Conscious Inch-Size Tao?

I n the previous chapter, we mapped out the physical location of the Tao and illustrated its bodily appearance. Yet, it serves only as an overlay of the sensible configuration of the Tao. The deep root of the Tao cannot be visualized in the head, nor paved beneath the feet, and never pointed to by the finger tip. Tao is never visible anywhere in the universe. Universe is the expanding mental illusionary space above. Tao is forever within; it is within the matter, the time, and the space. It is the source, the law, and the controller of all creatures. Within our human form, the empty heart is the structural Tao, the unconscious wave is the silent Tao, and conscientious expression is the expressive Tao.

Therefore, the conscious inch-size Tao is at the deepest connection, behind the subtle awareness, ahead of the vital expression, beyond the complete sacrifice, above the absolute freedom, through the ultimate truth, and within the forever peace. The conscious inch-size Tao is in every detail, upon each circulation, and through mutual vibration. It is when the heart's fire is not extinguished, completely cooled through a conscious and patient process of boiling. This is the refinement of the Tao within, the place where all the dust, garbage and junk dissipate before the anticipation of conscious understanding. They do not disappear, rather, they are being transformed. This is how the secret power of the Tao is expressed through the unknown tongue, the trackless step, the resonating heart, and the gracious spirit. It is the glory of Spirit.

To reach this infinite place, to capture this rapturous air, and to retain the morning-dew freshness is the next step in this heart-spaced cultivation practice. The ground is within the conscious heart. The seed of the heart is the window of soul, the vision of spirit, and the expression of truth. The soil is the holy water which constantly refreshes and renews all things. The freshness is the state of pure innocence, existing only in the condition of absolute honesty, awaiting in a state of spontaneous readiness.

The inch-size Tao does not have a specific location: it is a conscious flow, a moving spirit, a rotating wind, and a shining light. Within the body, it is a kind of bio-energetic vibrational sensation. Throughout the body, it is the active feedback in the interaction of body and mind. Beyond the body, it is the cosmic flow between the unbroken twilight and unfathomable void. The inch-size Tao does not have a specific organic attachment: it is alive, vibrant, vital, and exuberant, yet remains abstract, distant, remote, and mystic as it materializes. Why is this so? Ask your spiritual mind, your heart's intention, and your instantaneous gut reaction where they dwell in your body-mind? All these exciting indications and some encouraging aspects to their possibilities will be fully discussed in this character, which details and cultivates the heart in its cosmic make-up, to the degree where pure conscious intention arises naturally and returns immediately.

## The Characteristic Presentation

This Laoist character is constructed with three basic Chinese characters; ren meaning human, fa is to follow, and xing is the heart. The literal meaning of this is "human action should follow what the heart indicates." Ren symbolizes the most accurate initiative posture for human action, standing on two legs while facing the sky. In standing posture, before the body dances with the vertical spine, echoes the speechless sound through the ears, and directs its conscious execution through spirit, the hands are inactive, numb, and powerless. Like a cosmic tree, such a standing posture proclaims independence, strength, and demonstration of self-ensured control.

The Chinese character ren represents a standing cosmic tree. Legs and feet are the roots. The abdominal area holds the essence of the oceans, seas, and continents. The body, similar to the bodies of mountains, represents both the organic construction and dynamic function coursing between heaven and earth. Arms and hands are the wings which simulate the blowing wind, engaging in an interactive performance between the body and the mind, executing the decisions made by the mind and experienced through the body. When every decision made by the mind is experienced internally, it is cosmic, safe, and harmonic. The head represents the opening mouth at the peak of the mountain, symbolizing the fruits of action between heaven and earth, and the seed of God and Goddess. Spirit is the seed, consciousness is the fluid of cosmic water ranging from the purest form of wisdom and intellectual ability to the most highly concentrated thought patterns and belief systems. Eyes are that ripened fruits of Goddess's power.

Developmentally, when a baby is capable of standing on its toes, the pilgrimage begins its ongoing march for independence. When a sick person is again able to stand firmly, the body is healed. When a loser stands tall, s/he regains a new life. The act of standing itself ensures one's confidence, emerges into a healthy state, and displays its value. In humankind, standing posture gains its own supportive ground base represented by the water and land, mobility and flexibility. No one can survive for any length of time in a place with no clean water and fertile soil. Meanwhile, mobility depends on a stationary platform under the feet to enable walking to become flexible. It is not the feet that are important in carrying through one's life, it is how the feet connect with the earth, heaven and consciousness to construct the grounding importance. This grounding importance, just as it is in the Taichi position, is a solid nourishing of the supportive foundation. This is the first signal of right attitude, the first indication of right action, the first behavior of right performance. This is the primary step taken upon entering the Tao.

In a positive sense, standing on one's own feet is a declaration of independence from major financial and personal support. The two feet and legs adjust their positions and exchange the mobile information constantly through the directions given by the mind and the messages sent out of the body. The feet then report and transmit the information to the brain, which we refer to here as the mind, so that necessary changes or readjustments can be made. Learning to walk is a physical exercise responding to the mental growth. It is a spiritual pilgrimage and the earliest meditation practice. Walking meditation is the most powerful meditation in terms of physical healing, since through walking, the water of life and consciousness of spirit exchange information vertically, allowing all the toxic materials to be dissolved through feet and toes. In the present time, our life style requires educational background, just as it does in in business training opportunities. It means further that one should make one's own judgment and decision, being the possessor of adequate mental capacity and intelligence to express self-sufficiency. Another important consideration, of course, must be given to the physical requirement for the job performance.

At this point, take a deep breath and relax for a second. Upon awakening the memory cells that are stored in our environments, we are informed again of the numerous first steps taken, whether in learning or teaching, in love or understanding, in business or relationship. We often remember those very first steps in our personal meaningful life. How did they happen? Was it by chance or coincidence, by plan or synchronicity? Regardless of how it began, it changed us by redirecting our lives to a new and yet inexperienced domain, possibly expected mentally and spiritually.

Unlike four-legged animals, we humans journey with our two legs attached to our hips, using the two arms connecting to the shoulders to sustain and improve our life. We use our minds and hands to create, develop, and originate things. We can fly within our created inventions (not within the clouds like the enlightened Taoists) as the winged creatures do. Unlike angels that fly freely, we can travel in space psychically. We use our imagination to match this mystic function by immediately entering the cosmic reality.

Throughout human history, we have invented and manipulated everything possible in order to become more dominant and productive, and to live a more convenient life. The result is that, unfortunately, we have transformed ourselves from natural beings into socially accepted beings with a political bent or agenda. We have cultivated ourselves to a degree where we can no longer differentiate our instinctive behaviors from our cultural habits. Our cultural habits have, in fact, become important "instinctive tools" to suppress or indulge our biological instincts. We have driven our seasonal fear (cold, heat, wet, flood, etc.) into a commercially advertized obsession. We have lost our spiritual awareness to a victimized process of systematic conditioning. Worse, we have lost our spiritual ground by transferring it into religious practices. We execute God's justice by means of projecting our own selfish and institutional beliefs and by expressing our own (personal and cultural) love and hatred. We have also disconnected ourselves from our spiritual foundation by turning our attention outward and our heads downward. That is why we have lost our heads and our groundedness.

We did not follow our heart's intention in its first place. We follow only after the external invitations, attractions, and distractions, but not our true nature within. We follow, constantly and relentlessly, after our desirable shadows and egoistic expressions. This is why Laoism uses the three-character-description to introduce us to the right path of cultivation: human follows heart. It speaks for the nobility of standing up for our rights and for ourselves by following our own heart conscience. Heart conscience is the creative energy existing within the heartbeat but remaining beyond the structure of heart. It is the conscience of spirit. If we cannot stand up for ourselves, we cannot follow our own God's given path, the path of heart, the path of love. If we do not follow our heart conscience, we then follow only confusion and disorder.

This explains partially the characteristic construction of fa, the stroke of "gone" or "abandonment" with no support from water. It depicts the situation of fa having no peace, no grounding, but instead, abandoned, gone, disappeared. The Chinese character fa, representing the pronunciation of this tenth Laoist character, is a combined character between "water" stroke shui and "gone" stroke qu. In Chinese, it means "to follow," "to model after," and "to originate." It also means "rule" or "law." When the heart follows after water, life is alive with hope and joy, content with the flow of the life stream. When the heart is gone, the water and spirit are absent, rules are present and laws become the justice. When the water is absent, there is no flow, only stagnation and rigidity. When the heart is gone, there is no flow, only mad fire and rational justice. When the spirit is not present, there exists only dead mechanism (like a dead machine that stores our energy and sensations). Which way do you want to go, heart's way or rule's way? That is how "fa" wants you to follow the heart: standing in the mist of duality, pleasing and abusing the heart and body in the same time.

In spiritual practice, the heart must be cooled down through the water, as it boils into steam in its ascending process. This is the basic structure of Taoist practice, Kan-and-Li exercise, with Kan for water and li for fire. Water must be boiled into steam or mist or dew. Sexual energy must be liberated and then expressed unconditionally. Fire must be distilled, controlled, and refined. Heart must be emptied and then becomes content. When the heart follows its own mad firing power, it becomes the madness of the world. This is because the spiritual water in the abdomen either becomes frozen or discharged. To freeze is to become fearful, and to discharge is to express sexual lust. This is also because the fire, in the chest and brain, does not cool itself down in the water based body, in the abdomen or feet, but let it flame as a destructive force, a compulsive killing weapon. There is no steam of love being produced in the chest, and there is no stillness visible as the mental tranquility. This destructive fire ball is, literally, the self-destructive force of sin, the self consuming instinctive behavior, and passion of civilization. Civilization developed only conditions, built walls, created the endless controlling mechanism. It destroyed the life by burning up its precious life force.

The pictorial meaning of the character fa is to follow the flowing path of water. Naturally, without water, there would be no living creature. Water is life, is it not? To follow the path of flowing water is to follow the way of the Tao. This is the path of human civilization, living and dying along the flowing river beds. This is the second instance where Laoism uses the water element in the couplet. The literal meaning of the character fa ranges from "following and modeling" to "law and legislating," and from "against and confrontation" to "rejection and abandonment." The word "follow" suggests a very crucial moment, a heart-awakening consciousness, a complete sacrifice, and a life-or-death turning point. In terms of our behavioral action, "follow" can be identified with both self assurance and obedience, both gliding forward and chasing after, being both mutually respectful and uncommonly suspicious. Follow applies in either success or failure, either marching ahead or falling behind, either stepping freely beyond or being haltingly limited within. The objectivity of following can be both communicative and behavioral, both silent and active, both understanding and misleading.

This situation leads us to the final element of this tenth Laoist character, xing or "heart," with Xing representing the earthly fire within the body. The heart not only pumps the blood, but also stores the fire, especially when it unifies with the thymus gland in the chest and the golden egg in the Yellow Court around number #5 thoracic vertebra. Heart is the master of the body and the ruler of the spirit. It consists of all the countless myriad things in the universe.

In Chinese character, xing is constructed with a crescent shaped stroke and three dots adjoining one on each side and one at the top. The three dots represent the trinity of life, the masculine energy and feminine energy dancing together with a single combined heart. The heart is a central dot, the mutual spot, and the shining star. In spiritual Taoism, the crescent shaped line or stroke represents the circulation of the moon, the joy of the lake, the virtuous nature of the unknown (do-not-want-to-know). When the salty oceanic water is boiled by the fire of adrenal consciousness, the purified steam rises up to the chest to form lake-moon-holy-water through the anticipation of the thymus gland in front and golden egg shell power in back. The golden egg shell power is the origin of yolk, the cosmic Golden Shell. The thymus gland is the blossom of this shell-egg. When the thymus gland is charged by the unconditional love unified between the masculine and feminine energies, it attracts the central dot, the mutual spot, and the shining star. The heart can then become humble, still, empty, and peaceful. This heart is the Kingdom of God.

Heart, in Taoist tradition and Chinese medicine, is one of the five yin organs for generating and consuming the nutritional Qi. For every major yin organ, there is yang gland. For example, kidneys have adrenal glands, liver has gallbladder, lungs have thyroid and parathyroid glands, spleen has pancreas. Heart has, of course, thymus gland. Among these five major organs, the double (paired) organs have double glands. They are kidneys and lungs. The single organs have single glands. They are liver, heart and spleen. Liver and spleen's mating and battery-charging glands are closely attached to them. Only heart's peaceful-lake-like crescent hangs in the center of the chest, enabling the consciousness to be centered, souls dancing together, fire and water becoming unified.

Heart is empty by itself in the sense that, firstly, it relies upon the spirit to awaken the conscious spirit. Without conscious spirit, the heart is lifeless. The conscious spirit is the function of liver, the vision of eyes, the ability of awareness, and passion of dragon, the voice of thunder, and the Arousal of God. Second, heart relies on breathing air to make the "bellowing" body work. Bellow is the function of body-as-lungs. Without air circulation, bellow does not generate wind, and heart is airless. Third, heart must depend on spleen for supportive nutritious substance. The land of spleen provides all the digested nutrients to enable both the upper part of the body-land-mountain and lower part of the body-ocean-well to communicate with each other. Therefore, lastly, heart needs kidney water to distill its fire, calm its agitation, and purify its circulation, making the passion peaceful, death senseless.

Finally, human follows heart completes the eternal order of the mystic inch-size Tao. It demonstrates the exact order of the ascending process, the power of Te. Human life, personal and spiritual, is the first ascending character. This character's function is that of following, which is the second ascending process. These two processes are characterized by the third element, the spiritual heart, the illuminating light and Prince of Peace. This is the spiritual interpretation of the Tenth Laoist character.

## The Two-way Journey of Following

In Taoist tradition, there are two methods of following. The first is to follow in the footsteps of the pilgrimage. This pilgrimage is the searching and defining and knowing of the true self, the spiritual seed. On an average, this spiritual seed can be found during and after middle age between the age of 30 and 50. This occurs when the direction is found, the life is settled, and the heart is self-content. The second way of following is to be guided by one's present heart consciousness, which is about living with one's cultivated Qi and preparing for the last journey of cultivation practice, flight. This is the stage of producing the virtuous deeds, getting in touch with celestial bodies and their spirits, knowing the mystic character and function of the cosmic body as universe, and being ready for the flight to the heavenly realm.

There are always choices to be made, different paths to follow, choices to be made, which are to either the right, the left, or the middle road. Both left and right leads to distraction, disorder, and dysfunction. Only by following the middle path, the harmonious road, and the unified agreement can we live a happy, healthy, and spiritually "crazy" life. This two-way nature follows consciousness, which flows in both directions, up and down (appraisal and disgrace), self and other (inner and outer), left and right (right or wrong). The single spiritual self always requires peace, the echoing resonance, and the healing water. The single heart seeks the dual functions of energy where the space can be opened, and the spiritual self can be preserved.

This leads to a very critical point in learning and modeling from others or self. In today's world, the majority of people learn from others. They learn from each other by paying for their services and defining/rejecting one another. There is no true self involved. Only the shadow of spirit, the hope of dream, and reality of illusion. This leads, historically, to the establishment and the practice of institutions, from a random group to a secular environment, from gang to party, and from community to culture.

It is this process that makes following the most difficult decision to make, the most critical moment to live, and the most exciting environmental space to inhabit. There have always been two opposing laws governing us throughout evolutionary history: God's Law, and man's laws. In our society, God's invisible Law descends into man-legislated cultural laws. God's Self-moving-law becomes the rationally debatable and definable laws. In God's reality, God makes the law, Love makes the resulting/causing action. In man's reality, ego makes the laws, lust directs the profitable exchange. Fear pays the fee. As a result, God becomes a personal and cultural icon of an egoistic and selfish object. God's Law becomes self-characterized, other-multiplied, and ceaseless waste-polluted endless cycle.

Facing our average citizens is this dilemma; should we follow the laws, rules and regulations that have been set up by the others, those who have experienced their path of thought and behavior and bestowed their own gratification upon their decisions, attraction and rejection, or should we listen to our own internal firing and vibrating and emptying heart, which is our original and present heart's drumming? Following after others is a loss, following through is a transformation.

We know for certain the course our lives will take when we follow after others. We will lose ourselves by becoming the byproducts of others. Should we discover something that is new to us, we can then be sure that it has already been experienced. Rules, to a large degree, are established upon self interests, both self benefit and self protection. Rules and laws are not meant for the welfare of those who cannot benefit from them. The outsiders, with no thoughts or experiences in their domain, provide both the opportunity and income for those who had established those very rules and justifications.

Another example is the issue of sex. The sex organs should function normally after a person completes the pubic stage. That is a natural flow. But adults, both parents and law makers, do not want young children to be the participants. Their rules are that children are not in a position to support themselves. They bear the burden of self-denial and self-rejection. The financial responsibility is a decisive factor. If all the high school age kids were married and having babies, who would go to school and become an educated productive (for whom?) citizen. If all the people were self-taught, how could the learning institution exist? If all the married people were self supporting, as in an agricultural environment, who would choose a life in the cities and work in the factories? The agricul-

tural life is the healthiest life style and has the longest history in recorded human civilization. To work with light and clouds, land and self, water
and seed, soil and production has been a successful existence for many
centuries.

Education can never free the mind, nor the heart. It fixates the
mind; the heart is contaminated. The spiritual mind needs not to educated, only to be purified. God-given heart never needs to be educated, only
to be awakened. It knows everything that is right from its very conception.
Education may strive toward perfection while God's creative chaos is in
its perfect order. Education leads to class division, yet, God creates only
two classes, light and love (which are yin and yang, time and space).
Education may help one to understand oneself; yet, God's Selflessness
creates only two citizens, male and female. After all the years of school-
ing, the educated ones know no more than their counterparts in the eyes
of God, in front of the blank, within the darkness. Unknown is the teacher,
the educator, the master.

In our modern society, the majority of people are nothing more
than goods-consumers and bill-recyclers. When the social and cultural
environment does not ensure a safe and stable condition, how can the general population have self-esteem and self-confidence? When everybody
is worried about next day's income, from what source can they establish
a healthier and more spiritual environment? It is not the future income
that matters, but fear regarding it. The educational environment generates
a false hope which leads to further self-destruction. It is the illusion of
mind, the fat of ego, the drive for pride, and the control of fear.

Because of this, our modern society reinforces only two classes
of people, the educated and non-educated. The highly educated people
either enforce more rules and legislation, or enhance the mechanical
updates and further technological complexity. They possess the ways and
the means. The non-educated class listens and obeys the rules, buying and
selling the "educated" products, having no time or strength to educate
themselves, lacking the financial capacity to uplift themselves and raise
their standard of living.

Regardless of which road each person may travel, after retirement, it is the most educated and skilled who are inflicted with spiritual
"Alzheimer" if they are unable to free themselves from their old environment. They are completely lost in their educated dreams with no conscientious heart remaining. Their blood and fire have become old ideas,
dead theories, and used machines, all of which have rendered them
"stressed-out." Anyone who works in a nursing home must be aware that
the guilt for this lies within our compulsive education system. The education process liberates the most adaptable people, leaving those less able
to adapt with their shattered memories, their bodies numb and their minds
deadened. They become hidden prisoners in their own bodies,
sequestered in institutions.

When teachers work diligently at a pre-school or elementary
school, they are rewarded by the children's accelerated learning. But for
those who work in a nursing home, all that can be accomplished is keeping the status quo, at best. All the patients are dying. The rehabilitation

program means nothing to them. There is no energy left in their wasted bodies with which to revitalize themselves. What is the use? Have they not already been rehabilitated enough?

The teaching of Laoism advises that "the person who works according to Tao unites with Tao. In the same way he unites with action. In the same way he unites with loss. Uniting with action, the Tao becomes action. Uniting with loss, the Tao becomes loss." (24: 4;5) The education unites with the loss from the very beginning. God made our lives to be the loss and lost us from the very beginning in order that we can live breath after breath, love after love, life after life. Breath after breath ensures the existence of life. Love after love excites the meaning of heart. Life after life demonstrates the eternal Spirit. Life is a loss. Love is the action. Tao is the Spirit.

In life, those who have gone before us and experienced life have established their rules and justifications. If not for this, life could become a mutual interaction where each and every one of us is going on an adventurous trip together. This someone is God, the love, our new friend, and our new hope. God does not know us, He is within us. God cannot care about us, he is our vulnerable inspiration. God will not educate us, he frees us along our returning journey. God is not in our dream, he awakens us through our dream. This is the meaning of following through. Contrarily, if we follow through with our own created educational and institutional environment, we will never be through. We will be forever trapped within our own created "concentration campuses."

According to the path of flowing water which is the spiritual discipline, we all should follow our own awakened talents and capacities rather than follow in others' teachings or footsteps. If one follows, s/he should approach them as a reflective mirror and vision, not a respective status and prestige. Respect is the honor of heart. Prestige is the power of ego. The original stories of creation and inventions are much more appealing than a certificate, a degree, or a diploma. We all must follow through the collaboration with God's creative power. He has made everything from the beginning. He certified us and He completed us. He is the Ultimate that we must follow after and through at the same time.

To "follow" can also convey following each other, the mutually anticipated patterns, like the connection between inhalation and exhalation. Or to follow in a loving relationship where there is a mutual flow of both sending and receiving, energetically and selflessly. This is the true teaching of life, the harmonious flow of heart's consciousness of body and mind, sexuality and spirituality, self and others. In life, everyone can make a heart flow and no one can stop the flow. The big challenge is whether this heart flow is selfish or selfless. If selfish, then the person follows the instinctive drives and ignores the spiritual drumming. If one follows the spiritual drumming, there is no self within. There is only the vibration of inhalation and exhalation, the heartbeat of "lubb" and "dupp," and the pulsation of tapping and echoing.

In all situations, when you feel that there is a self, you find no-self, you are embraced by all the lost and undiscovered selves. By the time you feel that you are not yourself, then your true self speaks. The best advice is to follow the heart flow during your life time and the spirit-flight after this life. During your life time, the spirit awakens in your heart equally from God and Goddess. After the life, the heart returns to that original oneness of the spiritual state. Not the spiritual state as such during life on earth, but the true spiritual oneness between heaven and earth. This is the second passage of Laoist's explanation of the right action of cultivation, human follows from heart.

Once again, there is a distinction between being forced to follow after forcefully, obediently and following one another respectfully and with acceptance. The first instance becomes a total loss with no-self. The second is a loss of conditional selves into true self. This is how the life continues, how the Tao flows, and how the spirit follows. In spiritual practice, there should be no rules or laws or regulations. Rather, all living things are the mirroring, protecting, ensuring and guiding teachers. This is the role of a spiritual master, the model of mastering (God alone occupies this role).

It is common for many to know only how to follow after their masters. They don't know that there is another path, the true path once taken by the master. The reality at that time was that before becoming a master, there were no masters to follow. Therefore, the master followed after no one but self by following from the true teachings of the heart. Unfortunately, followers have been making the same mistake generation after generation, not following through the teachings after themselves. They follow only the rules/steps created by the others (including masters). These rules not only killed the true followers, but the masters as well.

## The Origin of Heart

Heart is, perhaps, the most commonly applied word in any language. It is the power organ in human life, not only in instinctive behavior but also conscious passion. It is also the most confusing and distrustful organ. Confusion arises from the lack of inner understanding, and the loss of inner confidence. Inner understanding originates in the liver which also hosts the spiritual consciousness. Inner confidence pervades through the self-conservation of willpower and essential sexual Qi. The will power is the power of self-preservation and self-projection. No further support or sacrifice need be made. The essential sexual Qi is the combination of biological water Qi of ovarian/testis organs and the instinctive firing Qi of adrenal organs. When you have the will-Qi, you are filled with self-confidence. When you have and preserve the sexual Qi, you are confident about yourself and your life.

The distrustful nature of human heart is its active power engaging without the presence of tranquil spirit. The tranquil spirit changes itself into the power of madness without being conscious of self-preservation. When the heart hosts other than spiritual beings, its space is jammed, its directions twisted and misled. Between the tranquil spirit and mad fire, ego plays the game with everything but does not take responsibility for anything. Empty promises and legal protection then rise to replace the role of trust and faith.

The organ of heart is housed in two disciplines. One is the Goddess's cosmic creative holy Qi, the origin of all creative matters and substances, cells and organs. It is the power of icy oceanic Qi, the joyful lake Qi, and the mystic cloud Qi. The other is guarded by the Will of God, the power of creation, the genetic construction of all creatures, and the celestial/alien spirits and animal spirits. Let us review these one by one.

We will first examine the creative holy water Qi, the origin of virus, the yolk, the ovum, the golden shell, and the mystic angel. The descending order of this formation transpires from the cosmic abysmal void of Goddess's creation. It stands for the oneness of everything, from water to seed, and from spiritual arousal to conscious formation. From the abysmal Void, called emptiness, comes the flow of cosmic water, standing for the Prince of Peace. Next is the creation of cosmic water (wind) in all the stars and constellations. Then we see the formation of water on earth, followed by the creation of fish, reptiles, animals, and humans. We humans, as the animated evolutionary products, are the latest, youngest, and newest member. Prince of Peace is our Cosmic Mother, egg is our biological mother, fish is our organic mother, animals are our biological sisters.

This power of creative force is blown by the cosmic wind, the conscious air, the organic breathing, and animated instinct: abysmal, aroused, and awakening. These are the processes of formation, from love to water, from harmony to egg, from marriage to ancestral courtship. Smell the ocean, the fish, your own body, the sense of those. Look into the whitish yellowish sprout to examine the golden egg within and golden shell surrounding. Feel the winged beings within and beyond the physical restraint. Listen to the sound of the night-mooning, the well-springing, and the breast-milking ways.

Lao Zi describes this evolutionary creation as "I am a fool at heart, as a water droplet is to the spring." (20:5) This is the only time Lao Zi mentioned abysmal fool, Mother fool, water fool, and milk fool. Fool is the cry of the Widow of Goddess. Water droplet is the power of Oneness. Spring is the joy of nourishment. They are all pumped by the blood (water substances) of heart. Heart is empty and heart is a fool; heart is peaceful and heart is joy. Emptiness is the Void of Cosmic Womb. Fool is the sacrifice of love into light. Peace is the oceanic stillness unstirred by the gravitational force. Joy is the lake of moisturized heart-Qi fogged in the chest. Goddess is a fool. Love is a fool. Water is a fool. Egg is a fool. Androgynous state is a fool.

The other side of the story of the heart belongs to the Will of God, which is the origin of the creative power, the penetrating light, the creative idea, the whitish envelope, and the decorating color. This Will is the will of chasing, penetrating, forming, ordering, and mechanizing. This Will is the origin of Spirit, which is the spiritual creation, the spiritual formation, and the spiritual transformation. This spirit comes from God's light, to celestial stars' powers, angel's flight ability, human's conscientious soul, animal's instinctive soul, plants' seasonal soul, and to rocks' eternal soul.

From God's Will of light, alien star lights become visible. From the Milky Way of whitish color, solar reddish fire is emitted. Because of sun's reddish fire, the moon's fogging water coming from the Heavenly Dog (the first star in the Bigger Dipper which receives the White Ice from the North Star) is steamed into the air, and cooled down on earth manifesting as oceans and seas. Through the orbiting discipline (as it has to be) and rotating order (no other choice), cosmic wind from the stars' interaction blows the oceanic water into air, coming together in the sky to form clouds. Earth's inner arousal pushes the oceanic water out of the mouth of the mountains to form streams and rivers. When the rain/snow and stream/river settle along the way, ponds and lakes are formed. This is called "Understanding the male and holding onto the female enables the flow of the world. This being the flow of the world, the eternal action abides. Knowing that the eternal action abides is to return to childhood." (28:1)

With the same order, the abdominal Qi of water flows in two directions, just like the orbiting power of streams and rivers, the rotating power of rain and snow. When these forces are aroused in humans, menstruation and ejaculation occurs. Menstruation is the volcanic power. Ejaculation is the watering sprout. The harmonious love making is the explosive earthquake. The death of self results in the beginning of a new life. This is described as "Understanding the pure and holding on to the impure enables the cleansing of the world. With the cleansing of the world, ongoing action suffices. When ongoing action suffices, it returns to simplicity." (28:2)

Equally, when the reddish solar light transmits into animal water, it turns into blood. When the blood turns into milk, it is the renunciation of love between fire and water, egg and sperm, yellowish yolk and whitish envelope. When the blood is not chilled with the abdominal water, it is the madness of fire, the ego confrontation, and the massive destruction. Disaster results, all due to the light being away from its star, the blood away from the milk, the lake away from the peace. The moon becomes disturbed, the light becomes cloud, the mind becomes crazy, the body becomes disquieted.

When the sun and moon work together harmoniously with other stars and planets, orders are established on earth, peace is ensured, and work is done. When heart and will are unified, love flows in life, peace distills, joy evaporates. When white and black are blended, forms are made thereafter. When masculine and feminine are united, offspring are produced.

When the biological cell is formed and diffuses into two cells, they become the yin and yang developing power of our body-mind. The yin cell forms the abdominal body, and yang cell grows into conscious mind. Within the yin body is concealed the true spiritual yang force, which is the primordial yang Qi of that eternal holy water. Within the yang mind rises the yin force of destruction and sacrifice for better or for worse, depending on the original conscious imprints. In between is the empty functioning of heart, the useful container of fire, and pipe station of blood. This is characterized as "Understanding the white and holding on to the black enables the formation of the world. Being the formation of the world, ongoing action does not stray. When ongoing action does not stray, it returns to the infinite." (28:3)

Unfortunately, most of the time these offspring are often off the shore, away from the mountain, aside from the land: aroused mentally and physically. They are racing and hunting: racing to compete with each other (to see who escapes faster and safely) and hunting to kill one another (to become a cannibal-like creature consuming the blood and meat of victim). After the race, education begins, ensuring further competition. After hunting, domestication begins, supplying more blood and meat. "Racing and hunting madden the heart." (12:1) The peace is destroyed, the lake is dried up, and love becomes selfish, the joy becomes lustful, and body becomes sacrificial. Conscious fire becomes the egoistic fire, the instinctive arousal destroys each other within the animal kingdom. Patriarchal life becomes the presentation, creating both political and religious orders and establishments.

## Animal Spirits

In order to understand the conscious fire and the biological instinct of the heart, we must know, chronologically, how the cosmic fire becomes spiritual blood. In the spiritual order, God's light is the Eternal Will, the Ultimate Power, and the Absolute Law. Through the Love between light and void, stars and planets were formed, aliens and angels are created. In the solar system, sun and moon were the matched couple for the creative beings existing on earth. The first animated couple on earth, spiritually, was the union between dragon and dinosaur. These two spiritualized animals were more alienated than the animal spirits on earth. Dragon provided the first spiritual soul of the arousal of thundering light of God by pouring rain of cosmic water of eternal peace within the Goddess. Dinosaur demonstrated the power of blue body, the inner strength of wooden bone, and the color dominance of evergreen. The green belongs to the dragon. The green-blue belongs to dinosaur.

The existence of dragons and dinosaurs was influenced by the seven East Star Group. This star group represented the Green Color of cosmic creation. This Color marked the first state of earthly existence, from dragon-spirit-inherited monsters on earth, to the gigantic physical green-powered dinosaurs, to the ever present green trees and plants. This is the reason that in Taoist tradition, green dragon is the conscious spirit arousing the liver organ, and green color is the creative womb of peace. This green color is the symbol of plant life, the image of a cosmic tree, the fashion of eyes, and vision of spirit. Confucius described Lao Zi as "dragon," a celestial spiritual being living in a human body on earth.

When the war between dragon and dinosaur broke out, it became the first battle of good and evil on earth. As a result, the good-spirited dragons became the spiritual deities of earthly creatures, while the evil-spirited dragons were punished by the image of the white tiger. The good-spirited dinosaurs became the symbol of water buffalo, and the evil-spirited dinosaurs became the model of suspicious wolf. These two spiritual forces were influenced by the West Star Group. The East Star Group is the creative birth and growth interacted with maturity and independence in the West Star Group, creating the order of masculinity of growth and independence, of passion and happiness, of self-formation and self-transformation. Formation took the form of creative water Qi. Transformation underwent the purification of fire Qi. Green is the ever present of peace, and white is the eternal strength of stillness. Dragon is empowered by the blood force of reddish fire Qi, tiger is individualized by the creative force of whitish water Qi.

This leads to the next descending transmutation from light to fire and from void to water in the existence of white tiger and grey wolf. Tiger governs the instinctive power, wolf projects the lustful spice. Tiger then transformed into the spirit of lungs, for breathing and other instinctive behaviors. The outcome was the creation of whitish fluid, the formation of white bones, the transformation of death. From the tiger's spirit, independence was ensured, the ego was constructed. Lust and control became visible. The wolf became the guiding power of the moon, especially during the mating period and immediately after menstruation. Suspicion and jealousy were alive with the emotionality and instability. Looking forward to arousal and being fearful of rape would swing back and forth. Psychic knowing awareness and physical gut sensitivity attract the wisdom power and intellectual fire. Menstruation invites the blood-battling between male hunters, inner peace welcomes the lost souls and surviving soldiers. Lost souls become the hope of future generations, and surviving soldiers become the ruling kings and martial lords. The body is protected and aroused, the peace is safe-guarded and house-ensured.

Domestically, the tiger changed into a cat, and wolf became a dog. Cat is more selfish and has more self-esteemed, and dog is more faithful and trustworthy. The corresponding pairing of tiger and wolf were represented by lion and buffalo. They were more family oriented than tiger and wolf. Lion established the kingdom of animal order, buffalo nourished it. Lion distinguishes the rules from foolishness, buffalo demonstrates diligence and sacrifice. This represents the matriarchal state of human evolutionary process.

The third order of this spiritual transmutation was the power share between snake and monkey. This stands for the healing and understanding, killing and liberation, sexuality and spirituality, instinct and wisdom. In I Ching, snake stands for the old yin, and monkey powers the old yang. Snake occupies the number of six, which is the constructive creation, the ascending longing, with its opening mouth ready to receive the seed of spiritual light. In human form, the snake starts from the abdominal area, which is the body of snake, the construction of small and large intestines. The two breasts represents the two eyes, and its mouth extends through the human mouth. The snake's tongue is the best and most reliable tool for self-protection. So also, is human's.

In another field, monkey's mentality is tactical, skillful, and forgetful. Monkey is characterized by the number of nine, representing sleep, dream, death, and transformation. That is why monkey is so tactical, so forgetful, and so unreliable. Who can compete against and trust a monkey head? Not scientists! Scientific mind is the power shadow of monkey's head, which is manipulation, controlling, and without spirit. There is no spiritual discipline, no spiritual honesty, and no spiritual obedience. Everything is concerned with looking, searching, and testing the facts. It is the dawn of scientific exploration.

The last transmutation of this spiritual order was the connection between horse and sheep. In the Chinese dictionary, heart and horse both harness the madness of fire. No other animal is stronger than a horse on a battle field. No other animal is faster than a horse as a means of transportation. No other animal spirit can so directly inspire human's passionate fight than a horse spirit. According to the description of I Ching, human spirit originated from horse and horse spirit originated from sheep. The sheep, representing the lust of the mouth and the concubine of the female instinct, received the fire power from God's transmitted light and solar light as well as the formative power of Earth Mother and blood sacrifice. Sheep is the only animal beside the buffalo (cow) which provides milk for human babies other than their biological mother. Its paired yin sister is rabbit, representing shyness, peacefulness, and gracefulness. Rabbit is willingly aroused by the spiring warmth, and sheep is diligently climbing the roof of the rock spirit to sustain itself. The rock spirit is the Shepherd, sheep is the care-taker. The white spirit is enlivened, and the white fur is milked. The white bone is strengthened, and the white hair is lightened.

How the mad fire within the horse was tamed and transmitted by the sheep's spirit is unknown, revolutionarily and mystically. The mystic figures of Pegasus, Centaur and Unicorn might provide a limited explanation. These monster-creatures did not occur in oriental mythologies. From white-tiger to spiritual horse power, there existed monkey's analytic consciousness, called thinking mind. This was, perhaps, the largest and the most encompassing celestial/spiritual influence imposed upon Western civilization. From bloody sacrifice for independence, from ego-oriented mentality to lawful obedience, western culture has finally been offering its greatest show on earth.

Originating from the seven West Star Group in the universe, this power structure is the color of white, representing the cosmic appearance (the superiority of the white race is based upon this cosmic appearance). Its material structure is the physical construction of bones. Its will power is the self-like-ego-and-pride due to its closeness to the creative power. Ego stands for the materialized self, pride is the quality of superiority. Its shadow power is the self-blame and self-contamination (guilt and sin). Death and transformation subsist within this paradox (crucifixion and resurrection). The heat is the power of summer and the meaning of absolute sacrifice (passion from the lust). Cold is close to the winter, ready to freeze the complete matured seed (death phobia). In between stands the power of fall, the season of harvest, the state of independence, the condition of coldness, the moment of happiness, and all in all the power of eternity. Yet, there is no unification there as in the Taichi structure or serpent worship found in oriental cultures.

The positive influence is the Christ-Love of spiritual discipline and spiritual sacrifice. Body has to die, lust has to be extinguished. Self has to be crystalized, discipline has to be established. The Christ-symbol of Love, which descended from a high celestial spirit, inspires the state of virtuous being, the order of self-discipline, and the willing-to-die sacrifice. In essence, Christ is the combined figure between holy father and holy spirit. He is never despiritualized into soul form. He is His Father's Image. By undergoing virgin birth and virtuous maturity, Christ demonstrates pure and ever presence of spirit. Biological birth process is a matter of materialization of spirit, carrying on the Father's teaching is both self-discipline and self-preservation. No vital Qi is wasted in human emotional and lustful forms. No spiritual essence has been suffused: virtuous, pure, absolute, and ever present. The matching power is the unconditional love, love for one and love for all. The products are the flights of thousands upon thousands of saved and ordained and purified spirits.

The negative influence is the scientific evolution taking over as the dominant show on earth. This trend is undergoing the same pattern as did the outer alchemists in Chinese civilization. What has happened is that instead of entering in and sustaining the pure state of spirit-form, out of lust, passion and pride, spiritual formation transcends into intellectual formation. The unconditional love changes into conditional obsession. The outcome is no longer the saved spirits, but manmade machines and justice. The result is self-destruction with the gate closing to the spiritual liberation, being guided by only mechanical operation. The inner conscious vibration is converted into electrical operation. Inner love turns into object-attachment. It is the monkey's head-star which represents self-centered and mechanically repeated mentality and forgetful heart which leads, ultimately, to the separation between spirit and matter, between water and substance (since the heart remembers everything, there is no need for researching and retesting procedure. It has learned and is liberated. It is done ).

The white color and white snow, the white bone and white hair are all part of the dynamics. Death is a struggle, independence is also a struggle. This is why in the Western culture, the acceptance of death is such a taboo, and fighting for independence is such a cultural pride. In modern science, there is a deep denial of (the power and significance) the instinctive behavior, which is breath. This may lead into the shadow part of the white-tiger's spiritual makeup, breath and nose, lungs and its energy being translated. This is the big issue for the white-tiger's spiritual existence. Meanwhile, white horse is the savior which transcends the power of breath, of seed, and of self-preservation. This is why even today in Chinese culture, the princess (any young girl) still longs for her "White Horse" to make the spiritual connection.

One thing is certain: the horse represents the number seven animal in Chinese zodiac, and sheep is the number of eight. Within the seventh of yang number, there is yin force which is peace. Within the eighth of yin force of nourishment, there is yang force which is spiritual independence from the biological body. Sheep is all nurturing, and concubine is spirit-free. In the Chinese linguistic construction, four numbers are used in the final I Ching illustration. They are six, seven, eight and nine. Six represents the oceanic state, the kundalini awakening and tantric engagement. Seven stands for the spring fountain, the transformation from seed to sprout or from sperm to fetus, and the growth of spirit within the body. Eight characterizes the independence after the union. Chest-to-chest embraced union (of six) is separated by spine-facing-spine co-depended existence (of eight), and announces the maturity of new seed coming from summer and courtship. Nine symbolizes the resting moment, the sleeping state, the hibernating conditioning, and the transformation from death to birth (see detailed material in chapter 14).

When we connect the animal representations with these four numbers, we will see the Chinese mystic tradition of the animal spirits being crucial in human growth and development. The four numbers range from snake, horse, sheep to monkey. Our human spirit is intertwined between body and mind, animal soul and human soul, sexual power and spiritual light. These four animals are the key animal spiritual representations in the construction of human spirit. Without them, we cannot build a bridge between instinct and consciousness. We cannot draw a line between grass-eating animals and meat-eating animals. We cannot find the deep connection between human soul and animal soul. Nor can we solve the mystery between biological hibernation and spiritual liberation.

In conclusion, the twelve animals in Chinese zodiac are commonly representative and native in the land of China. It does not include bear, lion, elephant, eagle, or many other animals which are important in cross-cultural understanding. The odd numbered animals are yang, and those named with even numbers are yin. The yang animals are rat, tiger, dragon, horse, monkey, and dog. The yin animals are cow, rabbit, snake, sheep, hen, and pig. Each animal represents one specific month, a time period, and an emotional/personal/psychic quality. These qualities deal with the direct energy quality, or persona. By understanding their characters and energy qualities, we can get in touch with our human attributes, organically and psychically.

The yang animals demonstrate the masculine qualities. They are rat (mouse) with crossing line, tiger of independence, dragon of dominance, horse of sacrifice, monkey of intelligence, and dog of faithfulness. The yin animals show nourishing qualities and sensitivity. Cow is diligent, rabbit is gentle, snake is swift, sheep is peaceful, hen is timing, and pig is earthy. The idea of the crossing line is always described as "crossing the wintery stream/icy water" in I Ching. The time is in the Winter Solstice and it generally refers to dog (the last yang animal) without taking the precaution of lifting its tail above the icy water. (Maybe, mystically, it is the reason that humans have lost their tails. They were frozen in the icy water at the beginning of the Ice Age. Eventually, the body turned into fish without tails and legs and arms. That is why the earliest taichi map represents two fish (black and white) biting each other's tail. Then the tail gradually became tongue. Makes sense!)

For the rat, tail is a powerful tool. A rat can stick its tail any place with a precise degree and angle, unlike the monkey which uses its tail only to hang the body. Rat uses its tail to demonstrate the power of crossing the line between safety and danger and between death and birth. According to the biblical mystery, woman is made from a man's rib bone. But which one? Anatomically, there are twelve pairs of rib bones. The first five pairs connect directly with the manubrium and sternum. The second five (sixth to tenth) join together to form the sternum. The eleventh and twelfth bones, hanging in the air, are called floating ribs. Which of these ribs were used to form female body? Could that be tail bone, as well?

Among these twelve animals, the rat or mouse is the most powerful (Buddha was welcomed first by the rat). It can go anywhere, from land to underground, due primarily to its sensitive eye and powerful teeth. Mouse is the medium animal in the ghost world of darkness waiting to be reincarnated. Modern scientific research relies on rat as the primary testing body which is no surprise in this sense. The smallest physical size of the rat, as compared to other animals, demonstrates both precision and accuracy, but yields no other social and cultural values. On the downside for us, the rat can manage to live inside the warehouse and stay in the roof. Among all the animals, only rat can stay above the people' head to rule the subconscious mentality connecting unconscious vulnerability with conscious ability. It is like a psychic backbone (the power of cerebellum) which deals with primary unconscious awareness. How do you feel when rats are chewing the roof or running and fighting each other above your ceiling? Can you take the roof off the world?

On this planet, the human spirit and body are a mixture of everything between heaven and earth. As mentioned above, human organic spirits come from animal spirits, and human conscious spirit comes from celestial and alien spirits which originate in God's Creative Light Power. The animal spirits are the highest representation of material spirit which governs the function of the organism on the one hand, but yet are the filthiest characterizations of holy water spirit. Animal bodies are the most complicated organs existing on earth. Without such organs, trees would be all that could live on earth, a representation of cosmic circulation between water and light. Without such organism, the only living creatures would be the swimming fish, symbolized as the cosmic Taichi with black and white within. Meanwhile, animal organs are even more filthy than earth's biological organ, oceanic fish. The animal organism is much more murky than earth's "hair," plants and flowers. Animal bodies have the highest development of parasites and worms existing between dust and water, from ocean to desert, from searching for purity to adhering to addictive behaviors.

Still, it is evident that the spiritual descending hierarchy ranges from God's consciousness to cosmic creation, from stars' conscious spirits to celestial existence (the most powerful aliens among all the constellations), from planets' conscious spirits to angelic existence, from earth's consciousness to human/animal existence, and from human consciousness to materialistic existence. In this structure, human spirit has the poorest energetic construction. It has the most innocent spiritual conscious makeup in the Cosmos.

In Taoist healing tradition, the human biological body is the representation of all animal organism, ranging from fish and snake, from reptile to mammals, and from beast to feast. It also ranges from virus and parasites to cells and minerals. Each organ within our body has an animal body. Every organic character in our body represents the biological/organic character of an animal. We are all one large family, maintaining similar sensitivity and instinct.

Another point is that since humans are the latest development of animal members, we have the highest concentration of all the animal spirits, including God's transmitted wisdom power and Goddess's psychic instinct. Therefore, each organ within the human body represents a specific animal behavior, whether it be fish or tiger, kidney or liver. This animal behavior is part of the conscious creation of God and conscious Love of Goddess. We are the messenger of the entire animal kingdom. No more dragon, no more tiger, no more horse. It is the man's power (not woman's) that controls the animal world, and the reason that many animal species become extinct.

Since there exists a set amount of spirits in animal world, all the extinguished animals' spirits are now reliving within humans. And there are more animal-humans than human-humans. As a result, there is a big gap between those who contain human spirit and whose who possess only animal spirits. People become more hateful toward one another rather than more loving to each other as brothers and sisters. This is the result of the spirits that are being killed constantly seeking revenge. The hatred is a combined human and animal hatred since humans condemn other humans and slaughter animals at the same time. There exists an equally powerful display between moral value and instinctive value. In moral value, there is no fear of death, since the spirit liberates itself from the biological death. Instinctive value treasures nothing but life, fears nothing but death, projects nothing but control, knows nothing but the existing temporary reality. Therefore, to most people, whether they possess a human soul or an animal one, their spirits are the prisoners of their poisoned bodies.

In the matter of killing, each time a person kills either an animal or another human being, s/he takes on the burden of spiritual punishment, since the spirit having been killed will energetically return to regain its position. That is the manner in which people and animals continue to annihilate each other. This is why meat-consumption is not inducive to spiritual practice. We transfer the energy of those extinguished spirits into our own living energy bodies, speeding up and intensifying further violent behaviors.

In spiritual practice, when one masters the heart, one masters the animal world as well, including the human family. Laoist describes this: "Poisonous insects and venomous snakes do not sting it. Predatory birds and ferocious animals do not seize it." (55:1) These enlightened masters are "Walking through, not avoiding rhinos and tigers. Entering battle without wearing armaments. The rhino has no place to dig its horns. The tiger has no place to drag its claws. The soldier has no place to thrust his blade." (50:4)

In this state, the heart is the true order of the spirit, the only master of the body. When the heart becomes thus distilled, no living creature can take advantage of the living spirit, and no evil spirit can haunt the precious temple. The true spirit lives eternally in its spiritual mansion, the cosmic womb. It is inside the body and beyond the organism; inside the mind and beyond the consciousness; inside the spirit and beyond the wonder. In order to live in such a state, distilling or taming the heart is the primary discipline.

## Celestial Spirits In Animal Form

In the spiritual law, the lighter matters rise up and the heavier objects sink downward. The light shines down and water evaporates upward. Matters and their forces co-exist with each other. Light and water are pulling and pushing each other at the same time to create all beings in the universe, consciously and materialistically. The energetic formation/circulation between light and water creates conscious/genetic formation, while material transformation creates individual matters of all. The water, representing the biological or materialistic form, comes from the self-rotation of the North Star. Following this, when the first star, called Heavenly Dog, was pulled by the North Star and pushed by other star groups, the holy water dropped from the North Star to the Heavenly Dog. Next it traveled from the Heavenly Dog to the moon. When the moon was rotated and pulled by the solar light and cosmic wind, water flowed from moon onto earth as a result of interaction between sun/moon and other planets.

During the first Ice Age, everything at the two ends of earth was icy, frozen water, as we see at the North and South Poles. In the middle was the fire ball, volcanos and earthquakes. During the course of earth's self-orbit and cyclical rotation, it gradually cooled down the Fire in the middle by melting the Ice on both Poles. Throughout its own evolutionary history, the single water droplet or water molecule attracted the shining light and solar power. The light became the conscious and biological energetic power source, while the solar light fused the water and sugar into the blood stream as the organic breakthrough from inorganic life. Fish and plants and animals then came to life.

In the opposite world, the spiritual and conscious world, God's Creative light then changes into Cosmic conscious makeup, from stars to planets, from cells to organism. When the spiritual power descends into Stars' consciousness, celestial beings are formed. Each celestial spirit is God's specific creative consciousness. Spiritual beings are Conscious beings. When a star's light consciousness works together with planets' water consciousness, angelic beings are formed. Angelic spirit is mechanical spirit. We humans are the mixture of celestial spirit and angelic spirit. The celestial spirit goes to the sun, angelic spirit goes to the moon. Human conscious spirit, as the power representation of sun, is one of many countless spiritual beings. Human biological structure, like all animals on earth, represents the formative power of angelic spirits, in this case the power of earth. Masculine power is closer to celestial spirit, feminine power is more closely related with planetary spirit.

## Behind The Science

When the celestial spiritual beings no longer lived their creative natural life in their own world, they were set down on planet worlds, such as earth, as a form of punishment. In our solar system, their spirits were either transmitted into human bodies or the bodies of gigantic and powerful animals, just as our human spirits were downsized into animal or hellish worlds as a punishment. When those celestial and alien beings are in human bodies, their spiritual makeup is far superior than ordinary human consciousness. They control absolutely the human conscious world, due to their own superior (superior to human's) consciousness. As a result, they would manifest their God's creative secrecy within as either an act of kindness toward the human world in their "salvation" practice, or would stubbornly continue to provoke God's creative power and wisdom as mechanical operation and intellectual manipulation upon human society.

These spiritual beings in human form have undoubtedly the highest power to discover and disclose God's creative wisdom which is either too distant from human consciousness or is buried inside human unconsciousness. They are also the worst enemies in spiritual discipline. Because of their spiritual and intellectual influences, human spirits are contaminated and human consciousness is poisoned, being manipulated and used without ever knowing why.

This is happening not only now in industrial and scientific evolution. This pattern has existed since the beginning of human life. Dragon and dinosaur are, perhaps, the best illustration of those. Christ was a living celestial spirit on earth, having the direct spiritual transmission from God's creative consciousness. The Western Mother in Taoist mythology and the Chinese version of human creation was the angelic spirit. When she lived on earth, her spiritual love attracted God's creative Light as the celestial spirit. She gave virgin birth to the Brother and Sister who were the ancestors of the Chinese race. Another account is, in Chinese history, that if a wife or maiden envisioned light or dreamed about dragon and other celestial spirits, she would give birth to a new emperor.

Alien abduction is not a new topic and has been occurring since the existence of human spirits on earth. As a matter of fact, this is how we humans and animals coexisted on earth initially. Animal life, especially human, is not simply a matter of an evolutionary process on earth from fungi and bacteria to cells and organs, it is the interaction between angelic earth spirit and celestial spirits above and surrounding the planet. When those high spiritual beings present their high wisdom and spiritual consciousness in humans, they become inescapably the powerful political, religious and spiritual leaders. They exercise both self discipline and moral restraint. They provide both warning signs and awakening advice. They become the greatest face of their time, a combination of physical power, intellectual capacity, and spiritual insight.

The ugly side is that when those highly advanced spiritual beings are transmuted into human forms, they take full advantage of human weakness, such as curiosity, lustfulness, obsessive and addictive habits, to compensate for their loss in their previous celestial world. This is where the danger lies in the scientific and industrial revolution. Since the beginning of the industrial revolution, the human mind took on a different role, and the human consciousness became a different reality. There is a clear separation between body and mind, good and bad, sacrifice and control, faithfulness and exploitation.

God creates spirit, science wants His truth. God is a Living Spirit, science looks into tangible materials, such as atoms and chemicals, cells and genetic construction. God is a Moving Spirit, science exercises control so the conditioned mind can feel safe and the instinctive body can be regulated and deregulated in a manageable way. God is the light power, whereas science converts everything into electrical operation and institutional practice. God is the conscious Spirit, science's purpose is to make everything mechanical. The final combination between human consciousness and the industrial development is the communication between the sensory world and mechanical world. It is the battle between man's power, which is egoistic control, and God's power, which is the spiritual awakening reality.

The scientific dream, from insight to invention and from fiction to research, deals largely with the relationship between human/alien spirits and God's Creative Spirit. Scientific mentality is more mechanical than spiritual, more materialistic than celestial. God's Consciousness is the most powerful consciousness. Since God is the maker of all things in the world, we, as God's spiritual children, do not need to rely on any of these matters and their mechanism to reconnect with Him.

In regard to Taoist tradition, the celestial world is one of the biggest trials in spiritual cultivation practice. When a practitioner becomes perfectly clean and still and peaceful, heavenly music can be heard, celestial and angelic spirits will dance "lustfully" to test the practitioner's inner stillness. They want to transmit their power upon the practitioner, to the degree that they will take on a human form. Thus, the practitioner becomes the "uterus" so that those high spiritual beings exercise their power in the human environment. At the very least, those celestial beings are frightening the practitioner's spirit and disturbing her/his inner stillness. Yet nothing can penetrate the spiritual inner stillness. No other spiritual beings can expel God's Divine Spirit. No other female spirit can discard the Goddess's Inner Peace.

## Taming The Heart

In Taoist tradition, taming the heart is always the major discipline. The purpose is to make peace with fire so that the heat in the body will not be wasted, and fire of conscious power will not produce any harm. This is the first priority in spiritual practice. It is not about being passive and submissive, but living a life of self-devotion and complete sacrifice. It is not about forceful devotion and blind and meaningless sacrifice, but the embracement of real liberation and total awakening. It is not about liberation from suffering created by mind and interpreted by the ego, but about fully transforming all the negative energy into positive and unconditional loving energy. It does not seek or long for the positive side of the mental projection and perfection, but embraces both positive and negative into harmonious flow and integrated oneness.

To achieve this is to transform the living world by first transforming your inner world. If the inner consciousness is not understood, the world cannot be understood. If the internal blockage is not liberated, the world will not be liberated. When the spiritual consciousness, which is the nature of unconsciousness as referred to in our modern psychological terms, is not the reality, there will always be an existent duality.

This spiritual consciousness deals with single-pointed fire, double-edged action, and triangular integration. The single-pointed fire is the circle of fire, the totality of the reality. When the point becomes small enough, there is no difference between what is surrounding it and what is inside. They are then one. When the double-edged action is executed, there is an embracement between the inner world and outer world, teaching and learning become the beginning and forever first time interaction. There will be a unified action between destroying the conditioned habits on the one hand and healing the old wounds on the other. There will be conscious present between dying gracefully and living peacefully. The triangle integration is the combination of water and spirit and love, of self and the other and mutual existence, of good and bad and neutral balance.

To tame the heart is to elevate the oceanic water into lake, and then transmit the clean water Qi of love into kind actions and spiritual deeds. Laoist method to accomplish this is: "Governing a large country is like cooking a small fish." (60:1) This is the metaphysical description of how to use conscious fire to steam the biological water. Country here means body, the entire body. Fish have both water Qi and spiritual yang Qi. The water Qi is the oceanic biological makeup, the spiritual Qi is the cosmic conscious creation. This is the pictorial representation of Taichi. This is the cosmic flow of Tao. This is the unconditional vibration of Love.

The small fish cannot be fried or boiled. It must be dehydrated and crystalized. This is the most explicit description of liberating spiritual seed from the vaporizing biological water. The spiritual seed is God's Creative Consciousness within the biological makeup of the small fish. The biological water is the representation of Cosmic Flow of Love. Fish should never be fried or boiled. This could cause the country to disappear, and people be killed. The country is the water, and people are the Love. It is not about Adam and Eve eating an apple. It is about Adam and Eve becoming an apple. The apple is the fruit, the seed, and the oneness of Love.

To tame the heart is to catch the sun firing and to chase the moon-lighting. When the sun-firing is caught, the thought is clear by itself. When the moon-lighting is chased, the dream is the living reality. Body then becomes the kingdom of Land, the country of a nation, the temper of the mind. "Fish cannot live away from the source." (36:2) We cannot live away from the peace and love. This source is the Creative Consciousness, the Creative Light, the Creative Love, and the Creative Oneness.

## Meditation Practice

Heart is empty, it resembles the cosmic womb. Heart is love, it attracts the chasing light. Heart is the center, it balances the conscious intention and its physical action. Heart is where the heart meets, the love dances, the body sweats, the spirit delights, and the soul cries.

Heart is an empty vessel, the instrument of the Tao, the maker of the unconditional love, the central peace for justice, the refiner of all wondering souls.

Heart is the caldron of inner spiritual fire, the wheel of life, the fortune of make-belief, the elixir for healing, and the igniter for liberation.

Heart is the source of life, the home of the couple, the school for education, the justice in the conscientious society, the temple of spirit.

There is no material in the heart, as it becomes visible through the materials of love. There is no vibration in the heart, longing and echoing are dancing through the heart. There is no sweetness in the heart, joy and happiness are produced within the heart. There is no lawful punishment coming through the heart, sacrifice and forgiveness are the justice of the heart. There is no projection nor rejection attached to the heart, acceptance and understanding are the heart.

Love is the instrument of the heart, thoughts are the vibration of the heart, mechanism is the suffering of the heart, faith is the examiner of the heart, children are the speaker of the heart, machine is the comforter of the heart, pet is the understanding of the heart.

Life is the inspiration of the heart, consciousness is the flow of the heart, behavior is the role-player of the heart, result is the reward upon heart, death is the birth of the heart, enlightenment is the bliss of the heart.

Light is the lover of the heart, colors are the matchmakers of the heart, wisdom is the spirit of heart, gut feeling is the arousal of heart, intellect is the eye of heart, love is the play of heart.

Feet are the longings of the heart, arms are the angels of the heart, embracement is the oneness of the heart. Being content is the attitude of the heart.

Dream is the art of the heart, wish is the planning of the heart, hope is the encouragement of the heart, success is the consequence of the heart.

Virtue is the judge of the heart, kindness is the response from the heart, compassion is the heart-blow, stillness is the heart-containment.

Heart for one at a time and heart for all in no time.

# NOTES

誠

# STEP ELEVEN: *FAITHFULLY*

Structure: reach 夆 + completion 成
Sound: cheng
Meaning: faithfully

### Faithful Heart

This Laoist character presents the solution to the previous three characters that remain unresolved, answering the question: where does right action start? Where is the first step to the right Way or the path of the Tao? Where does the heart lean? Along with these questions, there are two more questions waiting to be answered as well. They are "How to retain the empty heart?" and "What happens when the firing heart becomes no-heart?" To retain the empty heart is to utilize the cosmic energy inside the body-mind and circulate it in the invisible space within the empty heart. When the firing heart is charged by the solar light, the Red Sparrow's madness of God's passion is cooled by the oceanic stillness and cosmic tranquility, at which time the heart becomes no-heart. It then becomes the all-heart.

When a person's no-heart changes into the all-heart, sin no longer exists, and all action occupied by the negativity is transformed from its negative energetic compulsion into positive healing potential. The healing potential is the infinite energy power source rooted in God's light, to be used as a healing elixir for the existing wounds that accumulated from the past, and our inability to transform them. When we are able to do so, our future is no longer up to God, nor to the sickness, and is not part of our present entrapment. It is aroused by the awakening spirit, the conscious anticipation, and the flowing loving energy. This purification and revelation process is the portrayal of this eleventh character, the character of "innermost trust and outward faith."

In this character, we will see how the quality of heart, the volume of heart and resolution of heart work together as a unified oneness. The empty heart represents the quality of heart. The firing heart refers to the volume of heart. No-heart describes what the empty heart contains and how the firing heart is distinguished. These forces unite the original intention of action which is the trust within and faith without. Trust discloses the eternal quality as an energetic state, faith illuminates with the mental projection as the external space.

In reference to the empty heart, we must clarify that the heart is empty only to the degree that nothing can or should be contained in it. It implies that emptying the heart is the process of charging it with the energy of spiritual presence. The Eastern religions of Taoism and Buddhism, use the words "emptiness" or "nothingness" to indicate the state of cosmic entity, the condition of mental space, and the content of heart. This emptiness allows the cosmic light and spiritual power to flow freely in the vast space of universal body and in the presence of each and every spiritual body, filling the mental understanding with light and power, thus purifying the desirable heart.

There is no precise difference between emptiness and fullness, because there is no difference between a "solid" matter and its "containable" force. When these two religious traditions use the word emptiness, it is in reference to the vast and spaceless structure of universal matter as forceful empty matter through which energy can shine, vibrate, and circulate fully. Also, it is this vast and spaceless structure that provides an environment for the structural content and dynamic functioning to work with.

Laoist's explanation of the interaction between matter and force and between structural content and dynamic functioning is "Thirty spokes join at one hub, yet it is the emptiness inside the hub that makes the vehicle useful; Clay is molded into a vessel, yet it is the hollowness that makes the vessel useful; Windows and doors are cut out, yet it is their empty space that makes the room usable." (11:1) This is man's way, the replication of Nature's Way. Man's way is not as powerful as nature's. Although never as selfless as nature, it is always useful and valuable. The selflessness and emptiness of a hub/vessel/house are derived by the master self, man. The selflessness of man comes from the Master Self that is exceeding the Heaven Emperor or God.

This work can be explained more clearly by comparing the way bolts and nuts work together. Bolts and nuts tighten pieces together to make the tools stronger and machines more operable. When the nuts and bolts oxidize, they lose their strength. The tool becomes useless, and its operation ceases. In Chinese medicine, this bolt-and-nut theory applies to the energetic and organic functions in human body. A human body has hundreds of pressure points serving as the nuts, while bolts are the discharged energetic forces coming through neural transmitters. Since the human body is made of bones, muscles and organs, these organic bolts and nuts can be treated in a similar manner as they function in machinery. In the body, they too become "oxidized." When the toxins, waste minerals and undigested acids are backed up in a specific area of the body, a blockage occurs. This prevents the energetic force or Qi from flowing freely, resulting in sickness.

The Chinese medical arts use various techniques to unblock this area, either acupuncture or acupressure, herbs or Qigong treatment. For example, in healing with acupressure massage, the healer or therapist can literally come into contact with those "oxidized" areas. When you are informed of the problematic area, you can feel the dot-like spots in the "oxidized" area. The job then is to soften these dots and eliminate them by using healing energy. Chinese medicine doesn't use invasive surgical methods. It has been debated historically, that once the incision is made, it will deplete the vital Qi in that area, preventing it from recovering normally. Surgery would not only destroy the Qi-balance in body-mind, but also allow the evil-Qi to enter the body. This may appear to be a suspicious Qi attitude, but can be compared to punching a hole in a balloon. When the air is released, the balloon is no longer useable.

In conclusion, this bolt-and-nut theory is the business of yin and yang, of matter and force, of structural content and dynamic functioning, of spiritual light and biological water, and of masculinity and femininity. It is the product of "valley-spirit" and the light that "is exceeding the Heavenly Emperor." (4:5) What is valley-spirit? Laoist explains that "Valley-spirit is deathless. It is called the mystical female. The gateway of the mystical female is called the root of heaven and earth. Hovering, it seems everpresent. Put to use, it is never exhausted." (6:1;2;3) The mystical female, the root and the state of hovering are all about the empty condition of matter: cosmic matter, spiritual matter, biological matter, and mechanical matter. They are the matter of heart.

## Man's Way vs. Nature's Way

Since we use the manmade objects of hub, vessel, house or bolt-and-nut business to illustrate the usefulness of emptiness, it is important to have some comparative understanding between the power of man's way and that of Nature's way. Firstly, Nature's valley-spirit seems always empty, yet a man's heart never seems so. A man's heart is always filled with mental distortions, emotional agitations, and biological leftovers. We all know that the uselessness of modern man's and female's heart seem much more useful before the usefulness of valley-spirit, simply because we always place ourselves first in any situation.

Secondly, as mentioned above, creation lies within the power of valley-spirit, and not in man's creative patent rights. The mystic valley creates all forms and matters and substances in the universe, including our body-mind.

Thirdly, female power lies in the forming, healing and recycling, while masculine power fires, penetrates, and liberates. They are the activity of bolt-and-nut function, the mystic nature of I Ching's construction. It is a tragedy that in our modern Western society, the gift of creativity appears to be the entitlement of man, leaving no room for female. Consider the most precious, beautiful and valuable things in the world, consider their source. They are the children who are borne of their mothers' nurturing power. Even during pregnancy and labor a mother takes care of herself and the baby at the same time both consciously and subconsciously. Nobody can compare the link between a man-created-machine and a woman-created-man. The machine is merely mechanical and man is all humankind.

Fourthly, scientific creativity is no longer an imitation but has become a form of self destruction. Scientists rely on their ability to duplicate, replace and reproduce living things, most recently in cloning practices. They cannot ignore or overcome the notion and the obsession of self, nor can they replace the soul-source mechanism and spirit-descending power with their toys and machines.

Toys and machines are very useful and serve their specific purposes. I sit here typing my thoughts through a computer rather than using the time consuming, laborious script, handwriting. It is not possible to write with two hands at the same time, yet I can do so with a keyboard. Handwriting is already a printed form, but it is not an officially printed format. The printer does a much better job. Since I have developed the habit of typing, writing seems not as pleasant, relaxed, engaging, and creative. Typing is certainly more convenient. Typing words, like striking the keys of a musical composition, become the constructive substance in forming lines and roles. The scientific process has created a computer industry that generates the human mentality into a mechanical operation, digital communication, and visual expression.

We can now see ourselves more clearly than ever before, with a deeper understanding of our behavioral manifestations than we would in all previous generations combined. The machines have helped us accumulate and utilize all the generational information into a laptop function. We are empowered with more know-how and accumulated knowledge than could have been dreamed possible a mere generation ago. By the same token, a single action of pushing the buttons of nuclear arsenals can destroy the entire population and all of civilization. Are we still as destructive as we were? As Freud forecast: "the wolf within the man would always want blood." In the past men could only stab one person at a time, the enemy or himself. But now, the entire population can be snuffed out. What a difference the scientific revolution has made!

The question of selfhood today, between spiritual awakening and the intellectual mentality, is more hugely complicated than the early founders' minds could conceive. Look at our society today! Regardless of how hard we try to cling to our selfhood, how little of ourselves do we have? Regardless of how hard we try to perfect ourselves, can any of us be freed from our collective self, the representation of a group, a culture, a nation, or a global village? Could anyone live and survive alone? We have all the fragmented selves but no individual self. We have all the responsibilities but no freedom. In every instance, we are here for our intentions and calculations. Thus, our true self has never been freed. When the original pure self coming from the power of the spiritual descendent has been splintered into self-creative components, how can we live soulfully and spiritually? Have we not already cloned sufficiently?

In spiritual dialogue, I have observed varying opinions regarding the practice of cloning. One holds firmly to the belief that no spirit could live in cloned animals and humans since they are not natural beings. But what is natural? The materials of cloning are all natural. It is only a matter of changing the "bolts-and-nuts" action taken from a natural body to develop an exact replica. Can the spirit, willingly and with excitement, arrive at this test-tube environment? Another opinion suggests that the moment a body is formed, a living spirit will enter. Spirit does not care who made the body. The spirit's only concern is descending and relocating and continuing its existence in an earthly form.

All things are relevant. Nothing will become a common experience to each and every person in the same existing environment. For example, at a family dinner table, some prefer milk while others choose water or fruit juice. The reason is that there is always an immediate self, biologically or mentally or spiritually, but there is no absolute self. Nothing but God is absolute. But you cannot find Him! Yet how absolute could anything be without or beyond God! There is no separation between the one hundred percent single self and the conclusive and exclusive collective self. God is always in both our conceived reality and our expanded imagination, but never in between. We are then and now in between. Our body and mind are the in between. Heaven and earth are the in between. That is both the reality of God's life and our individual/collective lives.

As it has always been, the question of God and self may differ dramatically depending upon the mentality of the expectation of the person who constructs it, but the answers remain the same. The voices are different, yet the silence is the same. The language differs, yet the content never varies. Where is God and where is the self? They are everywhere and yet they are nowhere. They are all powerful and yet are nothing at the same time. They are the wind-blowing before the pro-creative construction and they are the echoing presence upon the dissolving resolution in the aftermath. The true self is none of your expectation and none of your concern. Nor is God. Religious or not, spiritual or not, sexual or not, none of it matters. The God's Self is always there before any conscious intention, and remains there after all the habits are broken. Yet it is never there when the consciousness is the reality, and when the habit is the belief.

There are two resolutions to the nature of man's way versus nature's way. Consequently, man's way can be said to be nature's way because man's way is natural. The personal and social and cultural are more inclined toward man's way because they are anti-nature or have been somehow abused. Even so, nature does not care! No man can change nature's destructive behavior within its violent acts of earthquakes, torrential rains, and fierce winds. Naturally, a person must always care about oneself, whether healthy or sick, awake or asleep. As do our social and cultural selves. Nothing matters more in human life than our selves. Anything attractive can offer an invitation. We become slaves to anything useful. How to maintain man's way in the order of nature's way is the content of this eleventh Laoist character.

## The Characteristic Representation

This Laoist eleventh character is composed of two basic characters, Zhi and Cheng, the character Zhi meaning "head toward ultimate" or "reach to an extreme." Nothing higher and nothing further. The original definition of this character in Chinese is that a bird descends from on high by following one and single-eye-pointed projection of ground. It pertains to "the flying bird in the air doesn't reach any higher and is ready to come down." In its literal sense, this would carry on the message of cultivation from the previous character from where the heart must return, be at home and grounded. In spiritual sense, the spirit must return to its oneness and never be led astray by the distractions and confusions. This oneness is the peak and highpoint where the bird (as each and every one of us) can see the self and world clearly. This is the power of single-eye, the third eye. The oneness is the landing point, the most ideal spot, and highest achievement. It is the dot of our one-self-ness. This oneness is the meaning of cheng or "highest completion, performance, or accomplishment."

Conclusively, zhi means that one has tried and done the best possible. Picture one running toward a cliff while looking back to the precious existence of self. This character allies two situations in life: One is the condition of effort, devotion, and sacrifice. The other is the situation of self-abuse, self-neglect, and self-contamination. Both situations embody the ultimate and the extreme. In its practical sense, one must realize the preciousness of life and the value of spiritual existence before the masonry-like physical existence. One must be grounded with the spiritual weight before the phantom ego alights.

According to the commentary of I Ching, "you can mystify the Ultimate of the world but you cannot hate it. You can act upon the Ultimate of the world but you cannot destroy it." The Ultimate represents the source for both spiritual and mental quest, physical and biological action. You should not, and you must not, either hate it or attempt to destroy it. When you allow yourself to hate it, you establish an internal action upon your own Ultimate divine. If you attempt to destroy it, you are destroying your own vital connection. The hatred emerges in the flight from the self and towards the self. The destructive action results in self-destruction. When the Ultimate links the form and image together in its spaceless picture, there is no way that you can project hatred upon it. When the Ultimate connects both the vital force for action and the final reward for interaction, there is no way that you can lose/disconnect its void-like vital root.

According to Tao Te Ching, this character can be defined as: "To know others is to be knowledgeable. To know oneself is enlightenment; To master others is to have strength. To master oneself is to be powerful. To know what is sufficient is to be rich. To act with determination is to have will. Not to lose one's substance is to endure. To die, but not be forgotten, is to be immortal." (33;1;2) In this sense, others are the extreme, and self is the ultimate. In order to accomplish this, one has to use the willpower. In order to achieve this, one needs to be centered by the enduring essence. Immortality is not a message of number, namely, the history of one's age. It is the living presence of the vibration of spirit. This spirit never dies and people will never cease to worship it. This is the ultimate extreme between the self and others.

In order to embrace and balance both the self and the other, one must be honestly, sincerely, extremely, and completely successful. This is the message of the second character. This second character cheng means that a person has been matured and honest and tested thoroughly in the cultivation journey for the success of complete accomplishment to be thus achieved. In its linguistic construction, this character is combined from the fourth and fifth characters of the heaven's stems. The fourth stem symbolizes the heart, representing all things that are due for harvesting in the summer. The fifth stem symbolizes the arms, signifying the twisted and entangled posture among six heads of five dragons. When the heart is centered, the six realms of the world will be integrated. When the heart becomes matured and completely honest, it will unify the five elemental Qi into a single act, the selfless love.

Thus, the six worlds are centered, the five dragons are tamed, and single heart is the manner in which it manifests. Success results and is distinguished by the accomplishment of all affairs, signifying that one has produced enough goodness for the reaction and interaction of a karmic situation to be completely dissolved. Nothing troubles the pure nature of the heart, nor interferes with the vibration of the selfless love.

The combined meaning of these two regular characters indicates that one has accomplished enough to raise one's arms skyward expressing exuberantly the winning, overcoming, and empowering message of victory. It also indicates that a person returns to (follows after) the altar where the empty heart becomes fully present, thereby accomplishing itself naturally according to the spiritual law. In humankind, this accomplishment is not concerned with accomplishing any particular thing, either deed or action, but overcoming the agitations and desires arising from the heart. It is about transforming the negative energy patterns into the positive loving energy of the heart.

This positive energetic form is the vibration of pure heart within the form of empty heart, or conscious light. When the heart finally becomes present, away from wandering and possessing and being mad within itself, the conscious light is the presence and success is the inevitable consequence. This success is not based upon succeeding but on how the empty heart allows the full manifest of all affairs around and within. This allowance absents all wishful thinking and desirable expectation. As Laoism has concluded "Success is consequent to all affairs." (34:2)

In conclusion, this eleventh Laoist character reveals that success is an act of devotion, not an exertion of will power. Do not allow yourself to be overrun by the various stages and temporary rewards before the final success is achieved. Going to the extreme without being chained by the extreme can be achieved by knowing where to stop, when to return, and how to embrace the extremes. In the unity of this is the accomplishment of all affairs, the ultimate success.

## The Meaning of Success?

To achieve success is the toughest endeavor in human life after health and happiness. Success needs health and happiness to accomplish its goal. There are two ways of measuring success: one is through common domain and the other is through spiritual outcome. Through common domain, success is seen as an accomplishment toward a specific goal driven by planned strategy. It is based upon the pursuit of either materialistic wealth or mental status. It is the attainment of a favorable position and reputation of a grander scale in terms of material gains and authority.

The spiritual measurement is the ability to master one's death while the life continues. It is how to retain the empty heart and sustain the vital force. The final success is measured not by the ego-driven or earthly opportunistic agenda. Status is an ego-certified position, and its crown is shifted routinely and often from one person to the next. Earth Mother recycles mercilessly both her own products and those made by man. Only the spiritual love, the virtuous deed, and oneness of the Tao can initiate and process success by itself. That is the Ultimate of spiritual success. Tao recycles the spirits but not the earth. Heart activates the spirit but not the matter. Success liberates the spirit and never restrains it.

Everybody differs in terms of degree and time preference on the scales of success, and each stage of life greets its own specific criteria in comparison to others. Since everybody's efforts and attempts to succeed differ, they all reach only their naturally rewarded success. As a result, each person naturally achieves her/his highest degree of success during the life time. Some gain fame and wealth at an early age, others struggle till long after their prime. Some achieve success along the way, others strive fruitlessly to tap into its secret door. Still others have to wait until the future generation (children or students) claim their successful results.

Success can be concrete and abstract at the same time. When the mind, the intention, the efforts and outcome all come together, success is a reward of both liberation and relaxation, gain and surplus, accomplishment and achievement. When personal feelings and attachments gradually slide away, success becomes as abstract as health and happiness. There is no status quo about it and it does require sacrifice. If the gain is more than the sacrifice, it is deemed a success. But if the gain is canceled out or there is a negative surplus, one must bear the loss. Success cannot be attached too closely with the personal and social components. To do so is to jeopardize success since one person's idea of success is another's rejection. Each person's attitude toward success may vary from time to time depending upon the primary needs and various attempts to achieve.

Success requires a certain degree of intensity and devotional sacrifice, enormous will power and energy consumption. If one always stands on the opposite side, there would be no such thing as success in this individual's life. Nothing can be changed and nothing will be achieved. The problematic areas standing in the way of success are:

1) There is no fixed scale to measure and clearly define success. There is no single way to define the requirements that meet success. One's success can elicit admiration in some people and contempt or hatred in another peer group because every one wishes for it and no one wants to abandon it.

2) There is often a gulf between what one attempts to do and expects to accomplish and what one actually receives and obtains. It depends largely on how well one knows and understands one's self and surroundings. The degree and completion of success also encounters the most obscured fateful fact of life, sheer luck and life-changing opportunity. Opportunity and luck are generally the last means to empower success.

3) Success is always personally defined and culturally determined. Personal needs are the demands, cultural glorifications are the

supply. Unfortunately, these two change from place to place, and shift from nation to nation.

4) Success has much to do with eternal qualities but nothing to do with eternal outcome, and is forever accompanied by a totally lonesome self. Nor does it entail the external manifestations of the inner qualities of happiness and love and selflessness as an attribute. In terms of the outcome, nothing matters more than accomplishing affairs. Affairs, however, are interpersonally designed and inter-culturally measured.

By contrast, the spiritual outcome of success differs dramatically from this common domain of achievement and measures. The spiritual success is characterized by the following:

1) One must overcome the dark forces rising from the karmic interaction in the past. This is the most difficult path because all the personal and cultural interactions coming through in this life are the accumulation resulting from the past. Why do some always gain more support than others? Why do some suffer greater misfortune than others? Why is everyone confronted with the same dark force and shadow again and again? Why does a specific personality structure or psychic aura meet the same patterns of both attraction and rejection? Why do good people encounter bad luck and bad people are gifted with good luck?

The successor in the common domain finds the gain and support and achievements through this karmic interaction, while a spiritual successor is able to transform them all. A spiritual successor realizes that no one can be successful in all things and no one can be pleased with every outcome of affairs. The teachings of Laoism are: "To know steadfastness means enlightenment. Not to know steadfastness is to act forcefully." (16:3) "Therefore, the sage is good at his earnest demands upon people. No one is left out. No talent is wasted. This is called being in the tow of enlightenment. And it ensures the good person." (28:3) "To know others is to be knowledgeable. To know oneself is enlightenment." (33:1)

2) One must stand up to all the trials along the road, including temporary gain and loss, attraction and illusion, distortion and disgrace. There is a similarity between this spiritual path and the regular domain of success in the sense that they both require effort and determination to strive forth and achieve. But the regular domain of success is measured largely through material gain, quantumized by the personal possessions, and inflamed by the cultural glory, while the spiritual success is measured only by love, valued by trust, and tested by faith. A successful life is surrounded by external gain and comfort. It is glorified by the eternal pride and satisfaction. Pride cannot enter the vast universal grace, and satisfaction can shrivel from the body at any given time. In a successful spiritual life, the gain is established by overcoming suffering in the Eastern term, and sin, the Western term. Its comfort is measured by the eternal stillness and external happiness.

3) One cannot be measured by the success of one's physical life, because it amounts to nothing when facing death. This is the hard and concrete rule in spiritual discipline written in stone. By no means can ordinary people come to terms with it before being stricken with the final punishment, which is always what they have earned. Success means

nothing before the final punishment or liberation. It is the success in the after-life that is paramount. Viewed in the spiritual eye, success is a warning sign and awakening call to take whatever opportunities available to transform life from the lower and mixed level into a higher and more purified level. Other than the spiritual liberation, death carries all the gains and surpluses of one's life time into a second cycle of life formation. In the next cycle the one who formerly gained less then will gain more. The person who gained more will lose more.

Therefore, 4) One must overcome the psychological and egoistic fear of the biological death process. Death is a safe heaven, and there is nowhere else to turn. Psychological fear can not understand it, and egoistic fear does not want to deal with it. In reality, egoistic anticipation, at both personal and group level, regards death as the hardest journey in life. That is why spiritual life values this journey by embracing it with love and light.

The meaning of a spiritual life in terms of success is far more than the accomplishment itself. It disregards the pride of achievement and obsession of its "ownership." As Laoist has further indicated, success "does not proclaim its own existence." "All things return. Yet there is no claim of ownership. So it is forever without desire. This can be called small. All things return. Yet there is no claim of ownership. This can be called great. The sage accomplishes greatness in not acting great. Thus can he accomplish what is great." (34:2;3)

The next step is giving in and giving up. Giving in is stopping at the moment of gain to share the presence of an accomplishment. It is an honor bestowed upon the mutual presence of the group. Giving up is not about relinquishing objects, but giving up mental obsessions and fixations on the material things. It is about giving up old memories locked within the spiritual consciousness. It is about giving up the ownership and allowing the spirit be free. Material things are useful and valuable in sustaining the livelihood of the temple of life. Why give them up? Food is always good, utilities are always useful. Why should one who spends all the life energy gathering the material things give them up? The spirit gives all things up, so should the mind let them go. The idea is to release them and enjoy them with a connected feeling and distilled mind. When there is no selfishness involved, the meaning of "ownership" does not exist. When the ownership does not exist, one embraces the small.

When a person is in the prime, physical appearance becomes a form of ownership. The male does not willingly surrender his strength, nor the female forsakes her beauty. When illness or an accident strikes out at that strength or beauty, the power of "ownership" is dissolved. When two lovers are getting married, each one's body is a "registered" or "licenced" ownership. When the relationship falls apart, and the life changes direction, this form of ownership no longer exists. When someone is madly in love and sacrifices her/himself for it, the love becomes a form of ownership. It is not the unconditional love which is eternal in itself. The love sacrificed is the loving energy which is sold. How can it be regained? It is a double loss that precipitates hatred.

In our institutionalized society, we are expected to own houses and cars, degrees and titles. How does it end? The status of President bestowed upon William Clinton has given him more troubles than any success he could achieve. To be elected and inaugurated is the highest success already and forever. Yet, a President is entrusted as a moral leader, but a human being encompassing a paired mortal body and moral deeds. Can one be excepted to be completely moral and mortal at the same time? Can one eat and fast at the same time? Can one breathe and drink at the same time?

Problems exist because people are brainwashed by the important titles and those of politically powerful names and consequently forget about being small and humble. Embracing the small allows the presence of the great. Recognizing the small allows the import of the great. Great people accomplish greatness by being small in order that both people and good fortune honor and impute ever more greatness toward their final accomplishment: the success of all affairs related to the personal growth needed in the spiritual enlightenment.

Contrary to this, many people fail along the way because the effort appears too daunting or they are mired in their struggling efforts. There is no more will power or the will power turns its energy to purely personal pursuits, losing sight of the goal initially designed. Laoism explains sharply that "The common people's engagement in affairs fail prior to success. So the saying goes, 'Give as much careful attention to the end as to the beginning; then the affairs will not fail'. It is on that account that the sage desires not to desire and does not value goods that are hard to get. He learns not to learn and restores the common people's losses. He is able to support the nature of all things and, not by daring, to impose action." (64:6;7;8)

In life, daily or momentarily imagined, there are many things done unsuccessfully. One reason is that it is not ready to be done and the time is not right. Knowing that one can accomplish something but not having done so only means that the time is not right. Over and above the hard work applied and the enduring will, the virtue of patience is necessary. Another factor is that the person wishing to be successful in the endeavor does not work in the objective and karmic fashion.

Setting aside this reasoning, many people misuse the meaning of success. Success is the result of managing and working through affairs to their rightful conclusions. The degree of expectation before the results are seen and the degree of intensity of devotion determine the variation of the natural consequence. The unexpected surprises come from having either low expectations or too high expectations. To have no expectation can sometimes elicit the positive aspect of surprise. High expectations always lead to the negative aspect of surprise, which is possibly a disgrace, as well. What the mind does not expect, anticipate and wish for is the opposite, or bad (but not necessarily "bad" as how things will turn out to be). They are not necessarily bad as were first thought so. They are only regarded so because they are opposite from what was originally wished for as good. Here, the teaching of Laoism advocates that "For everything that is good is the teacher of the good person. Everything that is bad becomes a resource for the good person. No need to honor the teachers. No need to love the resources. Though knowing this is a great paradox, it is a subtle principle." (27:3;4)

## Between Realization and Actualization

Few people realize the truth in the aphorism that "what you want is what you get." Even fewer can make it an actuality. Not many really know what they want, except for the egoistic, emotional, and instinctive desires. They do not actualize the vibration and manifestation and illumination of their pure love. In reality, the heart's intentions are what the heart receives. What makes the hearts vibrate is what the heart responds to. This is the realization process, while actualization means going straight to the direction your heart leads you. Let nothing mislead or misdirect your path, whether it be illness, loss of connection, or physical punishment. The persuasion should never be deviated, and the devotion should never be dimmed. There may be some yielding paths or relaxing times, but never wandering away. There will be pain but it will relent. The bones may be broken, but the spirit remains sheltered within, undaunted.

On the whole, realization is superbly visual and imaginative, while actualization remains graphic and painstaking. Realization paints an ideal visual map. Actualization treads through the maze of puzzles and pains and trials toward that the final destination. On the spiritual path, realization is much swifter than actualization. It has no karmic trials and blockages along the road, only the spiritual clouds floating in the mind. Realization comes only from the shining spiritual and visual light. For actualization, the road is immediate but the future is blind, unknown, mysterious. Each step taken is an independent success as one progresses through the imagined land. Each step is an isolated block. Having a good career, a happy home, good relationship and health is a mentally projected realization. They are all real conditions in the mind's projection upon that particular time. Their actualization may necessarily bring realistic punishment arising from an unrealistic expectation. When finally the realization and actualization become one, there is only success on either side of the story-telling activity, since the old successful story is relived by the new storyteller of the same old success.

History is an accumulation of stories of success and sacrifice behind the eternal spiritual presence. A storyteller imagines the old story and relives it consciously and personally. An institution is a story-telling place where education reinforces the continuous story-telling activities. There is a soul connection between the spirit in the old story and the person relearning and reliving it. In the same way, each growing stage of a younger generation is a story-telling experience. There is a common ground between those who have experienced and those who have not, since the old story repeats itself. Each seasonal game is a story-telling experience since the essence never changes. Only the numbers are different and players are renewed. So what is the final success? Ask the owners, the head coaches, players and fans. "What is next?" is probably the only reply in the media. But what is the difference between the first accomplishment and the ones which follow?

Each momentary and daily experience is a story telling activity, and each generation is a relived old story. That is both realization and actualization. The best story told is that of working well each day and enjoying a good rest at night. That is success. Everything possible has been calculated and all things are well taken care of. Nothing is missing and nothing has been rejected.

Continuing along the path of growth and liberation, each success along that affair brings a new crisis, a new blockage, and a new challenge. In many instances, failure results in a new progress leading toward the final success. A real success is welcomed only by final separation, the reality-check from the body and imaginative land formed by the mind, initiated by the firing heart and desiring mind. It is also spurred by the differences between realization and actualization. Realization is the reality where its action and the mental maps are representative. In actualization nothing is real and nothing makes sense. Every real thing has already been digested and experienced. What else is real and meaningful? Only the unknown murmurs silently. This is the real map of success and the real work leading to success. The unknown is real to realization and upon actualization. What else is real in the beyond, the future?

## Between Wish and Hope

Wish is a selfish expectation and hope is a projection of inner thought. Wish is more object oriented and hope is a vision or a picture of eternal world. Wish is extreme and hope is neutral. In front of hope, there is a mixture of desire and belief, and there is a mixed feeling of will and trust. When a wish comes true, it is nothing more than an actual display of pre-programmed mental thought. This pre-programming wants nothing more, nothing less, other than that ideal thought.

In this process, there are two things that wish does not want to encounter, the phrases of "I was disappointed" and "It was so unexpected." To further distinguish between a wish and a hope, you must understand that wish is very realistic, either because it is an unrealistic expectation or merely an illusion. On the other hand, you must understand that hope can embrace both the wishful and willful, both imaginative and trustful. In the lower realm, hope is a wish, especially if there is an objective goal. When hope is directed inwardly, it emerges as willful action. This willful action has the inner trust to support it. In its purest form, hopeful action is willful action. They are the substance of trust.

We must clearly distinguish the wish as the response of inner hope from the wish responding to one's desire. Inner hope is the presence of will, the absolute confidence and the absence of fear, while desire is a misunderstood form of wish, fixated pattern of mental obsession. Hope, in many instances, is an indication of liberation from restraint, attachment or fixation. It is a full commitment to one's inner vibration and calling, particularly in the case of inner hope which is the devotion of inner wish, for nothing other than its ingrained presence. This full presence is all-consuming, all that one has, can engage in, and seeks to accomplish.

The master support for this full presence is faith. Faith is total acceptance, complete understanding, fully anticipating, and harmoniously working through the process. Faith is not blind, it is as crystal clear as the shining light; faith does not agitate but preserves its steadfastness and opens itself to its awareness; faith is not giving up oneself, but giving the self up to the degree that the self is no longer an issue. That is when the self becomes the real issue. Faith is listening to the inner heartbeat, opening widely the space of heart, and accepting completely the self and all others as a unified oneness, not as diversified entities.

While this country, the U.S. was orenticed by the President's sex scandal, I couldn't but wonder about two prominent words seen many times: Hope, the President's birth place, and Star, the president's fierce rival. The Chinese phrase of "K. (for Kenneth) and Star' means rival or destructive star, pronounced ke xing (an expression often used to connote one's karmic company). Star is a single concentrated body of the vibration of heat and light. Hope encompasses both will power and spiritual longing, both realization and transformation, both awakening and illumination. To the President, his guiding Star was extremely powerful and distractive.

As luck would have it, the year of 98 numerically represented a form of masculine-feminine power. The masculine must obey the inner stillness and clarity of the feminine quality rather than illuminating itself vigorously and powerfully. When Star's power became the dominant factor during the summer of 1998, there was no Hope (no returning home) for the President to defend or retaliate. When the time shifted from Summer to Fall and Winter, the vibration and visibility of that Satanic penetration diminished gradually. At the arrival of Winter, the feminine power of receiving through inner stillness would diminish the vibration of a shining Star. This was at the end of 1998, preceding the final awakening power of healing and transformation begun in 1999.

(My prediction which I wrote at that time, 10-4-98 2:30 p. m. was that if the present situation continues into 1999, there is more support power arising from the President's forces than from K. Star's defensive power because no star can stand up to double yang. The President is one yang of nine, and his position is another yang of nine. He requires the healing transformation only from now till Winter of 1999. The feminine healing power will unite with his presidential power in this upcoming masculine year, assuring that he will retain his position. At the present time, the President should be concerned only with healing within and outward confidence.)

## The Content of Faith

When the physical trauma is healed, the awakening love is received, the organic Qi are unified, the practitioner will reach a state where the inner trust and absolute faith permeate the eternal need and external action. This is the stage of faith, along the spiritual cultivation practices. When this faith is established, self is all that one needs to trust, be devoted to, and anticipate.

Do not confuse the daily faithful trust with the deep spiritual faithful understanding. In our daily life, all situations are transitional, temporary, and stationary. Faith becomes a trust dealing with a specific situation or solving a particular problem. For example, "I trust you." and "I have faith in you."generally mean that the person trusts both your deeds and result, and retains the professional or personal entrustment. In this situation, there is little difference between what one has trust in and what one is faithful to.

In contrast, after the practitioner awakens her/his heart into love with light, trust becomes the pillar that allows the heart to continuously operate on full scale. Devotion will discipline one to defend against being side-tracked, lured from the path, express no hesitation, and waste no wasted time and effort. Anticipation is the joy of experiencing and engaging. When trust opens the door, devotion enters and invites anticipation to perform the task, ensuring both completion and satisfaction. These are the rewards of faith. Faith is the pure and loving heart. Its reward is the empty selfless heart. When one has a faithful heart, everything is satisfactory; there is no separation between a subjective dream and the objective course, and there is no defining line between the subjective satisfaction and the objective result. The word faith suggests the connotation of acceptance, understanding, and trustworthiness. It is an action created by ego absence. God or self, universe or body, energy or mind are all one.

Faith needs no promise. Normally, a promise is about clinging to an idea, an authority, being cloaked in bargaining posture, or engaged in a fearful situation. When someone makes a promise, it is an assurance that the matter will be controlled irrevocably, that the work will be performed well, and its personal evaluation will be authorized before its completion. Promises are pride, fame, ego satisfaction, and self glorified good performance. Hidden behind the good intentions are fear, frustration, suspicion, lack of confidence, and personal denial of one's inability to calculate the complexity of a natural outcome.

Any promise can and must be situational, personal, psychological, and cultural: smoothly handled, kindly offering the personality, peacefully demonstrating the psychological quality, and vulnerably sustaining the cultural environment are all part and parcel of the content of promise. The more one knows about oneself, the less one needs to promise. The more one understands the complexity of a situation, the less one tries to compromise with the inevitability of change in the situation.

Sadly enough, all the legal system is, to a large degree, predicated by the compliments to the pre-calculated outcome of a situation. Nobody can sustain an eternal calculation because the mind always changes, and no one can guarantee the outcome in an external world because all things are forever changing. The only way to judge the quality of a promise and to guarantee the outcome of that promise is with capital punishment at last, or leveling of a fine at least. Friendship merges into business deals, and personal relationships change into a victimized situation. When the ego attempts to control everything, when pride overshadows the situation, promises are the premise of justice and the best defense mechanism.

Equally, when fear confronts the relationship and desire controls the will, promise reflects the quality that connects the fear with basic needs. It also replaces the drive with a self-betrayed consequence. Indigenous dwellers, unlike civilized people, have a clear concept of the meaning of promise. What they feel is what they reveal and what they have is what they see. There is no need to promise anything. Everyone understands everyone else and faces the same dilemma based solely on obvious condition.

Before a child has been educated, socialized, and civilized, s/he cannot understand the meaning of promise since the trust is already there and the heart is up front. Later, when the eternal world is colored with information, educated with calculation, and envisioned with possession, promise will enter the picture. By the time the external world is painted with name, elevated with statues, and listed with obsession, promise compromises the outcome of life.

In return, what keeps everything going is the accumulation of efforts to victimize one another. "What is your promise?" and "You have promised..." become the gambling elements held on both sides. Laoism has summarized this as "Facile promises necessarily result in little trust. What is easy necessarily entails difficulty. Thus the sage, through extreme trials, ends up with no difficulty." (63:6;7)

In the matter of trust, the major consideration is establishing a self-trusting environment. Self-trust arises from pure energy channeling. This channeling power transmits the cosmic light and spiritual vibration into a conscious based, acknowledged, and well-informed field where there is no visible negativity. There must exist a complete purification in the mental, emotional, and biological distortions stored in the body-mind. A hungry person has no secure stomach. A clouded mind has no pure vision. A murky soul has no inner stillness. A ghostly spirit has no enlightening illumination.

Self-trust has all the components one seeks, searches, discovers and explores externally. When one transfers this portion of energy inwardly, the life essence is preserved, and true self is then revealed naturally. Even the last segment of self is hidden in the unknown, spaced with void, and imagined with God, a true knower is a self-knower. This is why Laoism claims that "to know oneself is enlightenment." (33:1)

One should differentiate between knowing and being knowledgeable because the structure of knowledge is already removed from the subjective anticipation. "The knower does not know everything. The know-it-all knows nothing." (68:1) Why? The knower is in a self-enlightened space of mentality. The knower does not need to know anything further in any given situation except for the digestion of the Tao and illumination of action. The know-it-all has no extra space or new information available. All s/he has is the already dead knowledge.

This is why Tao is always alive in person to person, situation after situation, and time through time. It is always completed and renewed at the same time. Nothing is left behind or dissolved. Nothing has been rejected or miscalculated. The knower places oneself in a pre-empted state. Through all the insightful experiences, the spirit is further sharpened, the mind is further purified, and the experienced knowledge become the living vibration. Through light, all is seen. Through holy water, everything is crystalized. This allows a pre-emptied state. "Preempty measures mean a great accumulation of Action. A great accumulation of Action leaves nothing to be conquered. When nothing needs to be conquered, no boundary is known. When no boundary is known, it allows the country to exist." (59:1) What does country mean to a person? Her/his body.

"The Knower does not know anything." also means that there are no preoccupied thoughts or beliefs whatsoever. There is neither pre-calculated intention nor ego-driven projection. When this state is the Conditioning, what else does the knower know? Nothing. What is the use of knowing anything? The knower is in such an occupied and grounded world that s/he becomes pointless, groundless, and functionless. This kind of knowing is not limited to the visions and words and calculations regarding the world. It is about the inability to reject any further and the capacity to interact in all realms. This is again the Flow of the Tao, not the flow of drives and instincts. When this self is the content of trust, there is no expectation and no misunderstanding. Silence becomes the action. When silence becomes the action, what is the use of speech!

This silent action is the substance of trust in the Tao. The teaching of Laoism explains clearly that "The marks of profound action follow only from the Tao. The substance of Tao is boundless and unfathomable. Unfathomable and boundless, in its center there is form; Boundless and unfathomable, In its center there is an object; Embryonic and dark, In its center there is essence; The essence is very pure, In its center there is trust. From now to the days of old, Its name never dies, Because it creates all things in their beginning. How do I know the source of all beginnings? From this." (21:1;2;3) What the minding spirit carries before the form is the boundless and unfathomable. What the profound action objectifies upon the pure essence is the trust. The substance of Tao is Trust. God's love is Trust.

## On Trustworthy Speech

Laoism pointedly states that "Trustworthy words are not beautiful. Beautiful words are not trustworthy." (68:1) The artistic beauty of a speech can promote the understanding between words and lines. It can also uplift the power connection between sonic vibration and silent action. But it never loses the simple notion of intention underlining the speech. Nor can it replace the plain truth of trust. Why? Because the beautified speech deviates from the truth, and artificial speech never builds upon the faith. "When faith is weak, there is distrust. Especially in the worth of speech. Results speak for themselves. This, people call me Nature." (17:2;3)

On another occasion, Laoist explains that the trustworthiness does not deal with the things or objects one trusts. It is about self-trust.

He demonstrates this by implying that action of a sage is: "The sage is always without his own mind. He uses people's minds as his mind. He is kind to those who are kind. He is also kind to those who are not kind. It is the kindness of Action itself. He is trustworthy to those who are trustworthy. He is also trustworthy to those who are not trustworthy. It is the trust of Action itself. In the world, the sage inhales. For the world, the sage keeps the mind simple. All people are fixated on the ears and eyes, while the sage always smiles like a child." (49:1;2;3;4)

When the sage inhales in the world, the Love and power of the Tao is alive and vibrant within. When the sage keeps his mind simple, his trustworthy action speaks for itself. What more can a sage do than smile like a child? Isn't the child-like smile loveable to the Tao, simple to the fact, and plain as the trust?!

## The Faithful Practice on Selfhood Tao

"When eminent persons hear of Tao, they practice it faithfully." (40:1) Why? They have a high spiritual base for cultivation and purification. Their energy patterns are more fitting and their personal structures move easily into the flow. The word "eminent" refers to a more spiritual groundedness. It is charged by pure yang Qi, instead of yin or mixed Qi. The nature of yang Qi is bright, light, pure, tranquil, and illuminating. Because of this vibrational frequency, those eminent people are not directed or influenced or changed by the present standard conduct, values, rules, regulations, social norms. Nor are they being measured or retrained by the numerous requirements supposedly to be met before certain achievements are accomplished. Everything they do connects deeply with the nature of the Tao.

Secondly, those eminent people are highly self-disciplined individuals. Rules and regulations do not bother them because they are with the flow and being with the flow is the ruling order. Their accurately anticipating, soulfully participating and completely transforming are the realities of being with the flow.

Thirdly and most importantly, those eminent people are honest to their behavior and true to themselves. As soon as the eminent person hears of the Tao, there is a complete understanding and integration with it. There appears no question, no cloudiness, and no doubts. The light is there, the understanding is there, the love is there, and the trust is all that is there.

The word "hear" is not limited to the content of ordinary hearing ability. Over and above that is the thorough anticipation. They not only hear the Tao, they listen to their inner voice as well. They hear everything about the Tao on the basis of self understanding and self liberation. They are not passive listeners, they are active participants. When the informed message of the Tao and the inner voice of listening to the Tao are merged, faith is the presence. All that is present is the faith. It is thus that they practice the Tao faithfully. This is not a blind faith, it is a heart opening choice and a light awakening voice.

In contrast, when the close-minded people, the so-called disbelievers, hear the Tao, they open themselves only to the degree of their habitual comfort. There is neither liberation nor freedom within. All they hear is what they want to hear, which is propriety, the things, and environment to which they are accustomed. Laoist warns that "Propriety is the veneer of faith and loyalty, and the forefront of troubles." (38:4) These people are not faithful to themselves, but faithful to their habitual comfort. So, where are they and where is the Tao?

## What Faith Means In The Art Of Healing

In the human healing process, whether it entails a surgery or a medication, whether involving drug treatment or placebo, the result comes from the faith within the heart. A placebo (whether for the purpose of experimentation or as an actual treatment) prescribed by a doctor to a patient is an extension of the use of candy given by the parent to console or cajole a child. Modern medical practice is an institutionalized and intrusive removal of the subjective healing ability and skill. The patient transfers her/his subjective healing ability to the objectified action, the operation, or the objectified matter, medication. Whether or not these actions or matters are effective, they are initiated from the subjective faith. And the medical profession utilizes this faith in its unceasing demand for business profits.

The surgeon sets about the action of removing and relocating the problem. Drugs are the vehicles for suppressing the problem. Rather than healing from within, they aggressively invade the body's natural bodily organic functioning, by using the virus or bacteria or heretical mal-genetic mutation as a means of separating matter from energy manifestation. The legal practice follows quickly in exactly the same pattern. The government, in turn, endorses this candy-treating behavior. In meditation, when cultivation is complete, the faith is complete; the completion does not lead to a condition that will make you healthy or wealthy or famous, but will open the way to immortality. This entails not only will and dedication, but most importantly faith, an ardent, passionate faith that connects oneself with the universe and our universal creator—God. It is the most complete encompassing devotion. It is the highest fulfillment one can ever attain, the most satisfying success one could ever reach.

## Meditation Practice

When one looks the world within peacefully,
The image reveals itself objectively.
Chewing the materials meditatively,
The body responds with surprise cheerfully.
Digesting the substances thoughtfully,
The mind acknowledges with light reasonably.
Feeling the gut's knowing authentically,
The trust of the world is all there originally.
Opening arms with heart sensationally,
The love tells the story back and forth individually.
Peering into the mind's eye intellectually,

Everything is understood completely.
Walking through the wondering path mindfully,
The journey completes itself successfully.
Sitting into the four corners of the world knowingly,
The substance of the Tao presents itself faithfully.

# NOTES

_____

_____

_____

_____

_____

_____

_____

_____

_____

_____

_____

_____

_____

溣

# STEP TWELVE: *IMMORTAL*

Structure: water $\dot{;}$ + heaven 禾 + well 井
Sound: yi
Meaning: immortal

## The Structural Content of Immortality

1 Reaching the ultimate emptiness,
  Concentrating on the central stillness,
  All things work together.
2 From this I observe their returning.
3 All things under heaven flourish in their vitality,
  Yet each returns to its own root.
  This is stillness.
  Stillness means returning to its destiny.
  Returning to its destiny is steadfastness.
  To know steadfastness means enlightenment.
  Not to know steadfastness is to act forcefully.
  Acting forcefully brings disaster.
  Knowing the steadfast implies acceptance.
  Acceptance is impartial.
  Impartial is regal.
  Regal is heaven.
  Heaven is Tao.
  Tao is beyond danger even when the body perishes. (Ch. 16)

The above chapter in the Tao Te Ching describes vividly the essential substance that enhances the journey of entering the Tao and the benefits received from following it through. The "ultimate emptiness" is the infinite space and energetic environment in which to search faithfully, submit honestly and embrace totally. It is called the cosmic valley or heavenly well. "Concentrating on the central stillness" provides the path as the eternal bridge leading into this ultimate emptiness. The Central Stillness refers to the most resourceful root for the formation, deformation and transformation revolutionarily and involutely. The Central Stillness is the Cosmic Void, the Valley Spirit, and the Holy Water. The Ultimate Emptiness is the largest universal space in and of itself, and the Central Stillness is the most minuscule substance in the infinitive space of the universe. This tiniest substance is the root of Tao, the resource of Life, and existence of Love. It is within the invisible space of heart.

Upon this root, both the mental realization and physical actualization are experienced. The mental frame of conscious acceptance is the reality. This acceptance creates the space for impartiality. Impartiality is the content of regal. And regal symbolizes the heavenly existing Tao. The natural process, eternally and externally, of destiny and steadfastness and enlightenment, unite within the realm of Ultimate Emptiness and from the stand point of Central Stillness. Since the Ultimate Emptiness provides the infinite space and the Central Stillness ensures all that is due, the faithful trust is enhanced, and the trustworthy faith is guaranteed.

Arising from the Central Stillness and entering into the Ultimate Emptiness is altered by the subject of this twelfth character, the heavenly well water. This heavenly well water is the substance of the Tao that never dies. Nor does the form, the Ultimate Emptiness, nor the content, the Central Stillness of the Tao. Thereafter, the faithful trust never dies. That is the true enhancement of spiritual cultivation practices.

This 16th chapter in the Tao Te Ching concludes that when the mind's eye or spiritual eye reaches the Ultimate Emptiness, there is no more space to be further explored by the imaginative visions. The Ultimate Emptiness is the remotest and the greatest void of the Presence. When the heart's faith is contented with the Central Stillness, nothing can rotate nor arouse it. Because of this essential stillness, nothing can become remote and empty. Everything that exists, living or dying, is present in the mind's eye. Every living environment, including the mind's eye, is embraced by the Central Stillness. This is the presence of the Tao. The Tao never dies, it is the structure of the Ultimate Emptiness and the material of the Central stillness. In spiritual world, the Ultimate Emptiness is the Ultimate Faith, and the Central Stillness is the Essential Trust. They are both charged and renewed by the substance of the Tao with the heavenly well water.

## The Faith that Transforms

When faith establishes the grounding, the right intention becomes both the mental awareness and physical engagement. When trustworthiness fills the empty heart, the right action pervades. In return, there is no contrast between the right intention and right action. Rationally, it becomes very simple; there is no disagreement between the intention and engagement, and no confrontation between the right intention and right action. Yet practically, this is the most difficult thing to accomplish. Why? Because

> 1) Complete transformation of ego-reality must be achieved. The ego-reality is derived from the situation where being a survivor and possessing material satisfaction are more important to you than the structure of pure heart and the essential trust of self. When the cultivation practice is enhanced to the degree where there is no attachment to material possession or mental obsession, the ego is transformed into the complete understanding, full acceptance, and mutual embracement.

Ego uses the spiritual intelligence, the emotional experience, and biological instinct to exploit the meaning of life in one respect and to extinguish the vital force in another. According to Taoists tradition, the word ego, or I, is a subjective awareness of the soul's existence upon the objective evaluation of body through instinctive drives. It is the combination of liver Qi and spleen Qi. Ego is both conscious and obsessive at the same time. When all the organs are required to live mutually with each other in order to exist, ego steps into the realms of the sensational, experiential, and analytical world. Before the five elemental Qi are unified and the thymus gland is reactivated, the heart becomes distracted and love is always selfish. Before the earth's Qi of spleen is changed into the Yellow Court's vibration, trust is always situation oriented and faith is its reward. This is one of the major elements in Taoist cultivation practices, aside from family responsibility, social anticipation, and cultural adaptation.

2) There must be a complete transition of the karmic path, assuring that all the karmic debt is obliterated. In the world of reality, the result of the karmic energy pattern sustains itself again and again. The karma is environmentally altered, spiritually determined, biologically constructed, personally detected, and interpersonally experienced. Within this addictive and vulnerable situation, the only method to alter its course is to work and clear the path by submitting oneself to Power of the Tao, or the God's light. To purify and distill oneself internally and to love all people and the world externally is the only path. When one's lower and condensed energetic patterns and forms are dissolved expansively, they will become meaningless and cease to exist. When the body becomes clean and the mind remains still, the self is then trustful. The world is lovable, the Tao is dear, and the Action is near.

3) There is a complete shift from the earthy watery existential life to the holy watery eternal life. This holy watery eternal life is a true spiritual life that enlivens itself upon the holy water, is guided by God's power, and channeled by the pure light in the cosmic realm. In its essence, Love is the Holy Watery eternal life, and light is God's spiritual power. Love is Goddess and light is God. The light shines, penetrating with force. Love embraces it breathlessly, enduringly. Together, it is the union of Tao, the harmony of action, the balance of opposition, and integrity of understanding.

This has been explained fully in this twelfth character in the couplet, which is antithetical with the fifth character in the first part of the couplet: one is perennial and the other is immortal; one indicates the cyclical eternity, and the other deals with the formless eternity. Since earthly creatures are counted yearly, there is no better way to calculate the time of presence other than accumulating it annually and conclusively. While this character deals with the essential destiny and natural process of spiritual life form, which is immortal, it is in contrast to the mortal beings' physical process from birth to death and to rebirth. It is the way of the oneness of the spiritual life.

## What the Faith Lives Upon —The Trustful Oneness

In our spiritual life, a single spirit merges to live from one physical being to another, from one animal life to another, and from one gender to another. It is the free will of choosing and participating, depending upon the last life's action or the reason for a new life experience. This is the oneness of spirit, being trustworthy and faithful. Laoist experiential explanation of this oneness is "Donning the spirit and soul, and drawing them into Oneness, can this come apart? Gathering in Qi and making the body supple, is this not an infant? Being clear-headed and eliminating any mystic vision, can even a speck exist? Loving the people and governing the country, is this not inactive? Opening and closing the Gate of Heaven, is this not the female? Comprehending the four corners of the world, is this not knowledge? Begetting and nourishing; Begetting but not possessing, enhancing but not dominating. This is Mysterious Action." (10:1;2;3)

In the phrase of "donning the spirit and soul," the spirit, in Chinese, is hun and soul is po. This has been discussed in the notion of ego realm between the liver Qi spirit and lung Qi spirit. In its essence, these two characters represent the duality of heaven and earth, and of masculine and feminine in both spiritual realm and biological world. This is the birth of oneness of spirit. The next oneness is the childlike/as in nature. A child's body is supple, but it requires milk and air and light for the body to develop and the mind to construct itself. In order to retain a child-like nature, the pure existence of spirit is required. Any mental beliefs, spiritual illusions and imaginative visions must be cast away.

Following is the nature of loving by gathering the Qi of the Tao, which is Love itself. By this action, the two openings for inhalation and exhalation, for sex and spirituality, for life and death, are naturally connected. Therefore, there is no gender restriction or addiction, and there is no energy block beforehand or as an afterthought. Through this feminine energy of Love, understanding enters the door of enlightenment. Therefore, begetting on love and enhancing on trust are unified. The trustful one is selfless with the potential for both and ability to unify both. Is this not the Mystic Action?

This Laoist teaching further details that "By attaining Oneness, heaven is clear. By attaining Oneness, earth is at peace. By attaining Oneness, the spirit is quickened. By attaining Oneness, the valley is filled. By attaining Oneness, the king puts order in the whole world. All these result from Oneness." (39:2) Under the natural rules and orders where each of the natural substances live and obey, oneness is the governing ruling order. Nothing can exist without oneness, regardless of heaven and earth, and anything in between. When the king puts order in the world, he combines his orphanage or brotherhood condition with his lost and longing partner— the widow or sisterhood—into a complete oneness. Rules and discipline naturally suffice, after which he continues to hold to this oneness without being distracted by either the praise and worship or the disgrace and impeachment.     The king represents our true oneness. Any person is himself a king. Any one who has developed thoroughly the highest of oneself, and achieved the best of self is the king. That is why we are all orphans, we are all kings, and we are all God's given self. This orphan is a wild self, this king is the awakening self, and this self is the one of self. Who can help us? Only Our God Self. There is a common saying coursing through people's fertile minds "Why doesn't he/she understand me?" The answer is that if you don't understand yourself, who else can. When you are pursuing something, that is your devotion, your personal journey. How can any one be expected to understand you? They do not and should not.

When you concentrate completely on your pursuit, you become a loner. Your mind's awareness is alone, and you are alone. You are one with yourself. You are alone with God and His creative power. You are alone with Goddess's love. God has given everything to you and sold you. Goddess has given all her love and her birth to you. Why should you expect someone not in your position, with your devotion to your destiny, understand you? Even though someone may have experienced a similar path, you are entirely alone. Every one is helpless in the depth of life. Even though someone has the compassion over and above the experience, you will not be understood because you yourself are not yet understood. Unless someone is one with God, you will be betrayed. Unless you are with your self, you are sold each time within each conscious contact, emotional attachment, false promise, and physical sacrifice.

Even though someone has experienced the same, s/he must remain silent, to allow you to complete the process yourself. God is silent before your action, Goddess's love is silent with your devotional love. So often, those who know make you stumble from the path you are pursuing because they also hope to benefit from it. This is unlike the spiritual path where the Master is eager to open her/his arms and share all, because s/he understands her/himself and neither fears you nor takes advantage from you. He is taking his advantage. All the "advantages" taken by your master facilitate your dying process toward enlightenment. The masters mirror your own awakening journey with their already enlightened path. The only advantage is their guiding you to your own self-understanding. That is the enlightenment! What greater advantage could there be?

The reversed situation is that "Without its clarity, heaven is liable to explode. Without its peace, earth is liable to erupt. Without its quickening, the spirit is liable to die out. Without its fullness, valleys are liable to dry out. Without proper esteem, the king is liable to fall." (39;3) The clarity of God's power is one of understanding upon light. The peace of Goddess's stillness is the content of acceptance. The fullness is the containment of emptiness for all that will potentially grow and develop. The proper esteem is the standard of selfhood in behaving, conducting, controlling, and letting go.

Laoist further explains that "Esteem is rooted in the humble. The high is founded upon the low. This is why the lords and rulers call themselves widows and orphans without support. Is this is not the root of being humble? Much praise amounts to no praise. Without preference, Being is as resonant as Jade and as gravelly as stone." (39:4;5;6;7) Widow is defined as the abandonment suffered by sacrificing herself and giving up her existence for the longing for Love and Union with Light and Power. Orphan is the rejected self, the homeless self, the hungry self, and the lost self. Over time and upon all situations, we are controlled and destined by our own divine orphan-state. No other person can help us in term of growth and liberation. Not even God. God has transcended His Power of Love of Light upon us enabling us to exist truly by our selfhood. All He has is us! He has already done all he can. We are as we have been constructed from the very beginning and we cannot change God's defined and Goddess's created nature. This Nature is One. This nature is selfless selfhood.     This is trustful oneness: that single intention, single awareness, single action, and single result from and for the action. Always and forever that One.

By the same token, when one abides as one, what would one prefer: masculine or feminine?  They are equally precious and they are impartial. When the mind becomes the cosmic flow, there is no  preference. When the body becomes androgynous, there is no preference. And when the kingship Self is Love, there is no preference. Marble and stone belong to the same chemical family. Brother and sister are born from the same mother. Love and hate run in the same addictive fashion. Sexuality and spirituality are charged by the same power light.

## Characteristic Representation

This Laoist character is combined with three basic Chinese characters. They are all pertinent in constructing the symbolic representation of Immortality. The first character is water, the second is sky or heaven, the third is well. The first character Shui, in Chinese language, indicates the preparation of a trip to the North, symbolizing the connective image of water and its virtuous deeds. This water is not the earthly water. It is the Holy Water. The Holy Water is the initial Love of Goddess's Valley-Spirit. In constellation form, this Holy Water represents the North Star. In our body, this Holy Water represents the unconscious nature of biological makeup, the combined  activity between sperm and egg.

The second character Tian is something "that covers the great, which is sky or heaven." It also indicates "the ultimate end and extreme territory." The two characters Shui and Tian unite to represent the blue sky of holy water, the substance of mystic female, or the womb of Great Mother, the Holy Water Above. Therefore, it stands for the oneness of heaven between God's Power of Holy Light and the Love of the Holy Water of Mystical Female.  Within, it is God's creative Consciousness, God's Conscious Space.  Surrounding it is Goddess's Image. Laced through is our body-mind. All the creatures, journeys and power-lines are in between.

The root of the Chinese character tian is da [great]. Great is the Magnificence of the Tao, the Peace of Love, and the Power of Rock. The one straight line above the character da is to construct the pictorial existence of tian. Laoism mentions four great things in the world, Kingship, earth, heaven, and Tao. This Line is the Great above all that is great. This straight Line is the Rock, the Power, the Light which pierces everything, emits light to everything, burns everything, and renews everything. This is why, in the I Ching construction, the creator used a straight Line to represent heaven, which is the Power, the Masculine, the Penetration, and the Independence.

Da or great is derived from the root stroke human. There is a line cutting through the existence of human. This line is the horizontal line of the earth that connects light and dark, day and night. It is the line that loves, changes, and returns. It is the gravity line that shines through the sun and directs and rotates the earth and other planets in the solar system. Water on earth is in this line. The surface of land before the eye's vision is in this line. Spine is in this line. Consciousness is in this line. This is the line of the first Nine, the first great, the combination between kingship and his Mother earth. This is also the line that connects the left hand to the right one, coordinating them in a straight line. This line forms the horizontal cross with the three nails in the crossing line: one in the heart, and one for each palm. This line is the balance line, the grounding line, the mutual line, the harmonious line, the right line, the fine line. This line is the line of breath, the thread of life.

When this line and the one above are unified, self and the other are unified. Earth and heaven are unified. Water and light are unified. God and Goddess are unified. This is the final representation or the meaning of tian, of Universe, of Cosmos, of the Home of everything including nothingness. These two lines signify the equality of function between holy/earth's water and the invisible hole, called cosmic well or valley spirit. This is symbolized by the third character constructing the Laoist Twelfth character. It is a man-made symbol for well. In the well is the holy water or sweet dew. Laoism describes that "Heaven and earth combine and allow sweet dew." (32:3 ) Well is one of the two hexagrams in I Ching dealing with manmade objects (The other is caldron, boiling the remaining sixty-two which are all spiritual/conscious hexagrams). It represents the content of an inexhaustible dispensing of the nourishing nature of female. It is, as Laoism has characterized "Hovering, it seems ever-present. Put to use, it is never exhausted." (6:3)

The physical construction of the Chinese character "well" represents the Cross. Assume you are holding a cross. Pay no account to the structural representation. Just remain focused upon the images of four edges; two along the vertical line and two across the horizontal line. Mentally visualize the open spaces where the four edges are formed, then the lines and points within the open spaces. What you will see should be four lines, eight points around and one square in the center. This is the Chinese Way of crossing. I Ching characterizes the function of a well by stating: "The well. The town may be changed, but not the well. It neither decreases nor increases." Historically, eight families form a social group in order to have a well, just as the eight points in the well character have been represented. This well also represents the image of our bodily lines and points as well, with two in the brain, two for the feet, and two in each hand.

This is the mystery of eight in the I Ching and Chinese mythology. Eight represents a young female with that inexhaustible energy, charm, lust, and virtue. Mathematically, eight is three times the two of yin and yang. Or as I Ching has demonstrated, the six children, three for each gender, and the parenting couple. Initially, these eight represent the eight phenomena in heaven and earth. They are: heaven and earth, water and fire, wind and cloud, mountain and lake. While in the high state of meditation practice, it is the empty space in the small square centered in the cross that powers the four lines and eight points. Inside the square is the inexhaustible substance of valley-spirit's power or the Great Mother's substance, Holy Water. This is the wheel-of-Love, the wheel of fortune/misfortune.

Metaphorically, the well represents our body, and within is the sky or heaven's water, which is cosmic water or holy water. Its color is white. This color is the white matter inside the brain, milk in the chest, and semen in the abdomen. Furthermore, it represents the white hair, in the sense that our spirit returns to its original color, white. This cosmic holy water is called Primordial Yang Qi in Taoism and Bindu in Hinduism. When this white cosmic water is fully cultivated, it is nowhere and it is everywhere. It is inside the body, along the flow of conscious streams, and out there in the light of the cosmic universe. So the well, finally, represents the Black Hole, the Valley of Death, the Heavenly Mouth, the Mystic Female, the Great Mother.

## Well, the Hollowing Well

Throughout the course of human civilization, water has been the primary demand, enlivening the body as well as one of the most catastrophic phenomena causing flood and destroying untold numbers of lives. This is the nature of earth after the Ice Age when Ice and Fire made torrential water raging madly over all the earth surface. Ultimately, the ocean base is created from the chemical reaction between earth's hot flaming skin and the light above the sky, with the racing water coming from nowhere. During that time, there were heavenly descended monsters living on earth, controlling the power of water flow, and abducting the angelic women living on earth. There resulted multitudes of cross-bred figures ranging from fish body parts, to animal and human parts, to celestial spiritualized intellectual parts. This was, perhaps, the earliest division of the human race, from the single biological mother, who descended from another planet to earth for the purpose of producing humankind, to assorted species of fathers and mothers leading their offspring. Each family/race lived upon its distinctive talent and character. The cultural proliferation, such as language, had begun. God's Power and Light and Rock and Message are carried out according to each and every family with the talents and power they have inherited.

In the early Chinese civilization, before the practices of irrigation and construction of dams and pools, well has been a vital channel to provide the drinking and agricultural water. In I Ching, the image of a well is the water being locked, trapped with no place to go, as the hexagram #47 Kun or Oppression represents. This portion of water then sinks down into earth. When a hole is dug out and a wooden pole is dropped beneath the water level, the water can be hauled up and life is saved. This is why in #48 Hexagram, Jing or Well, the wooden element below supports the water element above. When a well is constructed, it exists beyond the relocation of a family or changes between dynasties. Unless a jealous mind attempts to destroy others' livelihood by putting rotten food or poisonous substances into the well, the mentality of a well is tranquil, and the life of a well is inexhaustible.

Speaking from the Taoist esoteric point of view, the eight points extended from the cross represent the eight special meridians inside the body. Within the eight lines exists a dot of vital force. This vital force represents the wooden sun, the morning star. When this vital force is nourished by the distilled water, peace and tranquility are the resulting state. Without proper care, this wooden element of life force can be destroyed as represented by a broken jug or a rotting fish. When liver Qi is damaged and conscious spirit becomes lost, all the body carries is toxic waste contained in the liver. The broken jug results from the negligence, and the rotting fish has no life source (air and water circulation) to sustain itself. Without air, consciousness becomes numb, without fresh water, body becomes poisonous.

The next stage is represented by the #49 hexagram Ge or Revolution. In cultivation practice, the fire of heart's desire is channeled down to boil the water from the well, or abdominal area in this sense. There would be no any jealousy arising from the feminine water. Nor would the agitative feeling of an inability to penetrate with the masculine power appear. The conscious fire, the combination of spirit, intelligence, heart and emotionality, will boil the frozen water into a steaming state. Sexuality and emotionality are awakened into spirituality and selfless love. After the steam cools, it will be preserved in the caldron, as #50 hexagram Ding or Caldron represents. In caldron, it is a transition from Spring to Summer, a development from a wooden element into a firing element, a combination of passion and love. All the psycho-emotional energy is thus transformed into positive. The cold and fear turns into intellectual will. The agitation and frustration transform into spiritual consciousness. The jealousy and hatred channel into selfless love. Thus, the first of stage of cultivation, cultivating Jing and transforming it into the Qi is achieved. As a result, the only two manmade objects, well and caldron, will be fully crystalized into the body of light and vibration of Love. It will be the expression of flow in the next two stages of cultivation, from cultivating the Qi and transforming it into Shen, and cultivating Shen and transforming it into Xu the empty Tao.

The essential meaning of a well is not the constructive separation, but rather the embracing union. It does not abide in the usefulness of nourishment alone, it signifies the inexhaustible stillness. It does not apply to man's ability to construct a machine, it views a machine as a useful means to transfer the objectified self into its original place, the unconscious self. When man relies on the machine and not the spirit, life is destructive itself. When a man searches through a machine for the meaning of God, he gets only a strawdog where the birds are happily eating the ripening seeds. When man's intellectual wisdom rests upon the mere mechanical restructuring and manipulation, the spiritual power will lack fire. He loses not only what he is devoted to, the longing self, but also the self within. That is that summary of the ancient wisdom of I Ching. That is the tragic story of outer alchemists and their products, the materialized poisonous elixir.

In our modern society, the entire numbers of sixty-four human genetic construction are replaced by the use of machines, no longer male/caldron and female/well. A man's life, a combination of spiritual, emotional and mechanical, turns into a materialistically constructed function. Fortunately, there are only two man-made symbols in I Ching. How many, in contrast, do we find in science books? The Tao is always on a higher plane than the machine. And God's power is beyond calculation compared to man's meager power. Are we challenging with our man-made products or the natural ones? Are we competing against our energy consuming selves or applying God's gift of free self?

## Well, Well, Spiritual Well

When the earth was being formed between flaming rocks and flooding water, the heat was eventually cooled down by the cosmic light, and the flood was pacified by its own creative stillness within. The water sank down to form oceans, the water bed became plain, and the volcanic mouths became mountains. Gravitational wind circulated the cosmic air by lifting water molecules to the sky forming a protective living space for all creatures. Wind and rain created plateaus, rivers, jungles and valleys. This was, perhaps, after the Ice Age when the flooded earth surface created continents and oceans. The light sparkling in oceanic waters created fish. The light shining on land produced plants. The cosmic spirit diffused into the living spirits and their consciousness within all creatures in the water and on the land. Humankind became the highest representation of this spiritual descending power on earth.

When seven continents and five oceans hosted both holy water and flaming fire, it is unknown how the human races were divided. According to Taoist tradition, a different human race was influenced by the diverse celestial and planetaria structures and functions. It is the celestial structure and function that generates the human creative genes, from biological structures to intellectual characters. These variations range from hair, skin and eye color to thoughts, languages and mental capacities. Intellectual, religious and racial differences are the result of these departures.

The planetaria structures and functions influence the feminine construction, particularly those of sensitivities and psychic abilities. When holy water "fogs" through all the planets, Goddess power of loving and receiving and healing becomes the realistic power of the planets, including the creatures living on their surfaces. On earth, when the holy water shifted from moon to earth, it created the entire earth's power structure, seasonal and cyclical. Still, it is influenced by the cycle of moon. These sensitivities and psychic powers counteract the power toward creative light and inner conscious structures. Light changes the colors of various human races and inner consciousness and becomes the distinctive racial mental structure with its unique intellectual capacities.

In Taoist tradition, the green color is influenced by the East Star Group. The highest representation is green dragon and evil dragon monsters. The land structure is the color which constructs the plants, and in part, the water color. Green eyed people are the human structural representation of this. Liver and eyes are the organic connection. The green color can be the combination of blue-green as in water. That is the Chinese character for qing, which was covered in chapter eight.

The red color comes from the South Star Group, the celestial being is red sparrow. Animal representation is blood and heart. Red haired people are the physical representation and flying creatures are the animal biological and intellectual construction.

The color white represents maturity and eternity, independence and totality. It is influenced by the West Star Group. The celestial being is white tiger, and its biological representation is all the white materials, from white fluids to white bones to white hair. Earthly, it represents the metals, the salt and inner biological and intellectual structure of rocks.

The black color is the North power, the creative darkness which is both abysmal and impenetrable. North Star is the celestial representation, and the black tortoise is the celestial spirit. Black earth and night time are its planetary reflection. The kidneys are its biological representation, and black skin/hair is its physical definition.

In the middle stands the yellow shell, the yellow earth, the golden sun. The cosmic single rod is descended from the Middle of heaven to the sun and to the central point of the earth. Yellow color ranges between spring and fall, between liver and lung, and between creative arousal to mechanical manipulation. This may explain why and how the cosmic creation diffuses from the Golden Shell to yoke and spleen.

How the seven continents and five oceans formed remains a mystery to the human intellectual mind. Until the original creative memory is awakened within, there is no answer to this question. And there cannot be! The secret key to this is the function of Mystical Well. In order to tap into this Mystical Well, we have to know where the water stays and how the hollowing functions. We must also know where the Initial Spiritual Arousal forms in each and every creative being, from stars to planets, and from inorganic beings to organic beings.

The creation of human history is imbedded in memory, and its creative history is imbedded in the creative formation of earth. Throughout historical records, the management of flood control has been a huge ongoing battle between man and nature and between good and evil. In Chinese history, there are numerous records describing how a local virgin girl must be sacrificed in order to please the mad flood created by Monster Dragon and other celestial creatures living on earth within a human physical body. In biblical history, battling between the power of Rock Spirit and the power of Serpent's Blood represents the power structure between high spirit and creative manipulation among all the creative spirits such as serpent or dragon. They are definitely more powerful than man, but they cannot defend God's Creative Spirit, nor manipulate God's creative power within. This is the power structure of masculinity.

On the other hand, when the angelic Mothers were "raped" by the celestial spiritual beings to produce humans and other animals, constant fear of being raped and the dreaded apprehension became the living duality in the females' minds, especially the human females. In the case of Chinese history, when the Western Mother, who was a cosmic angel living on earth, gave birth to Fu Xi and Nu Wa, the brother and sister, they were all half human and half fish. Every female is fearful of being molested. This is, perhaps, the earliest psychological fear imbedded in female creatures. This is also the highest development of defense mechanism that females employ. All females have the best and highest sensitivity to either invite a male or reject the male's invitation by listening to their highest and earliest memory detector, sexual preference. If they accept it, they are open, receptive, and ready to receive the light of creation. If not, they transmit information psychically or biochemically to protect, defend, and secure themselves.

At the same time, longing for the light, the power, the direction and the penetration has always been a nightmare for all living females. Even today, there is a Chinese expression which says "that girl is dreaming of her white horse." The creative human spirit described in I Ching, the "white horse" represents both spiritual light, and biological fire. It encompasses the physical security and mental stability. It stands for the masculine Chasing power and inner Rocking character.

Therefore, the battle of earthly evolution is the battle between the light and water, God and Goddess, male and female, life and death. It deals essentially with the nature of sexuality and spirituality, which is harmony and oneness. Well, as a human creative symbol, represents this inexhaustible female power of receiving, forming, healing, and dissolving.

Laoist defines this cosmic well as "Valley-spirit is deathless, it is called the mystical female. The gateway of the mystical female, is called the root of heaven and earth." (6:1;2) First of all, this mystic female is the root of heaven and earth, the creator of all creators and the form of all forms. The sentence "Opening and closing the Gate of Heaven, is this not the female?" (10:1) indicates that the breathing activity of this mystic female is the combination of the inhalation of the Power of the Tao and the exhalation of the Action of Love. When the third eye opens, the power of the Tao is received. When the earth's gate (sexual organ) is closed, the Action of Love is expressed. When these two activities are harmonized, the spiritual life of an inner child begins. As for this inner child, its source is the life itself, containing the power of both creation and development, both maturity and return. This is the reason Lao Zi "wants to be wholly different from everybody else, by taking sustenance from the mother source." (20:8)

## The Nature of Holy Water

The nature of cosmic water is the most accurate representation of what this twelfth character has constructed. Cosmic water is the valley-based womb of all creations in the universe. It is the basic universal color, representing ever-present tranquility of blue sky. The blue sky breathes the white clouds, blends the sun and moon light, and supports the stars and planets in the universe. If the sky loses its tranquility, there could not be that chaotic order existing in the universe. If the sky doesn't have its lighter version of color, we would be unable to distinguish the difference between the sky based color blue and oceanic color blue. If the sky doesn't paint its face blue, our creative spirituality could not be awakened. If the sky doesn't contain its own special quality, it cannot attract us into its endless form, deathless existence, and mystic feature.

This blue sky is what our eyes gaze into, this cosmic water is what our spiritual mind swims with, this universal color is where our pure spirit returns, this holy water is what the couplet has highlighted. Therefore, to transcend from earthly and physical status to cosmic and spiritual being is the essential meaning of this twelfth character. Lao Zi became a fool to sustain the substance from the Cosmic Well of Mother Nature. Like a little baby, he preached his way through time without having a "hoarseness" in his speech. He submerged himself in his physical body to drink the cosmic well water within. He was forever "aroused" without the union state with his wife. He lived beyond the need to practice courtship and mating between a masculine/feminine spirit and male/female body. In spiritual practice, working beyond the lust, is one of the last stages to pass through before entering the place where Lao Zi was sustained. This is known as the state of the Prince of Peace.

When Lao Zi entered this realm, he no longer knew his wife or his biological mother. He was inside the cave, within the Cosmic Well, working with God's business of Arousal, of Lightening, and of Chasing, which is the ideal thought formation for the cosmic creation. He did nothing, became a fool, indeed.

When the Mother Mary approached her son Jesus in the temple, she questioned his presence in that place. He responded: "How is it that ye sought me? Wist ye not that I must be about my Father's business?" (Luke 2:49) His Father's business was His own business, and is our own business, individually and forever. The Lord Jesus was busy learning and preaching and performing healing works for the sickened souls, diseased bodies, and lost minds. As a matter of fact, he did not even recognize his mother. He asked, "Woman, what have I to do with thee?" (John 2:4) And He questioned further "Who is my mother?" (Mat. 12:48, Mark 3:33)

Biological bodies are the temples of spirits. Biological relationships are the renewed spiritual relationships. Yet, the biological family has nothing to do with spiritual family. We are all one spiritual family, born into divergent biological families. We all claim the same Spiritual Father and Spiritual Mother, but have our own biological parents. Our biological parents are homeless just as we are. Like our own lonely souls, our biological parents are orphans as well. What they have done is the production of the spiritual temple of our body. They could do no more. Having worked on such a project was our spirit's call and part of their life journey. They are spiritually responsible and biologically determined to rebuild the temples for the spirits when the old temples fall apart by the force of nature.

This is not to say that Jesus no longer recognized his mother or his brethren. It means that his spiritual journey of preaching and healing included all the races, young and old, single and married. All are members of his family. He is unbiased, having no preference. He provides with an equal unconditional love and indiscrete spiritual intention. Buddhists observe all women as their mothers, even though each woman lives through the journey of being a girl, a mate, a mother and a grandmother. Being a mother is the first and most rewarding role for a woman, and man is physically unable to perform such a feat on behalf of spirits. Man gives the Light, the Arousal, the Penetration for the spirits to be received, reincarnated, refreshed within new temples.

All men are brothers. There is One Father for all, and one Spiritual Father for each spirit. The One Father is God, and the One Spiritual Father is the God's inspired celestial being. All women are spiritual sisters. Marrying a woman is marrying a biological sister. Marrying a man is marrying a biological brother. In Biblical tradition, Jesus neither called his mother "mother" nor "sister." Nor did he call her "widow." Instead, she was just "woman." He used a neutral name to represent both mother and sister. Widow is the name of Goddess. She is the Mother of all creatures in the universe. Sister is His inner soul-mate, spiritual longing and unconditional love.

There is one more matter to be divulged in this area, that is, the act of fertilization. In spiritual discipline, the spirit descends through the third eye or mouth. In all the biological and medical books, the sperm is pictured as shooting lightening arrows (see the illustration in chapter eight). The biological reproduction of offspring occurs within the vagina. Painting both the third eye and lips with red is spiritually significant. There are mythological revelations stating that angelic women swallowed the shining balls of light, or the celestial spirits, through their mouth for the virgin birth process. Men will be aroused by this light, the red fire emitting through the female's third eye and mouth. It is a seductive invitation. Anatomically speaking, the mouth and vagina have the same tissue structure. Mouth is the mating organ for both fish and snake.

## The Magic Play of Holy-Water-Tao

As with the mystic magical play of the Tao, the teaching of Laoism has several explanations or refinements. "The Tao of heaven is good at winning without fighting, good at responding without speaking, appearing without being asked, good at strategizing while fighting. The net of heaven is broad and loose, yet nothing slips through." (75:4,5) This is the all power of the Tao. Nothing in the universe can compete against the Tao. No form can overpower the empty void of that constructive Tao. No matter can replace the complete substance of the Tao. No mechanism can include the immense system of the Tao. Observe the stars in the sky. Regardless of their incalculable number, none have fallen from the empty universal space onto the surface of earth. Nor has our earth rotated one iota from her normal orbit around the sun and other planets.

In terms of our human life, the net of heaven is inside our conscious awareness and intention. When we try to slip through and fight against it, it becomes a lesson in futility. We are slaves of our own conscious habits. When we make mistakes purposely but wisely or do something carefully but secretly, we think that no one will know because we were unseen and no one was present at the time. Be careful, there is always somebody with equal or higher power watching us. The term "mistakes" refers to the unpurified conscious action, arising from our self-contained capacity or selfish and egoistic intention. Any secret mechanism belongs to the magic play of the Tao (It is done). Any secretive action belongs to the returning journey of the Tao (to be aroused). Each and every intention has its equally intensified echoing response (the dual playfulness). Each and every action has its counter-reaction (mutual interaction and co-dependence).

Yet, through the sensory Tao, there is a pervading sense that no one in the world could have the capability to tap into our world of secrecy other than ourselves. Self is our most valuable asset, the most secretive key, and most reliable resource. When there is a complete understanding of self, the action is truthful, regardless of how others react to it. This is the true action of life. Therefore, mistakes are actually wrongdoings, and they are covetous in nature.

Unfortunately, our body contains all the information we have generated and our mind stores the messages permanently. Even when we say farewell to this world, information remains stored in our memory cells. God, and His angels, evaluate us, based upon what we have stored but are not judgmental. We are destined not only by our biophysical process of life but also by the mentally constructed information and messages stored in our memory cells, which in turn are our own deeds and conduct resulted from our own original action. The outcome of life is controlled not only by the biological process, but by our entire mental intention and conscious awareness. Without the mental anticipation of gathering, preparing and putting the food into the mouth, body cannot accomplish this feat. Even though the mind may order the mouth to receive poisoned food, the mouth is not responsible. It is the inner conscious reality creating moral action in spiritual discipline.

In terms of the usefulness of the Tao, Laoist's observation is: "The Tao of heaven is like drawing a bow. The high bends down, the low rises up. The surplus decreases. Insufficiency is supplied. The Tao of heaven reduces what is surplus and enhances what is insufficient." (79:1,2) This is the Tao of heaven, the circulation of wind and air in volcano. Volcano makes the mountains. Wind circulates the water molecules and sandy dust in the atmosphere. Rain forces everything down to the lowest place by creating spaces called valleys. Between mountains and valleys, between the combustion of the earthly heat inside and the vaporization of earthly water on the surface, everything is circulated, regulated, and balanced. The birth of clouds and the death brought by the flood/bloodshed make the water eternal. The birth of volcano heat and the death from forest fire make the fire eternal. The birth of bloody life and the death of bloody water make the body eternal. The circulation of water and fire creates the eternal harmony of heaven and earth.

In contrast, "The human Tao reduces what is insufficient and caters to the surplus." (79:2) The insufficiency comes from the over expenditure of the vital Qi of self, the surplus results from the mentally calculated and physically gathered material possessions. At the time we were born, there was already a deficiency in our vital Qi. Our spirit had been degraded as an earthly being and our one spirit manifests as two souls, conscious and instinctive. This was because instead of living with the oneness of harmony between ourselves and mother, we were now living independently, depending upon other vital forces of air, water, and food. When the body develops and mind matures, our true spiritual nature shifts into many selves, and our biological unification is recast into sexual conduct. When we are young, we have no knowledge, only the openness of virtue. We have no possession, but great vitality. As we get older, the useful openness of virtue is converted into a beneficial gain of knowledge. The truthfulness of vitality suffuses into the obsession upon materials.

We know that all things live upon the vital Qi: air circulation is the act of vital Qi, biological metabolism is the balance of vital Qi, water and food are the medium of vital Qi, and sexual activity enables the harmony of vital Qi. But do we practice or live in a way that can truly preserve our own precious vital Qi? Sexual activity, emotional turmoil and intellectual obsession drive this precious vital Qi to be used for the gain of material possession and the ultimate loss of the longevity of life. As a result, our true talent from the vital power turns into the action of stealing, as discussed previously about the notion of "thief." We cheat each other, steal from one another, and fight with self and all. The purity of body becomes lost into the sickness. The tranquility of mind is lost in illness. The more insufficient we become, the harder we try to increase the surplus.

To be a millionaire is good, fame is better, and health is the best. We don't realize that the millionaire cannot eat anymore than we normally consume at the same dining table. Wealth does not suffice to buy happiness. Famous people have no more names than those they have already been called. Health is but a mental awareness upon the biological process; it is nothing other than spiritual awakening into the biophysical transformation.

Therefore: "Who can use the surplus to benefit the heaven? Only those who possess Tao." (79:3) This is the mechanism of the Tao, the nature of which has Its mechanism to regulate, balance and harmonize everything that is part of nature. Without this, the irregular chaos could not proceed in its mystic order. The obscure structures could not have their exact constructions. And the unpredictable functions would not process their perfect discourses. The true surplus in life is nothing other than the accumulation of good and kind and virtuous deeds. "The Tao of heaven is impersonal. It enhances those who are kind." (81:4)

In rearing to the outcome of the Tao, Laoism instructs us that: "The Tao of heaven benefits and does not harm. The Tao of human-kind exists and does not compete." (68:3) What causes the harm is the form itself, without form, without harm. Lao Zi clarifies this by explaining that "It is only because I have a body that I have trouble. If I did not have a body, where would the trouble be?" (13:3) In life, what we beautify is the body, we can contain only what the body contains, we glorify ourselves through the body and die meaninglessly for sole purpose of leaving the body. The Tao always benefits us. It never harms us. How could a form-less Tao possibly harm us? How could an empty Tao destroy us?

By learning the Tao of impartiality, we are able to exist without competing, act but not behave, behave but not conduct, conduct without controlling. This ensures success becoming a natural consequence and its reward initiates a natural turning point. In human life, we try desperate-ly to complete with one another, not fully realizing that the person we are competing with is none other than our-self. In the Olympics, the athletes who overcomes themselves overcome others. Once you have done your best, there is no point in competing against others. It is a meaningless pursuit. How much further could you perfect yourself than being the very best you already are?

In conclusion, on the helpfulness of Tao, which is conclusive in the second remark, Laoism advises that: "The Tao of heaven is imper-sonal. It enhances those who are kind." (81:4) Even Tao is impersonal, it enhances those who are kind. Even Tao is impersonal, it enhances those who are kind toward those who are not kind, it is the virtue of kindness in itself. There is no need for recognition before, during or after we per-form kind action. We need only to be conscious of self. When we are conscious of self, others will recognize us with the exact conscious acknowledgment. When we can not distill hope into a conscious self action, we are destined to failure. How can others recognize us when we are not self-recognized?

In the 68th chapter in Mawangdui Texts, the last chapter in stan-dard version of Tao Te Ching, we read: "The Tao of heaven benefits and does not harm. The Tao of human-kind exists and does not compete." (68:3) Upon reading this, I felt that the message was incomplete. I sensed that Lao Zi had not said enough (There is, of course, never enough which is the reason we are experiencing the Tao right now). I have not completed my reading of the discouraging message. Even though it valued the goodness and kindness of noncompetition, it left me with diminished spiritual hope and no clear direction to where I might cultivate myself in accordance with the Tao. I became discontented.

After meditating some years on this during which I read the Mawangdui Texts, I had the realization that the extreme passivists promoted the philosophical concept of noncompetition and purposefully stressed the usefulness of this chapter. As a result, the noncompetitive act became the bestowed virtuous act in human conduct. According to Laoism, this conduct is derived from modeling the goodness of water. "Eminent goodness is like water. Water is good at benefitting all things, yet it actively competes. It retires to undesirable places. Thus it is near to Tao." (8:1,2) Water is active and water is competitive; if this were not so, how could it become pure and clean in the immensity of the murky and venomous mixture of the earth: if not, what other substances could occupy the biggest space on earth and exist in the bodies of all creatures; if not, what makes the air moist, sky cloudy, the body watery, and the land soft and inviting?

Instead of following after the goodness of Tao, these extreme passivists emphasized the importance of noncompetition, not realizing that noncompetition of water contains the power of competing to purify and clarify all the existing maladies and turbulence. Its noncompetitive reality is based upon the result of positive gain, or the surplus of good deeds. These good deeds come from transforming self and others from the murkiness and darkness. It doesn't signify that water is pure and clean, since it contains two elements, hydrogen molecules and oxygen molecules. How could it be pure when it already has two elements? It is the power of harmonious flow which creates its healing properties.

In the reality of mind, water is never pure and we are never pure. However, we are already as pure as we were in the beginning. The virtue of water is that it has the power to purify itself, and our spiritual mind has the power to distill ourselves within. Water has the capacity to maintain its clarity within the light and minerals. Water never competes with anything not belonging to itself, therefore nothing can compete against water. Water never tries to stay at only desirable places, it can be found in all places, from the open air to the solid metal. And water never harms marble and jade which are the color of water.

Noncompetitoin is a virtuous act. This virtuous act rises from the openness of heart, the expansion of consciousness, and the acceptance of self and others (Supposedly we are in God's State and Position. Why act and compete? Do nothing and it is Done). If we all behave in accordance with this virtuous act, what purpose can competition serve?. Noncompetition will "complete" with no heart and no desire, never "compete" with desire and drive (It co-exists). Do not think we should be incompatible before the reality of the competitive nature of energetic circulation (We cannot but fight through life every minute in the dual worlds). Rather, we should not be compatible when confronted with desire and drive. Noncompetition is a positionless act, and a selfless action. Noncompetition comes from the fully awakening to the natural position and responsibility carried by each and every living creature. Noncompetition is the deed, competition is the need. Noncompetition is the design, and competition is the desire. Noncompetition is the free act of spirit, and competition is the loss of life into action. Noncompetition always completes, and competition never suffices.

Competition is the core of marketing the economical and democratic political environment in this world. Yet, nothing competes against destiny, and no competition can survive in the face of the real submission to compatibility, which is the journey of a destined life, the gift of experiencing that life. The journey is our biological life, the gift is the mirroring spiritual life. This real compatibility is the true essence of vital force, the complete confidence within the self, and the absolute trust of self. The journey is planned, the gift is presented. Life is destined, spirit is duty free. What we are is what we are. God is helpless before this (God has finished His part). When we live with desire, loss/death greets us at the entrance to this desire. When we die, God within us dies. If we are awakening, God then awakens with us. Life is a gift which gives us the opportunity to awaken ourselves from the mixed living environment between heaven and earth. We will be awakened the possibility of clearing the path, paying the debt, and bidding adieu to ownership.

What has been planned is our original conscious makeup and biological construction. What has been unplanned is the conscious choice and biophysical experience rising from the conscious makeup of the previous life experiences. These experiences determine what we do and how we behave, ranging from our personal hobbies to professional choices, and from individual need to social responsibilities. A good athlete was born into an athletic performance, and a president was born with presidential character. The biological construct originates in the parental conditioning, physical and mental, as well as our previous makeup of soul, our personal character. If our parents are healthy, we will likely be healthy. If they are heavy, short or sick, we have the potential to become so.

Children experience resentment with the biological shortcomings handed down by their parents. When they identify with their biological and psychological components, anything they dislike becomes the reaction of guilt within. Anything they cannot correct or perfect produces resentment, or even hatred, toward their parents. When they recognize that they cannot be more attractive, healthy or successful, they blame their parents. When they cannot achieve the perfection they seek, they lay blame on themselves or their parents. They may lament, "Parents, why did you give birth to me?" "I wish I were dead, and I wish I were not here."

Don't give up on yourself, don't abandon your parents, don't fight what you already have, and don't blame your past. This is what we are now. This is the destined journey. This is the path, the debt, and ownership. Realistically speaking, if we want to do something, and this desire or dream or wish speaks constantly to us, we can never free ourselves from this conscious thinking pattern. Until we experience what we want, we cannot free ourselves. The desire will nag us. This is due to and what is meant by the gift of life. We must purify our body, clean our mind, still our heart, and cool down our emotional agitation. Until we have done so, there can be no pure and clean and healthy life. We must clear the path from the past, make positive gain from the debt, and transform the ownership.

It is not our parents' fault since our spirit chose them to give birth to our biological body in this life time. Our spiritual makeup, the body of soul, makes us as we are. It is not our parents' fault that we inhabit a heavy or short or sick body. Nothing is our parents' fault, we are responsible for making everything possible for ourselves. They are only our body makers, gene carriers, soul blamers, and spirit sinners.

In spiritual life, the path has been and will continue to be followed by someone else. All the positive gain will become someone else's game. All the ownership of spiritual masters becomes the obsession of their followers. We love the Christ, but we don't love ourselves. We want the enlightened Buddha, but we don't want to enlighten ourselves. I am writing the teaching of Lao Zi, but not writing for myself. Why? Because they are pure, clean, and powerful. Christ's love is more pure than any conditional love. Buddha's mind is cleaner than his own natural mind manifests. Lao Zi's teaching is more powerful than he could ever have thought. The Christ Love is the selfless love given through his selfless sacrifice. Buddha's mind was no-mind in itself but arose from his minding mind through the Cosmic Mind. Lao Zi's teaching is a universal echo through the silence that arrives from nowhere but his inner untraceable voice.

Because of our spiritual makeup and conscious reality, we borrowed our parents' love-making activity to structure our body. We used some of their personal and emotional characteristic to form our own lost personal structure. We lived together with them in the beginning in order to become ourselves again. But we can never be one hundred percent like our parents, especially in the matter of spirit. We may have similar likes and habits, but never the same spiritual makeup. This spiritual makeup belongs only to ourselves. This is what is meant by the gift. It is the opportunity to awaken ourselves spiritually within the reality of the biological experiential process. This gift is the virtuous deed, the full awakening power of our true spirit, and the impersonal kindness of the Tao. Then, what is the use of competition and where is the position of non-competition.

After completing the translation of the Mawangdui Texts, I saw the hope and felt at home. Noncompetitive attitude and behavior are good, but they do not go beyond the action of passive-retirement. Also, the passivists did not fully understand the function of the Tao, the active competition of water toward its naturally positioned environment. I now understand that it is not our wish to be noncompetitive, but to reach the state of noncompetition through the kindness of action. It means that before the dark force, light is necessary; before the desire, kindness is necessary; before the hellish world, spiritual awakening is the way! Noncompetitive action is not the only outcome, because Tao enhances me and you when we enter through the path of cultivation and kind action. Tao is kind but impersonal. Do not take anything personally, whether on the nature of life or in a situation of cash flow. Life is ruthless, and cash flow distorts the ownership.

We must remember to be kind to ourselves and to all. When we are kind to those who are kind, we gain the reputation of kindness, the kindness from ourselves and the kind reaction from those who are not kind. When we are kind to those who are not kind, we receive the double gain. What happens when the ruthless action meets the kind action? It has no choice but to be kind to its action and itself. The more kindness we express, the more bad karma we will negate along our path, and the more surplus will be accumulated for the future.

From the Taoists' perspective, if we can produce over three thousand virtuous deeds (based upon the cosmic circulation between four and nine), we will clean all the negative karma in the past, pay all the debts, and release all the responsibilities to whoever wants it. You may not be prepared to believe it, but you have no choice but to obey your karmic reactive play in this life time. If you do not accept it, you must realize that before enlightenment, there is only the enlightening path to liberation. This path needs to be cleansed from the negative life path. If you choose to continue to behave negatively, with habitual fixation, you cannot lose anything from practicing kindness. The kindness gradually cancels out the negativity, and surpluses (spiritual deeds) are under the way. But if you want to be clean and pure and healthy and loving, there can be no other choice than conscious awakening into the true path. The liberation from the old path clears the way for the new path made clean and pure and attractive. Do you want to walk the new path? Do you want to try it?

When we have the true kindness within, the Tao enhances us invisibly with inner promise. The Tao promotes us inaudibly with inner silence. The Tao grounds us intangibly with inner truthfulness. Then we have the magic enactment ourselves, harmless and deathless.

## The True Object for Enhancement

Simplicitly, the true object for enhancing the body is not only the water in the ocean, but specifically the water in the bladder. The true object for enhancing love is not only the water in the well, but the stillness in the heart as her essence. The true object for enhancing the Love into the Tao is not only the water on earth, but the milky water above as the eternal source. Therefore, the well in this Laoist character represents the awakening channeling of our spiritual mind. It is the white tunnel that guides our longing spirit. It is the eternal source of the Love of the Tao that permeates all beings in the universe. This is the true object for enhancement.

## Meditation Practice

Remember what you have sacrificed,
By retaining what you have purified.

Recall what you have remembered,
By refreshing what you have lost.
Rejuvenate what you have lost,
By reenergizing how you could be.
Reconnect yourself to the vitalized center,
By reactivating your original sense.
Relocate yourself into a high space,
By retrieving the creation of time.
Return to the eternal peace,
By reliving that immortal self.

# NOTES

俺

# STEP THIRTEEN: *SELF*

Structure: human 亻 + at 在 + inside 內
Sound: shou
Meaning: self

## The Character Representation

This character is perhaps the most accurate description of our biological representation for our spiritual self. What does "the human at inside" or "the man within" mean? Roughly speaking, it means that "you are with your self and you are yourself inside your body and mind." This character highlights the total meaning in the second part of the couplet, which is an effortless effort of cultivation. We have our human body but we live with our inner self. This inner self is the conscious self, the God's Creative Self, and our intrinsic spirit. Our body and ego and persona are the demonstration and manifestation of our inner conscious self, individually and collectively. Each of us is true, regardless of personal and cultural evaluation, to our individual conscious self in the sense that this conscious self transcends, represents, and symbolizes the image of our total being as a real and functional unity. The real being represents our real existence, biologically and spiritually. The functional unity defines the harmony and balance and integration of the body and mind, and the biological and spiritual existence as well. We are also our collective self in the sense that as long as we thoroughly understand our individual self, and are in the state of being enlightened, we can understand our universal self at the same place and in the same time. Collective self is universal self.

In other words, individual self is personal self, and collective self is impersonal self. The personal self is the subjective experience of the oneness of self, since we are already genetically coded, mentally informed, and spiritually independent. The impersonal self is the objective image of our self as a human being, which differs from that of our animal friends and families. Each of us is both a human being and a unique individual. The Taoists interpret the self that directs and transcends the personal self and impersonal self as the Pure Person, zhenren (We will discuss the word zhen in the last chapter). This Pure Person is the enlightened self who is a spiritually elevated self. This Pure Person is our original true nature.

This original nature doesn't exist for the sake of our biological presence even though it accompanies the existing biological body. This Pure Person or the original true nature is within our biological makeup, where it is the essence that mutates and pigments our temporarily real biological existence. And it is also inside the spiritual nature of the cosmic eternity that is beyond the comprehension of our mind and the match of our physical existence. The personal connection is the Pure Person that is inside our self existence, physically and mentally. The impersonal nature is the Pure Person that is inside the body of universe. This is how our biological body is lightened by the cosmic power. This power is transcended from heaven and originated from the mother earth. As Laoism explains: "Humankind takes its origin from earth." (25:4)

Constructively, this Laoist thirteenth character is composed with three individual Chinese characters, ren for "human," zai meaning "be" or "at" or "exist,"and nei meaning "inside"or "within." We have already discussed the character Ren in chapters nine and ten, the standing human body. The character zai indicates "the gate of harvesting and the mind of worrisome." It is composed with the "earth" stroke tu and "gift" stroke cai, meaning "the woody gift or talent grown out of earthly ground." The power of "harvesting" comes from the Power of earth, or tu. The situation of "worrisome" depicts the environment where the mind does not know how to manage the harvested products, which is due to the inability to utilize cai fully.

The nature of cai of any gifted talent must be rooted in earth. It relies on the pouring power of that earth's Qi to ensure its growth and development, but should not be bonded to earth. It exists together with cosmic light, spiritual wind, and intellectual fire entwined within the earthly oceanic stillness. This is the true meaning of spiritual "gift." Each and every one of us is a gift from God and His Creative Talent. His Creative Talent has been transmitted into our conscious makeup, which bridges heaven and earth, light and wind, water and fire. These are the three cai in the universe, namely, heaven, earth, and human.

Without the watering nourishment that comes from the mother earth, any gifted talent is nothing more than a dried and withered branch. All creatures on earth are gifted from the mother earth. It is the mother earth that ensures each of God's individual talented gifts. As for humans, without our specific feature, the gifted part is not talented, and the talent cannot be gifted. This specific feature is the combination of body and mind, of talent and gift, of love and self-discipline. When the body and mind are united, we see the true person within and hear the real person outside the voice. When the talent and gift are integrated, we feel the inspiration and connectedness. When the love and self-discipline are harmonized, we experience the longings and togetherness. It makes each and every one of us unique, special, gifted, and lovable. This specific feature also makes all the universal creatures individual, independent, and indigenous.

There are many talented people out there, but few are gifted. The majority of talented people either do not fully actualize themselves or are subjected to the exploitation of a system. To them, talent is like a rare commodity, a bargaining stance, or a disastrous object. Without such a talent, they would be plain, simple, and humble. Without the ability to polish this talent, the talent itself becomes a cutting edge, an intellectual spy, and a trouble maker. For the few who are gifted as well as talented, they are free to dance with their talent, and enjoy the party with the gift within. Yet, they are not enslaved by the talent, nor profiting from it.

Talents are like a diamond in the rough, rare, and unpolished state. Before becoming gifted, they must be smoothed, refined, and flawless. A talent is intellectually sparked and individually demonstrated, while a gifted talent is self composed and a duty-free character, since there is no nationality within gifted talent. Any talent is very inspiring, but without its individually sealed gift, it is nothing more than a conscious wave. When the talent becomes gifted, it will no longer be restrained by surrounding environments, such as demands or social requirements. It stands secretly, discretely, by itself and with gracious openness.

This gifted talent is within God's given power and ability. It is within the capacity and mobility of trans-personal realm. It is trans-personal in the sense that it flows with any tranced situation, between various spiritually inspired conscious communications. Most importantly, it is inside the spiritually toned God-given power. This gift cannot be transferred from one person to another, nor it can be traded. It transcends from a higher power that is beyond any individual capability. That is the power of talent and the beauty of gift. When an individual's power and collective beauty are combined, one is true with self, and the true self is selfless. The selfless self is true with myriad creatures, in harmony with all natural skills, and free from all restraints.

This is the application of zai. It is timeless and without spacial reference. It always stands by itself, solitary, waiting to be touched, ready to respond, unprepared, innocent. At the same time it connects with all that should be, from time to space, between action and interaction. With this gift, any interaction is a talented expression, any integration is a gifted transformation. That is the power of collective Spirit, which is forever hovering in the Cosmos and existing within the valley-ocean stillness. It is never exhausted, never dissolved. Nothing in itself is special, but taken together, the Commonality is revealed.

The character nei or "inside" demonstrates the posture of our "curling, coiling, huddling, and twisting self in its most primitive form." It is not the body that exercises these postures, it is the inner consciousness that drives the flexing muscles. It is not the given rationale that directs such mobile postures, it is the harmonic drummer within that beats to the vibration of empty heart. It is not the transmitted talent that makes the show, it is the invisible combination between a projected visible talent and a programmed hidden "camera" which activates the memory cells and neurotransmitters. Layer within the layer, the light is seen. Consciously working through the built-in consciousness, the inactive consciousness rises to the fore. Trial after trial, the gift becomes readily available. All God's given talents are programmed within the camera of Pure Person. The camera represents the built-in talent. The Pure Person is the self who upgrades the talent into a precious gift. This precious gift is "what is inside." This precious gift within is the refined spirit, the oneness of talent and love, one with light and water.

The character nei also resembles the sleeping postures of our animal friends, such as dog, deer, wolf, and tiger. Only when a creature is in such a state is the spirit revealed. Otherwise, the spirit is gone, having nothing to do with the business of body-mind. In its pictorial form, the character nei symbolizes a sleeping or dead body with legs and elbows curling around. The sleeping or dead body represents nine, which stands for the changing form of yang, a symbol of curling, the root of reforming, and the state of transforming. This dead-like posture of "nine" is the function of a tortoise, which is called Mystical Martial governing the northern universe. It is conceived within the darkness, with the light shining within and through. The Chinese character "nine" illustrates literally such a posture, position, condition, and state. This nine is again one of the essential strokes that make up the last character, elixir, or the flying self from the sleeping corpse.

What makes the curling, coiling, huddling and twisting are the four corners of the world, four directions of the universe, and four limbs in our body. That is how all the creatures in the world are. We humans are all scratching and grasping, biting and chewing, with the inability of curling and coiling, huddling and twisting. We are "frozen" within. The "third-eye-light" is frozen within. God's talent is frozen within. These "frozen objects" are moved by the skeletons, which in turn are moved by the four corners of the world, which in turn are colored by the Four Celestial Deities transmitted from God. The four skeletons are within the humans. The four corners are rounded within the earth mother. And the Four celestial Deities are the "skeletons" of the Heavenly Father.

This is where and how the Taoists' four deity-like celestial spirits (animals) are named. The Green Dragon arouses the East. The Red Sparrow inflames the South. The White Tiger matures the West. The Mystical Tortoise conceals the North. We are the corpses of these four deities. Our spirits are the corpses of these four completions. Our Pure Person is the seed of these four mystic beings. The Green Dragon arouses the Spirit. The Red Sparrow swallows the Spirit. The White Tiger rocks the Spirit. The Mystical Tortoise hibernates the Spirit. Arousing brings the birth, and Rocking announces the independence. Swallowing permeates the total growth, and Hibernating sleeps in the abysmal eternity.

The Green Dragon transmits the white drop into a white-yellowish sprout, a fountain, an ejaculation. The Red Sparrow steams the sprout, water droplet and light rod, and it sucks in the menstruation. The White Tiger pronounces the maturity, removes stems and dead flowers, and returns to its true self. The Mystical Tortoise whitens the true self, receives the discipline of self-punishment (being matured), and makes peace with the Arousal, the Fire, and the Rock. Centered in this is the real object of Pure Person. It administers the functions of the Four Deities, balances the edges and rounds, and unifies and expands Its Conscious Wave, which is the Law and Justice. This is the man within, the Golden elixir, the Pure Person, the God Self.

Then what is inside the programmed camera? What is it that exists within our human body? Is it water, sugars, proteins and minerals, or the ego, mind and soul? The answer is it is all of these and yet none of them. It is the spirit, the Primordial Yang Qi, the Cosmic Seed, and the God's son that exists within. As for this spirit, Thundering Arousal cannot overtake it. Bloody Fire cannot color it. Golden Rod cannot control it. Mystical Peace cannot suffocate it. It is there within and along with the spiritual consciousness forever. That is why Jesus the Lord is forever busy going about his Father's Business, never disturbed by the social and cultural conditions of family relationships and personal identifications in the society.

To program is to refine the talent, wrap the gift, and transfer the conditional love into unconditional. This is the most difficult program to be structured in human history. Civilization deviates from this program. Cultural implantation conditions this program. Life is the victim of this program, which is essentially the Work of Heaven within Its Four Nests: it is a living program, a moving progress, a changing wave, a shining light, a peaceful drop. No individual person can structure this program. No institution can compute this program, and no society can suffice without this program. It is the program of Love. Love is the innermost substance in the universe. Love is the most secretive talent inside the heart. Love is the most treasured gift inside the consciousness. Love is the most subtle object to be detected through Unconsciousness, which is Universal Consciousness. And Love is the most powerful light vibrating through the Cosmos.

From the cultivational point of view, this human within is the truly self-cultivated selfless-self that is in its original oneness form. This God enlightened self is free: not in the sense of being free from the physical matter and its social system, but in the nature of being free of matter and force, it may also already be in the state of creating or transforming. This is the son of God, the oneness of universe, the creator of all creations, the Mother of all creatures. It is the inextinguishable fire within. It is the undivided attention surrounding. It is the inexhaustible Well Water within the vibration of breath. It is the forever presence of Loving Spirit.

## The Literal Application

The man within is the man who died but is arisen. The man within is the man who is constabntly dead and renewed physically but continues to exist and leap spiritually. The man within is the man who becomes an immortal Pure Person. The man within is the Man who holds the Rock, shimmers in the Light, administers the Kingdom of Heaven. This description can be aptly described to this Laoist character. As for the man within, "You are not intimate by acquiring it. You are not distant in not acquiring it; You do not profit by acquiring it. You do not lose it by not acquiring it; You are not ennobled by acquiring it. You are not disgraced by not acquiring it. This enables the nobility of the world." (56:4,5) This nobility of the world is the man within. This man within is what it means, constitutes, and purveys.

When we are born, we are alone, homeless, and adrift in the wilderness. We must initiate who we are and what we will be called upon to do. Before our initiation, our sensory faculties must be intimidated. These sensory faculties are the vehicles for the conditioning process, which transform into personal habits and cultural fabrics. In order to hear the truth and see the light, we must cut through the flesh which connects between sensory faculties and inner truth. To cut through the flesh is to cut through the sensory faculties. These faculties must be deprived so we can see with the third eye, listen with the third ear, and smell through the Golden Shell. We must acquire this man within in order to become free. This is the meaning of "You are not intimate by acquiring it. You are not distant in not acquiring it." The spirit will never be intimidated. The man within is never distant.

After we become initiated, we are born again and we are at home in the cosmic spiritual House. In this House, everything belongs to everybody. Everybody is everything. It is the commonality of spiritual life. Everything is open: a guest to be introduced, a gift to be presented, and a tool to be used. We cannot profit from who we are, nor is this House subjected to profit by selfishness and personal consciousness. We are all members within, but we cannot violate the mutual agreement of existence with one another. This is the description of "You do not profit by acquiring it. You do not lose it by not acquiring it."

When we are born again, the seed is planted. It is the substance and power of faith. This is how "it" has been described in Laoism. This seed is forever with us. We will never lose it even though our conscious memory may lose it and our dreaming conscious may not recall it. This explains why "You are not ennobled by acquiring it. You are not disgraced by not acquiring it." When others are seeking nobility, they are not with "it." The faith can never be ennobled; it is the sacred man within. The truth cannot be disgraced; it is so simple and plain that no further instigation is required. When all the members are back home, no further pilgrimages should be conducted. There is no disgrace in not repeating it once again. Since you are at home, why repeat and reprogram and research? The man within has been acquired. It is within us forever. Since it has been acquired, no more education is necessary, no higher degree is required. It is empirical from the moment of being born again.

The cultivational practice to be at home with the man within has been detailed by Laoist's meditation exercise. It says "Close the mouth. Shut the door. Merge into light. As ordinary as dust. Blunt the sharpness. Unravel the entanglements. This is called mysterious sameness." (56:2,3) The man within is always the same throughout time and space within the spiritual seed. When the mouth is closed to all the poisons and the door to all the disasters is shut, the conscious and biological hunger are merged by the light gathered through pineal and pituitary glands. The world of self (body) is as ordinary as the blowing dust on earth; body is the dust which is scattered by the mind. The body is the dust of minerals, chemicals, thoughts, and conditions. The spirit blows them off the road to heaven.

When the mouth is closed, the needed nutrition will enter the inner organs and systems through the largest organ of the body, skin. When the mouth is closed, the verbal expression is transmitted into the cosmic vibration, speech is no longer necessary. When the mouth is closed, the tongue waits peacefully to receive sweet dew activators that flow from pineal and pituitary glands, no trouble can overtake this. The inner bridge of love is thus connected, and the emotional organism will be purified into unconditional love.

When the door is shut, no energy will be wasted, no secret will be disclosed, no troubles will result. This door stands for the erotic gate in the body where the most useful secrecy will be exposed and sold. When this useful secrecy is released, it will necessarily generate pride, hatred, fear, and violence. And more. When the erotic gate is kept shut, no secrecy of love will be released, no useful fluid will be ejected, no vital Qi will be emitted. The body is safe, the mind is at peace, and spirit is shining within.

This shining spirit within is the man within. The cosmic light has merged. The unconditional Arousal has been tamed, and the universal love has been concealed. This is the secret of life. The light shines within the power structure of pineal gland. When the pineal gland is activated by the cosmic light, there is no visual difference between day and night, there is no vibrational disagreement between the awakening state and dreaming state, and there is no separation between water and fire within. This is the process of merging into light: the light of power, the light of love, and the light of immortality.

Through this light, water within the body is steamed, the conscious fire is tamed, the elixir is produced from the steamed water and distilled fire. The spirit becomes light, water becomes love, and fire becomes self-discipline. The rest is the dust which returns to its original state; it is the lotion that softens the earth's skin. This ordinary dust forms the minerals, the soil, the land, the stone, the bones, the characters, and the rock.

In mental life, each sharpness is an action of discrimination, and an indication of separation. The intellectual life knows only how to cut through things but lacks the ability to heal them. There may be certain aspects of Arousal in intellectual thinking, but there is no healing love within. The Cosmos is an aroused rolling and whirling ball. All the required information has already been aroused internally by the Universal Consciousness. Because of this Arousal, the universe has been divided, the chaos has been programmed, and life has been destined. No further sharpness is needed.

In spiritual journey, mental acuity is too harmful to the tender soul and too destructive to the soft light of love. Sharpness is comparable to a single-edged sword, very talented but unrefined. It is a firing bullet, originating in the pre-matured state of arousal. It is not immature, but its short-lived maturity kills all by killing itself. Sharpness is very powerful but not refined, very useful but not blended. The original sharpness renders itself to God's Arousal. That is His Patented Right. Ever so, He has the Love to soften, blend, and level everything out. When sharpness of mind surfaces, the peace is disturbed and tenderness is strengthened. The loss is of nothing other than the vital Qi that will be consumed. The vital Qi is the precious loving energy itself. Why do that?

Entanglements are the poisons of mind, the illness of the body, and the karma of life. They must be unraveled. Entanglements are the sensory facilities, the working machineries, the hungry cells, and the crying souls. They must be upgraded with the unconditional Love and spiritual food of light. Thereafter, when the dust is disturbed, the spirit becomes the crystal elixir. God's sameness is revealed.

## Conscious Dying Practice

The preceding technique conveys the conscious dying process, which is the essential journey of spiritual practice. Only when we die at each and every given moment, will self be renewed, the body rejuvenated, and the dream re-interpreted. Only when we die completely, is spirit reborn, the home rescued, and the House reinsured.

The accumulation resulting from cultivation practices then goes to the spiritual needs and virtuous deeds. This accumulation is paid for by the death harboring the conditions, including the biological instinctive conditions. The evolutionary process of body-mind has accumulated its share. No further accumulation is required, but spiritual accumulation remains to be acquired and spiritual seed of faith to be prescribed. Only after we die, do we see that we are still alive, and know that we are here forever. This is the journey of entering the man within, which in turn is the flow of the Tao.

How to die consciously so we can see the eternal spirit is the highest degree of spiritual practice. "To die, but not be forgotten, is to be called immortal." (33;2) is the Laoist's dictum which characterizes the immortal self, or the man within. But how can we be not forgotten, by the self or by the others? What difference does it make? Essentially all the conscious awareness, mental intention and egoistic projection are the self and the components of self. The rest are the others, whether discharged selves and restored memories, or the names and images of objects.

Specifically, the motto is about the spiritual presence. As long as the spirit is present, regardless of whether the body is alive or dead, self is aware and others are conscious. Plato's dialogue continues through his unspoken voice and his followers' narrations. Lao Zi's way of life has never been forgotten. Edison's lightbulb continues to shine. Shakespeare's writings are read and dialogued constantly. Christ Love is forever the presence of love itself. This bespeaks the tragedy of death, the power of memory, and the glory of immortality.

The physical elements die cell by cell, memory after memory, and with task after task. They die quickly, allowing the continuous change to take place with the same momentum. Otherwise, we could not recognize that we are still alive and active and hopeful and in a dreaming-like state. This is what "to die" means. To live is to grow with development, and to die is to become atrophied by deforming oneself. To live allows the independent growth, and to die announces the unified resurrection. To live is to smile as when inspired by a sunrise and to die is to rest in the peace of a sunset. The spirit does not die and the sun does not disappear. To live is to breathe in the power of the Tao (not for the conditional habits but for the faithful self), and to die is to spread the seeds of virtuous Love (not only for the biological family but also for the spiritual community).

Only dying offers us a new space where new things can continuously exist. Without dying, there can be no new fresh air, no pure blood, and no clean life. To die is to continue to live anew. To die is to announce the retirement from one's own bounded growth and maturation. To die is to be reborn. To die is to discharge oneself from the temple of the body. To die is to be free again spiritually. To die is to choose new parents who will provide the body temple where we can house the same old spirit.

On the emotional and personal level, to die means to let go of persona by allowing the final curtain to fall on the stage performance and freeing all the past experiences. To die is to free the spirit, clear the mind, and ready the body. To die is to break away from conscious habits, destroy the mental structure, and abandon the physical performance in order that change can occur, continuation can take place, and transformation can be achieved. To die is to observe but not see; to hear but not listen; to sense but not grasp. To die is to be aware but not to intend, to anticipate but not to presume, to engage but not to be pre-calculative. To die is to lift oneself from the ground, to expand oneself from the established structure, and to live beyond one's limitation.

To die means to reexamine the valuable lessons, to recharge one's own vital source, and to renew one's own authorized decision. To die is to be child-like once again, to be uneducated once again, to be vulnerable once again. To die is to laugh joyfully and to cry tearlessly. To die is to learn from the very beginning, to remember from the very first moment, and to forget all that has already happened. To die is to become truly present with both death and birth. To die is to abandon the hope with reward, to reject the reward for the spiritual presence, to embrace the spiritual presence with undestroyable dark force.

On the physical level, the existing cells and memories and dreams must die in order to allow the transformation to take place. If the existing cells can not die and be replaced by the newly growing cells, we are dead from the beginning, as are the memories and dreams. How many memories deal with truth and are true to their original construction? The answer lies in continuously learning and experiencing. How many dreams are real and practical in their trustworthy reality? The answer is to dream on and on with the awakened spirit.

But along this changing, rejuvenating, reorganizing, and transforming, remember to be nailed in the spiritual ground, don't lose track of awareness, and don't become absent from the presence. This is the true meaning of "not be forgotten." Without this, who can recognize us? As soon as the mind changes, we no longer want to be recognized by ourselves or others. We need that change, the forever changing spiritual presence.

Do we remain as we were originally? In spiritual journey, the answer to this question is yes, always yes. The spirit is forever present, alive, and the same in itself, whether in celestial form or angelic makeup, whether in human body or as other sacred beings. "To die" is to cast off the conscious illusion, to purify egoistic expectation/rejection, to transform any second thought/guess into pure original conscious presence, to strip away anything that does not belong to the spirit, and to dissolve all the mystic appearance.

"Not to be forgotten" does not come from the physical evidence or conscious memory, but from the invisible spiritual fact. If a person, average or famous, does not generate the action from her/his invisible spiritual fact, everything will be forgotten, due either to lack of energy conservation or the inability to continuously refresh and renew. What is left behind is the old energy pattern that keeps repeating time after time, life after life. This is the part that needs to be forgotten by the spiritual consciousness.

(If the parents have a child and nurture it with unconditional love, this child will not forget them; when a product is marketable, the consumers will not forget it; when a fat spirit emits its well love, the lost souls will no longer forget it; when the Home is found, the son will never leave. He has no time to forget but forgives his innocence. He has no consciousness to remember but breathes cosmically. He has no purpose to forsake but be recycled by the presence.)

In life, the energy operation is based upon three disciplines, spiritual, personal, and physical. As a living organism, these three patterns are intertwined, and it is very difficult to detect which one is the primary in each and every reward. If the reward comes from the physical memory, it is the instinctive and obsessive memory that cannot be forgotten. The most difficult memory is the instinctive behaviors of breathing, eating, sleeping and sexual activity. They have their own distinctive energy patterns. In spiritual discipline, the major battle is between purification and transformation upon these built-in biophysical memories.

The personal memory is more perceptive toward individual energetic construction, or the power of soul. This memory is more subtle, invisible, and difficult to grasp than the biophysical memories. They are often mixed. Until there is a high spiritual awareness and conscious understanding, no one will be free from these two realms of energy consumption. This includes the cultural formation and group memories. The holiday seasons encompass the rigorous repetition of these cultural and group memories, which originated from personal history or group commemoration toward distinguished individuals and events.

Culture ritualizes the natural seasonal cycle for the purpose of self-gratification. The individuals within a culture are the memory cells of that cultural conditions. Holidays are, as a matter of fact, the biggest excuse not to move on, but to cling desperately to the long lived history. These seasonally based personal and cultural memories are the most downgrading energies for the spirit. They never let themselves go, nor the spirit. They sap the spirit's vital energy. They are the largest disasters in any given society.

Into the spiritual practice, the marked seasons, such as the Winter Solstice or the Spiring Equinox, are the reminding signs for the conscious reactivation and purification. It is a second chance, the last hope, the best resource, the highest remark, and the deepest call. How to catch such a moment to awaken, transform, and liberate oneself is the sign of power, the call of God, and the cry of Goddess. Theirs days are over. All their hope is to provide a chance for us to grow, an environment for us to interact, and a home to return.

Don't celebrate any holiday. It is a sad day, a terrible memory, an act of sin, and a self-punishment. Read the sign, breathe in the power; hear the voice, digest the message; catch the opportunity, liberate the self. Holidays are the old days, desperate days, and glorified days of Holy beings. Why celebrate them? Awaken now, awaken within. See the reality, embrace the duality. Make full use of time, save the Qi. Strengthen the character, march toward the wall/war of death. Then return to the original place, time, and reality. Holy beings used to live, die, celebrate, and then forget their days. Holy days are the Holy beings' anniversaries, the ghosts' celebrations; a conscious shock, an instinctive date, a shift of memory, a touch of new/old reality, and a cyclical footprint.

Don't invite the guests, nor buy the gifts. Don't please the host, nor satisfy the loneliness. Don't join the party, nor become depressed by the nothingness. Live fully every day, and not just prepare for the holidays. Enjoy truly all the time, and not just try to have a good time. Do not think about the birthday, it is the saddest day for the spirit (there is endless work to be done). Do nothing for it, parents have already been burdened. Remember that moment, return to the original place.          In spiritual awareness, the two above sets of energetic patterns or memories must be forgotten. This is the first part of Laoist's application, to die consciously through the living light with grace and joy. This dying requires only the pure heart and "innocent child" to be accomplished. To die is to be born again and enter a new body. Pure heart is the spiritual organic function, "innocent child" is the uncontaminated innocent mind which is the nature of spiritual consciousness.

When a practitioner has a new body with a pure heart and an innocent child within, s/he cannot be forgotten. The spirit lives beyond time and space. Time cannot take away it spiritual awareness and universal consciousness, since the spiritual body lives beyond the creation of birth and death of life. Space is nothing other than conscious expansion and interaction. This history of humanity and its civilization turns out to be the spiritual construction of biophysical memories. Those memories are the onset of all instinctive behaviors, including personal perception and conscious thinking process. Educational reinforcement is the cultural rehabilitation of these memories.

Since nothing can be further "deleted," nothing will be forgotten. In Taoist tradition, to forget about the family is to be born again spiritually. To forget about the society is to cast off the marks and imprints of human collective history, cultural and social and personal. To forget about self is to be conscious of spiritual self. It is paramount that these three things be forgotten. When these three conditions linger, the innocent child becomes an old experienced duck/dog, the pure heart divides into conditional obsessive selves, the biophysical body becomes the garbage container.

## What Does "Not to be Forgotten" Mean?

In Chinese, the Laoist interpretation of "to be forgotten" has different characters in Mawangdui texts and the standard version. In the standard version the character is "dead," "reckless," "presumptuous," and "desirably wishful." In Mawangdui texts, it is "forget" or "not recognizable." These two characters have the same root stroke "wang" which means "flee," "be gone," "disappear," "diminish," "die" or "conquer." The interesting part of the story of these two characters is that the "presumptuous" one has the "female" stroke at bottom. In the "not recognizable" character, it replaces the "female" stroke with the "heart" stroke. The original meaning of the first "wang" (with female stroke) means "disastrous." The other character "wang" (with heart stroke) means "having no recollection" or "not recognizable."

The disaster comes from not being centered with the body as the grounding rod. This usually results from the conscious mind not being present with the reality of physical existence. The mind flees, is gone, and body is dying and being conquered. In either case, there is no communication between the body and mind. In spiritual practice, the mind prepares religiously for flight but not to actually flee. There is no escaping point, only liberating reality. The standard version uses "presumptuous mentality" to calculate the conditional reality while forgetting that spiritual conscious memory can be real only when the blocking conditions are removed. The rewarding side of this mentality is the existence of a healthy physical life but with no spiritual afterlife. Body has to die and there is no need to either flee from it or conquer it. The best solution is to realize it within and then liberate from it without.

The Mawangdui version tells a different story, that is, "keep heart present." If heart is present, love is present, and connection is present. If not, nothing is present, the body becomes numb and dead flesh. The seed of immortality is the vibrational presence of heart. Only when the heart is eternally present (as it is), is the spirit immortal. Heart is the "caldron" hosting the existence of spirit. The conscious heart must boil and cook constantly to nourish the hungry bodies and souls, and allowing the dying spirit to then fly freely. This character advises "never leave the heart alone" "Never let the heart either flee or be captured." Heart has its own precious space in the heaven and within the body.

In comparison, these two characters deal with two distinctive sections of the energy consumption between "hanging on to physical body" and "striving for the conscious body." The "presumptuous" character deals with the physical level of forgetting. The Taoist aphorism is "The body is the country and mind is the ruler." This is the function of spiritual life on earth within the temple. Otherwise, there is no need to stay. Don't drive the body away from its own present job. Don't let the body be "conquered" or "captured." The love should always be present with the vibration of physical expression. The body should always be the instrument of love, the vehicle for the spirit, the caldron for the spiritual elixir, and the bedroom of spiritual art. This character concerns itself with the feminine perception of "not to be forgotten."

The "not recognizable" character is concerned with the mental faculty within the body created by the female. Goddess does not create heart. It is her unconditional love, the power of creation, the ability of healing and the mercilessness of embracing which generate the power of heart to vibrate through love. Heart as the pure content of spirit is created by the power of light and the power of creation. It is the son of God and the child of Widow. The conscious heart connects the power of God with the sacrifice made by the Widow. This Widow is the never dying Goddess's creative body.

In spiritual journey, the heart should never "turn away" blindly, nor be "unconsciously" forgetful. Not to go away blindly is to stay permanently at Home. Not to be unconscious forgetfully is to merge with light. When the spiritual heart is at home, there is permanent peace. When the spiritual seed is clothed by the light, nothing will go wrong. Nothing then can be forgotten. This is the practical advice of "to be immortal."

In both spiritual and social life, male and female have different reality checks. The female's priority of physical reality deals with the spiritual law of biological creation, which is the function between peace and water. The male's concentration on rationality or mind is attracted by the spiritual law of intellect, wisdom and cosmic creation, which is the power of steadfastness and fire. In modern society, even legal and justice practices deal with physical evidence, the hidden rod is the conscious projection. The physical evidence is concerned with either "conquering" the rival or "rescuing" the victim. To "conquer" the rival is to win consciously, willfully, and destructively. To "conquer" the victim is to "destroy" the crying soul, to "kill" the trembling body, and to "banish" the crawling will. To "rescue" is to "free" the body, to "save life," to "recover" from loss, and to "liberate" from suffering. In retrospect, it is the body which is subject to victimization, and it is the conditions which set the fire and invite destruction.

It spiritual practice, both these conditions must be abandoned. Otherwise, all the body can remember is the pain stored in the conscious mind, and all the justice practices destroy the innocent child, causing more damage to the pure heart, and further exploiting the body as victim. There should be no "cow boy" fights between the faster and swifter and the slower and more reluctant. There should be no religious or crusading wars for the futile purpose of rescuing those suffering from sin and injustice. When the heart is present, no wrong can be done. When love is present, no sin can be incurred.

Speaking chronologically, the original spiritual and biological makeup have already been undergone. It is done forever, by the design of God and the creator of Goddess. The sperm and eggs that formed us were dead from the time our fetus was conceived. Our infantile selves were different from adolescent selves, and our sleeping selves could not recognize our driving selves. What marks the difference between yesterday and today? The living self. What makes us unify our ancient past with an imaginative future? Our present self. If we were exactly the same as we were yesterday, we would not be here and now today. Either we are still there, dead or alive, in memory or dream, or we are not present here and now (somewhere else). If we are thinking and day-dreaming and hoping about the future, we are not doing the job here and now. Lao Zi remembers "to die, but not be forgotten, is to be called immortal."

Lao Zi is truly in that oblivious state of "look for it and not see it, listen to it and not hear it, and reach for it and not touch it." He is one with the Tao. Upon restoring himself, Laoist's experience is "These three are beyond reckoning, so when these three merge, they are One." Then he observes that "As for this One, there is nothing above it still to be accounted for, there is nothing below it that has been excluded. Ever searching for it, it is beyond naming." Since "It returns to no-thing." And "Its state is described as no state, Its form is described as formless." This is what he calls "the vision beyond focus." Seeking it, Lao Zi has been trying but failed. Why? He has experienced that "Follow after it, and it proves endless. Go before it, and no beginning is found." (14:1,2,3,4,5) What is this, the God, the Tao, or the presence?

The difference between a mortal being and an immortal being is that the mortal being is selfish, and immortal being is selfless. The mortal being thinks only from the ego self and works toward the ego expectation. It cares only for the result, the object, the match, the attachment. The world exists for it. The immortal being exists only, purely, wholly, and always with the presence. It doesn't exist separately with dust, nutrition, friends, and dreams. They are all part of the presence, the stage, and the show of presence. What else other than presence? This is why the teaching of Laoism has explained plainly but reservedly that "Employ the Tao of today in order to manage today's affairs and to know the ancient past. This is called the principle of the Tao." (14;6,7)

## Why "Employ the Tao of Today"?

Why we should "employ the Tao of today" is a very fruitful practice in life. Because it is today, here and now, God is here, life is here, hope is here, reality is here, and success is also here. Also, the masters are here, the teachers are here, and lessons are also here. Again, the problems are here, the distractions are here, the sickness is here, the enemies are here, and death is also here. When sitting at table, we consume proper nutrition, otherwise we eventually become either very hungry or fall prey to sickness from mal-nourishment. If we are not alert while walking or driving, we may get lost or have an accident. If we do not think in this moment, we cannot concentrate or engage fully in anything. In the face of problem or sickness or enemy, we must deal with them quickly before they deal with us. If sick in bed or in a hospital, we could die within minutes or perhaps seconds, our breathing becoming shadow and ineffective and finally terminating.

Everything is here and now at this present moment. You need not learn this from history, since history will always repeat itself. The layers will change, but not the substance. When reflecting on the city of

Jerusalem, we see a complete history of love and hate, the passion of devotion and sacrifice, the spirit of fight and rejection. You will witness all that history embodies, religion, nationality, the business, the politics, and the memory. Who is the Jew, who is the Christian, and who espouses Islam? This is the same question as "who is the self, who is the friend, and who is the enemy?" The self meets friends and enemies at the same time, feels love and hate in the same body, and lives and dies on the same ground. How can we presume to know what the purposes of life, religion, love and spirituality are?

Opposing this scenario is a Hindu Yogi or a Taoist monk meditating blissfully forgetting all but being fully present. All that accompanies them are the shabby cloth, the skeletal body, the drumming stomach, the firing heart, and the distilling spirit. They observe by experiencing their body and mind, being conscious and dreaming breath after breath, until their body deforms, and their spirit transforms. For them, passion is their mother substance: the breathing; love is a mental memory of counting: the breath; and hatred is the changing phenomena of everything that moves with a speed of light with the presence: again the breath.

What is the Tao of today? It is whatever is fully present yet remains secretly hidden. It is whatever it takes to get things moving, to make changes, and to continue with what the spiritual mind will direct. Why is the spiritual mind here? To enable the rational mind to speculate, the intuitive mind to sense, the emotional mind to vibrate, and the graphic mind to adhere. The spirit is the mind's best friend and the shyest company, with the most intimate understanding of how life works, how the light shines, and why the shadow hovers over all. Ego desires only gratification, emotion feels only the vibration, and sensitivity touches only the skin-deep rhythm. Faced with all these, spirit has no place to call as its own home, yet it is abiding in all, not engaging but ever present, not protecting but guiding. Without spirit, how does the human mind differ from that of an animal? Without spirit, what is the present?

## Reversing the Climaxing Mentality

In human life climax, sexually, emotionally and intellectually, creates an energy exhaustive state. The mechanical function of becoming aroused and entering climax is both biologically determined and socially influenced. Striving for climax, whether in union or performance, projection or connection, is the highest induced "drug"state, ensuring immediately the energy depletion. This is the perfect defense method that nature has designed within us for the sole purpose of diminishing ourselves without requiring outside aid. This could be a good state in which to face death, feeling no pain, only joy and bliss. Nature has preprogramed us in such a way that we do not know which is preferable, to live or to die, to be with the nature of self (spirit) or to be in harmony of duality (unified body and illusion). We are in the middle surrounded by everything.

We are in the mix of the harmony between psychic conscious awakening and physical peak performance. We are enjoying and dying in any given moment, it is so powerful and immensely energized. In this state, there is no preparation, no anticipation, and no expectation in the back of the mind. There is only absolute presence of peace and acceptance, understanding and liberation. Years (more or less) of preparation and devotion are finally displayed, we are both performers and audience. We know the moment is perfect, and we are prefect.

Unfortunately, we drive ourselves mercilessly into the end of life. We have sentenced ourselves. This preprogramed climax is such that only peace/death or hatred/violence can follow. What have we really done through climax? We have killed ourselves. Regardless of how rewarding the offspring are, how standard the project, and how valuable the inventions and creations and discoveries, the journey is over, the work is done, and spirit is gone. Why is this? We have transformed our spiritual energy into different energetic dimensions. Like a seed that has been processed as food or transmitted as a new plant, our soul became a different entity, a child, an art work, a book, a machine, a social fabrication. It is them that we have died.

Can art work speak for us? Will the book read us? Should a machine work for us? Does this social fabrication exist for us? Are we then, not forgotten? Whether the begotten child can remember us for a lifetime or the machine be useful to us for many years depends on how much of our energy we have put into it. It depends on whether or not we have invested our spirit into it. If the energy is from the physical level, it will be forgotten easily and quickly. If the soul energy is invested, it may last a few generations. But if it is from the spiritual essence, it will last forever. Spirit speaks for itself, soul protects itself, and body exhausts itself. This is why Laoism has concluded "Uniting with action, the Tao becomes action. Uniting with loss, the Tao becomes loss." (24:5) Spirit is the Tao, soul is the action, and loss is the body.

In terms of energy consumption, no other type of energy, such as intellectual and rational and emotional, speaks more strongly than sexual energy. In essence, sexual energy is comprised of all the above energy types. It is the harmonious melding of all these energy types engender-ing the mystery of natural selection. Everybody gets what s/he deserves and is rewarded by the equality of sexual energy, or the primordial yang Qi. Sexual energy is both the most valuable spiritual energy and the most powerful biophysical energy. Sexual practice results in both the best union and the most painful separation. The first separation is between God and Goddess. The first division is between yin and yang. The first race is between male and female. The first battle is between masculine energy and feminine energy. The first end results in death. The first return is the rebirth of the same eternal spirit. Along this energy channel, climax is the fine line, the actual mechanism, the final touch, the best match, and the highest peak experience of the sexual expression.

Whether in thinking or dreaming, physical or emotional courtship, praying or meditating, climax is the measure, the test, and the conclusion. Climax watches at the peak, measures within the degree, charges from the intensity, and focuses upon the concentration of primordial yang Qi. Climax defines a changing point, switches at a transitional joint, and then makes an unpredictable turn. Climax overtakes the spiri-

tual quickness, weighs the intellectual acuity, inflames the emotional turmoil, and triumphantly announces the unparalleled biological peak performance. Spiritual wisdom charges the climax, intellectual inspiration
initiates the climax, emotional expression intensifies through the climax,
biological breakthrough concludes the climax.

Through this matter emerges the force, inorganic being changes
organic being, vegetative state refines into emotional state, instinct
upgrades into intellect, sexual libido merges into spiritual enlightenment.
Through the climax, we experience God's secrecy, the Goddess's creation, the nature of mind, the power of expression, and the tragedy of life.
Life is God's inspired move and Goddess's designed mode, mind's
dreamed direction and body's trembling footprint.

Without climax, there would be no inspirational idea, no creative
thoughts, no heartbreak of passion, no life/death action. Without climax,
human life would be as plain as water, as peaceful as silence, as unsensa-
tional as numbness, and as meaningless as death. Without climax,
humans would breathe like plants, drift like clouds, think like animals,
and sleep like rocks. Without climax, spirit has no liberation, intellect has
no insight, emotion has no vibration, body has no discharge. Life without entering the realm and experiencing climax can never be a passionate
life, nor a powerful and meaningful life, but remains forever a vegetative
life.

In contrast, in the eye of the Tao, climax is against spiritual journey of retaining youth and sustaining a child-like state. Climax is count-
er-reactive to spiritual life. Climax sells out one's secrecy, breaks the
silence, exhausts the virtue, leads to loss, and announces the death.
Laoism states clearly that "Matter becomes strong, then old. This is
called 'Not-Tao.' Dying young is 'Not-Tao.' (30:5) And "When things
reach their climax, they are suddenly old. This is 'Non-Tao.' 'Non-Tao'
dies young." (55:3,4) This is the first point of Laoist's teaching on climax
and aging. It is a rather shocking and alarming advice.

The mystery of biological evolutionary process is a self consuming one. To become strong is the only way to reach a climax and dissolve
and deplete one's own special power. It is the only way to measure the
activation, and the most effective idea to be away from an inactive-smil-
ing-child-like state. Almost all personal, social and political life leads
toward an active process, which is a self consuming process. The power
line, structure and plant originate in the inactive state. The active behavior deals with the mechanical operation of life. The inactive state sustains
itself with the procreative power of the Tao. We all must live and we all
must die. This results from the action of the self consuming process.
When we relax or sleep, we are inactive: we preserve the life force, pro-
long the breathing habit, and produce immortality.

In Laoism, the inactive state preserves a simple life style. "Let
people return to: Use the technique of knotting the rope, enjoying the
food, appreciating the cloth, delighting in customs, settling in their living
conditions. The neighbor countries are in sight. The sounds of dogs and
chickens are heard. People grow old and die without interfering with
each other." (67:2,3) In Chinese history, knotting the rope is the earliest

method of counting and recording and distributing. When people try to figure things out themselves, no knowledge is needed, and no education is required, and no talent is exalted. It is a natural thing to do. To "enjoy the food" is to enjoy the life. To "appreciate the cloth" is to appreciate one's own precious body. To "delight in customs" is to delight in the freedom of self-expression. To "settle in their living condition" is to settle in one's natural grounding places, for body, for mind, and for spirit. There is no need to invent any further sounds than the natural utterings among all creatures, such as talking or the protective echoing and barking sounds of dogs quelling the spirits in the silent night, or being awakened in the morning by the crowing and chanting sounds of hens. Just to live and die in one's own life. No person other than the self could understand God's given self. Why interfere with one another. Do not create more negative karma. There is already enough in this life to live and to process.

The second point on climax deals with the returning process, from climax to inner stillness and from youth to childhood. "When you have the mother, you know the son. When you know the son, turn back to preserve the mother. Although the body dies, there is no harm." (52:2) This is the most crucial part of the spiritual practice explaining the need to unify between seed and its soil, between son and his mother, between light and its penetrating point. This Laoist advice deals with matrilineal culture where the son of God will receive his spiritual birth through his mother. But not the daughter. If it were daughter, there would be no God's seed to continue to the next life. This is, perhaps, the earliest fear of man, which may explain God's disappointment. If there exists only a female child, God must send another male from different stars and constellations to conceive his creative power. The rise of patrilineal culture explains the fear man has embedded within, the fear of losing oneself. This further stops the uninvited celestial spiritual beings trying to come and live with women and producing strange animal creatures.

Luckily, the duality of human yin and yang combines to ensure the dual existence of male and female. The spiritual nature of monoecism ensures the sameness. The emotional nature of dioecism charges both in positive and negative directions. The Biological nature of allogamy guarantees the equal existence of both male and female. This natural law ensures that each relies on the existence of the other. No one would survive continuously without interaction with the other. The spiritual sameness provides the conscious ground. The emotional nature of masculinity and femininity permeates the energetic flow of either discriminative or intuitive power. The discriminative quality separates self from others. The intuitive power accepts the similarity within the difference. The biological difference promotes only the bisexual quality for the continuation. The creative power of female exists only with the continuing/eternal power of male. The continuing/eternal power of male sustains itself through the creative power of female. Therefore, the patrilineal fear of losing oneself is nothing other than the fear itself. It is groundless.

This fear cannot be overcome without one knowing the self within, the complete self born by the mother independent from the existence of its creative mother. In order to know the self, one has to know the earliest place where the creative mode of Great Mother exists. It is the Kingdom of Heaven. Spirit lives with water and rises from the Kingdom of Heaven. Self is the Son of God, the Child of Widow. This is the depiction of Laoism "when you have the mother, you know the son."

This fear cannot be transformed unless one "turns back to preserve the mother." The masculine energy has to be kind with the presence of self-discipline in order that the feminine energy can express itself freely. The masculine energy has to be buried (frozen within the winter's icy snow-covered ground) and transformed through the feminine creative power of purification and rejuvenation. This is the reason the son (Self) has to retain the source in order to sustain the born-again-environment.

Through this process, the double loss we discussed previously (the sacrifice of love and need for receiving the love) will be utilized. To sacrifice for the love is to sacrifice the self for the rebirth. To receive the need is to receive the seed of true self. The true self will never be lost nor destroyed. When one sacrifices self for love, one transmits the energy of love into things other than self. When one is longing for the love, one is longing for the true self. Through Laoist's formula, The self will find itself at home when one is within the self. Nothing will be either lost or transformed. This is the oneness of Pure Person.

The oneness of Pure Person is the third point Laoist has defined. It deals with the unification of the longevity of life and immortality of spirit. "By attaining Oneness, the spirit is quickened. ... Without its quickening, the spirit is liable to die out." (39:2,3) Or "As a matter of fact, I hear those who are good at preserving their lives; Walking through, not avoiding rhinos and tigers. Entering battle without wearing armaments. The rhino has no place to dig its horns. The tiger has no place to drag its claws. The soldier has no place to thrust his blade. Why is this so? Because they have no place to die." (50:4,5) As for those who are good at preserving their lives, they understand then the principle of Laoism: "To die, but not be forgotten, is to be immortal." (33:2)

## Tao and Aging

"We live, we die. The companions of life are three and ten. The companions of death are three and ten. That people live their active life necessarily leading to the ground of death is three and ten. Why so? It is the nature of life itself." (50:1,2,3) In the Laoist history of this chapter, all the fights (verbal and written) are about ten [shi], the conjunctive character [you] between ten and three, and three [san]. The Chinese expression shi-you-san has fixed numbers with different interpretations: the fixed numbers are ten and three. The different interpretation arises from the conjunction character you. Numerically, ten is ten and three is three. This cannot be argued. All the historical fights are rooted with the connective feeling of the conjunctive particle which deals with the unifying notion. The Chinese character "you" means "has" or "again" or "and." Since addition is the basis of the entire mathematical world, the philosophical followers and average readers naturally put ten and three together, producing the result of "thirteen." This is the most common interpretation throughout the history of Tao Te Ching. Some scholars have reasoned that the number "thirteen" represents seven emotions and six desires. Others speculated that it is the function of five elements and eight hexagrams. This second statement sounds like the practice of fibonacci sequence where thirteen is the result of five and eight, five is the result of two and three, and eight is the result of three and five. The interesting part of this sequence is that the relationship between "Mother" and "Son" is equal. As the first two numbers —two ones— indicate along their unending sequential order, everything begins with one, and the number which follows after the first one is also another one. Two ones make up the first two sequential order. This serves well on behalf of Laoism.

The other common interpretation is "thirty," drawing from the idea of three tens, or using the practical idea of "thirteen percent"in each hundred (That still leaves ten percent out of the hundred.). I cannot fathom how there would be a similarity or parallel or correlation between the "thirty" in chapter eleven and the "three tens" in this chapter. The word "thirty" that makes up all the spokes in a hub is constructed with six sets, and there are five in each set. The six sets represent the dualities of the three dimensions of the world, top to bottom, front to back, and left to right. Each set has five and each dimension has ten. Therefore, ten represents the dual practice or mutual harmony of two sets of five, as with two hands and two feet. Five is how everything in the world, individually and collectively, manifests. Heaven and earth have five "thieves," and each hand has five fingers. Able to make use of these five "thieves" are the three talents: heavenly talent, earthly talent, and human talent. Able to use hand makes three talents mystically meaningful, mechanically workable, and magically playful.

Personally, before I put ten and three together, I have to know what ten and three represent separately and individually. After grouping them together, I ask my spiritual consciousness how the result agrees with my understanding of Laoist's original meaning in the text. Ten stands for the completion and the rebirth. Counting from zero to nine makes ten individual numbers, with zero representing the beginning. Zero is the invisible form, the empty Tao, and real beginning. Nine is the highest representation in the cardinal order. When one counts from zero to nine, then puts them together, reversing the order and making the resultant ten. Within the structure of ten, one is all and means everything, and zero is the very single beginning. This is the meaning of ten in Taoist tradition.

Three is the beginning state of changing and multiplicity, because "Three gives rise to all things." (40:1) Laoism frequently uses the word three: a) Look, listen and reach form the action of three; b) Invisible, inaudible and intangible make oneness of three; (14:1) c) Wisdom, intelligence and benevolence, plus justice, skill and profit make the interaction of "inadequate" three. (19:1) d) One, two and three make the universal construction and application of three; (42:1) e) The three administrators make the government work within a country; (62:4) and f) The three treasures Lao Zi holds: compassion, frugality, and not dare to act in front of the world. (69:2)

All together, ten represents the completion, the perfection, and accomplishment. Three stands for the beginning, the change, and the transformation. Among the three stages of life, youth, adolescence and aging, each stage has its completion. Without this completion, our life cannot continue. Each moment has its perfection. Without so, we cannot understand ourselves. Each action is a transformation. That is how we grow and mature on the one hand, and remain with our inner truthful oneness on the other. Completion is the life form, because of the combination of ten and three. Perfection results in death, because of the result of ten and three. The accomplishment is the meaningful transformation, because of the interaction of ten and three. There is no other way I can phrase it. The rest is up to you and Lao Zi.

What Laoism describes is that everything results from three and ten, whether it be life, death or life destined activity. In spiritual practice, the first and second part of three and ten are done. The birth is given, and death is predestined. This order is the flow of natural law. Laoism sums it up with "The companions of life are three and ten. The companions of death are three and ten." The most important part is not these first two, but the last, which is the meaning and reward of living an active life which leads to the ground of death. How to rely on human talent in dealing with the two sets of five thieves that life and death are conceived with is the answer to all the spiritual practice. We should intend nothing, desire nothing, expect nothing, and worry about nothing.

As a living part of the three talents, ours will embrace heaven and earth's talents. Everything will be done accordingly. If heaven and earth take care of their sides of threes and tens, how can we manage our side of the three and ten? The answer is by merging with them and embracing them. Then heaven and earth will take care of them. What we merge with and embrace is the union of two ones, mother and son. They are all there, planned, designed, and gifted for us. That is why we need nothing. This is the only method to elevate us beyond the power of death. All that is required is to blow the dust off the spirit.

## Meditation Practice

> Immortal, immortal, I'm mortal.
> Live or die, matters nothing at all.
> Standing and tall,
> One looks into things more.
> One by one, with wall,
> Piece by piece, as one can call,
> Color after color, a floating ball,
> Shape upon shape, till body is full,
> work and work, pay the bill,
> Life is but a fool.
>
> Drink into immortal,
> A smashed portfolio.
> Look at the photo,

A minded tornado.
Finish the battle,
A dusted bundle.

Immortal becomes a motto,
Mortal is within the portal.
Live forever is oh, so subtle,
Eternal means nothing to lie-to-all.

# NOTES

真九

# STEP FOURTEEN: *ELIXIR*

Structure: nine 九 + pure 真
Sound: dan
Meaning: elixir

### Liberating the Man Within

The man within implies the state of spiritual pregnancy. This state is the condition of being born again. Once one is born again, time and effort is required to nourish and promote further independence, spiritual liberation, and enlightenment. The spiritual liberation, in Taoist tradition, deals with the transformation from physical body to spiritual body. This liberation is established through transforming the strongest element within the body, the metal element or bone structure. Taoism calls this "dissolving the womb and changing the bones" or tuo-tai-huan-gu in Chinese. To dissolve the womb is to be born again spiritually, and to change the bones is to liberate onself from the earthly physical realm.

In spiritual practice, one should gain the power of the Rock of light, and not the strength of white bone. Bones are very useful to provide the structural foundation and networking. Without bones, muscles would not work properly, inner organs would not be housed protectively, the body, overall, would have no structural existence. In a sense, the strength of the body is the strength of the bones. The power of the body is the power of muscles. The interaction within the body is the interaction of the organs. The power line of the body is the channeling of meridians, veins, and arteries. The utility of the body is the utility of glands. The space of the body is the spacious spirit and conscious mind.

The greatest usefulness of a house is its open space, and the greatest usefulness of body is to host the eternal spirit. This eternal spirit is the man within as discussed in the previous chapter. This eternal spirit is the son of God and Goddess. It is the born-again man who has the power to dissolve the womb of physical body, and the ability to change the structure of bones, which are composed of calcium, phosphorus, and minerals such as magnesium salt, and to launch the body to the spiritual elevation. In the high stage of Taoist practice, how to use holy water and sweet dew (vital Qi) to replace blood and water is the practical solution to expand and utilize the marrow in bones. When the blood (the murky Qi) changes into vital Qi, and the holy water (the fire of love and essence of glands) replaces the bodily water, the weight of the body is lightened due to the expansion of the spiritual space. The metal elemental bones will be dissolved by the fire of love and sweet dew of glands. Thus regular milk will be substituted with the holy water, the cosmic air, and the essential body fluid, which is called sweet dew in Taoism. The process of "dissolving the womb and changing the bones" will be finally achieved. This is what the last Laoist character indicates, dissolving the sage's body into a Pure Person, and changing the white bone into a white spirit.

## The Resolution of the Man Within

The man within is the body of sage, and it is the fetus of the Pure Person. This man within is still largely controlled by the earthly and human realms. Before becoming a Pure Person, the sage is still a yin spirit. Sage has a yin-yang body which carries only one yang, the earthly yang or nine. This yin-yang or earth-nine represents the power of oneness which forms the creative structures of all beings. This earth-nine represents the Consciousness of God, the Shadow of God, but not God's Own Consciousness, which is the Purest Yang, the heaven-nine, and the Ultimate Consciousness. Sage's body represents the purest body on earth, but not yet an entirely cosmic body. He is not dead and not metamorphosed. His heaven-nine or the cosmic spirit is still a fetus within the earth-nine body. Pure Person is the metamorphic spiritual being.

The sage's body actually represents the cosmic or spiritual larva, where his heaven-nine is a hibernator within the earth-nine body. Enlightenment is the transitional state between larva and pupa. Pure Person is the adult of an "imago" which is the man within. The metamorphic animals, such as housefly or mosquito, must go through larva and pupa stages before becoming a fully grown adult. Larva is the immature and wingless stage, pupa is the immobile and nonfeeding stage between larva and imago. Imago is the adult insect.

Before a sage can fly, he must change his human and ordinary consciousness into spiritual and angelic consciousness, to accomplish this, he must travel beyond the earthly realm, visiting the heavenly home with ease. During this period, the physical body still attaches to the spirit or pure yang soul. When the body becomes charged by the star energy and cosmic wind, it is no longer sustained with regular food and water. It must remain in a "spiritual hibernation" state for a certain length of time, from months to years. Most enlightened spirits, such as Christ and Buddha had spent over a month in complete fasting before receiving the holy message and becoming enlightened. In Taoist tradition, Lao Zi remained in a cave for three years, and many other spiritual immortals have lived in caves for years and centuries. The pupa stage is the "cosmic psychotic" stage, in which one is not sure in which direction the spirit is heading, to the sky or within the regular consciousness. A "spiritual imago" is a very real immortal being.

In order to receive this Purest Yang, one must first become a Pure Person. Pure Person has double yang, carrying two nines: the earth-nine as the source of Goddess, and the heaven-nine as the son and creative power of God. The Pure Person has the power of light and power of creation in one single body. Physically and structurally, he represents the earth-nine creative power. Spiritually and consciously, he represents the heaven-nine creative light. Pure Person is the highest achieved Person in

Taoist tradition. Just as a doctoral degree is among intellects and master in all craftsmanship, Pure Person is the honorable title bestowed on those few enlightened Taoist sages. Zhuang Zi (Chuang Tsu) is named the South China Pure Person. Master Chiu, the founder of my spiritual lineage of Dragon-gate School is entitled the Everlasting Spring Pure Person.

The fetus of sage, or the man within, is characterized by the 54th hexagram of The Marrying Maiden [guimei] in I Ching. In this hexagram, the inner joy of spirit is willing to take on the role of submissive wife and mother in family and social life. This Joy represents the submission and humiliation in spiritual practice. Compared with the inner marriage between chian [God-father] and dui [Goddess-joy] in 43rd hexagram, this 54th hexagram issues biological marriage, where penetrating and thundering and arousing first son meets the joyous and lustful and directionless youngest daughter. The outcome of the 43rd hexagram Gui is both mental and spiritual, representing both oral power and written documents. In this hexagram, the inner discipline and stillness and creative power of God-father promotes the joyful yet lawful expression, in both verbal and written forms of ruling message. The individuals will be balanced between inner power and external expression, and society will be governed between the inner structure of God and external expression of people.

As in 54th hexagram, the result is marriage and family which leads to final separation due to either the death of one spouse or the inability of the two to maintain their ongoing relationship. The husband, even as the first son, represents the old masculine spirit. This spirit cannot sustain itself with the temporary joy and happiness executed through the marital relationship and be content with it, realizing the collapse of the unyielding and transitional state within the given permanent relationship. The permanent relationship is the symbolic term for spiritual union and its eternity. The transition results in the unbearable emotions and situations forced upon spirit as issued within the legal marriage where male and female function dutifully and lawfully as husband and wife. Eternity, as it always has been, cannot be situated with an energetic projection upon an external relationship, due simply to the nature of change. When the change occurs, the entire relationship changes. Nothing can stop this change. This is the force of nature.

The cause for the transition comes from the demise of the mutual spiritual affection as it existed in the beginning, and the eternal quality of the spiritual wish. Spiritual wish is an eternal quality. It is established essentially upon the inner awareness and spiritual connectedness. When this wish becomes projected, it becomes affection. When the mutual spiritual affection of mating and dancing beauty between masculine and feminine energy transcends into the promised relationship, dutiful position, ego bondage, and power manipulation and control, both sides share the loss. The male loses his spirit, and the female loses her virginity. This loss naturally brings about the separation which cannot be restrained by the laws and legislation practiced within a family and society.

Without realizing that the ability to arouse comes from the mutual affection between yin and yang, the male loses his power through the achievements of his own desiring approach, either offspring or machines. Without knowing that the inner quality of virgin is the sacred space of eternal love and virtuous deed, female gives birth to the children but loses the eternal beauty of virtue. This eternal beauty of virtue is the state of joy, the condition of happiness, and the quality of peace. It is this eternal virtue that arouses the spiritual creation of yang force. Before the arousing invitation, the penetrating and thundering and chasing power of Arousal must submit itself to the inner refined control. Without such, his vanity will be his down fall. Equally, the eternal peace cannot be stirred, disrupted, and chased without such Arousal. Through the power of Arousal, the inner quality will lead to a productive state. This productive state is the loss of peace and virginity.

The marriage characterized by the 54th hexagram does not convey the usual social marriage alone. It is the Ideal Loss of all "marriages" which humans long for and their hearts desire, including intellectual, inventive, and spiritual connection. Any connection is a form of marriage. This connection or marriage has been "promised" by the 60th hexagram which is Limitation [Jie]. The Limitation symbolizes the joint of a bamboo stalk. This connective joint is both a conjunction and a separation. The son, who has the spiritual eye and taste, must realize this limitation of bondage and restraint. In life, each connection is a limitation in itself. Since the heart and mind, the energy and devotion are connected to a particular sphere, there can be no space to spare, nor any freedom to be spontaneous. Any inter-connectedness issues a restriction, causing the transition of either change or separation. Change leads to separation, and separation is the permanent change which is the nature of individuality. The fine energy within the joint depends entirely on the mutual transition of change. And joint itself serves as a form of conscious restraint. The joint does not provide the equality of flow, but is separation in itself. Joint is an angle, an edge, a binding position, a hook, and spiritually, an empty promise. It leads no further than what was issued in the initial contract, and it expires upon the termination of the contract.

This is the advice given by the introduction in the 54th hexagram, "The noble man must realize the limitation of permanent completion." The husband must awaken from the illusion of a promised eternity which is guided by the wish and longing. His mind must be detached from this superficial realm and be in a condition of Wuwei, which is a non-desirable state, not a desirable engagement. The empty Tao is the governing vessel, no conscious form should be attached to it. The maiden must also fully understand that permanent completion of eternity is an ideal marriage, implying the end of one's maiden state, peak stage, and highest accomplishment. It is a submission to the man's way of eternity, fear and self-control. When the maiden becomes a woman, she is destined to become a widow, regardless of how well she will be cared for by her husband and children.

## Understanding the Spiritual Pregnancy

Upon realizing the loss of biological and social marriage, one must devote one's energy to spiritual marriage. In spiritual marriage, the seed is self, the spouse is the love of mutual affection between the masculine and feminine energies, the baby is the man within, the womb is caldron, the milk is love, and the food is virtuous deeds. The seed has no biological distinction, such as male and female. We all are God's children. We are the seed of cosmic creative duality. We are the center of joint and the representation of harmony. The man within refers to the spiritual pregnancy resulting from cosmic marriage. It is the match of Mutual Affection between God and Goddess, virgin boy and virgin girl. Sage's body represents the maiden, and his transmitted spiritual devotion and discipline represent the old man. Every spirit is an old man. Each love is a virtuous maiden.

The inner quality of maiden is the joy of life, the mist of love, the inspiration of creativity, the secrecy of understanding, the power of creation. This joyful state is the eternal union between God and Goddess, the ultimate harmony of the Tao as symbolized by the two biting and mating and dancing fish in Taichi. As the Joyous [dui, #58] hexagram has indicated, the power and beauty of joy is "in the midst of lecturing among friends." It is the combined floating voice uttering through the little girl's happiness and is, in turn, responded by the old man's inner stillness. The little girl, or the joyous dui, talks cheerfully and happily. The old man, or the sage, listens peacefully and with radiant illumination. The old seed is aroused by the little lake. The little lake is pacified by the inner stillness. The little lake is the innocent virtuous child within, the stillness is the accumulated Qi of experience, wisdom, and selfness. Even though the old man responds externally with an immense joy of relief, his inner stillness can never be aroused. Stillness is the Arousal of the lightening Rod. The virtue of his innocence will never be contaminated or abused, only joyfully expressed, spontaneously activated, and immediately renewed.

This state represents the happiest moment of life, the spiritual life, and presence of life, with only the flow of love being liberated from the blissful affection. This blissful affection ignites the spiritual arousal which leads further to spiritual liberation. Each receives the best from the other and nothing is lost. Oneness is retained, renewed, and reincarnated eternally.

The combined voice is the cosmic flow of Love, the voice of Joy and understanding of Discipline. This cosmic flow of Love is the drunken state of lecturing among friends, the drumming voice of the unknown tongue. It stands for the power of preaching individually, praying collectively, and worshiping selflessly. There is no other power that can match the joy of preaching, which is the joy of love, hope, and union. The two spirits are conducted by the power of air, blown by the spiritual wind. There results an endless drumming state of inhalation and exhalation. Just dancing, mating, loving, and being together and with one another. The body as an instrument of spirit will be liberated. The mind as conscious instrument for the spiritual wind blows and blows like a bellow. Spirit as the son of God dances together with the spiritual formative power of Goddess to announce the eternal marriage.

This eternal marriage facilitates the nourishing power for the spiritual fetus, the man within, to grow and mature. In this spiritual larva state, love promotes endless love, and virtuous deed promotes impenetrable virtuous power. The power of love and the power of virtue are the only food, medicine, and elixir to transform arms into wings and to turn human consciousness into cosmic consciousness. In this stage, love and virtue are no longer carried out by the physical expression, either through hands or feet. They are generated by the power of preaching which is centered at the crown point. Voice is a selfless expression, crown point is the spiritual antenna that connects the spirit with the heavenly light of Rod. When speech becomes voiceless, the energy charging the speech lifts immediately up to the sky, to connect to the heavenly rod. This is the power of plain talk of the Tao. This is the joy of eternal speech. This is the nature of preachment. Hands will harm people, feet will mislead people. Only the preaching voice can draw people's attention, retrieve the lost soul, fire up the power of love, and liberate the longing spirit from the sickened body.

Without the Joy of voicing, preaching, chanting, and praying, the man within will become individualized, materialized, and humanized. Each person voices individually, only God's consciousness makes the voice collective but voiceless. Each physical action leads to materialization, only preaching and chanting power can transform the material body into the body of holy water, and the conditional mind into an eternal oneness. Each human speaks an animal voice, only spirit prays in the heavenly tone. Through the power of voicing, the bodily fluid as sweet dew will attract the sparkling lights, which are the creative spiritual genes, to elevate the suffering and sinfulness of the human condition, raising them up into the cosmic House, where all forgiveness is freely given and purification is performed. One's own virtuous deed becomes ten thousand souls' virtuous needs. Is this not greater than any other action man can perform? This process highlights 13th and 14th characters in Laoism.

## Tao and Qi

In Taoist tradition, spirit is forever free: free from fear and conditioning. When death cannot control spirit, what else can? When the spiritual metamorphism is the living reality, what else can the other reality possibly be? Because of this spiritual realization, the Taoist mentality contributes two vital spiritual principles into the root of Chinese culture. One is "Tao is greater than machine" (tao-da-yu-qi). The other is "spirit is individual and cannot be institutionalized." The first principle challenges us to not cling to any conscious thought patterns that the mind might create, not stick with any object that the desire may reach out for, and how not to be conditioned by any footprint that life has already lived through. "Tao is greater than machine" does not mean that Tao is greater in quality, or more numbered in quantity, or more superior in use. It means Tao is above them all. Tao is above any spiritually created and mechanically formed qi or machine, whether it be star and planet, or chariot and satellite. This natural principle admonishes us "don't jeopardize the eternal spiritual consciousness which may transcend into the formation of mental instrument, don't degrade the power of spirit into a manageable tool regardless of how useful it may seem, and don't conform the ever present spirit into a controllable asset."

In order to understand this, we must know the meaning qi. The Chinese character "qi" refers to "utensil," "talent," "organ," "equipment," and "weapon." The original meaning of the character is "utensil, symbolizing a dog guarding the four mouths around." Initially, the four mouths represent the four hungry beings being guarded by the protective dog, as well as the four prominent canine teeth in the dog's mouth. The dog protects itself and four other hungry mouths at the same time. He stands in the middle, representing the creative spirit manifested as conscious wind charged by the breathing air. This middle ground also denotes the power of the dog's mouth and tongue, biting and licking and lusting for pleasure and growing in self-defense.

Biophysically, the four mouths placed around the dog represent the biological instinct of animal beings, such as water, food, sleep, and sex. The modern scientific system does not include breathing as part of the animal instinct. This system frees the spiritual wind circulation and conscious creativity at one level and materializes anything that the mind discovers and ego projects in another area. To disengage from spiritual inspiration is to materialize the spirit, to long for the secrecy, and to conform any spiritually conscious idea into mechanical operations, such as language and tools. To free the conscious creativity is a vulnerable excuse, and to project ego power is to be self-destructive.

In animal behavior, including that of humans, breathing activity is the primary charge of spirit into the body. It is the union between water and light. The photos within the atom of light transmit the spiritual creativity into the body of water, and water molecules then expand their bodies into the mass of air. Light then turns into heat and fire, and water becomes steam and air. The movements of evaporating and shining between water and light generate the dancing ball of the cosmic circulation of wind and rain. Wind quests the sacred spirit, rain creates the joyous life. This breathing power is the spiritual vibration of the cosmic tree of life.

Psychically, not to acknowledge the importance of breathing activity in the scientific community is an expression of inescapable vulnerability and an impression of death-denying rebellious compulsion. By not embracing the breathing power, the other four instincts will be mobilized. All the natural products such as water and food can be "decomposed" and "debriefed." By altering the genetic construction, food can be produced off-season. Food addictive behavior can be tremendously gratified. Diet and weight loss practices, the extensions of nervosa anorexia, exercise another form of the self-denial process. Sexual addiction can be further gratified through the use of contraceptive devices such as condoms and birth control pills. Sleep can be biochemically altered throughout an entire systematic practice from round-the-clock work schedules and refrigeration, to anaesthetic operation and synthesized drugs. Science is really busy feeding and pleasing these four hungry mouths.

Structurally, the four mouths stand for the four skeletons that extend and embrace the body trunk. When the dog becomes the embodied joint of the Cross (spiritual dogwood), symbolized by the structural formation in Chinese language, its spirit becomes a concubine, comforting all the hungry lusts. Dog also represents the spiritually transcended mode for all organic formation, the wheel-of-life, the maker of the souls, and womb for the body. Thus, spirit becomes flesh, unconditional love becomes lust.

In Chinese language, two separated characters are used to describe the dog. One is Quan, combined with the stroke of "great" or da and a "dot" on its top right applied in the character of qi of machine. The dot above the "great" actually represents the rope that the master applied to secure and domesticate a wild wolf as dog. When the dog becomes tamed, it bows faithfully to the master with its hungry mouth and lustful tongue. The dog must be faithful in order to be fed, it is the master who provides the nourishment. The dog must serve faithfully as a concubine to satisfy its master's need (creative spirit). This is the structure representation of the second character for gou dog, a combined character between a "dog" stroke and a "bowing" stroke.

When God created our spirit, He put a "rope" on our neck (to control our breath). When Goddess created our body, She made us "great" (the organic and soulful body ) with four skeletons. In front of our spirit and body, we are consciously faithful and vulnerably obedient. Faithful deed awakens into the spirit, and obedient attention is instrumental to the mechanical operation of the body. When we domesticated a wild wolf into an obedient dog, we put a rope around its neck. Its four legs (four mouthful behaviors) were tamed through the conditioning process (modern psychologists have re-tested this procedure) of eating habits which prohibit it from running wildly, viciously and cynically. These four legs then become the first four natural wheels of a chariot [qi] to transport master and his goods.

Spiritually, a dog is a spiritual bodyguard and a family policeman taking care of all the members in the family. The dog safeguards all the wandering souls through the dark nights, protecting the hungry mouths from starvation and becoming itself a food supply for other predators. Dog's talents of faithfulness, spiritual insight and straightforward honesty speaks for itself as the best friend for humans, above the diligent cow, the peaceful lamb, and powerful horse. The Taoist's astrological insight into the Big Dipper names the first star (the cutting edge of the knife) as the heavenly dog, guarding all the spiritual seeds or individual spirits descending safely to earth and returning faithfully to the North Star.

Dog, as the most respected pet in the Western culture, is by no means surprising or meaningless. The Dog Star constellations implied in the masonic practice may also shed light upon the Taoist tradition of the Big Dipper. The Canis Major called the Sirius is the brightest star in the south. It guards its canicular passion of fire in the battle of blood, which is animal spirit. Combining this Dog Star and Procyon which is between Orion and Gemini, the spirit of fire, of hunger and of lust shoots its star power into the empty formation of heart. Its power is a very high dimension of creative spiritual force. This star power creates the force of blood, the passion of heart, and the engine of flesh. Whether or not there were blood dragons and dinosaurs is not known. In Chinese mythology, dragon swallows the firing ball. Lusting for the power of North Star, the start of longevity and immortality, the Dog Star shoots its canicular power inside the spiritual water of the North Star. Together, the spirit and souls are created within the cannibal world. The mystical dragon's plant spirit emerges into a blood spirit. Masculine spirit of ego and feminine spirit of jealousy mutually consume one another. Violence and peace balance one another. The emptiness of heart and emptiness of fire support each other. The unconditional love (faith) and conditional lust (desires) destroy each other.

When the Dog Star's fire and the Heavenly Dog's water are combined, inorganic beings metamorphose into organic beings. The cosmic tree of life (circulation between water and light through air) adds consciousness and lust to the existence of an animal life. Food alternates waking and sleeping consciousness, sex sways between the biological recreational practice and spiritual returning process. Holy water and cosmic light turn into regular water and food supply. Air becomes both conscious thinking power and subconscious dreaming power. Sexual and sleeping behaviors dominate the shadow side of the qi (body-mind), gratifying the qi and destroying the qi simultaneously.

In spiritual journey, the four mouths in the character qi also represent the four sufferings of life, which are birth, aging, illness, and death. The four sufferings are the embodied spiritual hunger, which is controlled by the cosmic power and earth's cyclical change. The four seasonal changes "struggle" along the orbital and rotational "addiction," generating both biological and spiritual food for the dog (our God's domesticated body-mind). God has put a conscious rope in our head to make us faithful. The four realms of the mother earth render us instinctive. We are all hungry dogs in our spiritual journey.

All four realms of life are controlled by one action, faith. They are aligned by one behavior, instinct. Tao is faithful to Its Nature. Heaven is faithful to Its Oneness. Earth is faithful to Its Peace. Kingship is faithful to his Father. When we know that four great mouths exist in the universe, namely, Tao, heaven, earth and kingship, we must be faithful to our spirit in order to live peacefully with them. If we cannot, these four great mouths will suck God's transmitted spiritual power away from us, leaving us with no light to be conscious, no water to drink, no air to breath, and no food to eat. How to feed these four hungry mouths and to liberate the faithful dog within is the highest demand of spiritual practice.

While we are constantly feeding our instinct, we consume our own life-force for the existence of our body-mind just as we design and build a machine and feed it with our own savings. We can save money needed for our own illness, but we must also pay for the utilities in the house, take care of the bills, change the oil, file the income tax. Our body works intensively around the clock, against its natural rhythm, in order to feed both instinctive behavior and conditional fixations. The instinctive behavior, throughout civilization, has been converted to conditional behaviors, from thinking to drinking, eating and sleeping. Conditional fixations are the busiest business exchanges.

Instead of just feeding our body-mind, the God's creative machine, we add more and more manmade machines, cultures and customs, hand tools and automatic robots. We cannot tell whether our body is hungry or our conditioning is scheduled to be hungry. We cannot say whether we live for ourselves or exist for the culture. We cannot define the separation between our conditioned thinking ego and our spiritual insightful awakening. Tao is not Tao, God is no-God. God becomes a person. Tao becomes the way. God is a thinking machine within the body-mind, Tao is the operation assembled within the power of a tool. Spirit becomes remote, technology makes our conditions conveniently within their own fixated habits.

## Laoism on Machine-Qi

We first see the qi character's appear in Tao Te Ching chapter eleven. "Clay is molded into a vessel [qi], yet it is the hollowness that makes the vessel [qi] useful." (11:1) Vessel as the food container is perhaps one of the oldest qi made by man. Just as God created us from earth and spirit, we make use of a vessel with its body and usefulness. Earth is the body of all creatures, spirit is their usefulness within. Any Qi, according to this teaching, should have the "space" for practical use. This space first forms from the mental design. The human mental design originates from God's Mental Design. God's Mental Design originates from His Own Emptiness and Nothingness. Nothingness then creates the matter and body of all myriad things, Emptiness allows all the matter to be functional and the body to be useful. The Mental Emptiness then changes into physical space. The physical space is then molded into a vessel, a tool or a talent.

In terms of cosmic vessel [qi], Laoism firmly announces that "The sacred mechanism of the world cannot be manipulated. Those who manipulate it will fail. Those who hold on to it will lose it." (29:2) This warns that there is no way to manipulate God's creative secrecy as the sacred mechanism. Whether the scientific manipulation without practicing sacrifice and worship brings its own punishment or not, will be naturally revealed in its right time. It is not up to us to manipulate the sacred mechanism and profit from it. This is against the first spiritual Law which abides by the law of secrecy.

In the manner of governing a country, Laoism proposes the same teaching. "The sharp weapon [qi] of the nation should never be displayed." (36:2) Why is it so? Firstly, "The army is not the nobleman's weapon. As a mechanism of bad luck, he uses it only as the last resort." (31:1,3)Army destroys anything it combats, including soldiers themselves. When there is spiritual and moral discipline, there is no need for an army. Army is applied only in a situation of disastrous need for protecting one's power, land, and people. Army, in most cases, does not recognize what is good from what is bad. Formed by the power maker of a country, army is a body of instrumental qi for self revenge, self justification, and self protection. More innocent souls die in battle than serving the ego-designed need of justice. The combat soldiers and civilians are the most innocent souls.

The Emperor forms a body of doting qi, placing his commander-in-chief in charge of everything. The commander orders the soldiers to fight and die for the victory. Commander is the emperor's watchdog, soldiers are emperor's food supply (He uses soldiers to feed his hunger). Emperor is the watchdog of the Heavenly Order coming from the Power Above. If there are evil spirits abusing the land and people lustfully, the emperor has to raise himself up, obeying the order of heavenly justice. In so doing, as a noble man, the emperor should never make light of the army. The commander should never "shout out" an order lightly, unheedful of its dire consequences. Any misuse of an army would destroy the emperor's own food supply, people. Any mis-execution of an order would invite the commander's own loss, his position and his head. This is what is meant by the "last resort" in Laoism.

Secondly, when the sharp weapon is deployed, the secrecy is disclosed. "The more destructive the weapons [qi] people have, the more chaotic the nation will become." (53:3) It is not the sharp weapons causing chaos, it is the misunderstanding and misuse of weapons that cause chaos. Weapons do not contain any secrecy within, it is the sharpness of fear and self-protection built within by the mind. Weapons do not kill people, but are used by people to kill one another. Weapons are not sharp in themselves, the canny ego and distrustful mind are the tools which make the weapons sharp.

This fear and self-protection is the secrecy of the mechanism of life. Whoever understands this understands the sacred mechanism of the world. God Orders Madness. Emperor applies Madness. Passion is Madness. Peace is the container of Madness. This sacred mechanism of the world is the Prince of Peace. When peace is the order, harmony is the action. When male and female are united, there will be no war. When Joy and Arousal are harmonized, there cannot be any lust. When spirit and heart are one, there exists no longer any negativity.

Laoism also refers to "qi" as talent by stating "The great talent [qi] matures late." (40:3) If the talent is displayed at an early age, there is no maturity within and there is no virtuous love softening and blending and smoothing this "sharp weapon." Talent is the sharp weapon in life since it doe not recognize anything but itself. Talent respects nothing and discriminates everything. Talent has no virtue, it simply fires. Talent knows not how to embrace, it is capable of killing. When the talent has not been refined, it is the sharpest and the most dangerous weapon in the world. When man employs talent and not heart, nothing can be peaceful. Spirit is being misused. When woman employs talent without virtue, it is the pure spice. Intuition is being misused. Only when talent meets virtue, discipline, devotion, and sacrifice, does it mature as the fine qi. However, it takes years of cultivation to mature the qi of talent.

In spiritual discipline, talent represents the spiritual arousal, the penetrating sprout, and surging fountain itself. This arousing state awakens the spirit, fires the hearts, strengths the will. But there has been no time and space for refinement because it is too young, too tender, and too vulnerable. It doesn't understand what acceptance entails, what humiliation means, and what sacrifice is for. Talent is a virtuous quality, a precious seed, and a joyful hope. Yet, it relies on soil to grow, love to nourish, and heart to realize. Talent is the seed for idea, the power for development, and the treasure arousing admiration. It has been recognized as such from the beginning, yet to become such takes time. That is why "The great talent matures late."

## Qi Must Be Sold

Conclusively, in the eye of Tao, there is no difference between qi of talent as inner quality and qi of vessel as the refined product. God is molded in our mind, Goddess is our body. God and Goddess work together to make all the Qi-beings/machines useful in the world, from stars and planets, to talents and tools. God sold His Talent into us. We sold our talent into machines. Machines sold their talents into chaotic construction and destruction in the universe.

In spiritual Order, Tao is inside the nature, God is within the person. Spirit is inside the mind, soul is within the body. Mind is inside the mechanism, body is within the instinct. Mechanism is inside the consciousness, Instinct is within the change. God is in the light, spirit is in the vision. Goddess is in the image, soul is in the sensation. Spirit is in the creation, mind is in the illusion. Soul is in motion, and body is in pain.

Water and light are the most powerful machines in the universe. They produce each other and destroy each other. They then recycle one another. In life, an idea is a subtle part of a machine. A plan is a wishing machine. A smile is a happy machine. A pain is a dysfunctional machine. Spirit is a living machine. Consciousness is a thinking machine. Body is a biochemical machine. Cell is a magnetic machine. Soul is a feeling machine. Mind is a reasoning machine. Sleep is a battery machine. Sex is a life machine. Lust is a killing machine. Love is a changing machine. Peace is an ever present machine.

Therefore, body must sell it to the minding, pain must sell it to the healing. Mind must sell it to the reasoning. Reason must sell it to the visioning. Vision must sell it to the imaging, Image must sell it to the lightening. Light must sell it to the spirit-being, and spirit must sell it to God. God must sell it to the Peace. Peace must sell it to the Prince. Before the Prince of Peace, everything is sold to the above. That is the sacred machine of the Tao. That is the secret Power of God. That is the secrecy of life.

In our human history, talent and Qi have no opposing factors, body and machine operate in the same manner. In Chinese history, the qi as a talent has been rooted in the direction of refinement, whether intellectual Confucianism or some other technically oriented craftsmanship, such as was practiced by the outer alchemists. The intellectual qi promoted the ruling power to educate talented individuals to serve as officials. The mechanical qi has always been helpful and useful in society, but disregarded by the intellects. In this ongoing battle, the outer alchemists spent hundreds of years in wasted efforts to materialize a spiritual qi, called elixir, refined from earthly minerals and other substances. This spiritual qi is equivalent to the man within proclaimed by the inner alchemists.

Unfortunately, this materialized spiritual machine poisoned dozens of emperors and caused a backlash in Chinese scientific evolution. China has been haunted by the shadow of this spiritualized scientific pursuit for over a thousand years. To this day the Chinese continue to debate the two theories: "qi is not real" and "technology is everything." "Qi is not real" is an ancient call, meaning that any existential being is not real to spirit. Spirit is the real machine. Even though spirit does nothing that it can claim, it operates everything. "Technology is everything" is the cultural PTSD (post traumatic stress disorder) overshadowed by the Western invasion, militantly and technologically. "Technology is everything" is a hungry call for modernization and industrialization. Farmers have given up the farmland which has nourished us to work with machines, they exist on their working wages instead of their cultivated harvests. Between modernization charged by the Western pragmatic philosophy and the revitalization shaped by the ancient spirit, the educated scholars and intellects in China completely reject the usefulness of the ageless traditions of spiritual healing and medicine. They have become more scientific than any Western scientists.

Regarding the majority of the population, the ancient spirit still lives, thriving in their breath and being made visible through their conduct. Mao's pro-West communist practice of pure/absolute (Chinese scholars added "pure/absolute" to the original translation of materialistic idea) Marxist's materialism disappeared after his death. The old spiritual practices, labeled by many atheist-scientists as "federal superstitious poison," became revitalized. Qigong practice/healing is one of them, along with fengshui and other craftsmen's techniques once condemned by the Confucian intellectual ego. To this day, the spiritual root of Qigong healing battles with the Confucian scientific worldbeing promoted and regulated by government and health professions. Whether or not there will be a free spiritual environment in China, as was rooted in the U. S. constitution, appears gloomy and disappointing. The government is cloudy, wanting ambitiously to control people's freedom of spirit. People are then very disillusioned and hopeless.

## Individual is Qi

This ongoing ancient battle between people and their emperor is rooted in the second Taoist contribution to Chinese culture. This contribution is "spirit is forever individual and cannot be institutionalized." This implies that no individual spirit can be institutionalized in the format of a religious practice. Religious practice, similar in essence to marital practice, signifies the end to the joy of spirit. No one can transform the true spirit into a religious believer or practitioner. It is acceptable to the mind, but never agreed to by the spirit. The spirit has already been confirmed by the Goddess creation.

Since the Chinese emperor was unable to control the free-spirited Taoism, he projected his spiritual power upon the people by worshiping the Tao himself. This enabled him to establish a new dynasty which was rooted by the Taoist wuwei mentality. When he favored Buddhism, more Buddhist temples and monasteries began to appear. When the beginning emperor relied on Confucianism, intellects ruled the society. The mass population could never fathom the spiritual mind of Taoism, because Taoist's mind is not a machine-qi that can be either gratified or expressed. Tao is forever beyond qi-machine because Tao is beyond matter. Therefore, the Taoists' mind has ever been the ideal Chinese mind, whether in an ideal relationship or literal expression. Due to this spiritual power, there has never existed an institutional religious practice in the land of China. Taoism has no intention whatsoever of controlling people. Buddhism is effective in helping people to liberate themselves from suffering. Confucianism educates and promotes the intelligent and quick minded people into the established orders within the society, leaving only the mind to be honored and classified, without categorizing people into groups. Rich or poor, powerful or unattractive, superior or inferior are all the result of mental conscious affirmation. Education is the key to open all the doors of classification. Relationship defines itself as the grouping power.

There has never been a religious war in Chinese history. It is true that personal or cult-like verbal disputes abound, of course. There has however been religious punishment, such as publically burning a rule-breaking monk to death, but never a bloody battle between religious groups. The practical and quick minded people ultimately linked all the three religions cohesively in the same temple, allowing people to worship and conduct their business together.

When you are free, you are destined to free unconditionally and mutually other suffering spirits. There is a Way (Tao) somehow, somewhere, always for people to live according to their own chosen ways. It is not up to others to show them the way. There is an invisible Tao, but not an eternal Way. Tao is Absolute because of its affinity to be the No-Way. This No-Way flows with spiritual consciousness and loving practice. Love is eternal, but in each and every eventuality it is situational. This moment's suitable and absolute love could be followed by silence and rejection. One person's belief is countered with another's disbelief. That is why talking the Tao sounds plain, having a faithful heart for the Tao seems dear, dying a conscious death is rare. Only you can understand for yourself. Only you can pursue it directively and benefit from it personally.

This second idea also establishes a root power for the Chinese legislative practice. "Heaven and earth combine and allow sweet dew. Without rules, people will naturally become equal. At the outset, the rule must be expressed. Once it exists, stop speaking of it." (32:3,4) To not speak of it is to eliminate danger. Emperor changes the rule daily because of the changing situations. Each dynasty establishes its own laws based upon the karmic power of the founding father of the dynasty. Each region has its own natural law to obey. And each individual conscious behavior receives its own natural reward.

Laws have already been written by the Heavenly Emperor. They are done. All that an earthly and human emperor can do is to hear the Tao and follow the Way of ways. Each emperor knows that today's rule may invite necessary opposition tomorrow. Every Emperor is conscious of only one rule: submitting to the living reality of his own reality. The living reality is his living power under his egoistic control. No other person is granted this power and no other situation is allowed within this control. No disputation nor disagreement should occur before his living reality. Everything before his living reality is invited by his conscious living reaction. Anything existing before his living reality is controlled by his thinking reality. If there is a storm, escape; if there is war, fight to win. If there is a problem, resolve it and forget it. When there is a solution, discharge it and move on. This is the Ideal Rule of government in the history of China.

The first slogan "Tao is greater than Qi" signifies that when something is converted from internal love and joy into an external tool and machine, the spirit is limited within. Once the machine is invented, the creative spirit within dies. For every object created, the vital Qi for spiritual liberation is expended. The object is no longer the love but the tool, no longer the spirit but the machine, no longer the conscious connection but the binding bridge, and no longer the enlightenment but the death. Even the highest and most ultimate creation, the body, will surely die. In the face of this inevitability what purpose is there for the creations other than the joy of spiritual communication, preaching, chanting, praying, and worshiping? Even the sweetest union, marriage, will end, what further can we hope to accomplish other than being born again spiritually and raising the spiritual fetus? The permanent accomplishment created by Goddess and Her eternity is limited within each creation. What else has no limitation?

The voice is the most accessible tool for us to use. When the inner voice expands into a structural language, its directive power is replaced. Hands then become the most reliable tools. Once machines were invented, the creative magic vanished, like a devotion to a specific love with no return. When voice and hands transcend into manmade machines, the living joy is absent, the loving joy is over, and spontaneous joy is dead. When the living time is programmed and the living spirit is conditioned, the moment is gone, the present is over, the reality is dead.

Marriage is, perhaps globally, the most reliable institutionalized source of entering the "Eternity." Naturally, marriage is much more than the initial attraction and promise and licencing. It concerns the ongoing growth and change and adaptability, making the married state sound dismal at best, destined to failure. The parents are happy; they need not worry (hopefully) about whether their children will survive and prosper (like them). The government is happy; it hopes to make no further restrictions and regulations between boys and girls (never will be). When we form a marital relationship, our spirit renders itself the concubine of that marital relationship. This is precisely what the 54th hexagram indicates, the spirit being trapped as the concubine to accommodate the lust. From the onset of the marriage, the initial promise of marrying and living together forever will "limit" the growth of spirit, which questions the ongoing life activity, and is haunted by the final separation, divorce or death.

If one is not faithful to the spirit, to what can one be faithful! Must everyone be faithful to the promises and dutiful practices? Every person tries, but not every spirit. The sincere promises and dutiful practices are already withdrawn from the spiritual presence. The spirit has already been sold out to the fear (for promise) and lust (sexual practice) and relationship (social requirement). How much further can the spirit be divided? Already married couples, and those who are planning, struggle between two extremes. One extreme is to promise, to please, to sacrifice, and be dutiful to each other. The other extreme is to fight, control, abuse, and cheat on one another. Because the longing self is no longer there, the loving self is no longer the same, and the dancing self is not reliable. What has occurred? The arousal is absent, having been transformed into offspring. The maiden is killed and she is dead. Love is over and life is dead.

This tragedy results from personal, social, and cultural conditions. The personal conditions stem from the personal ego. The cultural conditions are borne of group ego. The mind dreads change, as does society. Therefore, the mind creates promises and rules, and society designates laws and justice forever trapping the spirit in the grip of collective egos. Idealization, conformation, personalization, and institutionalization are the protectors and defenders of such. To grow spiritually, one must separate from these conditions. One must be born again. This is what the man within advises and portrays.

## Establishing a Spiritual Family

How, as a biological or soulful couple, to support and promote each other's spiritual pregnancy is the beauty of this last Laoist character. Marriage has three purposes: one is to invite floating and wandering spirits in the other world to become pregnant in human forms again, one is to produce offspring for the continuous existence of the seed of love. The third is to form strong bonds of social and political stability, the unit of family and the foundation of society. In Taoist tradition, many married couples became enlightened. Along this process, there exists the real "middle life crisis." This crisis is the wilderness state, where a couple can no longer recognize each other, neither is at the spiritual home. Each has to search for her/his own sacred partner for the spiritual pregnancy. This spiritual fetus is nothing resembling their human offspring. It is the son and child of oneself. When this son is ready to become independent, spiritual enlightenment is achieved. The body then will be transformed, and the bones dissolved into the rock of light.

During the process of searching, one encounters many spiritual traditions, and various established religions. If one is lucky, as I have been, the spiritual vibration and religious tradition will be found within the same ethnic or racial background. This is not the case for everybody. There are those born into Christian faith who find their home in Buddhism or other spiritual tradition. Millions of non-Christians convert to the children of Christ. Sadly, when we conform the spirit to any religious practice, it is subject to abuse and has the potential of being abandoned.

Three outcomes may be produced from these evolving situations. The one group live beyond the ordained and trained background. They find both individual space and universal communality. After becoming enlightened, they live beyond the space where their religious group are housed. All spiritual traditions have their home both on earth and in heaven. They provide the colorful networks of God's spiritual creative mentality. Another group live within their converted religious group during life and remain with them in heaven after death.

The third group is either punished within its own spiritual and religious tradition, abandoned, or they reject their ordainment at last. They may join other groups on earth or in heaven, become ghosts or evil forces, or become self-isolated atheists. Either their spiritual foundation is weak, or the negative reinforcement they have experienced is very strong, they cannot make it to the spiritual journey.

I was twice a Buddhist, spent two lives as a native Indian spiritual practitioner, yet in this life time, Taoist is my home address. I have not forgotten what I learned from the previous disciplines, nor do I hate their specific concentration, but I feel surely that Taoism is the home for me. There is no rule governing, only kind advice. There are no commandments to follow, only shocking warnings to either disregard or yield to. There is no written formula to recite, only the teachings of life to learn and preach. Taoism does not create a religion, it provides a sacred space. Taoism does not convert followers, it relocates one's spirit from biological lineage into a spiritual one. Taoism offers no rule to obey, it awakens the conscious reality for all to see their own nakedness, contaminated mind, and non-conceptualized spirit.

I love Taoism intensely in this life time. I learned that, from Taoists' liberating voice, God cannot punish me, my life is in my own hands. Goddess cannot capture me, my own conscious longing is my spiritual mate. Culture cannot contaminate me, I speak only one language, love. Family cannot restrain me, I am at home by myself. I now have the seed of the Tao, the love of Te, the power of light, the flow of the Tao. Earth is my dust, moon is my lust, enlightenment is my must, spirit is my trust.

Taoism is native but individual: it echos in the land of China through all the aroused spirits. Taoism is natural but personal: body-mind is a natural gift, cultivation is a personal way. Taoism is selfish but sacred: it does not need to be known by everybody, it transmits its spiritual essence secretly and with no selection among the chosen ones. Yet, its voice is as originally pure as the silence. Its sound is as earthshaking as thunder. Its transmission is as complete as its beginning. Taoism is cultural but universal: it has a cultural voice called Tao yet it portrays a universal sound called Way. The mouth walks through the feet, the feet echo the power of voice. Each sound is different, yet the inner voice changes never. Each step is different, the inner journey varies never. Each individual behaves differently, the inner path differs never. Each belief is a gifted belief, the inner faith accepts forever.

## Entering the Eternal Home

Each person has three homes in a life time, the biological home, the personal home, and spiritual home. The biological home is where the spirit is reborn physically. Personal home is where one becomes established and continues to raise the family in cultural traditions. Spiritual home is where the spirit returns once it retires from the physical body. These three homes provide the three stages of life's growth: birth and youth with the biological family, adolescence and middle age in one's own home, and aging and death within the spiritual home.

During the first stage of life, our spirit is born into a married mating couple, our parents. Spiritually, our parents may be our past relatives or acquaintances, or they may have no past connections with us. They built the temple for us that our spirit could continue to exist in human form. In this stage, our parents' life styles may influence us positively or create illness in us physically and mentally. We are vulnerable and we are once again orphans on earth.

During the second stage, as we grow, mature, and become educated, we model ourselves after the family or/and cultural traditions, following the pattern of establishing our own family and raising children, building a career and possibly achieving fame. We search, define, struggle, and even die into this model of living, but our spirit is vulnerable and our soul becomes the widow/widower. We have given all to our children and culture, to our searching and consuming ego.

When the family cannot satisfy us, sex cannot please us, culture cannot answer us, government cannot control us, we are home alone on earth (again), wild, hopeless, having no idea where to go. Gradually, the inner spirit gently whispers and prods us, the celestial spirit arouses us, mountain spirit milks us, wind spirit directs us, rain spirit shows and renews us, land spirit supports us, ocean spirit swims with us. With the advent of the arousal, we are spiritually pregnant. Our Self is finally at home. Goddess becomes vulnerable. She becomes the Widow.

## Choose To Die

Everyone is gifted with the power and ability to choose. This is God's given power within, called spirit. All that follows is the renewable repetition, from breathing, eating, sleeping to dying and reincarnating. Each action is a complete action that most of time leads fully to the next, changing the patterns and characteristics without changing the essence and eternal quality. Each race has a chosen color, each culture has a chosen voice, each individual has a chosen spirit. Ancestors pass down their original body-makeup to us, shaping us into exact replicas, physically. Culture produces our original conscious voice, empowering us to mimic exactly after this endless echoing between spirits and ghosts, sensations and thoughts. Spirit is our true origin, we repeat the same spiritual entity life after life.

In human evolution, human ancestors were cross-bred between planetary angels and celestial beings, between animal spirits and inorganic substances. Besides the unique spirit we possess individually, we all share the same animal spirit, from our bodily structures, to our instinctive behaviors and our conscious abilities. This is the power of animal recycling as we face our death journey. The body returns to a state of water and dust, becoming the food supply for others, including animal research and organ donation. Conscious ability changes from swimming and crawling, to walking on two/four legs and flying with wings. The physical behaviors range from vegetable-eaters to meat-eaters, from seasonal reaction to perennial hibernation.

Among the availabilities and activities, exists something that is beyond them all, that is the ability to choose. Upon the forever existing duality, spirit mediates between conscientious and conscious choices. Conscience is the moral justice, consciousness is behavioral display. Conscience is universal and spiritual, consciousness is cultural and personal. Conscience embraces the simplicity, consciousness echoes the loss. Between the two there exists the power of choice: how to listen and how to follow. Able to first hear something, then following it is the power of spiritual consciousness, not able to first ground oneself before following anything invites the loss. All the actions of hearing lead to liberation, and all the actions of following lead to death.

How to die is the ever-looming religious and ethical question, and how to choose to die is ever more challenging. Spirit always knows when to leave the body, even in the time-compressed catastrophes. Soul slowly removes itself when the body ceases to breathe. In Taoist tradition, it takes 49 days for the vegetative spirit [Po] to leave the body. The conscious spirit [hun] normally leaves the body within three days. Spirit makes the choice months ahead.

Death is all conscious to spirit. But for the survivors, the judgment is waved between natural and accidental. They do not realize that even an accidental death is a perfectly natural choice, the only difference existing is how the speed of time changes the physical reality. On the highway it is accidental, in bed it is natural. Explosive in the air, painstakingly through sickness. A natural death takes months and years to be prepared for, while an accidental death is unbelievable to the thought and shocking to the conscious reality. The choice has been made, either by the deeds accumulated or the karma which is repeatable. One suicidal death necessarily repeats itself many times until the spirit gets tired of it. One violent death invites another violent scene until a peaceful solution is under way. Any peaceful rest promotes a new auspicious beginning. One enlightenment action elevates ten thousand suffering souls into a crowded-cloudy-jet-flight. Consciousness is very tightly packed with crowded information. Clouds are the breakthrough. Jet carries the precision of spirit, and flight announces the final liberation.

## Final Launch

Just as the outer alchemists designed the fireworks by experimenting with the timing of various explosives, inner alchemists refined the biospiritual fluid into golden elixir to enjoy the cosmic communication. Just as scientists invented and launched the satellite, hoping to discover and receive accurate information of either self-projected or alien habitation, Taoists returned to the deepest basement of earth-building—cave—in order to launch the spiritual flight and understand the cosmic construction within the watery muscles and shining bones.

In 51st hexagram, the second line expresses vividly this journey of transformation. "The arousal thunders with lightening by bringing forth the critical transition. You must lose a hundred thousand shells and climb the nine hills. Do not go in pursuit of them. Within seven days you will be back home again." The "arousal" is zheng or the first sun, representing God's Arousal. Its power is lightening and thundering, bringing forth necessary crisis. This crisis stands for the critical transition. Like a hatched birth pecking through the shell and becoming individual, the spiritual liberation lies precisely in the power and ability of the transforming spirit from bodily realm to cosmic home. It relies on the swift speed of lightening to burn the flesh, in order to free the spirit. It is a massive arousal to the spirit, and the most surprising shock to the consciousness.

Therefore, the consciousness must prepare to sell a hundred thousand shells. Shell represents the skin and entire body, the number represents the total number of individual parasites within the body. Each parasite is a spiritually transcended conscious cell and a concrete object based in a breathing shell. In order to fly, consciousness must die, spirit must liberate from those shells.

The only choice is then to climb the nine hills of the brain palace. There are nine openings in the brain skull, each forming a printed mark, a suppressed hole, emitting the light coming from the star. The middle hill is called crowning point, where a hundred thousand spiritual conscious lights unite and become as one singular spirit-light. When the power of lightening and thundering comes through the journey of climbing, the spiritual fire rests at the crowning point, readying its flight to heaven.

Seven days represents the seven layers of cosmic creative foundation, the seven holes within the face, seven colors of the rainbow arch, one hydrogen and six oxygen molecules, and earth's seven conscious days of creation. When the spirit travels across the seven layers of cosmic creative foundation, it is finally home. The Pure Person is welcomed by all the enlightened sages and celestial beings. The journey into the Tao is actualized. It is the conclusion of sacrificial indebtedness that faith is rewarded.

## Character Representation

This character represents the final outcome of cultivational practice. It is neither the death nor the rebirth of our physical existence, but
rather the elevation of the spiritual elixir into the cosmic ozone. The spiritual seed (golden elixir, Pure Person) enters the root of heaven. His deeds
becomes the fruit and carriage for the common people. As has been
described in the last line of 23rd Split [Bo] hexagram, "The grand fruit
cannot be eaten. The superior man receives carriage. The inferior man and
his house are split apart." In Chinese, the character for grand [shuo]
means "big head," "master" or "stone." In spiritual outcome, it is the Pure
Person within. Shuo-ren or superior person is a person who has contributed the deeds of fruit. His virtuous deeds are the fruits of people.
Even these fruits are mean to be enjoyed vocally, but cannot be "eaten"
orally. It is to be "digested" consciously, wholeheartedly, and faithfully.
Therefore, this grand fruit [shuo-guo] cannot serve the stomach. It is for
the hungry spirits.

Through the lifetime's cultivation, the superior man or shang shi,
translated as eminent persons (40:1) in Laoist word, not only obtains the
seed of enlightenment, but also the carriage and road to transport and support the people. His virtuous deeds are the carriage of the people, and his
spiritual seed is the guiding light above/ahead of the crossroad and
upon/through the crisis. The four wheels (the enlightened realms) render
the carriage to move successfully and efficiently. The carriage makes the
four wheels useful, thereby providing the foundation, as the land and
road, for people to overcome their four hungry mouths, the four instinctive behaviors.

In contrast, the inferior man splits the spiritual seed from its temple, the house. He not only destroys the house, but the spiritual power as
well. The house breaks down, and spirit flees. Unlike the superior man
who has transformed his spirit into Pure Person and his body into the consciously awakened carriage, the inferior man suffers the loss of both.
There is no way that the inferior man can crystalize the biological essence
into Grand Fruit, not because he lacks a spiritual base, but because he will
lose everything he has. Instead of refining one's consciousness into the
deeds to construct the carriage, he wastes it along the way by gratifying
his pleasure and searching his mentality, all controlled by the four hungry
mouths.

The Grand Fruit in I Ching is the Pure person in Laoist last character. The Pure Person is a cosmic fruit, the golden elixir. It is surrounded by the house, the relaxing, sleeping and deforming body. This house is
represented by the dynamic function of nine. Nine is the highest representation of yang's manifestation which is invited by the change and transition. In ordinary life, when the work of the day is finished, the yang Qi
of mental energy has been consumed. It then requires relaxed sleeping
environment for the pineal gland and adrenal glands to generate more
useful energy for the next day. While in spiritual work, the yang Qi is
never consumed, it is accumulated through the cosmic circulation.

Through unconditional love, compassionate action, faithful devotion, and gracious sacrifice, the Grand Fruit is produced. Nothing is wasted and nothing is dead, even though the body dies, the house splits. This split is more blissful than any earthly pleasure one can experience or imagine. This split is the final launching process.

Nine is the highest form of maturation, the turning point, and the changing moment. Nine is the accumulation of seven rainbow colors, plus black and white. The White color fluctuates between the base of cosmic color and the ultra-violet. The ultra-violet is the light that is higher than the light power of the North Star. The black color links the mystic valley with the infrared ray of solar light. All things on earth that are red perceive their base color from the solar light, which is guided by the light of the Dog Star. It is the purple or violet color that connects spirits to the North Star. The remaining five colors belong to planetary groups in the solar system, each in turn is influenced from different directions by the star groups out there.

Should a specific object , whether the elixir of a Pure Person or an inorganic being out there in the universe, have a power that is higher than the ultra-violet light, it could not be contained on earth. The earth does not harbor a strong enough attraction to hold it. This is the elevating power of our spiritual form, or the power of a sage. The literal explanation of Pure Person or Zheng means the sage drops his corpse and flies into the sky. Out there in the vast universe, Pure Person is the lower family, as is the fungi on earth. The Pure Person is free from the cycle of birth and death, and He is shining day and night and visiting the heaven's valley caves. Above the Pure Person, according to the Taoist literature, is the Spiritual Person. The Spiritual Person has the transformative power of changing things between heaven and earth e.g., relocating the earth's mountains and oceans. The next highest is the Absolute Reality, or Juijing in Chinese, jiu for absolute and jing for reality. The Absolute Reality is the highest form of spiritual matter or cosmic being.

## Meditation Practice

Jing is essential to being.
Qi works as if the meaning.
Shen lights above the formation of dreaming.
These three cannot be further examined through reasoning,
Nor be captured by feeling,
They are the substance for ever changing,
Presenting the trinity of returning.
Working through the journey of continuous processing,
Until the conscious dreamless thinking mind reaches its awakening.

When the light is invisibly shining,
It clothes all substances with its precious dressing.
When water becomes madly swimming,
Nothing else has that power of fleeing.
They are joining together to make all beings as becoming,

Like the flying objects rotating and revolving.
Through the volcanic power of sprouting,
Then weightless sinking and deepening,
Till heavily locating in their proper places of living.

Not knowing the meaning of suffering,
Beyond the accountable reaction of numbing,
Pushing through the unbreakable air of drumming,
Enjoying within the suffocation of transforming,
Clinging carelessly in the breathtaking spinning,
Dazzling in the space of incredible saving,
Presenting with an image of incompatible smiling,
Realizing that all things are ruthless being,
In the situation of endless acting,
By the light-split disappearing,
Beyond the timely catching of crying,
Unflinchingly forever existing,
As still as the very forgotten beginning.

Wondering is an impenetrable believing,
Practicing zealously till all things are naturally dissolving,
By the power of embracing,
Within the step-by-step ascending,
To the point where there is no beginning,
Illuminating the map of returning.

Could that be a wonderful celestial being,
Symbolizing God's catching,
Distilling Goddess's felling.
Enabling the Tao of fulfilling,
Entangling the three-in-one-no-thing.